MORNING STAR OVER AMERICA

Twentieth Century Anthology
AD 1997-1999

Transcripts of Messages
The Blessed Virgin Mary

William L. Roth Jr.
Timothy Parsons-Heather

The Morning Star of Our Lord, Inc. is a nonprofit, tax-exempt, (501)(c)(3) religious, charitable organization that is incorporated under the laws of the State of Illinois. It has been created for the dissemination of various apologetic works in defense of the Holy Gospel of Christianity. It is the role of this Roman Catholic corporation to provide pastoral consolation to those lacking in faith, the infirm, homebound, incarcerated, deprived, dejected and those who are otherwise suffering-humanity for the Glory of the Kingdom of Jesus Christ. All proceeds from this book are being donated to other charitable causes to help feed, clothe and house the poor, and for the reproduction of Christian media for distribution across every continent of the world. If anyone would like to contribute to this worthy cause, you may do so through the following website address.

The Morning Star of Our Lord, Inc.
Springfield, Illinois
www.ImmaculateMary.org

Published by The Morning Star of Our Lord, Inc. Used with permission.

Publish Date: May 16, 2010
Canonization of Saint Joan of Arc

ISBN10: 0-9793334-2-3
ISBN13: 978-0-9793334-2-2

Cover Image: Giovanni Battista Salvi (1609-1685)

The Morning Star of Our Lord, Inc. has published twelve works to date by William L. Roth Jr. and Timothy Parsons-Heather, the initial being their nearly sixteen hundred page, two volume diary that meticulously chronicles the opening days of the miraculous intercession of the Most Blessed Virgin Mary in their lives. These two men are under ecclesial obedience to the Roman Catholic Bishop of the Diocese of Springfield in Illinois who reserves final judgement concerning their disposition.

DEDICATION
and
INVOCATION OF INTERCESSION

Pope Pius IX

Ex Cathedra
Infallible Declaration
of
The Immaculate Conception of Mary
Ineffabilis Deus - 8 December 1854

Pope Pius XII

Ex Cathedra
Infallible Declaration
of
The Assumption of Mary into Heaven
Munificentissimus Deus - 1 November 1950

The Mystical Revelations of the Morning Star Over America

Official Deposit of Works

The following twelve manuscripts comprise the syllabus of the official public record of the Revelation of the Most Blessed Virgin Mary as the Morning Star Over America. The dates of submission of each work to the Bishop of the Roman Catholic Diocese of Springfield, Illinois has been recorded.

In Our Darkest Hour
Morning Star Over America
February 22, 1991 - December 31, 1992
Volume I
Submission Date: February 9, 2000

In Our Darkest Hour
Morning Star Over America
January 1, 1993 - February 22, 1997
Volume II
Submission Date: February 9, 2000

Morning Star Over America
Twentieth Century Anthology
AD 1997-1999
Submission Date: No Bishop in office at time of publication.

At the Water's Edge
Essays in Faith and Morals
Submission Date: May 8, 2001

When Legends Rise Again
The Convergence of Capitalism and Christianity
Submission Date: March 13, 2002

White Collar Witch Hunt
The Catholic Priesthood Under Siege
Submission Date: June 26, 2002

Babes in the Woods
With a Little Child to Guide Them
Submission Date: March 18, 2003

To Crispen Courage
The Divine Annihilation
Submission Date: August 8, 2005

Supernal Chambers
A Resurrection Prayer
Submission Date: July 11, 2006

Morning Star Over America
The New Millennium
AD 2000-2002
Submission Date: September 5, 2007

Morning Star Over America
The New Millennium
AD 2003-2005
Submission Date: September 30, 2008

Morning Star Over America
The New Millennium
AD 2006-2008
Submission Date: August 22, 2009

"When we speak about the origin of Christianity, we are referring to the Holy Roman Catholic Church, *Sanctae Romanae Ecclesiae*, an eternal institution that itself has been maligned through the tropes of atheists and secularists since its beginning, that has never once conceded to its detractors or persecutors, and that will prevail in triumph forever beyond the extinction of the created world."

-William Roth Jr.

MORNING STAR OVER AMERICA

Twentieth Century Anthology
AD 1997-1999

Preface

AD 1997 1

AD 1998 67

AD 1999 139

"Our refuge is Christ Jesus the master griever, the succulent fruit, immortal rector, comforter and consoler, bewilderment of the learned, Abraham's eye, the shoot of Jesse, perfect sufferer, anointed one, keeper of the flame, compass for the lost, servant of paupers, virgin brother, key to the heart, banner for the people, spirit of wisdom, King of kings."

-William L. Roth Jr.

Preface

by
William L. Roth Jr.

How many parents have chuckled at the spectacle of their young child with a favorite blanket draped across their shoulder, coat donned to the chin, small knapsack in one hand and the thumb of the other pacifying their insecurity, heading out the door supposedly running away from their taskmasters whom they have decided they can live without? Imagine how those parents humourously questioned the intentions of their small charge, knowing with far more enlightened vision that their ultimate destinations before their retreat to their loving arms would be the front step, the end of the sidewalk, or the edge of the yard. So many naively state that they can see no evidence of our Eternal God, yet His near-perfect reflection has stood at many a doorway watching resolute nestlings turn their backs and launch themselves on temporary courses into the unknown. Indeed, humanity stands no more beyond the paternal gaze of the Almighty Father at this moment than any of those toddlers who momentarily effectuated their emancipation from their parents. Now if we consider contemporary events, both secular and spiritual, does not the miraculous intercession of the universe's Holy Matriarch echo the same parental inquiry in our hearts? Do we not hear the words—"Where are you going? Have you decided not to live with us anymore?," as we stand with a death grip on our materialism, intent upon engaging the foray of a godless existence, free of the protection of our more noble spirituality. To what destination can our nation ultimately arrive once shunning the wisdom of divine grace, our recognition of definitive truth, our faith in the wisdom of our forbears, and the Christian knowledge of societal unity that rescinds all human impulses to strike out into cold-hearted antipathy, bloody division, and finally fiery oblivion? Does not the same rogue spirit that seeks an insatiable epicurean independence also badger Christianity to step-aside into some non-influential, private sphere of obscurity? To what end? Around what story will the shining seas serve as bookends once our homeland is vacated of Christian virtue and self-discipline, love and charity, generosity, mercy, forgiveness, purity, and care for the least fortunate? Nay, how long can we outrun the reaping justice of Almighty God for the slaughter of His enwombed children? Should we ignore Holy Scripture and allow our patsy version of His mercy to fool us into thinking there is no justice standing like an avenger behind His patience? What will the hallowed landscape of our scenic plains resemble after all moral principle and noble aspiration based in selfless love are finally disparaged into nonexistence? Conflagrations, indeed! Do all the haughty antagonists of the great Traditions of Universal Christianity wish this historic experiment in democratic self-government to succumb to the infernal siege of atheistic secularism that is poised to destroy its very nature without so much as a twinge of conscience or apology? The majestic Lady of Mount Calvary once petitioned us to look for Her when Her pedestal came into full bloom. Many have assumed this pedestal to be a reference to the Moon upon which She stands depicted in the twelfth chapter of the Book of Revelation and has appeared in Her many apparitions worldwide. If anyone were to ponder whether God acknowledges His earthly creatures as they reach-out for the stars, then they must affirm, even if accidently, that we have venerated Her as our Heavenly Queen and Patroness of the United States of America, for we have rocketed to Her orbiting pedestal to be at Her feet and have placed our nation's colors there. And God has indeed responded reciprocally, sending this Heavenly Queen back to us as the Morning Star Over America, and that is the defining essence resting providentially beneath this mantle of revelation. The honorable legions who have always hoped for Paradise are awakening to Her mystical reveille rolling a sweet melody of conversion across our warring fields; and the sky-rattling thunder of historical change is beginning to roll. We see this hallowed nation that we call our motherland having been forced out into the terminal frost, to its encampment at the Valley Forge of our ideals; starved for unyielding truth, shivering and dying beneath an encroaching darkness being pulled over our souls by the most dead consciences mankind has ever allowed Satan to invade. Yet even in the inevitable approach of torturous nightmares, noble Americans of Christian fortitude hold sacred an ethereal promise of greatness that calls us all beyond our slumbering patience to the final battle that looms at the edge of the mystical frontier which will define us as worthy for the halls of Paradise, there awaiting the assault of divinity to call us to the salvific fields of the Holy Cross. The God of Heaven has always yielded fortune its saintly heroes, given them saber and steed, and anointed their spirits for glory, that humanity be called with His own voice to the tides of the highest destiny which flushes the enemies of righteousness back across the chasm of their audacity to defeats they could not possibly have envisioned through the blindness of their ages-old arrogance. The Most Blessed Trinity took the side of the Original Apostolic Church upon a mountaintop called Calvary 2000 years ago and has never suspended that allegiance; and this righteous God pauses inflicting His unimpeachable Will throughout His earthly vineyard in deference to the Son who was crucified there to make it holy. Thus, imminent are our trials and tribulations whose assessment will not be found with badges and statutes. Personal tragedies, internal sorrow, helpless grief, insurmountable crises, and dooming depression. Then, where will be a public law? What of accusations, adjudication, and disposition? The lifeless jurisdiction of the claims of man will convict himself for the record. For these trials will be the conflagration of the heart, the confounding incineration of the arrogant self. Gone will be the futile elitism of pride and procedure. Reduced to ashes will be our wasted experiences from which will rise the last fragile images of a fraudulent and deceitful mankind. Coming is the acclamation of every mortal whose last breath will be "How Great Thou Art." Gone will be fashion and formula, process and equation. At last will be infinity. Upon us is the last age to be detained by time, the final to be lost, so sayeth the Mother of God. No public consensus can weigh against this Truth, and no private revelation can destroy it. It is time for our awakening from the sleep of mortality and escape from this horrific night of sin. Humankind will be "all" again, with no role or class or hierarchy of self, rather completely selfless and one in God. This last age, marked by revolution and revelation, is the time into which all human existence has flowed since the fall of man.

Every time God reissues the white light of dawn over the eastern horizon, He proclaims that Truth on the Earth must go on. It can be rather discomforting at times, and the Lord spares no venues to remind us that the only real dignity we have comes from Him. While we work the land, groom the fields, stock our shelves, spread the commonwealth, commute, transact and confer, Jesus is busy overseeing our transition from sinners into saints. Rust belt, corn belt, bible belt; they are all the same to Him; but what we do with our appointed years in exile has permanent effects on the ethereal realms above. Yes, Christ goes to work every day too. His acreage rolls inside us, often rough, dry and steeply offensive, but always fertile, tillable, and seasoned for sowing good will. We know that people are individually distinct, and humanity has a collective identity as well. And, just like our commonness with the sea, we rise and fall according to our groundswells of pressure and atmospheres of social concern. We drink when we thirst, bleed when lanced, recoil when frightened, and cringe when we are ashamed. The world is in turmoil these days because of our unholiness; and while the birth of our children is God's decree that we have not yet outstayed our welcome, we are surely on the verge of eviction. Our excesses have taken us to new levels of disobedience and depravity. We have crashed the gate of incivility, shredded our nets with egoism, and knocked down partitions that were supposed to separate us from the seediest parts of life. Every time we draw another breath, we are taking something that belongs to God, exhaling our frustrations over life's heavy burdens, unaware that someplace in His infinite Wisdom, there is a given number of blinks and heartbeats allotted to us all. We are moody creatures who must fight against the temptation to insulate ourselves from the imposing aspects of being human; there are times when we must remove our shirts, pick up a shovel, pull a rake, wrap a line, and heave a bale. Again, Jesus does His work even so. He raised a hammer above the Earth the moment He ascended into Heaven that struck humanity straight in the heart at Pentecost. And, with that impact, He fractured the world from surface to core, redirecting our attention to Peter the Rock, the Vicar of the Roman Catholic Church, whose spirit and vigor still reign in the Papacy. Even though the sun goes down in Rome and it looks like nighttime again, it is never dark at the Vatican.

No culprits could conceal their crimes near the Necropolis of the resurrected Popes. And, there are no days off at Saint Peter's; everyone serves a Kingdom that is just beyond their sight. The Holy See is the home office of Christianity, the place where the buck stops and our marching orders are given. It serves no democracy in its Kingdom of the Spirit, but preserves by divine decree the dignity of every man. It is where forgiveness is extended and mercy is held on high. No government can exempt us from the authority of the Pope; and no leaves of absence or midnight escapades should distract us from heeding his sacred commands.

Do we remember that the Father wept seeing the selfishness of Eve and Adam? This is what Jesus feels when blessings and graces are accorded without an intense spiritual response from humanity. We should perceive life in the context of stirring the heart of the universe, making Nature feel approved, and sharing with the heavenly hosts everything that fulfills their desire to be united with the Church. Life should be a prayer of the highest magnitude and deepest meditation. It is not a strike and run event, not like skimming stones across a pond or taunting a badger in the woods. We should breathe-in the environment around us, all the facets of the earth, everything we see, hear and smell in union with our Creator on His throne. Through our acceptance of the Cross, the Lord is delivered to satisfaction wresting His creatures from the jaws of spiritual death. We must be on guard at all times that evil might corrupt the hour. If we are careless, we will not be shielded from the sight of villains or invisible to the enemies of our work. Let us not yet force the dawn of Armageddon! Any arrow of persecution can sail from east or west, high or low, even from the netherworld. Our prayers in the light of day induce the most brutal thugs of night to haunt us; snarling, fuming and famished to devour our holy domain. Our only armor is the Crucifixion, our knowledge that victories are replete with risks, that we stand to lose everything we have gained if we concede to sin. Once we forge a platform where we can sing the Lord's praises through the expression of the self, symphonies begin to play, the Saints assemble, the Angels rejoice, and the Holy Spirit lavishes such ethereal eloquence upon our hearts that the earth shudders in space. Our spirits awaken, our immortality intensifies, and we take command of our weaknesses while our innocence reprises confidently from the past. It becomes so obvious that reparation for humanity's transgressions is taking place that we belay our reticence and bask in the applause of the Church Triumphant. Our subconsciousness feels knightly, our souls quake, our piety flexes, our senses stir, and everything unique to our 'being' roars like a lion, too brawny to be felled by far-flung spears or boulders catapulted in midair. We gather as indomitable creatures in Jesus' Holy Sacrifice until He comes again. This Love springs-forth the Truth from lying beds and perpetuates confession from the wicked. Love is the holy inquisition of God toward Creation. He makes and proves Himself by the work of His own hands. He reproves and reproaches, yet forgives and enfolds. What Divinity from the Heart that humankind attacks! Love assures our rest. We are transformed from mechanical nature to unity in a singular trinity of power and omnipotence. Love delivers us again to the Deity we all once abandoned. We face this flourishing truth at the break of each new day. The strobing passage of dawns is proof that we have yet to reach eternal light. But, our sense is clear to anticipate Him. We are both hungry and thirsty, and too unsatisfied. Coming is the day when we will neither be too cold nor hot, and not weak but strong. Now is our chance to shed the deprecating oxidation of sin once and for all; to gain an untarnishable sheen to allow our souls to rival the sun. God is not so much captivated by what besets us as mortals because He realizes our propensity to sin. He is more interested in our own identification with the suffering of His Son for our sake, for the expulsion and expiation of our sinfulness and salvation of our souls. To this end, He gives us grace for our trials and refuge in His Love. What captivates God is our loving care of our fellow sisters and brothers, the elimination of their suffering by our sacrifices, and our realization that His heavenly Saints and Angels, accompanied by His Virgin Mother, are our intercessors to Jesus' merciful Heart which bears the approval of God in all it receives and proclaims.

Why then Morning Star Over America? Why a title of such transcending omnipresence whose object of affection-laced admonishment is keenly the United States of America? Is it because we have lost our blanket of decency on our way out the door, and that we needed a parasol of protection under which we could hide during the strong-willed chaotic societal descent that is occurring? What is going to awaken this grand nation to the perilous path we are treading? Is it the biting cold of incivility; the perpetual feud and folly of ideas in conflict with moral reason, or just the outright mockery of everything that portends holiness and the sacred, a rancid arrogance that will leave our culture fated to be nothing more than life littered with one lonely application of grief after another, flavoring our palate with such bitterness that we would finally concede to a better course? Is it going to require such desolation for beauty to rise again? It is interesting how some ask why the Most Blessed Trinity would send the Holy Virgin of Bethlehem to advance His Glory instead of allowing Jesus to reveal the facets of His unseen Kingdom Himself. Somehow those who commit spiritual suicide by falling on the sword of "choice" at any hint of an immoral cause wish to deprive our Heavenly Father the decision to send anyone whom He pleases as His vested emissaries to petition our faithful compliance with His Will in our time. After all, was it not Jesus Himself who commissioned sinners as His evangelizers to go and make disciples of all the nations 2000 years ago? Did He not expect those pagan societies to listen to His messengers, and promise those who did that they would be granted eternal life as a reward for their compliant faith? You see, neither the spiritual dynamic nor God's modus operandi has changed since those early ages of revelation. He is the same yesterday, today, and forever. Now, how great is our responsibility to respond in our day with the same faith as our ancient fathers in the face of such supernatural grace and mystical phenomena, be it through the appearance of angels, voices of warning in our dreams, inexplicable healings, Eucharistic Hosts that bleed, statues that exude blood and tears, luminous signs in the sun and moon, images on glass panes, and especially in the testaments of visionaries and seers who witness to the miraculous appearances of the Most Blessed Virgin Mary who has come to the rescue of our times? God is responding to our contemporary needs, both historically and spiritually, so it would behoove us to see these questions as rather rhetorical. The more important question is, are we going to heed the enlightening admonishments of the Mother of Christ and lift Creation to the peak of sanctity upon our sacrificial backs, or ignore Her and perish together in a flaming pit as self-possessed fools. Our Lady asks each person, seasoned and amateur, high born and poverty-stricken, backward and mensa member, to make the conscious decision for Jesus Christ! High and low, across and back, forward and aft, processing the past and advancing the future, Our Lady projects Her miraculous presence to those who are willing to invoke the most minuscule smidgeon of faith. She offers Her beatific vision and devotes Her Immaculate Heart still after surrendering Her Divine Son to a horrifying death on the Cross at the hands of sinners who were no more decadent than ourselves. Why? Very simply, She loves us beyond our ability to imagine, but not our power to imitate. We are the children who were bequeathed to Her from the Cross and She knows that Her little tykes, in our nation particularly, need to be reoriented in vision to better understand that Everlasting Life is a gift that scores of millions of Americans are being distracted from embracing in our time—and horrific consequences loom like a vulture peering from the shadows of a rocky crag. She wishes instead that our hearts become tendered to the Truth of the ages, to live by its soothing comforts and revealing light, and willingly prepare for an Eternity that will consume us even in the here and now if we would become like little children and accept it. Heaven rests in peaceful pining for the moment where it will be allowed to overwhelm every human heart with joy. Thus, the Queen of Paradise manifests Her miraculous intercession in a multitude of astounding ways, each offering and challenging our next step in faith, hoping the mystical collage of Her unrivaled beauty and intelligence might be enough to inspire the flagging faith of pagan and prelate, alike, to come alive in witness to the centuries-old Gospel which is the only thing that can save humanity from a global conflagration so intense that the hardened steel in all of our skyscrapers will melt like butter. Our Lady has said that it is an ancient myth to believe that one cannot be perfectly united with

God in spirit and Truth while living exiled on the Earth. Jesus has proven, the Church has proven, and the Saints have proven that oneness with Divine Love can happen as we serve in Our Lord's vineyard. We know what needs to be done; we have known this long before Our Lady ever came speaking to any of us. We must come to realize that supernatural charisms and miraculous signs do provide necessary service to the purposes of Redemption because those who believe respond by way of grace and keep alive the possibility that millions of their doubting brothers and sisters will come to believe in a Heaven that flourishes amongst us through the mystical evidence they present, notwithstanding the heckling from those who will never believe. It is all about the essence of that faith, the unique quality of receiving the gift of trusting the Word of God in our openness to accept what our liberation from exile and transference into the Afterlife will bring. The essential faith about which Our Lady speaks is the clear comparison between the suffering of the world and the peace and brilliant Light of Heaven itself. The Incarnation of Her Son, His Conception in Her Womb, is the fulfillment of the Annunciation of the Archangel Gabriel, and the object of the angelic choirs who announced news of great joy to men of good will at His birth. Our acceptance of suffering in this world, our determination to conquer it, our defiance in the face of the horrible odds against our success, and our knowledge that we are living the Resurrection of Jesus produce everything we need to stand upon our faith and see the edge of Heaven's floor. Why suffering? Because there is a difference between Light and darkness. We are opposed here in this world because evil knows there is complete acclamation in the realms of Paradise. Our bodies bend and break because our spirits already sense the ultimate perfection we will embody when we break past the veil. There we will be set free in ways that will not be known to us until that time arrives. However, all that said, Our Lady reconfirms that our lives here are not encumbered by confinement in the way we have always known the term. It is not as though we cannot walk the entire circumference of the globe, even if we had the strength. We are not held in measurable boxes that are smaller than the dimensions of our physical world. This does not make us as free as a spirit can travel, but it nonetheless assures we have full access to the parameters of the world that God created for us. The question remains to be answered as to whether we realize there is an ultimate freedom that is greater than we have ever learned it to be. When speaking in the spiritual terms of the Church, the answer is obviously that there exists such a liberation. Our Lady has asked us personally for nearly two decades, as my brother and I have recorded, to look at the world as She sees it. Realize that those who listen and heed Her messages benefit from a special discernment of human existence which transcends every boundary ever thrust upon us. She spares us the process of learning about the beginnings of Salvation through the deeper penitential means by revealing them Herself as a reward for our faith. It would seem that it is a loop of sorts. Our Lady has told us that the way to lead a perfect life and sense the glorious nature of Heaven is to practice it to the letter of the Gospel. And, that Gospel sends us right back to the ground on which we walk, sanctifying it, cultivating it, and preparing it for the generations who will succeed us, should there be any.

Indeed, the Sacred Scriptures tell us plenty about preparing for death, about reproving ourselves in all things sinful, and about anticipating with joyful hope the return of Jesus in Glory. All the faithful Christians before us have done as much. However, the Virgin Mother has also told us plenty about these times of chaos and revelation that are different from previous times and ages, although it is the same stirring darkness fomenting it all. The Serpent of the Garden is jumping from horizon to horizon like lightning, entwining himself in the tree of life, and falling everywhere that men provide him a venue—and many are the venues. It is not simple rhetoric to say that we are closer to the Second Coming than any of our ancestors; it is a fact. God knew that the previous centuries would expire before Jesus breaks through the veil of our exile to reclaim everything that is His. It is not that Jesus knew how long to wait, but that it does not matter to Him. His entrance and Judgement will be the same if it would require another 10,000 years. But, we know by the season upon us and all the signs and the mandate that the Queen of Heaven has given that there are many fewer than that. Her commission all along since the past 200 years alone has been to warn humanity that the end is near. She has referred to the End Times in Her messages all around the globe, and specifically to my brother and me, because this is the era that will bring the great reckoning and the closure of the ages. We are participating in establishing the definitive pronouncement which prophetically announces this impending series of events. We are seeing that the world's societies are committing themselves to self-destruction in ways that have not been seen. Instead of the unilateral annihilation by America's foreign enemies, the United States is being destroyed from the inside out. Diversity is a demon who has no conscience but to liberate evil from the chains of Christian restraint so that the father of lies can run rampage to bring death and destruction to everything that would instead provide us a beautiful future. Principle, devotion and sacrifice have been cast to the gutter and mocked with impunity, along with every tradition of decency a towering civilization could have ever revealed. Our Lady has told us many times in a whole host of ways that our country is rotting like a hollow tree infested with termites. Ironically, She has told us amidst our righteous concern that this is not necessarily a terrible thing from the vantage point of Heaven. The core of America needs to be cleansed if it will not convert of its own volition. The scientific secular humanist and atheistic diseases must be eradicated and replaced with the visionary Spirit of the Church. Rather than complain about the things we see happening, She says that we must see the transition of our country as She does. Believe that it is purifying and rectifying, that it is the Lord's way of allowing the imperfect to become permanently extinct. The Roman Catholic Church will always be in place, and the Holy Mass will always be the renewal of mortal life into newer times.

Let us speak more about this faith that She has come to address. It is not our senses that matter. It is not sight nor sound, nor the fragrance of Heaven, and not even the touch of our fingers on the handles of the Gate to Paradise. Our faith, however, is our tangible foothold to the Afterlife. It is like the cloud upon which Jesus will descend when He comes again in Glory. One would not think that somebody could stand on a panel of air that cannot be seen, but this is what our faith does. There are physical references too numerable to count. When we stand on our feet, the ground seems to push back to sustain our weight. Even though we do not feel it, physics tells us that the mass of the Earth is pushing us upward while its gravity keeps holding us down. This balance is what gives us a platform upon which we stand upright. It is force-neutral in that our body can rise and collapse based solely upon its own strength and physical attributes. Now, let us look upon this as a parable to our faith. My brother and I, along with millions of others worldwide, live every day knowing through faith that Our Lady speaks to and through the Church, and that we should listen. We also know that the Gospel is true; the Roman Catholic Church is the original church founded by Jesus Christ on Earth, and that the future will culminate in the Triumph of Her Immaculate Heart containing the Second Coming of the Son of Man. In essence, there is a perfect balance in the faith we live, the mystical events that are occurring throughout the world, and how we are sacramentally preparing for the future that is about to arrive. This does not imply that Jesus' Second Coming would not occur if we had no faith or if the Church was thought to have been disparaged beyond credibility or somehow snuffed from existence. It simply means that we are at peace with God and our role in Creation because we choose to believe through a comprehensive spectrum of fidelity that is responding in concert with the works of the Holy Spirit who is closing out the ages with the elevation and glorification of Revelation's Woman Clothed with the Sun. This is part of the unique balance that sustains the reason for our birth and our inheritance in the Cross. This balance is what is missing in those who choose not to believe, and they are the ones who delve deeply into meaningless science and philosophies that have nothing to do with the end of the world and their appearance before the Throne of God, or how they will be dressed once they get there. This balance is missing in politicians whose policies disagree with the teachings of the Church. It is missing in mothers who choose to abort their children and the doctors who perform the murders. And, it is missing in any clergyman or pastor who summarily dismisses the miraculous intercession of the Queen of Heaven. Further examples here are quite endless in number.

Our Lady has always told us that the perfect balance in human existence is at the juncture where our exile greets Eternity at the veil of our faith. The valley of tears in which humanity lives and the Glory that will accept us as Saints is divided by the smallest margin. And, this veil for some is actually permeable by their prayers and the acceptance of supernatural events. Each time Our Lady speaks to my brother and me is an example of that permeation. For all of us, it is prayer from the heart that moves us closer to the instant of permeation. We also know that for some, the veil might as well be a mile-thick wall of brick and mortar. The point our Holy Mother always asks us to make is that mankind is who decides the thickness of the veil. I repeat, it is mankind who decides the thickness of the veil. What does this mean for the Church composed of millions of individual souls? It means that it must be universal and centrally focused. All eyes must be one eye, and the reverse must also be true. There must be one vision, one focus pulled by many who compose the Mystical Body of Christ. Is this vision yet perfect? Not even close. Far from it. Is this vision being corrected? Yes, and the Church, the Gospel, all the apostolates, all of the Virgin Mary's apparitions, and everything else serving to awaken the consciences of men comprise the single "corrective lens" that aids humanity in seeing where the world is going. This also implies that the lost must not only be able to see, but they must be willing to look. They must be hungry to perceive what the Lord would have them do instead of being satiated by all the distractions that lure them away from Him and doom the possibility that they would one day find themselves acceptable before His sight. These people need a vacant place to look with untrammeled sight at their very existence. Hence, the rotting of the core of America is making way for spiritual faith to take its place. We are back to the original premise. This is why we must not be overly saddened when we see the demise of long-held patriotic institutions or the financial destruction of the government. These things are making way for the introduction of the Gospel Truth where instead so many millions have invested their lives and futures in a college of lies. If one is to be healed, he must ingest some awful-tasting medicine at times. If America is to be cleansed and redeemed, it must be gutted of everything that corrupts it. And, for disorder to disappear, there must be epic conversion or conflagrations to rival those of the worst in history, likened to the most gruesome battles in the annals of the world. Our Lady suggests that a spiritual renewal will unfold to lay waste to everything that stands in the way of the Church. It may require Armageddon, or it might be something as simple as the cry of a lamb. This will be decided by the choices of men. At present, our conduct and almost total lack of acceptance of Her miraculous intercession are an ominous petition to the heavens for

Armageddon. Our Holy Mother wants us to understand the connection between human faith and the unfolding of future events. She prays that each person realizes that the faith that is dispensed from Heaven can retrace the steps of our forbears and reverse the tides of time. It is all based on human love intermingled with Divine Love in such a way that the former becomes the perfect likeness of the latter. The Blessed Virgin is trying to step us forward in time from our limited space in exile, effecting our movement toward the Kingdom of God and allowing us to rendezvous with Christ as He simultaneously approaches us to end the world. She is a gift whose miraculous beauty of Divine origin precedes Jesus through Her obedience. Instinctively, She has come to rescue Her children from the throes of perdition. Her honor amplifies Her perfect Motherhood. The crown She wears calls us like the stars to look upward and live the dignity we gained through Her Crucified Son. This Mother of God chooses Her own to magnify the essence of Her being and the meaning of Her prayers. She is uniquely stationed and perfectly adorned to reflect the awesomeness of Heaven. Perfectly united to Jesus, She leads Him by the affectionate grace that soothes His immortal Being. Hand-in-hand, they come to us united for the cause of our conversion through the genius Spirit into the people whole, the uniform purpose of God for our existence. Mary is the tabernacle of universal love who brings us freedom while binding us dictatorially to our monarchical God. Through Her, we are blessed for a life in a liberty we have never known. This Lady springs magnificently from Her maternal office to command the world. She gives life to the parched of conscience. Her hope collaterally lifts our hope. In no other creature do we find such bliss and beauty in the feminine form of a mother. From inside the Colander Crown of Mary flows the Divine Mercy of Christ the King, a drop to every soul in time. Her mandate is from the Hand of God Himself because She is the sweetest fruit of His Love.

What is it then that has impeded Her success in touching the world deeply enough for it to be shocked into changing? What is dampening the response to Her unprecedented intercession? Where is the push-back coming from? Sometimes it seems rather rhetorical to say that humanity's faith is not meeting the challenge. But why? How do the dominos begin to fall when most do not even know there is an active faith required of them or a challenge from Heaven marked by such serious urgency? There is something called a subliminal hierarchy of influence within each human being, meaning that there is a collage of things within each person weighted in particular orders according to their unique personal development, secularized social poise, and exposure to the Truth that has influence over how they respond to situations and events. It is why we accept some things immediately, while being indifferent and dismissing others as irrelevant to us that would seem obvious to another segment of the population. Most are not consciously aware of what truly influences them to make decisions or has undue power to grasp their attention, nor are they sensitive to the scope of grandeur and consequences enjoined in those things they are brushing aside. For simplicity of discussion, there are three camps of people in the world. The first is comprised of those who are beyond the boundary of being influenced by Christianity as it presently engages them. They are the people immersed in beliefs and cultures outside the gravity of understanding the tenets of Christianity. The second are those who have submitted their hearts to the Gospel through the historical Traditions of the Original Apostolic Church. And, then there are the rest who have a semblance of Christian faith but are either scattered into conflicting persuasions as a result of unfocussed religious pluralism, or who are comfortable being a Christian in name only while refusing to tender any meaningful sacrifice for their ascendancy in holiness. For those outside the boundary of influence, usually cultural authoritarianism and unimaginable pressure from sectarian and atheistic peers squelches the environment where through liberty of conscience Jesus might fluently touch them in a realm of peace. And for those in the last group, few arguments for Christian solidarity matter because Satan has inoculated them with a wall of distractions which they are pleased to indulge in, thinking their simple knowledge of Christ and their interpersonal interpretations of Scripture are enough to manifest Jesus' desire that we be one body. They enjoy being only an island, while the massive continent of Universal Christianity lies off their horizon. It is this last group who are important for the moment. In realms of religious belief and in the arena of faith, nearly everyone sheepishly defers to those who can generate intellectual arguments that are beyond the average person's ability to understand. Most people are intimidated by complexity of thinking without realizing that it is oftentimes nothing more than that. They believe that since they have not concocted ideas in as convoluted dimensions, they must defer to those who seem to have found the key. And in many cases, this could not be further from the truth. Obfuscation by inundation is the main characteristic of much of our intellectualism, particularly amongst the "miracle police." We often tender blind faith in other sinners who simply have an aptitude for orderly brain functions where they can construct complex multidimensional arguments. But, what happens when those with this intelligence are wrong, who have built their arguments on rickety foundations that they have obscured with their cerebral hubris, who would move beyond themselves in faith only after God Himself conquers them with miraculous power rivaling the parting of the Red Sea before Moses? When this misplaced devotion occurs, millions become complacent in their thinking and paralyzed in their conduct, and an impenetrable indifference toward anything outside their perception or allegiances ensues. Their subliminal hierarchy of influence has enslaved them because they do not realize that they have laid their confidence, lives and dignity in the hands of others who are as fallible as they are who happen to be sorely misguided through their own arrogance. In this anemic state of faithlessness, it becomes nearly impossible to loosen the thinking of these individual sects unless one has evidence that renders the intellect irrelevant. This is why the Blessed Virgin Mary is miraculously appearing in the world. She is the earthquake that splits the very bedrock of their sectarian intellects. She leaves the stoic mentalities of the supposedly learned speechless and their agendas superceded, and they know it, therefore they reject Her with hyper-zeal. It is like debating how the pyramids were built, and suddenly pharaoh's chief architect and engineer walks in the door. All the supposition and speculation becomes moot at that point. The Mother of Jesus is attempting by miraculous means, but still within the boundaries of our faith, to align those who have the courage to believe Her so the domino of the wicked will subsequently fall at seeing authentic Christianity glimmering like a city in the distance with such spectacular brilliance that their hearts break at the beauty. She wants them all to wonder what they are being left out of, and hopes that fear of the Lord would finally bring them to the wisdom of their sacrificial obedience. But, what has been the response to the Mother of Jesus Christ from those who refuse to align themselves with the Truth She is revealing? The learned who are filled with more facts than faith purposely ignore Her, and encourage everyone under their influence to do the same, as a way of not having to deal with the seismic temblors She is generating within their perception. They are actually more enamored with themselves than they are with the Queen of the Universe, if you can imagine that. It is the grandeur and the consequences that they are dismissing out of hand by refusing to consider what they are. They would generate entire theologies, just so they can stand justified saying, "I am not required to respond to your private revelations." For the record, they are not "mine" and they never have been. These lost individuals eschew Our Lady's twisting them into focus and reject the opportunity Our Lord Jesus Christ is giving them through His Divine Mercy. And if one places them in the proverbial gun sights by speaking this truth with a bold confidence they cannot ignore, the clandestine hellfire of backroom slander, rebuttal, and rogue judgement descends like a monsoon from their lips and actions, not only upon those courageous enough to speak the reason of why we are not responding as a collective body of believers, but also upon the principals of influence to whom everyone else is looking for guidance so that these leaders will be as skeptical as those who are chiding them not to believe. Point blank, the Mother of Jesus Christ is appearing to Her children all over the world who have no influence, authority, intellectual prowess or reason to lie, and these same ones are so far down the subliminal hierarchy of influence of those with authority and intellectual aptitude that it is nearly impossible for the Holy Spirit to gain a footing from which to move the conscience of humankind through the wholeness of Christianity's Body. And in this rational conclusion rests the great test of faith being laid before humanity in our time by our loving God. He is unfolding Redemption in a way that requires faith from both the weak and the powerful. Did He not do as much when He chose to be born in a manger as opposed to the satin-lined bassinet of a worldly king? The story is consistent, the Gospel is unfolding to the same integrity. The Lord of Creation will dispense Divine Mercy and change our world if we will but open our hearts, summon our courage, and respond in every authoritative and creative way the Holy Spirit inspires, all defined by our holy sacrifices. Nothing more need be said. So far, the Virgin Mother is being treated as if She is irrelevant, given lip service as our response, left to succeed on Her own, and challenged to deliver earthshattering "supernaturalitate" before the stodgy dominos teeter in allegiance to Her Immaculate Heart and drop the entire body of Christianity into alignment with the Truth which would instill confidence throughout its ranks to accept and fulfill the charge of the Holy Gospel with urgency because time is so short. Once the principals of influence tender their fealty to the miraculous nature of Jesus' Queen openly and confidently, scientism will be superceded and the subliminal hierarchy of influence will align like a beautiful picture; the lake will become peaceful as a millpond which drives a sifting wheel, and the world will descend into the arms of Christ like a feather coming to rest upon a pillow. The new springtime will stir us into stunned amazement at how quickly the sunlight of better days came out. This is how God sees it, and it is as simple as that. At this point, the faithful millions who do believe are required to sacrificially stand as victims in witness to the truth before the disinterested religious intelligentsia dominating the arena of faith who collectively refuse to do anything more than sniff and walk away like a persnickety cat that does not like his food. Then, the moment Satan senses the division, he highlights, stirs, pries, and exacerbates the strained relationships and coerces people into opposing camps; all caused by the obstinance of those who refuse to surrender their pride, get on board, and accept that God may be summoning their faith to higher realms for the purpose of converting the world before it is too late to avoid a global holocaust. Self-acclaimed theologians who have no use for miracles or the supernatural intercession of the Virgin Mary unless it happens to them are one of the greatest instruments of Satan that the world has ever known because they project stifling force at the pinnacles of the subliminal hierarchy of influence without much effort at all. They do not have to convert millions to their faithlessness; they only have to poison the perspective where millions of people are seeking direction and the strength for their faith. And they do this so everyone will listen to them instead. Even the secular forces of the world are more than pleased to assist them at any juncture where they need a greater venue. It is much like the partisan political advertising agencies that portray themselves as journalistic news media. Candidates with views outside their prejudices do not have a chance of dignity on their airwaves. These theological influence peddlers are the domino that will not fall in love with God enough to believe Him, His Queen, or their brothers and sisters who have been sent to them by divine decree. They handicap the faith of weaker Bishops, they disguise their faithlessness as prudence, they turn the Holy Eucharist into nothing but a symbol, they edit the Word of God according to their heresy, they dismiss the existence of Hell, they explain away every miracle of the Gospel, they deny Jesus' Resurrection, they advance slanderous revisionism of the heroic lives of the Catholic Saints, they have manipulated the Second Vatican Council to suit their pluralistic agendas, they disparage the supremacy of the Catholic Church, they attack the Papacy at every opportunity, they abhor obedience to the Pope, they turn evangelization into a political docket of social justice, they depopulate seminaries of sacred orthodoxy in alignment with Rome, they besmirch the Holy Rosary, they exhaust the courage of holy priests, they scatter the allegiances of the faithful, they pontificate in word, writing and attitude as if they have direct communication with the Lord, and are the first to challenge, nitpick, cajole, slander, mock, and poo-poo anything that does not resonate with their personal estimation of the grand knowledge of God they think they bear. And the Most Blessed Virgin is the prime target of their derision because She renders their heretical, religiously populist agendas irrelevant while declaring to feminists that She is the real Lady of Creation! Conqueror of Heretics, indeed! They believe they are the infallible ones who know the wisdom of God above every other mortal, simply because they have created a structure of thinking so complex that simple little children do not care to understand it. Thus, their pride claims superiority in all matters relating to the Kingdom of God. These individuals are scattered throughout the world in deep places of influence and in most university settings as instruments of darkness who disparage and diminish Our Lady's influence through Her miraculous intercessions at every opportunity. They downplay whatever they cannot destroy outright. The Virgin Mother believes they should rethink their purpose in life and their contribution to human redemption before they are called to an accounting of it. Whatever the devil cannot discredit and slander in the moment through the lips of their cerebral subterfuges, he encourages to be dismissed to future generations to decide, if at all. Our Lady has told me that Her obedient children are more the theologians than they are! The greatest manifestation of the Holy Spirit in the human heart is not defined by human intellectualism. Yes, She has spoken to me at length about intellectual thought and the pride it habitually engenders. And, these thinkers would rhetorically deflect their culpability while donning sacrosanct disinterested demeanors for this messenger even saying so, and they would be believed by the gallery of the lost who have subliminally hitched their insecurities to academic accolades which do nothing to confirm supernatural approbation in the eyes of God. Our Lady gives no regard whatsoever to intellectual learning if the faith is not present to accept the works of the Holy Spirit such as Her miraculous intercession, especially after these influxes of grace have been displayed so profoundly and convincingly before their very eyes. Upon how many church domes and between what number of spiring steeples does She have to stand? How much rejection must She have to endure? To how many simple children must She appear, and how many mystical phenomena must She bestow before the learned begin to shiver in their boot soles at the tepid nature of their faith? Do they realize that these graces have come from Her unimaginable suffering, an Immaculate Heart broken open by swords and daggers of colossal pain which now inundates our lives with salvific wonders? If they had the faith they claim, they would have already exhausted themselves and their careers traveling the unbelieving world reveling the works of God in our midst through Her divine intercession, diving into the cabal of the faithless to become either martyrs or the evangelizers that would change the course of the ages. The record of history will show that they did none of this, and our country and the world are the spiritually poorer for it. Our Lady knows they are lost in their mental macrocosm of conjecture and deconstruction, and so should we. Everyone should cease being intimidated by the supposedly learned and discern their actual motivations instead, because far too many of them have forfeited their capacity to respond to anything requiring their authentic faith many textbooks ago, and their shunning of Our Lady's appearances proves it. They deserve the righteous rebuke they are soon to receive from the very lips of Christ Himself. My words are simply a premonition of the lambasting that is going to descend upon them like incandescent fire. These things must be said because the truly faithless mind-set held by these imposters is one of the major reasons the world has yet to respond to the Queen of Heaven with the abandonment that Our Lord demands. The Church looks to them for the assistance of their intellects, but also for their stellar humility and fear of God which bestows upon them the wise flexibility to respond and testify to the Will of Almighty God. It has never turned to them for their definitive decrees as if they are the origin of the Deposit of Faith or the auditors of its splendorous life-giving effusions. The Church petitions their contribution of multidimensional spiritual and mystical knowledge perceived from the spectacular lives of the Saints coupled with their own healthy mystical holiness to be presented in a flexible manner that protects and confirms the unique genius of the Holy Spirit in our time, while remaining steadfast in the anchoring of history that the Church may preserve its unity with the past as one Body in allegiance to the one Savior of Man. Since it is evident that previous ages of Christians have proven far greater faith in Our Lady than our contemporary example testifies, who is it then that is not preserving unity with the past? Alas, multitudes function as spiritually-anemic excuse generators in opposition to the King of kings because the wings for the mystical sensibilities are not spread to accommodate the lofty winds of the Holy Spirit. They are like a captain of a sailing ship who is revving the seldom used engines in a direction opposite the course intended by the billowing sails. And when the benevolent winds overwhelm their intellectual engines, they throw the anchor to impede its progress by force of will. Anything at their disposal they will use to sully the agenda of the Mother of God, because they do not have the faith to become participants at Her side in the conversion of the world through Her Immaculate grace, even though no other will be sent to deliver us from the approaching nightmares of our own making.

Those who believe themselves to be sophisticated religious intellectuals are sitting at their drawing boards, many with no more benevolent inclinations than to create a framework of reasoning to hoodwink everyone else into accepting some inordinate personal or societal agenda, be it the defense of homosexual conduct, the justification of women priests, the defense of same-sex marriage, the assuaging of feminine radicalism, the plurality of every religion, the maligning of the hierarchy of the Church, the dilution of the unique nature of the Papacy, or a whole montage of other illicit nonsense that their ego-stricken natures could seduce them to delve into. Jesus gave them seven instruments upon which to build the transportation for humanity's return to Paradise. These instruments are the seven Sacraments of the Catholic Church and what they coalesce into, stand for, and the sanctifying grace they bestow. These Sacraments are the outward signs of God instituted by Christ to give grace to the human soul for its elevation into the eternal realms of the Almighty Father. Theologians are like automobile engineers. They must make sure these seven instruments are preserved or incorporated into any plans that are designed for the advancement of civilization upon the road to Redemption because they are the source of humanity's unity with God. If these thinkers do not fulfill this simple purpose, they are not in alignment with the Holy Spirit. It is like making sure every car that is built has a steering wheel, passenger compartment, headlights, windshield, windshield wipers, rearview mirror, and an engine.

Windshield - Baptism
Windshield Wipers - Penance
Headlights - Confirmation
Steering Wheel - Holy Orders
Engine - Holy Eucharist
Passenger Compartment - Holy Matrimony
Rearview mirror - Anointing of the Sick (Last Rites)

The great theologians of Catholic history were all humble children who drafted their vehicles through the centuries in deference to these elements. Others who are presently touted as religious giants have been duped into whittling them to a fewer number. Imagine setting out on a trip in a car without a steering wheel, windshield wipers or an engine. You would end up sitting in the driveway in a rainstorm for a week with the wheels chocked sideways to choruses of, 'Are we there yet?' And, the answer would always be 'no.' Anyway, the point is, many theologians have appropriated an authority over the Divine Will of Jesus Christ which was not given to them. They have not only decided to audit the numerical incorporation of the original seven elements, but have also assumed the responsibility to determine the color of the paint, the style of the rims, the shape of the body, whether there is an air conditioner or the windows roll down, and are presently in the process of drawing the map where the vehicle will travel. Then, our Holy Mother appears in our midst and they find themselves walking toward a great public venue beside the driving lane that has been set aside for transporting patrons by tram to the stadium, and a Greyhound tour bus flies by with Her children hanging from the windows screaming with glee, and these pithy thinkers hurl epitaphs because She did not submit Her vehicle to the inspection of their drawing boards in advance. Her tour bus is not the subcompact that they had designed for everyone to cram into. The salvific Truth is larger than they believe allowable. They fail to notice that the bus still has an engine, steering wheel, passenger compartment, headlights, windshield, windshield wipers, and a rearview mirror in which every person on that bus sees them as trailing miserably behind in dire need of a lift, because chances are, they are not going to be in their seats at curtain call of the first merciful act of Eternity. Please do not succumb to the temptation of believing that my descriptions are harsh, especially when one has not yet experienced the purifying sword that Saint Michael the Archangel wields. In his Light, my words by comparison are a gentle suggestion. I would never in a million years have had the spiritual strength to advance these sentiments had I not learned them in the midst of Our Lady's statuesque perfection. These things must be said because the perspective of these lost individuals must be wrenched around to face the Will of God again. And the King of kings has charged me to grab them by the lapels of their collective ego and shake them if need be. Spiritual mediocrity is of a rotting, egotistical flesh that must be cut from the body or we are going to perish from the infection. If they see a shimmering sword of admonishment slashing down upon them, it is not to run them through, but rather to shear away the chains that Satan has wrapped around their souls so they may taste a freedom and a strength that they have never experienced in their lives.

I asked our Holy Mother one day how so many intelligent men and women who portray such sincerity came to be in this debilitated state. She said their sincerity is a facade behind which they are hiding their unchecked pride. They exist within a frail condition that is not unlike developing a theory to understand the physical universe. The forces that make-up the cohesion and movement of the tangible heavens have been in place and functioning by God's divine hand since the beginning of Creation, despite man's lack of complete intellectual understanding. No scientist or physicist has ever been able to impeach the movement of the heavens; they move no matter what equations would supposedly disallow them from doing so. And that is the analogy. It is noteworthy how astrophysicists return to their drawing boards like giddy little children when their intelligence is stunned by more revelatory phenomena in the heavens. They know they will be left behind in the development of astronomical knowledge if they do not participate in seeking out an understanding of what is occurring before them. Even though they are relegated to mere observation in the face of planets and stars that will never allow them to participate in their perfect galactic grandeur, they search for meaning in the phenomena they witness with openness and passion. These honest inquisitors have developed a pliable paradigm explaining the orchestration of the heavens through the language of mathematics based on observable phenomena and rigorous experimentation. Yet, in the scientific arena, this paradigm is simply a lens for observers and not the truthful essence of that universe where they would be participants in the forces they witness. This is the difference. While the unseen world has always moved according to the invincible Will of God, the truth of His spiritual Kingdom becomes seeable only by our active participation in the faith that reveals it. The essence of the Most Blessed Trinity is not a theological construct of the mind or a structured fabrication of mental argument, no matter how precise those cerebral descriptions may be. The Truth of the Most Blessed Trinity is rather a love that reigns in the heart which bestows an inherent confidence in Eternal Deliverance based in the historical facts of Jesus' Sacrifice on the Cross. This revelation of the unseeable Kingdom is what the Catholic Church has sustained infallibly throughout the ages through Her dogmas of faith and sacramental structure. Through faith and our communal prayer, we possess a mystical sense of the unseen Kingdom that is the grace animating our existence as an effect of the Sacraments that preserves humanity's future in Heaven. Jesus was so simple and gentle to human hearts which were open to Him because He knew our unbridled capacity to generate thought and vision, but He also realized our tendency toward disjointed relativism in the face of sacrifice, and thus how confused we can quickly become. Let's face it, humanity wanders away like any toddler does the minute one turns their back on them. The heart needed to be spacious, vibrant and uncluttered, with the capacity to contemplatively grasp the multidimensional flourishing of grace that would permeate human existence and draw the soul back to the original Garden of

Life. But, its attributes of vision must be solidly imbedded in our sacrificial participation in human redemption in imitation of the Crucifixion based in the exercise of faith infused by the Holy Spirit, instead of being grounded in the dead function of grouchy observation supported only by intellectual biases dismissive of every work of the Spirit of God that does not occur in the systematic environment of a theological paradigm. And in all this somewhat frank admonishment of those in intellectual bondage, I bow before the humble genius of the Spiritual Doctors of the Roman Catholic Church who made themselves true instruments of the Holy Spirit for the Salvation and conversion of men in a multitude of creative ways. All of them believed deeply in the miraculous and the wisdom gained through the mystical grace of the Holy Spirit. Saint John of the Cross and Saint Teresa of Avila, for example, both wrote at length trying to describe their miraculous relationship with God which they found to be difficult to commit to a page, but knew was open to every person given the breath of Life. And, let us not forget how deep was the mystical heart of our late Pontiff, Pope John Paul the Great.

The necessity exists for the Church to remain true to the commission and revelation that it was given upon the Feast of Pentecost. Fairly few people realize what this actually means. When the Holy Spirit descended upon the Church at Pentecost with our Holy Mother present, they knew that power in tongues of fire was given to them. This power transcended everything they knew about human exile and all the reasons they ever had for living. It took their hearts and thoughts to higher, metaphysical levels, to places that they had not yet gone when Jesus was with them in the Flesh. We know that the Apostles were the first Bishops. And, this lineage of grace and knowledge has been handed down to every Bishop who has been aligned with the Pope in Rome. What this means is that these descendants possessed The Faith according to their inheritance from those first Apostles. Our Lady has made it definitively clear that She stands by our present-day Bishops with clarity and emphasis, as do my brother and I. It is not that they are perfect by any means, nor are they infallible in their preaching about faith and morals; and neither are we. This is why it is imperative that we remain loyal to the Vicar of Christ who instructs us, who is capable of leading us from the Chair of Saint Peter toward that perfection, toward that infallibility. When we hear declarations from those who disparage and despise the Original Apostolic Church, we see the bitter jealousy of rogue theologians and hedonists who see the Church in a way that it does not truly exist. Some of these people believe that the Church exists to serve its own dogmas, but it is the other way around. Dogmas are the doctrinal revelations of Divine Truth that have existed from the beginning, that have served and supported the mission of the Church from the Apostolic age. They are like jewels that have lain in the Heart of the Church since its inception that the Holy Spirit has chosen to definitively impress into the crowning history of man by solemn declaration at certain points in time. And when someone sees it the opposite way, they perceive their own writings and teachings as autonomous from the Supreme Pontiff in Rome. In essence, their own pride in their assumptions about what God does and allows causes them to feel as though they are the infallible ones, as if their thinking is ageless. The only ageless thinking is that which is in communion with the dogma and teachings of Roman Catholic Christianity. The Holy Spirit has grown the Church according to world circumstances through human history; in other words, harmonized with the ability of men to understand one another in different countries by their capacity to communicate and share their view of mortal existence. These abilities and capacities have changed through the centuries because of new mediums of travel and communication. The Lord has taken advantage of these modernizations to spread the Holy Gospel to lands far and wide. Pope John Paul II utilized both of these media to the best of his talent and the extent of his health. He traveled, spoke, and wrote with eloquence and urgency. He delivered the Gospel message exactly the way it was handed to him from Heaven, and through his holy predecessors. The problem some theologians had with Pope John Paul is that they had previously never heard some of his proclamations, such as his Theology of the Body, or encountered his ecumenical kindness. But, just because something is finally brought to the forefront does not imply that it is new. It is the same with the present scope of Our Lady's miraculous intercession. Notwithstanding its seemingly unprecedented magnitude in our time, She has been an instrument of Jesus' engagement with humanity from the beginning, and it is only the Church Militant who awaits the Holy Spirit's clarifying pronouncement of the final dogma revealing Her maternal station as Co-Redemptrix and Mediatrix of All Graces because the Church-Triumphant and the Church-Suffering already know it. In this final Marian dogma, Her miraculous intercessions throughout history will be given context, instead of them being seen as an abstract accessory to the principal nature of Redemption. Our Lady's historical intercession is going to be matured from the definition of "private revelation" into the realms of "dogmatic example" in much the same way as the Holy Mass is the dogmatic example of the Eucharistic Dogma. The animation of the Eucharistic Dogma is the Holy Mass; and the animation of the Dogma of Our Lady as Co-Redemptrix and Mediatrix of All Graces is Her miraculous intercession throughout history. God has saved the crowning revelation of His Mother's dignity for the close of the ages, while theologians and advisors are looking for historical precedent in Her words and actions when there seems to be none on any scale they recognize. Should we reject a fully open rose because we have never seen one at any time other than in its budding stages? Pope John Paul the Great taught with prudence the beliefs of the Original Catholic and Apostolic Church with as much accuracy as Saint Peter and all the

Popes, and He loved Our Lady. They all loved Our Lady! If we told a group of people that a Cross was erected on a rocky peak in the Andes mountains, their instinct would be to ask when it was put there. If we said that it was placed there around 1972, many would state that it could not possibly be true because they surely would have been told about it before today. These people actually believe that they already know everything that the Holy Spirit has to say, that the Sacred Scriptures are dead statements locked in an antique document, and that Jesus does not have the right to enhance or clarify His own teachings even in the face of the near extinction of Christian evangelization in our contemporary era. This is why so many theologians are reluctant to advise pastors and Bishops to allow their followers and parishioners to share our Holy Mother's appearances and messages within the orthodox realms of the Church. These new manifestations simply do not fit into their perception of the Church fixed in the first centuries. They say that there could not possibly be a Cross in the Andes mountains because they would have already known about it. This is why we should pray for our Bishops. They are human beings whose hearts are as simple and gentle as our own, who are trying to maintain an impregnable relationship with the Holy Spirit, but are burdened with both the eccentricities of those closest to them and also belabored by a stiff-necked world of human beings who rarely follow any leadership unless it capitulates to selfish cultural whims; and this is cause for sorrow. Our Bishops are charged with the sacred responsibility to preserve the integrity of the Church and to protect it from deceptive forces that arise from every earthly direction, while expected by Heaven to summon a courage through almost supernatural faith in order to trust the integrity of authentic messengers who are themselves sinners whom they have oftentimes never met in their lives. Who would not have difficulty finding the faith to transcend such a dilemma? Can we imagine being asked to believe a near stranger claiming something so extraordinary without a supernatural sign to prove it when such a magnitude of consequences are in play? Yet, God asks for that faith nonetheless. We should recognize the strength that is displayed by the Bishops who do believe and openly witness to Our Lady's miraculous intercession. When all is said and done, it will be seen that they trusted Jesus Christ to protect their judgement; they trusted their own hearts and believed in the honesty of their spiritual children, and most of all, they believed that God would never fail them. And with this trilateral faith, they display the strength to be unafraid of being out upon the waves because they know the Lord will ordain events beneficially for the Church in response to the personal sacrifice of their fears. Only love, stability, faithfulness, patience, and an obedience that nurtures trust ever bridge that gap between reticence and truth in these periods of discernment.

The Holy Scripture speaks about the long-shared statement that there is not enough room in the world to place all the books it would require to record everything Jesus did and said. We must remember that Our Lord is still saying and doing through the power of His Holy Spirit. Theologians who reject Our Lady's apparitions are not attuned to the Living Spirit of God or the historical witness of the Church, and they seem to refuse to pray for discernment which would separate their skeptical intellects from the trust in God they should have. For if they prayed as they should, they would not be opposed to such mystical beauty. They cannot seem to admit to the miraculous unless they see the miracle occur for themselves, because they always harbor the fear that they might ultimately be proven wrong. Saints are not afraid of being wrong because they know Christ is their front and rear guard. The fearful walk up to the smoldering remains of a house and remain unconvinced that there was a fire. They encounter a tree that has piles of succulent apples scattered beneath it, but will wait until the next summer to see a new crop of apples actually hanging from the branches before they will admit that it just might be an apple tree. The analogies are quite endless, yet they all reveal their same hyper-scrupulous faithlessness. They cry with their actions, "Come down from that Cross, and then we will believe." We must get past "whether" it is truly the miraculous intercession of the Queen of Heaven, and proceed to the obedience which She is trying to effect through Her salvific intervention. Imagine what would occur if the skeptics would employ their intelligence like those giddy astrophysicists, and return to their drawing boards to engineer plans to magnify what the Queen of Heaven has had to say to every nation and tongue. It is then that Heaven would be at the beck and call of their intellects with all the power and majesty that Paradise possesses. Can you imagine referring the content of Her messages to the secular world in the context of the miracle of the Incarnation? Or, the miracle of the Resurrection or the Eucharist? Physicists took Einstein's ingenious knowledge of the relationship between matter and energy and built an atomic bomb. What could be done with an exposition explaining the interaction of mortal humanity with the supernatural grace of the Queen of the Universe, while incorporating the nature of the Church they know so well? Think about it. Her supernatural appearances for the conversion of humanity are as essential in the deliverance of men as the Descent of the Holy Spirit, and they flow inexorably from that same Pentecost. It would be prudent if we would ponder what it is like to be a theologian who listens more to scientists and pragmatists than the Spirit of the Lord trying to open his heart. People like this are hardened in thought and reticent in their actions. And, ironically, they are not so much worried that certain miraculous manifestations may be from the devil as much as it may actually be the presence of Heaven trying to tell them that their reluctance to adhere to Heaven's calling is from their disbelief that God can do anything He pleases without their consent, and demand their concessionary faith in the process. He asks for the obedience and submission that they are so diligent to exact from others. We have seen throughout the years while conversing with the Virgin Mother that She has little regard for these theologizers because they desire more to watch the Church than participate in its sacrificial mission. They refuse to ante up and get in the game beside the heroic witnesses to the Truth. They are the proverbial peanut gallery of self-possessed snobs much like the secular media in America today. They are self-appointed critics who put more stock in the Protestant Reformation than in the miracles of Fatima, even though the latter would have snuffed out the former on its first day had God so deigned His power to be revealed on All Saints Day in 1517. If you look at their history, you will see that this is true. They are poring over the Scriptures with their anemic pedagogies, trying to locate a sentence that asks them to allow room for the influence of Our Lady's apparitions in the redemption of the world. And since they cannot seem to find it, they assume with self-ascribed authority that Her appearances have no theological purpose and are extraneous manifestations that are products of spiritual zealotry, delusionary fanaticism or diabolical regulation. We have gotten to the point where theological intellectualism has become the excuse for this trite breadth of faith as if it is all ordained by God Himself. The arsenal of our greatest allegiance is locked in chains in a cell no one can free themselves from without knowing the combination they have put on the door. It is an armory filled with weapons that have never been fired, and at Our Lady's first volley, the thundering report causes them to run like gun-shy bird dogs on their first hunt because they have no idea what the weapons sound like. Think about it! That is why when they see that Heaven has transcended to Earth and personally unleashed the power of faith in millions of children, they are at best radically indifferent to the expression because it is the only action that they can engage by force of will in the face of having lost control over the Holy Spirit whom they fear is going to ask something of them that will require a faith they do not have the courage to display. Is this any way to evangelize a world that is sliding off the ledge into the abyss? How many countries and states have to be gutted of Christianity before we accept Our Lady's divine assistance and begin to call the world to repentance like carnival barkers? Faith does not originate in the mind of man. It does not arise from finally learning enough. It is a revelatory explosion in the heart that dispenses grace to all that man says, does and believes. It is a metanoia which concretizes and drives conviction into the realms of sanctity. It creates heroes from cowards and geniuses from simple little children. The devolution of our capacity to believe in all that is yet to be seen occurred slowly over time, and it began with the writings of dissident revolutionaries and other nonconformists who thrust the Church into a defensive posture based in scriptural argumentation and textual parsing. Further, there appeared in time the lingering need of early Christians who wondered how to reconcile and bridge to the teachings of the Ancients. Could

Socrates and Aristotle be so far off, they asked. Hence, there became a melding of the philosophies of the Ancients with the teachings of the Church, without careful discernment regarding the historical path being charted for a human species of profound intellectual diversity which is naturally reticent to believe anything before seeing or understanding. The input of explorers and astronomers even exacerbated the problem. These early curious men did not know what to do with their seemingly God-given intellectual frameworks whereby they were trying to define the mortal world. It was like being given the ability to run and not first considering the obstacles before leaving the starting blocks. God wanted a 100m dash, and man was intent upon engaging a steeplechase. We can remember the depiction of Forrest Gump who ran from one coast to the other and back again and said, "I was just runnin'." No purpose, no destination, no vision of the heart, just cerebral motion. What was the vast imagination of men came to be seen as being dispensed from the mind of God. It streamed from the same pride and disillusionment that felled Adam from the Garden. Through the centuries, succeeding intellectuals came to see themselves as prophets because they had no one who could compete with their mental engineering to call them down; they had no global voice that could reach them in time to prune the forest they were planting. If the Popes in those times had the communication mediums available today, this could have been stopped. And, we could add countless other reasons why intellectualism has grown over the centuries to the detriment of faith. Take into account the influence of mathematics and physics, and the growth of empirical studies and hypotheses. Remember that as science grows larger, the need for faith seems to grow smaller. This is a false relationship because science will never touch the realms of God; it only observes His will after the fact, while faith allows us to prophesy what God will accomplish next. All of these things have contributed to the lessening of the prayer for faith that Jesus addressed so many times during His earthly ministry. The Holy Spirit will guide Creation if we are willing to listen to the heart and unite as one humanity in the Church. I asked Our Lady one day what would be effective in dislodging the steel grip of intellectualism; what kind of argument? She responded that I should highlight the 'relationship' between Heaven and Earth that is hard to explain and difficult to recount on a page. She said I should show them Morning Star Over America! In other words, what was Pentecost all about? What does a person receive through the Sacrament of Confirmation administered by Saint Peter through his succession of Bishops? Simply put, how do they account for the many miracles around the globe that cannot be attributed to orthodox Scripture? Do they simply dismiss these Parousial graces out of hand because they do not fit in their framework of theology, and then declare that they are unimportant to the spiritual growth and faithful convalescence of the Church worldwide? Our Lady continued by saying that they dismiss the direct actions of God because of their impenetrable impression of the Sacred Scripture, believing accurately that nothing else is needed for human Salvation, but believing inaccurately that anything further that is miraculous is not prudent for conversion. They draw the dichotomy between Salvation and conversion, when they are actually inseparable. They make a distinction between orthodoxy and miracles as though the latter is somehow strictly unorthodox. Miracles are instead essential to the Church because they reflect and reveal the consistently living Spirit of Jesus through His Mystical Body, who is the Church itself. Transubstantiation is a miracle, after all! And yes, orthodoxy is a miracle too. Hence, it is a paradox. One cannot speak about the Church as a member and be separated from all that it spiritually generates. One cannot be diagnostic without having a part in the diagnosis when it comes to the Church. It is not like a physician and a patient. Here, when the doctor draws blood, it is equally as much his blood as it is the patient's. This is one of the reasons that Scripture states that the physician should heal himself. Some theologians perceive themselves separate, as though they are not part of the same body. This is why they utilize their intellects to make false judgments. When Jesus told the Church to 'put on Christ,' He meant to wear everything that the Holy Spirit hands us, including whatever manifestations dispensed through Our Lady that will make us more acceptable in the Father's sight.

So, let us look at the impeding intellectual mechanics of a person's receptivity to Our Lady's revelation as the Morning Star Over America. The Blessed Virgin has infinitely many ways in which She is able to communicate with humanity, not the least of which is through the complete spectrum of languages that man has ever attempted to speak. Yet, there are so few ways that human beings will allow Her to engage them. It is as ridiculous as someone saying that the Holy Mother must speak in Her original language from Her youth or they could not possibly be authentic messages from Her, as if Her being released from the bonds of Earth and assumed into Heaven as a perfect creature bestows no greater abilities than being consigned to the limitations of the audible inflections She learned as a child. Too often the scope of our discernment is far too limited or disoriented to make an accurate judgment on whether the messages are actually words from the Mother of God as testified. For example, if a person were to read the New Millennium works of the years 2000-2008 without first being exposed to the seminal events of the original Morning Star diary from which they were born, one could disavow the supernal intercession of those later years because it is so overwhelming of anything that Our Lady has dispensed throughout history that mankind is aware of. All comparisons fail. It has to be riddled with the seer's own thoughts, they say, and therefore unacceptable of belief, no matter how beautiful is the wisdom that it reveals. It is too big a leap of faith for most to accept that the Virgin Mother has been allowed to speak to Her children so deeply, profoundly, intimately, and extensively over a period of years. It is too much for them ever to have hoped for, therefore, they conclude that it could not possibly be true, notwithstanding that they would then have to admit that the recipients were theological, spiritual and literary geniuses to have produced such a body of work on their own amidst the pummeling of familial opposition, personal sacrifice, and mundane daily duty over an uninterrupted span of two decades. Our Lady endures an arduous task speaking to humanity because She knows that the more revelatory She becomes, the greater the opportunity for the "intellectual discerners" to concoct reasons to disqualify Her before the masses as being worthy of their obedience, and then the scandal and discredit of Her work begins. Simply look at those who are in diabolical legion against Medjugorje and you will find your example. She has great difficulty interacting with mankind openly because human pride will not allow it. Her messages often surpass the faith of those individuals who discern them based upon menial criteria whereby they limit Her freedom to intercede as She sees fit. And their trust in the integrity of any messengers is most always out of the question because they are more convinced of a sinner's ability to fail than they are in Our Lady's power to succeed with whomever She has chosen to deliver Her warnings. We must remember that Her purpose is to challenge our stale faith to make it grow by offering manifestations that are just beyond our present parameters of belief, hoping we will step out that tiny increment farther into Her arms. Imagine a mother assisting her child in taking its first steps. She steps back the smallest distance upon her knees, leaving the child tottering on their own, and holds out her hands. This is exactly what is happening through the Virgin Mary's mystical appearances. She is just beyond the reach of so many skeptical intellects, and is beckoning them to take that step. But, what happens? Intellectual dust-storms are kicked up within the doubters because they do not trust the Queen of Heaven, the scope of Her power, the urgency of Her intentions, or the integrity of their brothers and sisters with whom She has chosen to speak. They stand frozen in terror, wobbling in their tracks, simply trying to maintain their stoic balance, just like that tiny child; and then they wince and begin to cry. Historical precedents relating to Our Lady's numerous intercessions throughout history are scoured for incongruous irrelevance by square-peg personalities who are hoping to somehow incarcerate or disqualify Her will to nurture and guide as She sees appropriate as a Mother. Hear me now! She will not allow the magnitude of Her intercession to rest upon some sinner's assumptions of the dimensions by which She is allowed to engage Her children, no matter what they will have to suffer for being the recipients. She will do as She pleases, and oftentimes intentionally to defy those who have audaciously attempted to define Her by the reservations of their own sinful blindness. How many times has She fulfilled prophecies during Her apparitions in ways that are completely unexpected by the skeptical discerners? She wishes our faith to be implanted in the strength of the human heart supported by Her immaculate grace and illuminated by the Spirit of Christianity's King, even to the point of our own suffering and death. By an immersion in the original Morning Star diary, one is given a chance to grasp the daily dimensions of sacrifice from which the loving relationship with Heaven unfolded to produce its miraculous fruit. We see the dedication, single-mindedness, devotion, abandonment, perseverance, obedience, and the impregnable bond of love between God and His children. We see an example of miracle-supported faith that is so strong as to have opened a conduit between the seen and unseen which the Almighty Father advantageously poured the waters of Heaven into the lap of humanity through His Heavenly Queen. In this, one can recognize that only the Most Blessed Trinity could have been the initiator of something so ingenious and beautiful, all wrapped in the power of faith. A tangible lifeline has been thrown from the miraculous to reasonableness by which one can find stability and comfort for their budding acceptance of the mystical realms which stand poised to assist mankind in these darkest hours of our time. In other words, this expansion of faith provides a peaceful composure to support the belief in miracles where fully-inflamed evangelization might then ensue with the power of the first days of Christianity. The original diary allows one to be factually drawn into the "heavens of the miracle" where the reader in turn becomes a facet of the miracle. Heaven then overwhelms the Earth by virtue of this expanding faith which is validated at the Altar of the Roman Catholic Church. The messages that opened the new millennium reflect the maturity which grew from the simplicity and surprise that closed the previous century which was markedly inscribed with horror, heresy, desecration, destruction, and mankind's inhumanity. One can see in literary form both the test of faith and the dispensation of a relationship with the Heavenly Hosts, and how it was engaged with abandonment because the love was so strong between the triad of the Virgin Mother and Her two faithful sons. She placed my brother and me in Her lap, and then sat down with us before Jesus and began to pray. It is all about an example of the spirit of Saint Paul who declared that all should imitate his faith. It is a picture of a relationship that has been eternalized. My brother and I have been repeatedly taken beyond the boundaries of the world, past the edges of our perceptions and existence much like a balloon being inflated to larger dimensions. But, imagine if the balloon was confined within a box instead, and not allowed its natural expansion. Our heretical beliefs, sinful biases, inherited absurdities, misguided judgements, worldly perceptions, and even at times our orthodox religious perspectives are the box, while our transcension into true freedom through the buoyant interior grace of Our Lady occurs in lock-step with our familiarization with self-denial. Why self-denial? Because if we cannot deny our incarcerating dispositions, we cannot transcend anything. It is like letting go of the ballast holding down our hot air balloon, while Our Lady is the burner expanding the canopy. If we wish to fly, we must invoke our faith and believe! Over these particular years of life in union with our Holy Mother, She used our trust and devotion to the best of its composure and stepped us into realms where the Saints have walked in order to understand the love that emanates from Jesus' Sacrifice on the Cross. Only rarely did we know explicitly where we were going or what each day would bring; but we knew who we were with, and that any sacrificial engagement was worth the cost of the discomfort. I have said it before, who wants to walk around deluded and ego-stricken in the shadows of their own pride? It is comfortable to stay in the darkness until we realize the Love of Heaven, then our movement toward the Cross, one cleansing step at a time, begins to be something we live for. And if we can take giant leaps in that direction, all the better. The Holy Virgin's appearances are that giant leap for mankind. She has taken us by the hand and processed us through scalding bath and excruciating compliance, demanding the best from us without excuse, challenging our trust in Her while offering beatific encouragement, and asking us to be scrupulously honest about worldly perspectives as She pushed us past the mortal deceit that we were cowering from, until we now stand poised in Her immaculate grace, free from care about any infliction that could be heaped upon us through men. A great confidence has been ignited within us by Her coming into our lives that allows us to abandon ourselves and our lives to Her guidance without question. The reality of Her presence in our lives and in the life of the Church is manifested to us and through us. Is this not what the Catholic Church has always taught about the Most Blessed Virgin Mary and Her care for us? I am oftentimes taken aback by the disposition of skeptics, not so much that I am offended by them or surprised, but that I am incapable of understanding them. Their view of the world is foreign to me. I cannot contort my mind into the shape by which they view life. It would be like watching the President of the United States standing at the podium preparing to deliver a State of the Union address who starts cooing and babbling incomprehensibly like a six month old baby before the eyes of the nation. How would the chambers of Congress and the American people look at the man? Skeptics are standing with their ankles wet on the promenade deck of a sinking ship and are worried whether the ark that has proudly pulled alongside is seaworthy. Think about it! How does one live with the uncertainty and helplessness in which they are immersed? What kind of arrogance goes down with the ship because it does not like the captain of the rescue vessel? Verily, I will tell you—'the kind that will sink into the pitiful fathoms of creation and be destroyed, foundered in the icy depths beyond the memory of the future's nobler age.' They have no prescription for the elevation of humanity in any venerable way, yet act as if any agenda that presents itself must come through the blessing of their uncooperative pride.

I tell you, Redemption has already arrived and deliverance is rocking against their compromised hull! They better take the converting leap of faith, or they are doomed! Divine Mercy is dispensed through Jesus Christ's salvific agenda, and no other!

It is so difficult to crawl back into belief once one stumbles at the outset and travels down the path of intellectual skepticism. Once one engages their pride, it is so difficult to crucify it. It is like a grand thoroughfare unfolding before them that they believe must first be strewn with house-size boulders to be cleared through monumental sacrificial effort before anyone travels upon it, notwithstanding filling the craters that are created by their colossal impacts. When I was confronted by the Holy Virgin's miraculous intercession, in those first moments, a virgin grace of ultimate, unsoiled, breathtaking perfection was present in my mental constitution just as it is for everyone, a pure moment—the beatific thoroughfare splays its grandeur in front of us—and my choice was to set foot upon it and believe with all my heart in order to be taken to the destination its very manifestation prophesied. That is the example, the leap of faith, when compared with those who begin by allowing their skepticism to dominate their thinking through aberrant discernment and personal fear, as if throwing down a gauntlet before God, challenging Him to conquer their unbelief because they will not accept unless He does so. The ego says to God, "Kill me if you can." And God responds, "That has always been My intention. My Son has already killed your ego. Do not persist in your dead unbelief, but live the certainty of Everlasting Life through the power of the Holy Spirit inside you. Take up your cross, tender your sacrifice, place your ego on the pyre, and unite in the Eucharistic Sacrifice of My Son through your faith." Our immediate compliant response is the echo of the original Fiat. Our Lady did not engage an intellectual confrontation with the Archangel Gabriel at the Annunciation, nor did She engage any "healthy dose of skepticism," while we can see Zechariah's punishment for doing nothing more. Our fiat has allowed the Blessed Virgin to guide my brother and me into realms where She pines to take all humanity in the same way, and by the same sacrificial example. We are not in an extra-natural relationship with the Hosts of Heaven—we are in the normal state of spiritual communion that everyone should reside in and can attain through reception of the Most Blessed Sacrament, a small measure of faith, and by clasping the miraculous hand of Our Lady's intercession. Our Holy Mother has assisted us with the virtue of patience to remain on a mystical plateau of elucidating grace that is allowing the most skeptical to be given pause as to what they are witnessing. Experientially knowing the love of the Most Blessed Virgin jettisoned all our trepidation, and silenced the questioning intellect which possesses the innate tendency of our fallen nature to seek out conflict with Heaven because we cannot plainly see its parameters just yet. Those who engage their minds to seek out reasons not to believe will find that Satan is positioned at the periphery of their thoughts, poised to give them the evidence they are looking for, because he knows the discernment of human beings rarely reaches levels of laser focus to winnow speculation finely or accurately enough to proceed without him being allowed his impediments. Our Lady's miraculous presence definitively conquered my perception leaving no gap to span between believing and knowing. Although I understand what the human mind is capable of in this regard, I have never been required to engage the mental hurricane of trying to discern the authenticity of every moment because I know it is the Queen of Heaven who is leading us. And this knowledge of Her overwhelming presence and power in our lives renders the minefield of human thought irrelevant, not just for me, but for all mankind. I have never been anxious about being deceived by the devil in regards to this miraculous charism, nor have I ever questioned Her even for an instant. I have never tested the Mother of God, nor do I ever intend to. I have instead challenged every spirit which has attempted to coerce me into non-belief; and none have passed the test. We did not see Abraham test God; we did not see our Holy Mother test the Archangel Gabriel. My choice is to follow their example. Scripture confirms that it is the right choice. Therefore, with this intention, it is easy to trust completely like a little child because there is no other option. It is like never talking back to your parents, while their wisdom protects us as their children. I trust our Virgin Mother so much that any worries that could be generated by the evil one are thrust so far down the subliminal hierarchy of influence that his ability to impede my clear discernment is almost nonexistent. And even if he were to raise his head even an inch, She would shine a light on him so intensely that I would scamper back beneath Her most intimate care faster than a lightning bolt. It is still a pilgrimage of faith after all. When one is outside this relationship with the Holy Spirit, they place their trust in their own mental perceptions fraught with their worldly biases and vanities, and they inevitably stumble punch drunk through the domain where Satan pummels them into submission before his deceptive lies. I not only trust the Holy Spirit within me, but I trust God's Spirit in all whom I meet who reflect Him. This is our bond. It is our solidarity. It is our fraternity in divine grace. And this is why it is so easy to be united with our Holy Father, Pope Benedict XVI, and His Bishops because they emanate the Divine Light of the Holy Spirit.

I wish to reveal a personal dynamic that is rather obscured related to our relationship with our Holy Mother. There are so many people who when discerning miraculous intercession become disconcerted, wondering how it is possible to accept mystical phenomena with openness and confidence, and also remain elevated and unafraid of being deceived. Let us consider the relationship between the Virgin Mary and any child with whom She has engaged a consecrated relationship. Would God allow anything evil to infringe upon or influence that relationship if there was perfect obedience and blind trust submitted by the child toward Him? We already know that deceitful influences will never come from Our Lady; and we should also know that God will not allow any unconquerable deceptive influences from the unseen world. He will no more allow the devil to carry away an innocent child with miracles and wonders than a father would permit his child to be abducted by a sinister figure in an alley offering candy. Our Lord knows that all we have is our trust generated by our faith in Him when engaging the mystical realms. He knows we are walking blindly in faith, while asking us to trust that it is in His hand that we find our own. Therefore, should we not have confidence that He will never violate that trust we are extending? Does Scripture not state that He desires we believe like little children? Do we actually believe that He would allow Satan access to one of His children who was totally abandoned in blind faith to the emissary who was sent to miraculously dispense His guidance? Do we actually think that Satan had a snowball's chance in Hades of coming between Gabriel and the Virgin of Nazareth at the Annunciation? In other words, if God knew that a child fully intended to never doubt the elements of His mystical actions, no matter what challenge to faith that He might throw down before them, that they would believe innocently without question, follow His leads immediately, and accept His mysterious guidance with the faith of Abraham, could the child not in turn know with confidence that God would not violate that gift of abandonment? When we love God to the complete abandonment of the self, nothing sinister can breach that bond. Upon the basis of this reciprocal union of love, Our Lady has led us through chambers of existence where it is certain that most intellectuals would have denied attending Her. She has tested the strength of our solidarity with the higher realms from every dimension and from many angles. It is as if God was essaying the tensile strength of our faith, our devotion to the Sacred Heart of His Son, much like He did with Abraham being asked to sacrifice his own son. And in union with this Patriarch, my brother's abandonment and my own have yet to falter, while humbly knowing we have never met a mob who wished to actually torture and crucify us. We have faced fear, confusion, ostracization by many close to us, along with deeply sacrificial circumstances which rent our beings, but the power of the Holy Spirit in Our Lady's presence brought a recognition of immortality where we knew our spirits would outlast these things and be clothed with glory, no matter what men's judgements may be in time. Consider the trust that God wishes we would have in Him. Imagine the innocence of a little child, and holding a piece of candy out to them in your hand. And when they reach for the candy, you pull it away. They look at you incredulously, and maybe with a giggle. Then, you extend the candy again; they reach and you pull it away again. What impression strikes that child's heart? Their trust in you is destroyed. They begin to wonder whether they can ever trust you to bestow the candy into their possession, in fact they feel tempted to never trust that you will ever give anything desirable to them again. This is the work of the devil. Through our personal relationship with the Virgin Mother, I have realized that God would never allow the faintest twinge of that experience to touch our childlike hearts if we remained in Him. He will not fail in His part. And from the poise of that realization, our Virgin Mother has been allowed to dispense a complete spectrum of supernatural graces that She has been otherwise unable to impart to humanity at large because of a lack of abandonment on mankind's part, particularly from those who claim to be walking by faith. For us, all has been light. Even the times of darkness have produced light. The moment we choose to disavow our portion of this reciprocal bond; the instant we choose to invoke our will outside the union of our relationship, entertain doubts, and move from complete alignment with Our Lady, Satan is allowed entrance to the arena, prying and prodding and deceiving until faith is lost. All markers become obscured in a haze of duplicitous uncertainty. The faulty human will begins to stumble around in the darkened intellect of a sinner, like a blind man who has lost his grip on the hand he once held. Imagine being blind and someone with a beautiful voice took you by the hand. Great confidence would well up within you, and you would travel with them in confidence anywhere. But, if at any time you lost that person's hand amidst the hustle and bustle of the worldly crowd such as in Times Square on New Year's Eve, you would either stand paralyzed or flail through the air reaching out for that hand again. Terrible fear and doubt would arise within you, even if an unknown hand suddenly grasped yours again. Is it the same one? Is this the person I have trusted before? There is mental disarray and lack of peace until one hears the soft voice they have always known. My brother and I are like these blind men, but we know the voice and have never released the grasp on Our Lady's hand even for a second. We follow, imitate and embrace Her vision and guidance without question. We are not afraid of stumbling over curbs or falling off cliffs, or even plunging into the masses of humanity at any given place on the globe upon Her direction. With the Queen of Heaven, we could travel the perilous *El Camino de la Muerte* (Road of Death) in La Paz, Bolivia blindfolded, and it would be a joyous adventure. In union with the Virgin of Nazareth, there is no deception possible from the unseen world. That is why She is the conqueror of heresy. The darkness is eradicated by Her presence, where our commission is to continue the battle against the constant haggling by doubting sinners to renege our part of the union where the Virgin imparts eternal vision. It is this openness to Our Lady that we are trying to lift before humankind by engaging those who are terrorizing humanity with their portrayal of Jesus as a Messiah who takes candy away from a baby. They are trying to characterize the Queen of Heaven as the fiend in the alley because they do not have the faith to believe in the commanding power of Her presence. The only way the devil can succeed in depriving us of Our Lady's wisdom is if we fail to trust that She is in complete control of the dimensions of Her miraculous intercession. All we really need to do is obey Her and follow wherever She leads by surrendering our faculties to Her mystical itinerary. If one cannot find Our Lady's hand, then take ours because we are holding onto Her with our other hand. It is true that even messengers possess their own individual weaknesses and sometimes stumble, but usually because they have broken trust. During the trial and being all too human, they have sometimes dropped the Virgin Mary's guiding hand for a moment, become unsure whose hand they grasped next, surrendered their discernment to other sinners, and have allowed the fallen world entrance into the sacred realm of influence within them, then they flee from the Cross which would bring them back into alignment with the grace of Heaven. Diabolical circumstances spawned by others' lack of belief surround their insecurity like a pack of wolves, and they give those forces influence in the relationship they have with the Heavenly Hosts. Satan senses the breach in their spiritual defenses and enlists his minions to descend upon them, demanding an engagement with the debilitating forces of the supposedly discerning world, eliciting compromises from amidst their doubts; and the deconstruction begins. (Matthew 15:14, Luke 6:39) Jesus could have been the greatest secular king ever to have been known had He surrendered the sovereignty of His Sacred Heart to the Sanhedrin to save His life. They would have elevated Him to the pinnacles of worldly influence and rode upon His power to secular heights and kingly riches, but He would have forsaken His hypostatic being with the Father had He done so. He would have broken trust with His boundless confidence in the First Person of the Most Holy Trinity and placed it instead in the opinions of the scoundrels who surrounded Him. He did not compromise with sinners, and neither should we. Consider the satanic ploys used against Saint Joan of Arc to get her to disavow the authority of her mystical experiences. Her rational fear of abandonment to the Cross which happened to be the fire of a burning stake was the only thing that could have gotten this young maid to flinch, and Satan employed it. But, should messengers have to go to spiritual martyrdom or even death in the image of their Savior to validate the message they are bearing? If true, then so be it. In most cases, seers have had no better fortune than so-called witches who were dunked to discern their integrity, albeit simple character assassination as opposed to outright murder has blessedly been the method usually employed. Human nature has not changed all that much through the centuries.

Further, it would seem that the discernment of many people requires Our Lady to always speak to Her children as if they are toddling infants. Consider how parents speak to their smallest children. They play goo goo games with them, speak in funny exaggerated voices, make faces, and coo them. But, as their children grow to adulthood, they engage them with composure, respect, intelligence, depth, purpose, and at length. They put away childish things for greater wisdom. *"But when the perfection comes, the partial will pass away. When I was a child, I used to talk as a child, think as a child, reason as a child; when I became a man, I put aside childish things."—1st Corinthians 13:10-11.* The perfection has arrived in the Morning Star Over America. Our Lady has been speaking for centuries to humanity in measured ways, most often to children because their intellects are not solidified, leaving them able to listen and respond. Does this not show us how human intellect often requires stupendous amounts of faith or miracles to overcome it? This is a shame. Our day sees Our Lady speaking to spiritual infants whom She is determined to see to maturity in preparation for the close of the ages, therefore She is elevating the profundity of Her wise guidance. No message, no matter its depth, comes from a vacuum or without purpose, thus everyone should see in the original Morning Star diary the planting of the seed of faith that was nurtured and grew the forest of revelation that flourished into the New Millennium messages. Faith allowed the door its opening, seeds were planted, and a comprehensive cultivation of souls commenced in those founding moments. Yet, the door never stopped opening wider as the years passed. The saplings grew into a timberland. And now peering into the valley from the cliffs of grace, we can together ponder the Immaculate Heart who has planted it, nurtures it, and sustains its posture of glorification. Articulating Our Lady's beauty is like trying to describe the ethereal resplendence of the Grand Canyon bathed in the rays of a western sunset to someone who has seen nothing more than a county gravel pit in the gloom of a rainy day. Those who disregard Our Lady's miraculous intercession are failing humanity for selfish reasons, and the weight of scholarship that is thrown behind misguided motives is the millstone around the necks of those who refuse to tender their participation in Her agenda. Many base their discernment on criteria such as that the messages are supposedly mundane, repetitive, predictable, or of too great a number, as they often state regarding the great shrine of Medjugorje. For the record, there is no foundation in Truth for such brash determinations; these are simply prognostications wafting from the pride of doubters like the stench from a dead carcass. They testify that Our Lady is too effusive for them in one way or another, or speaks of worldly things that they think She should not despoil Her station to be interested in. Some even reject claims of Her intercession because they do not like the idea that the Virgin Mother would be so accessible to Her children by appearing so predictably and consistently over such a long period of time. They even have the audacity to inform us that Her appearances damage faith. What?—there's the infantile babbling from the podium again. This is from the same people who would tell us from the other side of their mouth that the Blessed Virgin is our Mother whom we should be confident is caring for us at every moment. Can we not see the disconnect between their bipolar beliefs and the consistent faith they should be displaying? And ironically, it is these same scrupulous malcontents who would disqualify the work of the Morning Star Over America because Her messages are anything but mundane and repetitive; of a scope that they could never have envisioned in their lives, and that She has been intimately apprehensible to we who are Her children with simple motherly interest and affection that everyone should have been taught is present in each of our lives from the moment of our birth. One could wonder what they would accept from Her. They cannot imagine that Jesus would allow the heavens to interact with His people in a way that would require their faith too. Our Heavenly Mother has taught me to neither grovel nor pander to the egos of these unbelievers, hoping for support that will most likely never be forthcoming. They are the lot of sinners who will inevitably shout for God's children to be sent to the Cross.

"I called you to Medjugorje for the purpose of revealing Myself as the Morning Star Over America. I called you there; this is what I do for all who travel to the Saint James parish. It is curious, however, that some go there and refuse to believe, even though I have summoned their acceptance. This is a function of their human will. It is also the impact of their pride. Some say that if I were appearing in Medjugorje, I would say more, I would make more emphatic gestures about the condition of the world. Others maintain that My only role in Salvation history was to give birth to Jesus in Bethlehem. The latter is correct to an extent written in the Scriptures, but I come now not only to urge My children to accept the Cross, but to overcome their own humanness, to bridle their opposition to the teachings of the Church. My role in Medjugorje and here in America is not so much about redeeming humanity, but converting humanity. Jesus has saved humanity outright. There is nothing I can add to His Sacrifice. Remember that I told you that Jesus did not ask Me to carry an ounce of the Holy Cross. It was completely His to bear. I never shed blood for the redemption of lost sinners.

Therefore, you see that My role as Mediatrix is to ensure the cultivation of the hearts of mankind either with kindness or the rawness of the cold facts. I speak with impassioned overtones when I see My children straying from the path of holiness, and this is the way you have learned to speak and write. I am not suggesting that I am not still the gentle Mother sung about in those pretty melodies, I am saying that gentleness comes in many forms. How could God allow Me to sit idly by and watch His children walk such crooked paths? How could humanity, all born from motherly wombs, not grow in enlightenment by the Wisdom of the Immaculate Womb that bore their Salvation into the flesh? There is an obvious correlation between being born into the flesh

and being reborn in the Spirit. There is a great heaviness that attends the mission of teaching lost sinners right from wrong, and you have felt that weight upon you at times. I wish to make clear what I said before. You have the faith, love, and will to remain calm in oneness with the Holy Spirit. You have the power to tell evil around you that it has no authority to shape your thoughts, actions, and feelings. I realize that this sounds easy when it comes from Me because I am already in Heaven. However, think about My sorrow in seeing the Son of Man tortured and crucified before My very eyes. This is a grief that no one should ever have to suffer again. I have said on many occasions that it is replicated by mothers and fathers everywhere, those who lose their sons and daughters in the battles of war, accidents of all kinds, diseases, and outright carelessness. These losses unite the sufferers with the Cross to immeasurable degrees.

How many words have I said to you in almost two decades? It is nearly unimaginable. You should be pleased with yourselves, even righteously proud, for caring enough about your brothers and sisters to help Me convert them to the Cross. There are moments in history that account for thousands of years of change, and your lives here in this place are filled with those times. What humanity will see the most on this side of the veil is not the dailiness you have invested, but the earthshaking product of that investment. While you have lived hours at a time, they will see an eternity of beatific grace. Why? Because they could not have lived your agonies. Someone had to be called. A certain soul or two had to be touched by the miracles from afar, where the Angels tread and Saints repose, and you and your brother are these fortunate and yet unfortunate souls. Your sorrows have been real, your burdens toilsome, your suffering intense, but your hopes remain alive. The Lord will reward you with the presence of your friends beside you at the foot of the Cross and the gate of Paradise. You must realize that you have been chosen because you are capable. You are worthy because of your compliance. You must know that the Holy Spirit is consoling and advising you and that you are doing well. You have given your life for the Church and to the Church."

There is no precedent for the revelations of the Morning Star Over America, only that Her Love is larger than anything humanity has yet conceived. She is closer than the air we breathe, and more overwhelming than any fire that could come from the skies. The scope and depth of Her work bear witness to its spiritual grandeur and the ominous urgency for mankind to listen and obey now, not generations in the future. Let none of these frank admonishments cause anyone to believe that I consider myself anything more than a child whom God has lifted from his sins through the Sacraments. We must all give credit where credit is due; and that is to the Lamb of God who died and conquered death so that we may set upon this new beginning. Notwithstanding our primitive lapses in conduct and devotion, we must proclaim our new identity with confidence and how we attained it, and be thankful beyond the heavens for it. The Christian apologist C.S. Lewis made a profound statement when he said, "*I would prefer to combat the 'I'm special' feeling not by the thought 'I'm no more special than anyone else,' but by the feeling 'Everyone is as special as me.'*" This more closely resembles the view that Our Lady wishes we would have of ourselves and one another. No one in Heaven, on Earth, or under it, will ever be allowed to diminish the dignity of Her children in Her eyes. She is even taken aback at the instances where the Saints were reportedly to have described themselves as worms for penitential sake. Her Immaculate Heart shudders that these monikers be applied to any one of Her children. She would have loved in those moments to have descended from the heavens in Her raiment of Glory and scooped those Saints into Her arms to caress and console them, don them in the robes of kings, and tell them that their fears regarding their missteps were unfounded and had been wiped into nonexistence by a Holy Sacrifice on Calvary so profound that only their tears of joy would be accepted by the heavens now. Humble before God we must be, but beaten down by ourselves or the vengeful world, never! Not one time in all these years has our Holy Mother ever thrust my spirit into despondence or allowed me to diminish my dignity in unfounded apology before Her. In fact, She has taken me to task for groveling apologetically over my sins, saying that She did not wish to hear how weak that I believed I had been, but instead how strong in triumph I felt standing over my weaknesses after being absolved and lifted above them. She rejoices at that faith in Jesus. She told me to repeat as many times as I needed to believe it, "When I am strong, I am strong; and when I am weak, I am also strong because Christ is my strength." It is false humility to claim we are wretched once Baptism has divinized our souls and the Sacrament of Penance has further wiped them clean. One who wallows and refuses to accept their recreation in Jesus' perfection does not really believe in His mercy and forgiveness. It is an outright rejection of the restorative grace of the Sacraments. How many people walk through this world knocking doves out of the sky, saying they have no right to fly. How many sinners slander saints because they refuse to accept their own absolution and rise to the occasion of grace with Eucharistic thanksgiving? Our Lady wishes Her children to tender simple repentance and accept absolution, then—*Stand and deliver your giantness of heart!* It is a lie against the Holy Spirit to flounder in self-pity because we are children of God now, purchased by the Sacrifice of the greatest Man ever to have lived, our brother The Christ! He is the Descent and also the Ascension within us. All is forgiven of those who believe, repent, convert, accept, unite, and obey. All is elevation, grace, support, assistance, strength, confidence, identity, devotion, heroism, gallantry, nobility, honor, sacrifice, love and the Cross. Heroes process to hilltops marked by crosses, while worms simply feed on the decaying earth that is saturated with the beatific scents of their hallowed victories.

So, what does the Most Blessed Virgin Mary want? She wishes an arena of peace to prosper where life on Earth can become like Heaven; a solidarity within the Roman Catholic Church, amidst its flourishing fields of sanctifying grace through the sacramental forgiveness of sins. And from that domain where Heaven comes to Earth by Eucharistic Sacrament, She desires that we come to understand Love spiritually in its infinitude as opposed to our defining it within the limited affections and frailties of our human condition. She wants us to recognize the urgency of being connected to the origin of life and not simply its practical facets. Being formed in the womb as a human is nearly irrelevant when compared to recognizing ourselves as undefinable spirits temporarily burdened by fleshly frames. Our mortal flesh is confined by parameters and impediments, but the spirit is infinite and eternal. And when our spirit moves into union with the essential divinity of God through Christian Baptism, we allow ourselves to be impressed, mortified, and motivated by sanctifying grace so that the enfleshed soul of mankind becomes animated toward perfection as a united creation through the diverse avenues of Jesus' sacrificial nature, which is Divine Love itself. And in this, the world becomes our dreams. Philosophers from ancient times to the present have pondered the nature of humanity and the definitions of our existence upon the earth. Suffering people strewn across the ages have testified with their tear-drenched mortality that the heart is encased in flesh for something wholly more beatific than the simple endurance of discomfort, pain and affliction. We aspire, dream, hope and envision things that the world seems incapable of delivering. Why? Where does it all come from? From where do those original visions arise? Where do the ideas originate that have never before been conceived? They are from the Father of lights (James 1:17) who is revealing His Kingdom which we are being prepared by the Holy Spirit to enter. The Most Holy Virgin is asking mankind what kind of future he desires. Will we rise in the closing hour to become humanity at its finest? The most intelligent, the most life-giving, the most faith-filled, the premiere species of consciousness that the universe could have ever produced? Are we prepared to manifest all that mankind has ever dreamed of becoming, the noblest of the noble? Will we rise to imitate the sentiments of our greatest art, the courage of our soul-shattering epics, and the splendor from which legends are made? When the dawn opens to our sun going supernova millions of years hence, or maybe the fateful day an asteroid splits our fruited fields to their core, or the night comes which is lit by man's final obliteration of himself, or the moment when the Son of God preempts it all by appearing in majesty, upon the morning reveille of all life to the crowning Glory of His Kingdom, what will we see when panning this burned-out orb bobbing in silence through the solitude of the cosmos, the spectacular lighthouse of man gone dark, knowing the marvelous story of mortal existence has finally become only a memory to the universe? Will our tears flow and sorrow burn, or will a hallowed reverence instead overtake our souls? Verily, in the midst of that apocalypse from the pinnacles of Resurrection, we will see the luminous spectacle of mankind's penitential opus locked forever in the mind of Eternity as the definition of the sacrificial work of God's Only Begotten Son. We will witness the one Cross beaming like a beacon out of the midnight of the mortal ages. We will see the last faithful priest consecrating a piece of bread upon a Catholic Altar, the final Rosary bead passing between the fingers of a child, the last kiss being placed upon another's cheek, the concluding kindness exchanged between enemies, the crowning morsel being passed to the lips of the last starving person, and the final crying baby being birthed from the womb by a mother who wished to testify to the ages with the last act of her humanity that bearing her child was her ultimate witness to feminine perfection. Yes, there will be a last child with no one left to kill it. Life will stand victorious over all death. It is these special ones whom we will see with exceptional fondness, the last of humanity's many who witnessed to the power of Christ within them, they who embodied the collective beauty of what was once mortal man aspiring to human perfection upon the Earth. What kind of person says 'no' to the highest aspirations that rage in every man's heart, while knowing we are headed for that exulted age? Who wishes not to be seen as part of the sparkling fineness that defined what the spirit of humankind rose in the flesh to be? Our Holy Mother says that mankind has been saying 'no' to his heart for too long, and is here to change that defeatist knell into a triumphant affirmation of the dignity of the human race in the Cross of the Savior of this world. Then, let those disasters come, let the stars fall out of the sky, petition Our Lord to join us once again, call down the celestial Hosts to winnow the wheat from the chaff, and dare evil to crucify us because we know our lives are etched in the permanence of His Eternal Kingdom—and we will live again! Everyone, no matter their plateau of observation upon the globe, can see the contrast between the highest ideals of our nature and the expedient compromises which characterize those who are feasting and festering on the dignity of man's future. It is obvious that the world has not completed its storied progression to the pinnacle definition of human excellence personified by the Lamb of God. Therefore, we must awaken and do better.

Our Lady engaged a conversation with me in these veins by referring to the world resting stagnant in substantial completion as opposed to striving for its optimal completion. Each of us knows that we were born helpless in an unfinished environment which possesses harsh circumstances resulting from human sin. We all recognize what impales our hearts, the things that impede or outright destroy the beauty of how we wish life would be unfolding. While we recognize that Jesus "finished" the world on the Cross, meaning that He perpetually united the seen and the unseen worlds of Creation by His Holy Sacrifice, and finished the resurrection of all men by His Paschal Resurrection, Our Lady's idea of completion refers to the spiritual reciprocity of collective humanity as Jesus' Mystical Body. Our Lord did not come amongst men simply to "save" us as if we had no part to play in our liberation from the fallen nature we inherited from Adam and Eve. If that were the case, we would have been forced to recognize that the heavens opened and consumed our mortality at the instant of His birth, preempting everything that has labored us for the last 2000 years. Why did this not happen? Obviously, God wanted something more from us than simply being claimed as booty plundered for His Kingdom. He came to deliver humanity from this fallen nature with the words from man's own lips. Jesus asked for man's own sacrifice in union with His own. He asked for mankind's faith in Him. What would the last two millennia have been had all the world believed those simple shepherds on the first Christmas? The Savior of the world endured His Sacrifice on the Cross to exonerate the human race from the debt we owed for offending the Perfection of the Ages, and thus granted us the opportunity and authority to rise through our sacrificial invocation of faith into oneness with the God who created the universe. Our part is to be sown and cultivated toward that ultimate perfection in the seasonal fields of His forgiving grace during this age of mercy, to be convinced of our immortal strength through trial, to recognize our invincible divine nature through our acceptance of every atrocity that the same creative human intellect could engineer in its darkest hours, so that upon arriving in the full Countenance of Paradise, we would know a crown awaited us even before hearing the words, "Well done, my good and faithful servant." "Completion" is a term that recognizes this transition of humanity into higher states of grace which renders our mystical garment more seamlessly stitched to the Will of God at each point in time. Hence, it is appropriate to recognize those whose religious faith is still growing who have not yet reached the plateau of understanding in unseen matters pertaining to the Church, their own Salvation, and the agenda of God that will define the closure of the mortal ages of the world. When they give themselves in submission to the Church, it is their faith-filled moment of commitment to their unity with Christ upon the Cross, their initial acceptance of the transformation inaugurated at His Birth; and it marks a major milestone toward substantially completing their future. In contrast, let us compare these people to Pope John Paul II or Pope Benedict XVI. The latter two have optimally completed their unity with the Holy Trinity by virtue of their sacred office, even though at any time in their earthly lives, they were both sinners in the flesh. Obviously, Pope John Paul the Great has superceded even the optimum completion of a faithful mortal life and has reached seamless unity with the Father. For example, when Jesus said that Saint John the Baptist was the greatest soul born of woman, He still said that the least in the Kingdom of Heaven was greater than he. Saint John the Baptist is a biblical example of an optimally completed life given to Jesus. So, you see, Jesus Himself talked about the greater and the lesser in terms of maturity and identification with the Spirit of God, hence those who believe that all you have to do is say, "Yay Jesus!" and you are saved, are terribly mistaken in their minimalistic approach to spiritual completeness. Their attitude at best reflects their substantialism, but is a far cry from the optimal perfection that Jesus desires of them. The point being made is that everyone we know is on the pathway of God; some are moving forward, some regressing, and some dead still in the middle of the road, celebrating that they have already reached their destination. If we think about the inferences that can be drawn from the concepts of substantial completion versus optimum completion, it is almost tellable where certain people are. People of Christian faith are more optimally complete than non-Christians. Catholics are closer to their optimal completion than Protestants, and so on. Consider this analogy that most everyone would accept. The physicists of the 20th century were ingenious men and women who understood great depths of the physical world at the opening of the last century. Yet, Albert Einstein sent them reeling in stunned wonderment with his theories of relativity. No longer could the worldwide college of physicists consider themselves the premiere scientific intellects. Einstein revealed his optimalism in physics, while the rest had their substantialism revealed by his transcending genius. With this discussion, the attempt is to focus our vision on the fact that all humanity and the earth itself are in an ascending transition, and that the Faith of the Roman Catholic Church is the transcending genius that is being articulated by God through Her Dogmas and Traditions to succeeding generations since the Crucifixion of His Son. This phenomenon of the maturing spirit is why Jesus and His Mother have always had to exercise extreme patience waiting for lost sinners to convert to the higher realms of perfection. And not only that, they have been patiently waiting for good Christians to finally decide to do something positive with their faith instead of standing like weaklings in the shadows. Those who have embraced Our Lady's miraculous intercession have engaged a prolific step in optimally completing their perfection within the optimal framework of the Catholic Church. It goes without saying that there are many people who practice Christian faith substantially, but only partially. Our Holy Mother never suggests that any soul is less worthy than others while they are on this road, rather She is concerned with their progression forward upon it. No one ever arrives in Heaven saying they wished they had not made so many sacrifices for Jesus, instead they nearly always question Our Lord whether He feels they had done enough for Him. Very, very few look into His eyes and know Him as one mirror facing another, each seeing the essence of the other in themselves. Every living being is in the process of becoming this image of Jesus Christ. If we are not, we are failing the greatest opportunity that human life could ever present, much to our total desolation at the juncture of life and death. Many people have given the years of their lives, their treasure, their heart and prayers, their grief and suffering–all of these things so that the Church would be prospered into our time, elevating humanity like a ship upon Her crests of divinity to the conferment of Salvation. They see the Cross with perfect vision, which means that their perception of their life's purpose is as finished as the world Jesus set aright on the Cross. This is only to say that their purpose is finished, while their execution of that purpose is still ongoing. As long as we have air in our lungs and living blood in our veins, we are maturing the Church by our life. Once we commit our heart's work to the page of human history, nothing in Creation can remove it again. Our lives are a rendering of the contents of our hearts, and in the case of my brother and me, a literary explication of our love for God in our relationship with His Queen. It represents our hope for humanity that materialized from the celestial mists of our greatest contemplative awakening, that all men will embrace the pinnacles of spiritual potential and proceed down the path of their lives for the glory of the Cross. Every person must become even more than substantial, all the way to optimally holy, lest they regret ever being given the breath of life. Holiness, after all, is the worthy goal to be pursued. There can be no holiness without true love, and there can be no authentic love without spiritual holiness. We must become passionate participants in the conversion of lost sinners, where we see and feel what it means to have our intentions spurned and ignored. Like Jesus, we desire for our brothers and sisters to come to the sweetness of His Divine Love, so much so that we ache inside wondering what else we can do, what sacrifice we can make to advance Light in the world. Our Lady has told us that it is the self-will of other men that causes them to cast Jesus aside and evade the call of God's Kingdom. Our interior heartache is the way the entire Church feels knowing so much suffering must be endured in reparation for those who refuse to engage an optimal life in grace.

There are varying degrees of holiness in individual men that we have seen rise and fall, depending on how they feel and the circumstances of daily life. However, as long as these degrees keep them moving in the direction of optimum completion, they are as blessed as the Saints already in Heaven. Even though they are sinners walking blindly in the dark, they have given their own will to the guidance of the Holy Spirit, and they will arrive at their destination intact by virtue of the redeeming Sacrifice offered by the Roman Catholic

Church. They may not have reached their optimal completion just yet, but their momentum is taking them there, while the prayer of the Holy Mass is the wind at their back. And, believe it or not, most all the people we have known in our lives are like this. They have never been intentionally malevolent, but more ignorant about what choices should be made and unaware of the forces from aloft that are driving them more toward their optimum holiness. There are thousands, however, who are headed to damnation in the unquenchable fires of Hell. They are not progressing in holiness; they reject everything it stands for when connected to the Church. Doctors who use their profession to perform abortions are on their way to Hell. It is as simple as this. While our Holy Mother has never explicated the realms of Hell with as much detail as Her revelations regarding Heaven, saying it would serve no purpose, She did tell me the name of one abortion doctor who condemned himself to the flames of Gehenna when he appeared at the Throne of Judgement. She said so had most others. This is where they have chosen to go, and that we should feel no sorrow for them. Hell is a place of unending fire and punishment, and there are a lot of people in it, especially those who mocked its very existence. Therefore, the pursuit of holiness is an important process that is not as easy for some as it is others. Much influence is made by the way someone is raised and other matters that affect their view of mortal life. There are Saints-to-be incarcerated in death-row prison cells right now. This is why the Church is not quick to judge the ultimate destiny of the human soul, yet tells us explicitly what to avoid. The Mother Church leaves the issue of judgement to Jesus' Divine Mercy, but we do have the authority to tell someone how they might be judged based upon the criteria written in the Holy Scriptures and proclaimed through the spiritual guidance of the Catholic Church. And, this is where the concept of a substantially completed life versus an optimally completed life are best discussed. Some people know when they get there. The Apostles knew they were works in progress. Many disciples never had a doubting moment. Even Saint Paul said he was confident of his prize in Heaven. Our Holy Mother told my brother and me that we will someday bask in the Light of everlasting life, and we believe Her. But, it is not as clear to billions around the globe, and this is why She comes to enhance our understanding of our responsibility to respond to the overtures of God, especially through Her miraculous intercession. If everyone applies themselves to the teachings of the Church, the lessons of Jesus in the New Testament, the wisdom in the Beatitudes, the intentions of the Blessed Virgin as our Mother, and their own good consciences, we will collectively as the human family make it to the Promised Land. This cannot be accomplished without sacrifices, suffering and the reorientation of our beliefs. We will be despised and rejected for what we believe, not only about what has been taught for the past twenty centuries, but what we dare to do, write and say about how the final ages of the world will play out. It is in these faith explicating writings, speeches, good works, and obediences that our optimum completion occurs. Yes, we can attain the status of Saints like John Paul II and all the Saints while here on Earth. It is possible for men to exist on the same earth and live in different worlds. It is a measure of blase substantialism versus heroic optimalism. One might ask how people who have no intention of any kind of spirituality are related to substantialism? Does the fact that they have simply been given life play into the substantialism? The answer is yes, because they still have potential, as minimal as it may be. As long as they can receive The Word, they are not irretrievably lost. As long as they do not reject the Holy Spirit or blaspheme the origin of their redemption, there is still hope for them. How does one know when a state of optimalism has been reached? It is specific to each individual. The human spirit knows when it has been touched as much as the heart and conscience will permit, based upon the psychological construct of the person. In other words, if the seemingly worst person in the world feels as though they know and love God more than anything else in the world, they have reached the optimal completion of their faith. If they would choose to die a martyr's death defending the Cross, they are there. When a person has embraced the conviction strong enough to lay down their life for those whom Christ loves, and would without doubt respond in the testing moment, they are living by Divine Love alone and stand with Christ at His Crucifixion. No greater love could be generated; no impediments exist; it is beyond the world in the realms of the infinite; they are optimum. This is the love to which God responds in the Sacrament of Holy Orders. Our priests are clothed with the Crucifixion through their devotion to their sacrificial vocation. They live and breathe the testing moment every day of their lives, like beacons ignited in perpetuity. Husbands and wives surrendering their beings to each other in the Sacrament of Matrimony is an equally luminous example. On the other hand, when a billionaire gives ten million dollars to the poor, he is still in the darkness, walking the slow road of substantialism. He has been generous only according to the standards of those who do not know what it is like to have that much wealth. He has not faced the loss of what composes his life and uttered the word "yes." The same can be said for theologians who have no use for Our Lady's miraculous intercession. They are walking the slow road of substantialism, even though they feel they are optimally fulfilling their faith. And based upon their knowledge and their unwillingness to concede to the Will of God, they might judge themselves in the same way as those abortion doctors. Divine Truth is unavoidable, and always exists as the backdrop of life against which all men must measure their actions. The Cross cannot be avoided by anyone headed for Heaven, all are martyrs, either spiritually or physically, who triumphed with grace over the pummeling this life inflicts. Whoever wishes to save his life will lose it, while those who lose their life for the sake of the Gospel will preserve it into the realms of Eternal Life. (Luke 9:23-26) It is much like a paradox in that it is impossible to dream that you are asleep unless you are really asleep. Therefore, substantialism is characterized by the word "velleity," which means volition in its weakest form, a mere wish, unaccompanied by an effort to obtain it. Substantialism is the defining essence of lukewarmness. Those who subscribe to this practice in their knowledge of God are also practitioners of secularism, even though they may claim that they are Christians. Their diluted faith is not what Jesus asks of them; it is not what the Church warrants. They practice velleity when they instead should be deeply consecrated to the pursuit of human sanctity. Hence, velleity, substantialism and lukewarmness are synonymous. When we pray every day, our hearts remain soft and we see more clearly that most people are more indifferent than prone to evil, although one is as malevolent as the other. Our Holy Mother wishes to highlight the phenomenon where people, including many Catholic Christians, declare that they are religious in nature, but not really in fact. This is why Protestants hold the Catholic Church at arms length no matter what their version of ecumenism declares. This is how Catholic politicians make decisions against the teachings of the Church and in defiance of the Will of God and their Bishops. Both of these examples speak to the falsehoods about their alleged allegiance to the Holy Gospel. Many Roman Catholics are as injurious to the faith as those who belong to other denominations, but they will be held more accountable at the Final Judgement because they knew better and also claimed to believe. Is it better for someone to hold an errant position based on false information than to practice outright disloyalty to the Truth they claim to embrace? The latter is the worst hypocrite in the world. It is the same regarding Our Lady's miraculous intercession. There are those in the Church who hail the Virgin as our Mother and profess to the world how accepting they are of Her guidance. Then Jesus sends Her to us and allows mystical manifestations of Her profound relationship with the Church as a test of the optimal nature of their professions of faith. But what do these people do? They hear His voice and harden their hearts anyway. They fail the test of their claims. They believe in miracles, but only if they occur in distant lands to unknown people in former generations. The faithful of America must reconsider how close they will allow God to come to them. What kind of hypocrisy do they believe is acceptable? The Most Blessed Virgin Mary is the Patroness of the United States of America by divine decree, but masses of the population, including many who are our brothers and sisters in Christ, believe that She has no right of persuasion here. This is diabolical nonsense and a declaration of the substantial nature of their faith, as opposed to a thundering ovation of welcoming approval from a sanctified nature that is optimally electrified by the Holy Spirit. The final goal of our Holy Mother's intercession is not to confirm that miracles can occur, but to initiate our interior contemplation of the true motivations behind those miracles, and to commence the radical reorientation of our allegiances to come into alignment with the Holy Sacrifice of the Cross. We will either adore it or endure it. The entire body of humankind is being asked to come into full communion with the Roman Catholic Church come hell or high water, because there is no true optimalism outside the sanctified realms of its beatific domain. We must become participants in the Holy Sacrifice of the Mass as if together with Christ we are laying down our lives for humanity, or God will bring us to the Cross by placing us upon it so that we can taste its magnificent desolation intimately, and thus come to know how beautiful Divine Love actually is. If one is at odds with the Catholic Church or holds any animosity toward it, their soul is wounded, possibly mortally. If one is advancing an agenda in opposition to the Magisterium, their soul is dying. If one hates the Catholic Church, their soul is already dead and is simply waiting for its interment in the abyss of eternal fire.

Our Lady knows that Her children are steeped in the throes of world violence. We are perpetrators and victims of human selfishness. The elements of the Earth keep us too busy, it would seem, to be curious about the Lord who has fashioned every inch of our surroundings. And, it is lost sinners who ultimately give up on themselves. In that vein, one need not be totally lost in secularism to be blind to the Truth of the Church. However, secularism is the Church's worst enemy. It wears a cloak of common ground which is actually a veiled agenda of diabolical detachment and moral darkness. If we looked at America from abroad, we would see a nation that has delved into the oblivion of materialism and lust which has been adorned in a devilishly deceptive image of freedom. Is it not true that materialism has caused the bankruptcy of the United States? Although Our Lady cares very little whether our country is fiscally solvent, She is the defender of the poor and cares what affects them. It is glaringly evident that those with wealth tend to always take care of themselves first. The Virgin Mother has spoken at length about this in times past. The real focus is the spiritual solvency of America. The fact that most young people are reared by single parents, that they are impacted by lust and consumerism every day, that they are given no foundations in prayer or the Church; these are the issues that matter because these are the issues that are defining mankind's response to God and the ultimate composure of our future. Their hearts are like purses that contain the spiritual riches that Heaven has to offer, but they will not open themselves to receive the profits of Jesus' Crucifixion. Our nation is headed on a disastrous and destructive course, and Our Lady believes that this is not a hopeless case. She is doing Her part to help Her children avoid the collision that is about to ensue. Her messengers and seers in communion with the mission of the Church are making a difference in families across our land and around the globe. The Queen of

Angels is touching the minds and hearts of those who will eventually bask in the Eternal Light of Heaven. Thus, we embrace every word that She speaks to us. We continue with the hope that each one will bring solace and peace to those who are searching for understanding and fulfillment. There is meaning to our lives, and there is purpose because joy is undoubtedly the achievable goal for those willing to be embraced by the Light of the Love of Jesus. Our hearts are the conduit through which Heaven penetrates the veil, and the Face of God is glimpsed in preparation for our reconciliation with the ages. This is why Our Holy Mother asks us to pray from deep within ourselves. And, this is why we continue to kneel before Her, eagerly anticipating the affections that She bestows upon us through Her Eternal Love. I hope with all my heart for the day of God's Light to come quickly and decisively. I long for the world to immerse itself in the beatific brilliance of Heaven because the goodness of Our Lord Jesus Christ is so much more enjoyable to share than the despicable tyranny that we witness throughout the labored globe. The inebriating cup of suffering is filled to the brim with humanity drowning in the desolation flowing over its sides. Yet, I joyfully embrace an immeasurable confidence that what we are seeing is a tide that is flowing away from us like a waterfall into a canyon, never to return in the history of mankind. There will never again be a century as the one we have just completed. God has always harbored the triumphant culmination of Creation within the Sacred Heart of the returning Messiah. Christ Jesus owns the ultimate victory that each of us will soon witness. Oh! there will be unending jubilation as has never been conceived by the collective human heart! Our worldly championships will be forgotten amidst the ecstasy that will ignite with greater power than a billion nuclear explosions. The aged-holy will shriek with the glee of children as they watch every hope that dashed itself upon their despair resurrected with convincing fulfillment in front of their sorrow-singed eyes, while their infant grandchildren giggle beside them as if they had known God's secrets all along. Our Omnipotent Father is about to answer the smallest whimper that ever escaped our soul the way a mother responds to the cries of her newborn child. We are at the threshold of watching every prayer heaved from the desolate recesses of each human heart unfold into history, striking and destroying with the very power of the Almighty every shadow of sadness that ever touched our beings. Creation will be re-created by the undefiled Heart and desire of Heaven. The mortal history that millennia of Saints could not seem to pray into being will appear like a river of pristine grandeur, rolling and bubbling with an immortal grace that will be visible to every eye. At the break of this jubilant day, we will recognize that our prayers were the invincible, transforming power of God as the answers float into our laps like a tide washing over a child playing in the surf on a sandy beach. God will say YES to each of us again and again and again, until our hearts are too filled to utter another request. Then, the meek shall inherit the Earth and the Kingdom of God will be ours with no tear to burden an everlasting peace called Eternity.

These transcripts from Our Lady's Immaculate Heart that my brother and I have placed before the eyes of the world project from the location of Heaven's repose. They are more than a collection of literary religious works, they are en masse a means by which God has touched the people He loves. They breathe the same Life as the Gospel itself while never superceding it. They are sustenance for our joy, knowledge for our understanding of God, and help during these times of trouble. Do not hold them back from those who need them. These miraculous works are meant for a humanity that is parched for compassion. Our Lady's decrees and reprimands are dripping-wet with beauty and liberation. Their themes and cadences stir the heart of man to realize that Christianity remains the only vibrant cause in the universe. It has been said that there will always be new generations of men, but our Holy Mother says that this will someday not be the case. There needs to be a means to that end, and the means is the Will of God for His creatures to repent, to ratify what Heaven and Nature have done, to fall on bended knee and recognize that the inevitable passing of humanity is coming very near. What the Mother of God has done here in the heartland of America will grow that repentance; it will speed-up the day when everyone alive will come to the conclusion that there is no life, truth, or resurrection without Jesus Christ on the Cross. Her divine grace can be felt by everyone through these strains of revelation. She intends to melt every hardened heart, knowing the icy indifference of man cannot withstand the rays from the Eternal Sun, even in the deepest cold of our sins. The radiant warmth of Her Love is evident, apparent, and powerful. Each of us is already a participant at Her side in this grand march toward Eternity simply by reading the words She has spoken here. Each of us has already been transformed from pauper into prince and traitor into warrior, ordained beneficiaries of the Divinity who is Love Himself. Everyone is rich because grace is touching us and imprinting Life upon our being. We are perpetually accepted by God and reciprocally called to accept this beatific fact so that our joy may become complete in this world that needs nothing but Christ to return into its midst. There are many visions within the human heart that are authentic, but remember this one. We are loved! Despite everything the world has used in its attempts to destroy the hierarchical origin from which this comforting beauty flows, it is the living fire that God will never allow to be extinguished. Even if it were possible to totally obscure every hope within every human soul, there will still live within us the flame of Jesus Christ who promises to love us. History will still declare that God appeared on Earth in the Person of a Perfect Man and proclaimed with His Blood that we are acceptable to Him once again. Healing given its divine venue will restore shattered dreams. Now is the venue, now is the time!

Forever hope matched to eternal dream! They are alive! And, nothing can stop the Queen of Heaven or the Messianic Son whom She bore! I ask everyone to augment the overwhelming triumph of God through your best effort at optimal completion. With your heart, join the parade marching toward Heaven. With your prayers, invite the whole world. From the darkest hovel to the most adorned mansion, let us lift our hopes that all may be one, as You, Father, are one with Your Son and the Holy Spirit. Who can doubt this story of Infinite Love emanating from the Heart of Christianity? We are witnessing the premonition of heavenly victory through its hierarchy while passionately striving for a heart ever pure, a Truth beyond lofty, and a vision finally clear. This is the Spirit for which humanity must yearn to call its own, united as one. This is the essence of life that is the fulfillment of our primordial longings. It is the image of our restoration to the unstained original, within our expanding capabilities as it flowers from our beatified vision. Of its own accord, it transcends the prophetic distance, spanning the gulf between what we have become and what we are commanded to be. Pine to be Love; to heal, to elevate, to reconstitute, to consecrate human hearts back into the Womb of the everlasting. Oh! to be birthed into Immaculate Hands, into an embrace with almighty-powers who stand in ranks and columns determined to defend the perfect essence of man and transport our spirits aloft like eagles soaring above the mountain of our mortal chains! It is now that we must ascend and take flight beyond the world which is failing beneath our feet. We must go to God together, arm-in-arm and comfort-to-wound. If united in this common destiny, we will not fail. If there be only a remnant responding to the call, then let that misunderstood oddment advance toward the heavens like a thundering rocket into the blue, climbing from the bowels of Creation with the masses of humanity in the grasp of our hopes, booming into the firmament past barrier and boundary with a piercing honor that will split the veil of man's darkness and reveal the Face of God to the Earth once again. Let the courageous summon the strength for which the weak pine! Let the reborn breathe Light into the shadows where tepid souls linger in stagnant darkness! Let heavenly vision chart the new course leading to the treasured day of Resurrection, toward the Cross that marks the hallowed spot where the riches of Heaven were deposited from the hold of God's sky-faring Heart, into a land of mourners that have looked heavenward for its soothing riches since the first clap of mortal time. It is the Eucharist Who lives within the Tabernacle which stands with preeminence above every Altar, the very Presence of God, a Treasure so profound, the Grail of every courageous explorer and unfulfilled expedition, the beatific array of total splendor that commands the humble gasp of Creation itself. God is emanating the streaking rays of His Bounty from the Marian vaults, soothing and searing sinner and saint alike. We must partake of this life-giving Jewel and spread its glistening reflections across the world! In this way and through this purpose, humanity is transfigured into the sparkling diamond which the Almighty Father has every intention of placing in the crown of His Only Begotten Son. Hail to Christ the King! Hail Messiah and God! Blessed be the Lamb! Empower us, O' Holy Spirit! And, all honor to His Mother and Queen!

Dear Blessed and Sacred Virgin, two decades ago, I heard your beautiful call within my heart. I did not know you, but the sound of your voice was the caress for which my heart had always dreamed. In your grace and love, I found the reason why I was born. I have found purpose, fulfillment, joy and most of all, a hope that I know is powerful enough to change the world. I know the Father listens now, and will respond because He loves me. You have given colossal meaning to my every act and inspiration. You have given me vision where once I was miserably blind. I am thankful for finally seeing Love, oh! so simple and yet beyond every earthly dimension. I am thankful to be blinded again, but this time by the Light that emanates from your blessed soul and the sacrifices you bore. I love the Light and I love you. I thank you for the longing you have ignited within my soul; the longing to honor your Son Jesus with every beat of my heart and breath of my spirit. I wish to bestow upon Him every moment of loving affection, praise, and honor that the world has thus deprived Him from the moment He came to save us through your virgin womb. Mother, your Son deserves to be loved with nothing less than my perfect love for Him, indeed the perfect love of all humanity. So Mother, please sustain me in this giantness of heart. Make me little so my heart can grow big. Nothing in this world is worth bringing the faintest shadow of sorrow to His glorious Heart who has loved and sacrificed so much for us. I repent the shadows that bear my name and offer them to the penitential Sacrament so generously bequeathed to us by your Son.

Mother, please look upon your children with compassion as I know you already do. See us praying to return home to you. See us desiring your motherly protection. See us longing for peace and purpose. I pray for those whose souls are dying in the wreck of this world. Heal those who have stopped looking for Heaven, who no longer desire and have ceased longing. Dear Mother, you have worked the miracle in my heart that has delivered me into your arms. You called, I answered. You beckoned, I came. You desired, I obeyed. You spoke, I listened. You asked, I complied. You hope, and I am now scouring the world looking for your fulfillment from every human heart. I am asking them all to come to you. I pray for this miracle within every soul. I wish to call every person that God created "my brother and my sister." I will accept everyone who comes to me in your Son's Name with gracious love and tenderness, for I remember how you have received me who did not know how to love you until I saw you. I was thrown into the furnace and only my love remains. Jesus is made happy by love. He died hoping that we would understand and be transformed by His resurrecting grace. How happy He must have been while hanging on the Cross looking down at you, Mother, knowing that at least you understood and allowed no resentment into your Immaculate Heart. With every reason to hate the world for such an act of horror against your beloved Child, you instead loved with the complete capacity of your infinite being. And Jesus was fulfilled and happy to have died while gazing at such great love for Him. Yes, Mother, you have helped Him love us. With Him, you together transcended Creation on Calvary. What must those eternal moments have been! There atop Golgotha, you and your Son so high above the world, too high for any human being to grasp, lost in a Sacrifice that redefined Creation and saved all that was precious in the history of an entire universe. Please sweep humanity into those heights, please help us to enter this sacred mystery, please help us accept, please make us worthy.

Among the mountains of Medjugorje, you have come; throughout the world you have visited, and as the Morning Star Over America do you shine! Hear my petitions for the holy priesthood, these heroes who profess your Son to this darkened hostile world which needs to be led to the heavenly altar for its very survival. Grace all your priests with the courage to respond to your loving voice. Protect the beautiful universal Pastor you have given us in Pope Benedict XVI. Allow him to lead the world to peace. Give him length of days to see the victory he is cultivating. Let him feast on the fruits of his labors. I pray Holy Mother especially for this country of the United States of America whom you have admonished with genuine affection. No nation has ever been so blessed by God, yet wretched multitudes still reject Him with malice aforethought. They reject that which is honorable and pure. Raise a legion of spiritual patriots to once again secure our motherland, and drive from our shores all that corrupts it. I pray for the miraculous change of our nation by the power of your intercession as the Morning Star Over America. Encourage my fellow countrymen to share, to care for the least among us, to teach their children virtue and nobility, to set every good example of holiness and witness with our generation to the next that Jesus Christ is our only source of peace. I humbly ask for Heaven to be unlocked to all my brothers and sisters in Purgatory, those who spent their lives being recklessly indifferent toward their presentation before the penetrating Light of judgement at the Throne of the Almighty Father. My God in Heaven, I ask that no one have to suffer anymore, but if it be Your Will, grace us to engage it well. I pray for the end of this suffering, and also the end of the need for that suffering. Help the wretched and irreverent to know that the world is suffering for them, and then maybe they will see love once again and contribute their part. Father, please see these words and let their souls come to you for reorientation, peace and joy. I ask you to recall that Mercy triumphs over judgment. Please invoke the complete triumph over suffering!

My greatest prayer of thanksgiving arises to you from the deepest depths of my heart. Thank you for my brother Timothy. You have given me a brother who loves me perfectly. He has endured it all with the grace of a prince. No one would ever believe, nor could they comprehend what he has suffered so the world could be granted the words of the Morning Star Over America. You have given me a compatriot worthy of the call, with a lion's heart and a spiritual strength that I have never witnessed in another human being. I not only believed him, but he believed me, and we both believed you. It has been a reflection of your Trinity. You have given me a life bonded in grace with him in service to You, a life of testament to the blessings of the Holy Cross from Canada to Mexico's Gulf and from sea to shining sea. Please give me an eternity at his side. Upon this, I will have received all from you, and my heart will be forever contented. I hope that you will soon allow all Creation to share the love you have given us to manifest through your Holy Roman Catholic and Apostolic Church. All my heart I pour out to you. I ask nothing more for myself in this life except to proclaim the Morning Star Over America with convincing power and saintly composure. Please do not let me fall to any of my weaknesses and thereby damage your Mother's work. I ask for all the abilities and faculties that I need to move the world to loving you. I beg for infinite miraculous graces for the souls of the world. Shock them into belief if need be. Bring to fruition the sacrifices of the Saints, and unleash their power upon the Earth. I pray for every hue of grace, every kind of miracle, every facet of your supernatural love to be revealed, sparkling and radiant before the eyes of humankind. I cry out for Revelation! Victory! Triumph! Life! Peace! Healing! Joy! Come, O' Love! Come Divinity, Redemption, Transformation, and Light! Bring the Triumph of the Immaculate Heart of Mary!

Hail Mary, full of grace, the Lord is with Thee.
Blessed art thou amongst women,
And blessed is the Fruit of Thy Womb, Jesus.

Holy Mary, Mother of God, pray for us sinners,
now and at the hour of our death. Amen.

MORNING STAR OVER AMERICA

Twentieth Century Anthology

In the Year of Our Lord

AD 1997

"We recognize the cyclical nature of human life, the repetitive errors and accidental yields, the reassuring days and enviable nights, the shy phases of the Moon, our comedies borne and skirmishes lost, the love and loathing, the keen and outlandish, the scarce and opulent, and everything else that bridges the gap between our tallest mountains and deepest dreams. All things come and go; we either hand them to our descendants or commit them to the past. Nothing but our soul in Jesus lives on. Indeed, even the town mortician is eventually laid to rest."

-William L. Roth Jr.

Saturday, March 8, 1997
7:45 p.m

"Good evening, My children of Light and Love. Thank you for joining Me at the window of your hearts through which you focus upon the paradisial summit awaiting your challenge of its heights. Together, we have taken you near the heights of human holiness. It is your obligation to finish the journey as I watch and pray. My little ones, your final journey to the top is equivalent to the journey of Jesus upon the Mountain Calvary where I also watched and prayed. God will never allow you to be either alone or abandoned. It is I who keep your footsteps sure. I will always tell you where to place your next step... The world must remember that it was I upon the Earth who brought your Savior the first time. It is also I who now prepare the world for My presentation of Him again. That is My Love. That is why I am speaking to you now. The time is near. The end of the Earth as you know it may well come tomorrow or in that next century just months away. Oh! pray that Jesus comes in great Mercy! The last century has been horrid and treacherous for all that is good and decent. The past hundred years have brought the diminishment of human holiness never-before seen in Creation. Industry and technology have replaced good works. Entertainment has replaced meditation. Materialism has replaced prayer. Scientology has replaced faith. Despair has destroyed hope. Selfishness has replaced charity. The slaughter of millions of innocent victims of wars and the scourge of abortion has left a very cringed brow over the eyes of God. Impurity and poverty are the dead weight of a doomed age. And, of all the mockery one could imagine, a sinner has given birth outside the Sacraments to a child named for the holy land of Lourdes. I must tell you that God is not well pleased with human destiny of the 20th century. His Church has been divided and ignored. And, one of the most holy and reverend successors of Saint Peter is being treated as a lame and ignorant servant of only indifference. I assure you that this Pope has yet to raise his voice to all in the way that he will! The most responsible Vicar of Christ on Earth is now in the Chair of Saint Peter! He is all that is keeping God from crushing the Earth! One day, all will see what I am telling you is true. But, he will be at home in Heaven by then.

My children, the ravages of the last hundred years have deteriorated the collective conscience of humankind to its lowest point in mortal history. What a fitting time for the Master of the house to return home. When Jesus is least expected, He will come. But, thankfully, those who are My children will not be caught by surprise. You will be ready, indeed. That is because you are obedient. And, to those who are not, I assure you that My Grace will convert them. They cannot get away from their Mother. They cannot out-run Me. They cannot hide under the furniture. I know each child given to Me by Jesus from the Cross by name. I know where they are playing. Many can already hear My voice calling them Home. Those who are not listening will indeed feel the pinch of My fingers on their ear lobes as they come with Me, complaining all the way to the bathtub. Oh! you will hear the water splashing, but I will not let them go until they are clean of all that offends God. Have hope in this promise and pray for many. Pray, indeed, for all. I will provide prophecy, revelations, and graces as numerous as the stars. I know the Heart of God and He knows Mine. We will not lose. We will reduce the transgressions of the past 100 years to a point on the tip of a fiber of straw. They are already no more as the Cross has timelessly destroyed them. But, it is the acceptance of the Cross by many transgressors that is the key to this Mystical revision of human history. That acceptance and that Cross are the union that makes all things possible between God and man. My son, you will see that all I have told you is the Truth, and will come to pass in your day."

Saturday, March 15, 1997
7:01 p.m.

"My pretty little children, you are My special ones who pray to change the world. You are obedient in your supplications, strong in faith, and loving in your desires for the destiny of your brothers and sisters. You do these things for God, and because I ask. I know God. I have lived His beautiful Face as you will soon live that same Blessed Visage, your homeland and your peace. You live in a very corrupt and clandestine world. I call your hearts out of the world. Where your heart goes, your soul will follow. I can assuredly capture your heart while Jesus simultaneously accepts your soul and takes you to the Father. You do not yet know Heaven. You have not reached your holiest destiny or seen the brightest Light of an ageless Paradise. But, you stand now at the doorway between Earth and Heaven. I have led you there. I have elevated you to the podium, at the lectern from which you may speak the Truth to the world. The Holy Spirit has composed every speech that any human need hear to reach the heights of happiness. It is not material wealth. It is not even perfect health. It is simply "perfection" of all human capacities, made one and Divine through the Blood and Cross of Jesus Christ. As you journey to that perfection, your worldly desires fade, but too may your faculties wane. You may feel the cold steel of ill health or captivity, but you will always be well and always be free. And, if these words were being spoken from a mountaintop, I would address tens of thousands through the plea: Come to Grace! Come united and without conflict! Cast aside all that divides you! See no color or nation, nor race, nor creed. See not disparaging language or sadness. Be not afraid to be one humanity! Be all of God's children under His guiding hand. There is no prejudice in God. All who come to God are one

Love in many parts. If you can hear My voice, you can be saved. If you fear your past, take courage in your future. If you feel sorrow for your sins, take delight that they are no more; Jesus washed them all away. I call upon all who live to walk toward the Light. Cast your shadows back to the darkness in which they will not be revealed! Yes, turn your back to the darkness. Your face seeks the sun like a flower seeks the rain. Believe Me when I tell you, the wheat and grain that lie as seed beneath the Earth celebrate in their own Divine way in anticipation of breaking through their veil of soil. They are blessed by the life-giving water and living sun to seek life. Be the seeds of righteousness! Anticipate your break through the veil of darkness into the Light! Answer the call of the living Son: Come out! Drink-in the Life-giving waters given you at your Baptism. If the world is to come to fruition in time, now is that time! If you have courage to invoke, bring it now! If you have hope in your heart, let it live now! Creation has been waiting hundreds of thousands of years for the crescendo now near its peak. The groaning of the Earth is its dying gasps! The Earth will soon be replaced by a New Earth, and Heaven will be made new because you will be there. All of these imaginings are not just lost hopes. They are real and true. The family of humankind has neared its thanksgiving meal. All will sit together in harmony and will feast upon Salvation. And, your Lord Jesus will return thanks to God with His hand in yours. Jesus will be the Grace for your Eternal meal of heavenly bliss, just as He is now at Holy Mass. And, all the Saints whose ranks you will join will revel with you the Lord of all. You will be able to speak to God to His Face, an ever-present prayer of thanksgiving. And, as His Son says, *Let us return thanks,* He will have to wait the first ten-thousand years to say Amen because all the new Saints will still be returning thanks with every fiber of their being.

I am very happy to bring you this news. I am grateful to God for allowing Me to come to the Earth bearing words of encouragement. I bring you the Truth, just as I brought the Truth into the manger in Bethlehem. Jesus is the fruit of My womb, a fruit that will always live there. Oh! you should have seen the Life inside the Tomb as the angels witnessed the Resurrection of Jesus there. The happy tears, the dancing, the praying, the meditation! God's Word of Truth would not die! Jesus suffered and died as a mortal, but as Truth, He would not die. And, He has yet to relinquish that Crown. Indeed, He never will. I wish to bring you ever-closer to that bountiful Resurrection; for as a mortal, your body will also die. But, like Jesus, you need not die with it. You, too, are Truth when you live in Jesus. All Truth is one, and you are one in the Love He brings. Jesus wishes to melt your cold hearts, to render them a molten lava of Love which He will pour into His own Heart to cast you into the perfect shape of Love, a beauty fit for Paradise. God has plans for you! No heart is too hard for the pulse of God's loving hand upon it. No soul can resist the Love that God gives if their heart is shaped by Jesus. And, it needs very pretty attire. I have come to adorn you in beautiful Easter garments for your presentation to God. Easter morning is your invitation to accept Jesus' Resurrection. Easter is your premonition of your own victory over death! Rise with Jesus! Rise to new Life. Come to the top of this mountain to be with Me! The view is beautiful. The gate is near. Thank you for listening to these words. Thank you for your holy prayers. I will seek from God the granting of every petition you have offered. I love you always, indeed, in My Immaculate Heart."

Friday, March 21, 1997
7:14 p.m.

"Greetings this springtime evening! I come to you in the magnificent Love that makes all benevolence one and united. I come in peace, the Queen of Peace and Love, to visit you where you serve. Amidst God's paradisial summit, the Angels joyfully anticipate their next mission to your side, dispatched there by God to comfort and console you. The veil that holds you fast in mortality is breached by Love. God perpetually transcends the veil to bring you Wisdom through His Spirit. He permeates the veil beatifically to bring you the Body and Blood of His only Son, sacrificed for the Salvation of your souls. And, My children, God grants you His Divinity by bringing you to perfect holiness, a Divinity you can attain in these mortal days. I ask you to remain open-of-heart to always remember these blessed attributes of your relationship with God. Always He is Love; always He offers His Love, and forever you will be loved. And He gently asks each of these reciprocally from you. My children, despite the terrible sinfulness in the world, there are still great moments of Divinity, many acts of perfection, many places of beauty. The most beautiful place on Earth is a converted heart. The greatest act of perfection is the offering of love to others. And these things need not be rehearsed to be perfect the first time. There are many acts of beauty that are incidental, brought by Grace, talent, effort, and conviction..."

Our Lady gave me an example of the perfection and divinity of which She is speaking. Recently, I was listening to some of my favorite songs. One in particular was sung by a young lady who was gifted with one of the most magnificent voices ever heard. The Blessed Virgin told me that the recording I was listening to was the first rendition that the singer had ever sung. Her first rehearsal was the version released to the world. It was perfect the very first time she sang it. Our Lady continued,

"This is how deeply you must know your own love. You must be able to predict that you will love always perfectly well under any circumstances. There is no rehearsal for perfection of that nature because Love is perfect from the foundation of Creation. I call you to this anticipatory action and life. The former world is passing away as we speak. Change is now occurring in the world. While much of this change is good, it is still met with widespread opposition. The last months of this century and millennium have arrived."

Saturday, March 29, 1997
Holy Saturday
2:43 p.m.

"Greetings I bring this solemn afternoon in observance of the anniversary of Jesus' Body lying in the Tomb, the Tomb of the Universal Soldier. My children, tomorrow you will again celebrate the grand Feast of Easter, the most glorious Sunday of the Church year. Please pray that every soul now living in darkness rises to the Light come the dawn. Pray that the Light of the Resurrection will chase the darkness of sin out of human hearts forevermore. Indeed, hearts given already to Jesus enjoy that brilliance today. I am the Mother of Perpetual Light, your Eternal help. Please pray with Me that conversion and belief come to the world. You are in the hour of observance of Jesus in the Tomb. Jesus' Body represents the highest state of expectation known to humankind, next to His Second Coming in Glory. You can imagine the feelings of those who knew Jesus as the Christ, the Anointed Son of God, as His Body lay in the Tomb. Their faith was tested as never before. They yet had no way of comprehending or understanding that they themselves and multitudes of generations to follow would fight to their deaths defending the Truth which rose at dawn the next day. You know the life of Jesus now as you would have known Him when He was crucified. You would have been beside Me praying with the firm belief in your heart that soon would live again the Son of God. This is the faith with which you now kneel beside Me."

Before the tomb which held Her Son, Our Lady summoned the victory into Her Heart. Her faith convinced Her that Her Son would rise again. The joy of the world was preserved within Her expectation. She anticipated the overwhelming surprise that would be felt by every heart which was at that moment swallowed by grief. She triumphed over human desolation and death. Before the tomb, She says, "Do not take your eyes off that stone." And indeed Jesus moved it, coming forth just as He said. It is with this expectation that we await the triumph of God. Can you anticipate the indescribable surprise on the face of humanity? We must have the convincing faith of Our Lady as She stood before the tomb. Our Lady continued,

"Imagine the Love of the Angels which God dispatched to the Earth awaiting Jesus' Resurrection. They waited as I ask all My children to wait now for His Second Coming. Become the Love of the Angels! You must realize with great importance that Jesus was resurrected not so much to make the world believe, but rather to reward the believers! It is the same today. Your resurrection will come because you believe, not to make you believe. The Soldier who died for the greatest cause known to Creation rose again. The greatest battle for human freedom was waged by Jesus Christ against evil and indifference. And, though He died and because He died, He became the Victor. Those who believed that Jesus would rise from the grave asked others, *'Do you know where Jesus is?'* When others would answer that He is dead, the first Saints would say, *'He is resting. He just conquered the world. He will be up soon to do His final work before He goes to claim His crown next to His Father in Heaven. And, He so loved us, He will come back in us.' (Pentecost)*

Although it was painful to endure death on the Cross, Jesus knew that His pain would end the pain of all His brothers and sisters for eternity. His stripes would heal the wounded, His Death would destroy the death of all humankind. Although Jesus did not utter these words audibly, He said them in His Heart, *'Adam, I love you dearly, no longer will you be weak. Neither can the grave contain your soul, never will the sting of death stain your eternal happiness.'* And, Adam was indeed vindicated. He was set free with all humanity from the bonds of sin and the sting of death. The Soldier answered the call to which His Father had commissioned Him. A perfect Body was now perfectly scarred, ribbons and medals of bravery and honor. He walked the Earth as the Son of Man, the Omnipotent Prophet, the Servant of humanity, the Conqueror of evil, and the Champion of the ages for all Eternity. You are blessed and fortunate to know Him. So, come sunrise tomorrow, remember the happiness that God brought the world with Jesus' Resurrection. Know how different the world is, and how high Heaven is above what they might have been. Among many things that Jesus destroyed on the Cross was human sadness. The world still needs to realize this blessing. Humanity exists in a new state of Grace that it needs only to accept. Still, there is human sorrow. Still, there is suffering, just as in the Incarnate days of Jesus. But one day, He will come and wipe away every tear from your eyes and help you to live peacefully in the new world He will bring. Until that moment, God asks you to be Christ for others. Be His anointed children, consecrated by your baptism and the Blood of Jesus. When you see sadness, supplant it with joy. When you see suffering, destroy it with love and servitude. Do all the things you know from the Beatitudes, so beautifully recounted by Saint Francis of Assisi. Help the world live expectantly and prayerfully as your example of kneeling hopefully before the Tomb on this day hundreds of years ago. As I was then, I pray beside you now. I pray in unison with you and ask that you resonate My intentions to God. You have a humble response to My call for which I am forever grateful. If you can only imagine how timeless Love is! You see the days and months pass before you, but they do not diminish your faith and hope. The years escape your grasp, but you happily let them go in favor of the Eternity to come. Indeed, the world is passing before your eyes! You are living the End Times. Millions do not realize the Truth before the world, but I am helping them. One day, you will be united with Jesus when He gives you a glorified, perfect and incorruptible body. Thank you for accepting your just share in Heaven! Thank you for never leaving My side. I will always know that you are My holy children. I love you."

Friday, April 4, 1997
6:59 p.m.

"I greet you, My beautiful children, with a holy and reverent kiss of Love. You are My special ones, My prayerful children whom I love with endless compassion. My children, I know your hearts. I see your suffering. I feel your sorrows and pray for your strength. You are part of the faith that keeps My Son's hopes living in the universe. Thank you for being participants in God's plan for the destiny of humanity. Thank you for answering the call of God without questioning why. I have come to ask you to continue to pray for the Mother Church. Pray for all souls who compose Her, who lead and guide Her, and who serve Her in so many exemplary ways. You know how God loves His Church on Earth. He asks you to know Her well, to embellish the sanctity of Jesus' Spirit who dwells in Her. Please pray for the Holy Father. Pray for the hierarchy, the Bishops, priests, all those called by God to serve. Know that in all of the longevity, Grace, and beauty of the Church, She is still a tender and sensitive faith and order. She still knows pain and weeps over Her lost sheep. Please pray for Her, be kind to Her, and treat Her gently, for She is the source of the salvific Sacraments that are guiding you Home. She is the blessed Body of the Salvation of humanity. Treat Her with dignity and respect. The Mother Church is the seamstress who made your holy baptismal garment, and through whose grace you are kept clean. The holy and Universal Church is God's Love for you and the vehicle through which, in faith, you return that Love. Exult the Catholic Church over every nation and principality! Honor Her all of your days and She will bring you to Jesus through Me.

My children, I have never before told you of My tender love for the Holy Church on Earth. I wish you to know that the intercession of the Saints is invoked by your petitions to God through His Faith-Church on Earth. It is there that the Saints have left their inscription and legacy. It is there that you are greeted by them as you enter the doorway of the sanctuary. They relish the time they are allowed to speak through you. They are happy to have the opportunity to pray for you and simultaneously with you for the peace and healing that you seek for the lost world of humankind. When you go into the Church, especially for Holy Mass, you are flanked by angels who usher you to the site from which God wishes you to observe and participate in the Crucifixion of His only Son. The Holy Church Universal is blessed because it belongs to Christ, the Anointed One. Thank you for your compliance and participation in the one Body of faith and love for Jesus. With Him, I bless you and guide you. God knows both your heart and your faith. He knows how you pine for peace in a world so reluctant to love. He sees the cynicism about you and the persecution you suffer for His sake. He also knows overwhelmingly your impatience in waiting for the coming of His Kingdom and justice. When your faith is perfected, you will know that He has taken His first steps toward you. Any time you see a Baptism, you see the footstep of Jesus coming to save you. When a child is fed or a sickness healed, it is Jesus laying His foot down on His journey back to the Earth. Each time you pray for the lost, He lengthens His stride. When you reach-out to the lonely in His Name, your Lord increases the pace of His steps toward the mortal world.

My children, if all the faithful would pray in unity for peace and healing, Jesus would come running at full speed back to you with the power and pace of the Champion that He is. You already know Him and He assuredly knows you. The pendulum came to a stop on Mount Calvary and has ever since been swiftly swinging back to you. One day, all will see. All will hear. Please be ready, My children, because that pendulum is also the clapper in the bell of Creation about to hit the other side of time, a ringing joy that will end the world as you know it and ring-in the new age of Paradise and peace. I promise that I will be there and help you come to complete Love. I will help you put your little hands over your ears if the joyful ringing seems too loud. I will not allow the mightiness of the fireworks to frighten you. Stay close to Me and hold-on to Me because that day is coming very soon. And, it will be then that your eyes will be blessed with the perfect vision of Mercy personified. It is then that you will know what your life was for. The perfect purpose of your life given by God will come peacefully to rest in your heart. Until that day, your heart will be restless. Until then, you will ask the question, why? From now until then, you will continue to wonder "when" is "then." It is not offensive to God for you to demand His attention. That invocation is a righteous call for the elimination of every evil that befalls humankind. God has already answered your call. His solution was brought nearly 2000 years ago. You are just now realizing it. Call upon the power of the Cross! Call Jesus into the world to quench the fires that burn the human spirit, and yet, to ignite fires where souls are frozen in hatred and indifference. Call upon the Blood of the Cross to cleanse souls lying filthy in sin. That Blood is the fuel you need to carry-on your journey, the Life-Blood that can resurrect a dead world. Yes, indeed, the Life-Blood of the Church is literally the Blood of the Lamb of God who takes away the sins of the world. And, in that Life-Blood flows the Mercy of God.

This is the special Sunday that His Mercy will be especially fluent. At the designated hour of Mercy this Sunday, you will know a portion of the ringing-bell that heals the ages. Please participate in that Divine Mercy and know that God will hear you. If you have a prayer, pray it! If you have a petition, lift it up to Him! If you have a dream, dream it indeed! You awaken God's compassion and Mercy by your call to Him. God is a God of Love and His Love is for His children. His New Covenant is your only chance to board His outstretched hand about to reach your soul and recoil into the majesty of the heavens. His outstretched arms and pure sacrificial hands are that train that is traveling the Earth seeking passengers bound for Glory. And, once you have boarded, you may look to your feet and notice that you are standing on rough terrain. If you ask, God will tell you that it is where there was once a spike that pierced the holy Palm that holds you. I ask you to remember these holy things and meditate on the happiness coming now in time toward you. Thank you for listening to My words of holy encouragement. I am here because I love you. You cannot fully comprehend how I love you. Please remember that your passage into Heaven will come swiftly, and you will wonder where time went. You will wonder how your mortality could have passed so quickly. Thank you for praying to heal such a wretched world. Thank you for yearning for Heaven, for knowing the petitions and intentions of My Heart. Though your passing days often seem strange and conflicting, know that they are a part of your passage toward Eternal Life and perpetual Light. Hence, they are a gift from God to prepare you to embrace Him perfectly. Thank you still for honoring Me through the Holy Rosary. I am your Advocate, your counsel to Jesus, who is your Savior. I sincerely love you with all My Heart."

Friday, April 11, 1997
7:01 p.m.

"My Love is with you and My Son brings you peace. My dear little children, you are God's lost artwork for which He has come searching. From the ravages of sin at the influence of Satan, you were shaken and fell from display in the halls of Paradise. But, Jesus came to pick you up, to repair your souls, to restore your perfection, and to again elevate you to the holy halls of beauty for all Creation to see. I am very happy to see so many of My children lifting-up their brothers and sisters, leading them, forgiving them, and teaching them. Jesus is happy to see brokenhearted children mended through the love of others. He is proud of His artwork. Jesus' Sacred Heart is touched to see

His little children wearing apparel that says, *I am special, God did not make any trash.* My children, you are living in a world that is near its Reckoning. I tell you this constantly; and each time I repeat it, you are yet closer to that Truth. Soon you will see the destruction and obsolescence of such phenomena as complacency, indifference, egoism, and hatred. It is time for change, and the change will come by the power of judgement. While God prefers that judgement be preceded by conversion, He will not hold the world statically in mortality for the wait. God is the only true Master of time and timing. He has already decided when to bring His Kingdom to Earth. That Redemption and Judgement is so close that He has consistently invited Me to come to Earth and serve as the *New Gabriel.* Gabriel comes with Me each time I visit the world, ushering Me and clearing My paths into your hearts so that My messages can be heard. Do not be afraid of this New World to come. Do not believe that you are not worthy of such Deliverance. Indeed, Redemption seeks you with as much life as you desire it. You are like a lightning rod while Redemption is the lightning. God has found you. The world was illuminated by the Cross of Jesus on Calvary like God shining a light into a dark pit. He came looking for you with the beaming Light of His Son. And, Jesus flashed your vision that allowed God to say, *Oh! there you are*! He is now reaching down to pick you up. My children, God picks you up by the heart. You speak to God with your heart in answer to His words I love you from the Cross. Jesus is the Truth and the Earth is His palate. The Cross is His tongue with which He pronounced the words, *It is time to come Home.* I am here today in advance of the harvest of souls. Many hundreds of thousands still labor in the vineyards for God..."

Today, my brother attended the funeral of a middle-age woman whom we saw nearly every day at Holy Mass. She was very reverent toward Jesus in the Most Blessed Sacrament, while suffering a terrible physical ailment. Our Lady mentioned Her to us,

"The new Saint of the day has said, *By the Blood of the Cross, we are saved.* She is in Heaven. Please know what that means for the world. Know how happy she is to be redeemed and made new again. For all Eternity, for the perpetual Day for which you seek, she will be ecstatic. Your brother is to be thanked for coming to pray at her funeral Mass. It was very kind. He did, indeed, attend the funeral Mass of a great person. The world must come to know greatness as defined by Heaven. Please remember all the Saints. They will assuredly remember you. You are the tabernacle of Jesus' Spirit. Jesus does wish to reside in every heart. Where He lives is blessed with peace. You are the souls whose charge it is to sanctify the world you know. You are doing such work well. For many years, day after day, I have been watching you work in God's vineyard. Your labors have been sweet and your prayers very powerful. God gives your intentions and petitions power to change the world. For two decades, you have been seeking ways to interpret, understand, and overcome the world and its influences. I watched you grow and waited joyfully for many years to bring My intercession to you."

Our Lady then manifested visions in my heart of all those days that She patiently watched over me waiting for February 22, 1991. My spirit welled-up with the peace and lightheartedness that I had as a child during my play. I began to cry as I was able to see and feel my childhood as it was miraculously brought back into my heart. Through these visions, I transcended into the joys of my past as they were presented as premonitions for the future. Our Holy Mother continued,

"Those days give you cause to smile. They are behind the veil, days that are gone, but ones that you will see again from the purview of perfection. You will live the sweetest moments again. All of this hope is real. This is not magic, fantasy, or a dream. It is real and a part of the Glory of the New World Jesus brings. I am happy to bring you this Good News. There is nothing or no one that you desire in your heart that Jesus will not give you. Each day that you live, that reality comes closer. You will soon see the comets from the Light-side of Creation. They will look like tiny lights under your feet. Remember that God not only desires that you have a joyful heart, He requires it! I give you My Motherly blessing. ✞ Thank you for your prayers. I will speak to you again soon."

Friday, April 18, 1997
7:00 p.m.

This evening, Our Lady offered simple words of encouragement to give our hearts strength. Our daily labors are often heavy and exacting. The world is rushing at such a rapid pace, and there is very little room for peacefulness. And so, Our Lady has come again to bring peace into our lives.

"Peace. May the Peace of the Holy Spirit be with you always. My children, the holy men and women known to Creation as Saints are praying for you, and also with you. Along with them, I come to ask your prayers for the lost world. My special children, your daily work is an effort in the Lord. Do not allow your weariness to affect your peace. Through these words and in response to your call, I bring you messages of Divinity and Salvation. You are very interested in Heaven, and I bring Heaven to be with you. I am happy with your lives and your prayers. I have been sent to ask you to continue to be peaceful and happy. God is filling your lives with grace. If you comprehend the good standing you hold in Heaven, you will smile the whole day through. By your holy prayers, you are helping sanctify a very sinful world."

Tuesday, April 22, 1997

It is Time to Try

Brothers, can we hope so large as to cast our shadow on the bulging sun?
Will we call our consciences home in time to catch the parting train?
Is all that is not right too wrong to change?
Do we dare to fight the indiscretion of invincible wills?
Can we focus our vision upon what is yet unseen?
Can we hear the faint calling of weakened souls, too tired to stand?
Is our collective human spirit on its dying bed?
Are our inquisitions wrought by pain, temper, terror, and fear?
Then call Home. Run Home. Love Home.
This hallowed Spirit we call Jesus is the boulevard to human completion, our rendezvous with perfection, where lives of love are cast into grateful hands.
Shed of winter hearts, the fatal Earth will die no more.

Friday, April 25, 1997
7:09 p.m.

"My dear children whom I love, I am your Mother who has come to tell you that holiness is the catalyst for human conversion to Jesus Christ. Holiness unlocks the door to perfection. This is a good day in Creation because God owns the day. His Love breaks the bonds that make hearts lonely and sadden feelings. My children, it is a glorious day in Paradise because thousands throughout the world have joined those basking in Eternal Light. There are thousands more whose souls are confined in Purgatory who will be released into Heaven because of the prayers you are now offering. It is a beautiful Easter spring. I know that you love the spring, and equally the autumn. While your climate and season say that it is springtime, it is the autumn of time for the world. The harvest is near. You must continue to pray with all the Saints to Jesus and God Himself for Divine intervention and for miracles to help convert the world. Along with this Feast of Saint Mark, the next two Thursdays are days of great grace for the world. Next Thursday, you shall honor My dear spouse Saint Joseph, and you will have yet another pretty evening of Ascension Thursday. I will be with you as I am always to pray for you and with you during these last times for the mortal Earth. God is very happy to continue to send Me to you, and He is very happy to dispatch the

Angels. You are living your life as Jesus asks while seeking the Kingdom of God. Indeed, you are bringing God's Kingdom to others in a beneficial way. The heavens are forever grateful, and God will always answer your holy prayers. It is a very special time on Earth when you pray. Your love, prayers, and holiness mitigate many of the wrongs that others commit that you so fear. This is why it is so important for you to continue. Thank you for your prayers and desires for the coming of God's Kingdom."

Friday, May 2, 1997
6:58 p.m.

"My beautiful children, I am your dear Mother, the Queen of all loving souls in Creation. It is indeed a very pretty place to which I come, as I visit the center of your hearts to join in your prayers and take them in union with Mine to God. Today, My children, I must remind you that evil still lurks rampantly to take away your happiness and good health, even your mental health. But, remember that no evil can survive the power of My Love. Please invoke the assistance of the Archangels and all the Saints. It is a pretty world about you. God lives in all places and brings peace to them. It is My pleasure to accompany and represent Him in the universe. I will be present when all Creation has been closed and reopened again in Glory. The door is moving on its hinges with each new day. I wish to remind you of the great gift your Diary is for the world, a gift which must be presented at all costs. You can see its power, and you know its grace. This is why it is so opposed by Satan. However, I care not what Satan demands. He has neither power nor authority over the Kingdom of God or its children. Suffer what you will; you will never leave the beaming eyes of the Lord whose suffering you complement. Jesus' suffering preceded your own and makes your own perfect because you do it for Him, for all the sacred souls who will come to the Light because of the burning embers of your love for them. Many children have proclaimed loudly in tears, '*Lord, I have loved your people.*' And Jesus the Lord knows your love. Your participation is what truly perfects the suffering of others in the way that My Visitation perfected the life of Saint Elizabeth, the mother of John. It took the union of our hearts and souls to manifest the Mystery of the Visitation. The Visitation is My example to the world. It represents service to those who precede the Second Coming of Jesus. The tiny unborn children are the little Johns who are to witness for Jesus, to prepare the world for His Return. This is why it is so important that they be given birth. Unborn children are the future baptizers for Christ. It is imperative that the world recognizes the grace of Baptism. You are now preparing to receive Jesus again. You are evangelizing and flourishing in the Holy Spirit. Others will look at your life and recognize the signs of Jesus in you, and indeed the signs are there. I wish for you to know how blessed you truly are. You share My Grace in God and in the Truth of Love. The state of Heaven is made complete by the fruits of your lives and the gifts you bring to others. Those gifts consist of your prayers and sacrifices that many to whom they are given will not realize until Jesus comes again. However, do not allow this veil to diminish your hope and effort. Believe in your heart that what you do is for God. Be at peace, and comfort and console others. This is a watershed time for you and your work for Me. We must pray that you progress to the completion and fruition of your blessed work. Please keep praying and adoring Jesus. I am at your side at all times. I hear your little voices calling Me to your side. I do as the Father wills. You are never forsaken, even when it may seem so. While you must be confident in God's response to your prayers, you must not flippantly expect an answer at a given day or hour. Please continue to pray, and God will do the rest. Thank you for not giving-up when it would seem easy to do so. Jesus' Love is Grace enough for you. I truly love you beyond your comprehension."

Friday, May 9, 1997
7:29 p.m.

"Good evening, My blessed little children. The Virgin of Love has come to pray with you. I am pleased with your peaceful lives and your desire for the conversion of all humanity to Jesus. Please do not fear the world. Your souls are in the hands of My blessed Son, Jesus. My children, the world is sore from the many wounds inflicted upon it by wretched sinners. Innocent and blameless souls are being scourged and abused. The holy suffer at the hands of the wicked the world over. It is your prayers which will rectify this terrible condition. Give your lives to the Holy Rosary and to your Mother. I will not allow evil to tear your love from your hearts. I am your Mother, your Protectress, who cares for you like no other. Call upon Me in times of trial and trouble. I will answer your call because, on so many occasions, you have answered Mine. When you ponder the wondrous Love of God, you realize that no evil can truly conquer you. You will indeed suffer much, but suffering is a milestone on the road to victory. Live by faith and prayer. Time is growing short, and Satan is striking everywhere and at any time. I wish for you to always remember that God does not always reveal His motivations, especially through My intercession. His main motivation is Love and whatever brings the world to greater Love. I am happy with the composition of your Diary. The many blessed messages and holy images are filled with meaningful parables and examples of sacrifice and obedience. Be confident in its success. I ask you to pray for the unborn, for those in prisons, for the elderly and infirm, for the conversion of sinners, for the poor souls in Purgatory, for world peace, for the Holy Father and all the clergy, and for all the many other intentions for which together we pray. I am very happy with your lives. Thank you for beginning a new novena. I will pray with you. Please pray, pray, pray. I will speak to you again soon."

Friday, May 16, 1997
7:11 p.m.

"My prayerful children, your Virgin Mother has come to pray with you. Indeed, I am with you whenever you pray to lift your petitions to God. Please know that you never pray alone. When Jesus told you that whenever two are gathered in His Name, He is in their midst, He included those who pray alone because He knew that I would always be the other one present. God has designed a special future for you because you love Him in return. I am the center of that future. All valleys lead to Me, and all streams of life roll into the benison of My Immaculate Heart. When the faithful call Me blessed, they speak for God. It is the Holy Spirit in you who proclaims My Grace. My Special son, the power in your Diary is a gift from the Holy Spirit. Its words are most beautiful. As your heart is deeply touched, so will the world be touched. Each time I come to pray with you, My appearance is in reflection of every message I have ever given. I echo each word with My simple presence; and My reaffirmation of Love to you is for your soul, not just a repetition of words recorded in your mind. This is a very blessed time for you. Together, we have been building a great ship of faith and love that others will board willingly in time. Please continue to pray. All you need for survival in this very dangerous world is the Grace from My Immaculate Heart and the strength given you through the Holy Spirit."

Saturday, May 24, 1997
6:57 p.m.

"Good evening, My joyful children. You are the hopeful ones, the faithful ones who trust God to lead you back to Him. I have come to direct your way and to give you the nourishment of Love you need upon your journey. My Special son, before I go any further, I need to give you a warning to keep you from being seriously and permanently injured. When you light the candles, do not hold the lighter upside down. The flame will crawl up the chamber and ignite the fuel. It will explode in your hand like a grenade and burn you and ignite a fire in this holy place. When you light the candles, always hold the candle in a horizontal position and then the lighter in a horizontal position to light the wick. Then stand the candle vertically. Do you understand? I wish to protect you, and your obedience makes that protection possible. I am happy to have come to share another hour of prayer with you.

This is such a great time of anticipation and opportunity for the world. A little work along the way is fixing your home as you wish it to be. You are helped by Saint Joseph because he loves you so. Please increase in veneration of Saint Joseph. He understands your kindness to Me. He sees your compassion for the poor workers. He sees your faith. Veneration of Saint Joseph is a great sign of predestination for those wishing to know God. Saint Joseph is a powerful Saint! I am the submissive spouse of Saint Joseph, and he is the father of the house. You sit around his table like olive plants. I am happy to defer to My spouse as you invoke the intercession of the Saints. While I am your most reliant intercessor, Saint Joseph is God's most powerful Saint! I promise that I am telling the truth as defined by God. It seems that the injuries that your brother has sustained are being mitigated by your prayers. While he will not fully recover, he will be better than in past weeks. Your Diary is a very beautiful text which will draw tears from the readers in the same way that you wept in reading it. I have come simply to speak with you and cheer you today. I have come to pray with you and bless you. Many exciting things are happening because of your love and your wisdom. Thank you again and again for your holy prayers which convert the world.

Friday, May 30, 1997
7:13 p.m.

The Cry of the Messenger

"Dost thou not know, O Israel, that on this day hath fallen thy most gallant warrior?"

"Peace. The peace of the Holy Spirit is with you always. My children, the Spirit of Love protects and guides you. He gives you Wisdom, confidence, and good strength. My dear children, I do not come to warn you of a terrible scorn given to mankind by God; My words do not portend doom and hopelessness. Instead, I come bringing you hope and happiness. Of course, the world is filled with heresy and hatred, but such have already been defeated by Jesus to be manifested completely in your time upon the Triumph of My Immaculate Heart. In that, My little children, is constant hope. Do not fear the day, for the Light is Christ the Victor. You bask in His Holy Light. You are cleansed by the healing waters from the side of the Champion, pierced beautifully for your souls. I must tell you today that unless you hope in your success, you will not succeed. Believe in the power of your prayers and you will be successful. Know your courage with which you convert others and you will savor such victory. Accept the Love in your heart as the Truth which guides your days. My children, today I have come to remind you of the Reign of the King that you so adore, yet cannot see Face-to-face. Your King is not only the King of Creation, He is also the Prince of Anticipation. Jesus anxiously awaits the word from the Father to return for His blessed children. At each new day, He turns to the God of all to say, Is this the day? Jesus knows His own and waits in every possible emotion to come to take you to your mansion which He has so beautifully prepared for you. With toil, suffering, sweat, and His holy Blood, He built that mansion for you, and many mansions there are. They are a New Zion for a New Man. Man-Zions. Mansions. I have seen the Glory of this New Jerusalem. I have come today to assure you of My intercession to assist you to get there. In your heart and in your love, you have seen this New City from the firmament of faith. Your vision is from the perspective of your trust in Jesus. No despair or fear can stop you from attaining this joy. The King who reigns there has announced His desire for your attendance at His Eternal Feast. And, the King's wishes are always fulfilled. But, these days are the precedent to that Glory. Now is the time that will take you there. Yours are the prayers that will usher-in His Kingdom. You are His evangelists. You are His baptizers. You are the last age to say "Yes" to a salvific plan for humanity that began at the Annunciation of Saint Gabriel. What Grace you must now know! You recently viewed a motion picture depicting the passage of mortal men through time. You are doing so at this very moment because you are praying simultaneously with all the Saints in Heaven who lived centuries before. Prayer is timeless as your Love is timeless. I assure you that there is no better place for you to be at this time. You are doing God's work in the vineyard where He needs you. You are wielding tremendous power over evil and influence over the indifferent. Please know that God is pleased with your progress. The King is smiling from His Throne and knows that you are a messenger of His Holy Will on Earth. This King protects you and gives you the gifts you seek. My children, I am grateful to God to be allowed to bring this news to you. I am humbled by the gift He made to Me of yourselves as My little children. Heaven does not take your sacrifices lightly. We share in your grief and celebrate in your joy. You are one with Heaven when you realize, reveal, accept, and live the Life of Christ. There is no better way to make God happy with you. As you adore Jesus, you concurrently venerate this Mother who gives Him to the world. So, do not desist in your hope and prayers. Do not be despondent about the travails of a passing world. All is said and done. It is finished. You are just now learning about its happy ending. To the Victor-God belongs the souls He saved. Many are among them, you have not time to count, but all you will soon know. My children, I have been about the world blessing and dispensing graces. As terrible as the world seems, it is only Satan's facade in attempt to destroy your hope in Jesus. He will not succeed because your faith lies in the Sacred Heart of the Son of God, the Crown Prince who is already King. My son, your faith is enough to bring all that you seek. Your Love can conquer any ill. Please never dismay at the world. You know already the Truth which Jesus has given you to know. God has allowed the world to see an image of your Love for Him. It is especially important for you to protect that image. Before, no one had any means to determine its limitless magnitude. Now, however, if you do not emit that perfection, they will know it. I will help you to be the perfect Love that you wish to be. I am always with you and join My prayers with yours. I will speak to you again very soon. I love you."

Friday, June 6, 1997
Feast of the Sacred Heart of Jesus
6:57 p.m.

"Good evening, My precious little children! I come to you in Love, as I am the Mother of the Eucharist. I come on this Feast of the Sacred Heart of Jesus to pray with you for the intentions of the suffering Heart of Jesus and for the advancement of the Will of God. My children, I have told you before about the Sacred Heart of Jesus. His Heart is filled with Love, and although encircled by the thorns of human sin, it is beautiful to behold. There are many hearts created by God, and many are holy. However, there is only one Most Sacred Heart. There is only one capable of dispensing the Divine Mercy so needed by the world. And, My children, it is My Immaculate Heart that begs you to desire Jesus' Mercy. While Jesus is the lesson, I am the teacher. Once you have kissed Jesus' Most Sacred Heart, you have committed yourself to His Mercy; you have accepted the Love that God desires you to know in Him. My children, God wishes your hearts to be holy like the Heart of His Son. Then, you will be acceptable in His sight. Then, He will know you, and you will know Him. It is the intention of God that you live in the bounty of Jesus' Love because you will never again be lost. The father saw his prodigal son with his heart. Saint John saw Jesus on the shore with his heart. I have been sent to ask you to likewise know Jesus by opening your hearts to Him. God will deliver you to His side when you do. My Special son, a loving brother-Saint of yours has asked to attend My visit with you today:"

Our Lady gave me a special gift today by bringing a great American saint and martyr with Her who spoke profound words of light, just as he did in mortal life. He told me the Holy Rosary is our source of success, and declared that I continue obeying our Holy Mother.

"Please allow this day to renew your vigor for the holy veneration of the Sacred Heart of Jesus. Please remember the refuge all will find there and the Mercy that flows from its depths. Jesus' Heart is the fountain of God's Mercy and Love, intended for all sinners to take refuge there. Thank you for the pretty remembrance of Me in your invitations to your prayer group. This is the month of the Sacred Heart. Find your strength and peace there."

Wednesday, June 11, 1997

Time does not serve man, nor should he be deceived by it. Its sole purpose is to lead humankind to the Truth; that he must not only observe, but in which he must participate for the glory of God and the transformation of human mortality into beatific Eternity.

Friday, June 13, 1997
7:00 p.m.

"Good evening, My holy little children. You are the salt of the Earth and sweetness to My Heart. God is served by your lives, and My presence here today is proof. My loving children, your faith has made you the happy children that I ask you to be. You are fluently imitating My loving gestures. I love to see you smile. These days are the continuance of your journey back to God. Heaven is a better place because, by your prayers, you are allowing more souls to enter. Every soul that you win for Jesus takes many more with them to Heaven's gate. You cannot outdo the kindness of God. He loves you, He is proud of you and blesses your work. All of the beautiful images that I have given you over the passing years are living examples of God's Love. Through His Will, I have come in your midst seeking your assistance. My work cannot be accomplished solely by Me. I need your help, and I am grateful for every prayer, act and thought that you offer to God. My children, God wishes for My happiness. My happiness is contingent upon the conversion of My children. Hence, God will convert My children to ensure My happiness. And when this is complete, I will complement His work and reward your service by incorporating you in the Triumph of My Immaculate Heart. It is Holy, Blessed, and yours. You have nothing to fear. You have Heaven to gain. What is the suffering and commitment that you give to God compared to the Kingdom that He will bestow upon you? What is one dark night compared to perpetual day? These are the times for which you have been waiting to actively participate in a sacrificial way to bring the conversion and Salvation of souls to the hands and feet of Jesus. You sought a role, and you are fulfilling it. Yours are the hearts that light the way for those blinded by the darkness of their sins. Your prayers warm the coldness of other lives. When you follow Me, others will wonder why, and I will show them why. You may tell them why. My children, of all the things I could say to you today, I wish to simply say that I love you. You cannot yet imagine the immensity of My Love. You should invoke the intercession of the Archangel Gabriel, and He will try to show you.

Thank you again for your holy prayers last evening. I was brought to happy tears by the words you offered by the power of the Holy Spirit. This is why Jesus asks you to pray the Rosary. It gives Him opportunity to praise Me through your hearts. Today is such a pretty day in your lives. You enjoy making progress, and I enjoy seeing your progress too. My Special son, I am not convinced that you realize how grateful Jesus is for your help to your brother. Your reward is great, and is already waiting for you. However, you assuredly have much more work to do. Many will be vindictive prior to their comprehension of the purpose of your work. Many will flee from you and call you arrogant. Be strong and humble in Love! I could have done nothing for you without your consent. You said 'yes.' The most important thing I seek from you is your happiness. I wish for you to boldly plead guilty to being happy! Love is a perpetual state of being in unison with the Will of God. This encompasses all things. Thank you for praying to convert the world, comfort the lonely, and heal the afflicted. The daily Mass is your greatest prayer."

Thursday, June 19, 1997
7:33 p.m.

"My Grace I bring you today, My children, a holy gift that is yours. I come in peace and wish you Love. My entrance is into a world in which I once served God and to which I return to serve My children. I am your Mother, your voice in the Heavenly Court. I represent you before the Holy Jurist, Jesus My Son. Your justice is indeed an identical image of His Mercy. Given venue, righteousness will eternally prevail. And so, My children, it has come to this. God loves you so profoundly that He gave His only begotten Son to save you. And too, His Love manifests through that Sacrifice to include My miraculous intercession as a gift for your acceptance of the Holy Cross. Hence, I come not only to seek your prayers and obedience, but to also thank you on God's behalf for surrendering your will and your lives to Him. The world is steaming and stirring about you, but you are not impressed. Evil clips at your heels and tries to sadden you, but you are not at all moved. Materials and worldliness cry-out for you to embrace them, but you are not seduced. These things are true because you belong to Me. I can see you from the vantage-point of God. I bring you the opportunity to enjoin that venue. Your vision is derived from Love and is nurtured by holiness. Therefore, after these past special years, you have at last learned that you can achieve success only through prayer. Your prayers are the lifeblood of your holiness. In holiness, you are of the Love of God; you reside in God and belong to Him. You are not a culture of the Earth, but of wholesome life given by the heavens. So, where is the world that you should search for it? Indeed, it is not at all. It is only passing, transient, temporary, failing, mortal, finite, and unholy. You have transcended the boundaries and bonds placed upon you by Adam. Jesus set you free! The human will was capable of casting humankind from the beauty of Paradise, but had not the power to regain it. Jesus restored human perfection and sinlessness. He also simultaneously reaffirmed the power of the human will. You can now choose Jesus as your Savior, an act of your will, and you will be saved because God has reciprocated in Love. Adam chose to sin, but God now asks you to choose the Blood of His Son. As you ponder the world in your prayers, you will be reminded of many saddened places and broken lives. You will meditate upon places whose inhabitants do not know God, and others where He is outrightly rejected. These dark dungeons are those for which you should pray. God sees the same world for which you pray; and if you ask, He will heal their lands. God the Father is depicted as a left eye in many church windows, and Jesus is the right. He sits at the right hand of God and will soon come again to reclaim His Kingdom. He is doing this for you and for all those He loves. He also knows that the anticipation of His Return is met by the faithful with concurrent anxiety and fear. Every soul that Jesus knows will go with Him to Paradise is asking, *'Am I doing the Will of my Father in Heaven? Is my life worthy in the magnificent eyes of God? Have I manifested the Beatitudes in the spirit through which Jesus gave them to the world? Am I listening to the Wisdom echoing through the generations from the Mount of Olives? Have I accepted the Sacrifice still alive through those same generations from the mountaintop of Calvary?'* Those souls who ponder these holy attributes and affirm their allegiance and dedication to Jesus have already conquered time. There is no grave or destructive ash that can kill their spirit. When a dove flutters from a branch to a new perch atop an evergreen tree, his beauty flies there with him. That evergreen is eternally alive, paradisial, and unaffected by adverse elements. Such is the eternity of your souls and the beauty they carry, perpetually alive for the Hosts of the Heavens to venerate and love. I ask all My children, 'Why not fly? Why not be free?' There is not a weight in the next world that can burden a soul, not a thought, a feeling, or emotion. I ask My children to lift your hearts high. Fly to the highest branch of the everlasting Tree of Life. All the Saints and Angels await your arrival. The view of Creation is awesome from there. You are above the groveling creatures whose fate is to crawl on their bellies over the rocks below. Fly high and sing a new song! My Special son, knowing how beautiful your vision is, consider its magnitude at the highest place in Heaven. I promise that you will make it because I will help you. Thank you for remembering to pray as I have asked. I will make sure that the dogs do not harm you. They are deathly afraid of your brother when he looks into their eyes. They know that they would be easily defeated by him if they tried to attack. He can stop them in their tracks. He does not condone evil of any kind."

Saturday, June 28, 1997
7:14 p.m.

"My dear, dear special little children. It is, indeed, an amazing Grace which sustains you! The holiness and Light which you have so willingly embraced are your guides to Paradise. They are the beacons which Jesus has brought you to lead you Home. And yes, you are sustained in the life of perpetual prayer. You are perfected by all of these. The breath which sustains your life is faith, and your love is your life itself. My children, God is maneuvering the people He created into the positions which best please Him. You are being aligned at the right hand of Jesus to fight for Him and with Him. You have courage because you need faith, but you have valor because you invoke faith. You greet the day with the perspective of anticipation and revelation. You do not fear because God is in you. I have seen you live these realities for the decades of your lives. Today, your greeting of the world is again through a simple heart. You are sitting in the carriage waiting for it to begin its final journey Home. Imagine the eight beautiful steeds standing with dignity, strong and still at the front of your carriage. They are tall and handsome, and they occasionally turn their heads to the side just to say, *Whenever you are ready*. These mighty steeds represent the magnificent pillars upon which God has placed His hope to take you back Home. One steed represents *the pillar of Saints*, another *the Angels*, another *the Great Sacrament*, a fourth *the prayers of the faithful*, a fifth *the fruits of the Holy Spirit*, a sixth *the collective human spirit*, a seventh *the great steed called Hope*, and the eighth is *one single Hail Mary*, the power of all other pillars combined. Yes, My son, all of these pillars are the strength built by the Sacrifice of Jesus on the Cross. The horsepower that will deliver humanity to God is derived from the Blood of one Lamb. One Lamb created eight steeds. And, so stands the magnificent assembly waiting for the God of all who is sitting at the seat at the front of the carriage called Redemption to shake the reigns in His hands and nicker, *Let us go now homeward with our cherished cargo of souls. Let us go proudly to the homeland which I prepared for them.* And, then, the eight Glory horses will raise their heads proudly and walk in cadence to the beat of the mighty Sacred Heart. Their manes have been beautifully braided by the holy women of old. Their coats have been brushed by the calloused hands of those faithful to Saint Joseph. What beautiful horses are prepared to move at the initiation of God's call. When this happens, you will know. You will be both in the carriage and also watching the carriage. I have made some pretty ribbons and bows to place on this carriage of Redemption. I have given it My motherly touch. Yes, God has aligned His people, His Hosts of Heaven, His Holy Sacraments, and all the power of righteousness to bring you Home. When you hear the clapping of the hooves on the golden pavements, know deep within your heart that God's

Kingdom is come. Yes, there is a distinct majesty about horses. They are strong and confident, peaceful and obedient. It is with this same majesty that God touches your lives to allow you to know the valor of a mighty steed. My Special son, I try without end to describe the jubilation you will know when you come to Heaven. And in understanding My metaphoric parables, you are coming already to know the beauty from within. All of this has come from the Sacrifice of one Man, My Jesus. You will see Him Face-to-face and He will know you. And best of all, you will know Him. Indeed, you are already one Love. I share this truth with you with the confidence that you will continue your life for Him. You will endure many horrible battles for Jesus before He calls you Home. You will always be victorious because of your faith and your love for God and for Me. I give you My promise of Love and commitment to your Salvation that I gave to God through the Angel Gabriel. I will speak to you very soon. I love you. Goodnight."

Friday, July 4, 1997
7:27 p.m.

"Good evening, My little children. You are My pretty hearts that flicker and glow perpetually in a world of darkness. Your love is not derived from flash powder, nor is its resonance but a bang ringing through the air. No, My children, your service is of a higher making. Your light never fades, and the sound of your love for God is ever upon your lips. Your Mother is the Patron Saint of your country. Hence, this is the Land of Motherhood. For that reason, I again plead for your prayers to end abortion. I indeed wish your country a happy anniversary of its founding. And, I ask you to recall the reason for this foundation, that you may honor God freely. My Special son, these are the years during which I have addressed you upon this occasion—1991, 1992, 1993, 1994, 1995, 1996 and 1997. These cumulative years represent your true freedom, not the country in which your heart resides or its government. How many years is it? With the Grace of God and your prayers, we will continue. We will continue to redress the grievances of broken hearts, to fight evil and indifference with prayer and holiness. We will strive to usher the Kingdom of God into a world which is at its peak of rejection of that Advent. We shall not desist. We will continue to hope in the fruits of our prayers. No other nation in the world is so developed as the United States of America; and yet, no other which knows God so well is rejecting Him so willfully. I assure you that I am advocating and interceding on your behalf. Today is a time of reflection for your country. But, not enough of its citizens are in unison with the God whose Grace you beseech. When Jesus returns to the world, it will not be a far-off event announced by wise men. It will be the fatal realization of all mortal men and women. There will be no time for theology or reflection. As Jesus reclaims His Kingdom, only the voice of 'yes' by the human soul will be important. This 'yes' must be as swift as the 'Fiat' which first began the downfall of evil at the Annunciation. Those who proclaim and live in accordance with the Apostles Creed have already pledged this 'Fiat.' I am your Mother and teacher, and Mother of your Teacher. You will never go astray by heeding My call. You will always know your lessons by praying to understand. I have spoken with you for many years. But, from where I come, I have only begun and am already finished. Your patience and effort make these simultaneously possible in the passing world of time. I love you dearly. I have always loved you dearly. It is not possible for you to comprehend at this time where you are in My plan. But, you are on course and in union with the march of Creation toward the victory of My Immaculate Heart. You know Me, however. In your love, you know Me best. There are many changes and constant motion in the world. Your bodies are growing older in an exile subjected to pass. But, your heart will never grow old. Your heart does not age. Indeed, it perpetually feeds your wisdom to anticipate God and fully accept His Will. Through glory and pain, alike, you know Him. I assure you that God will end this seeming repetitive pulse on Glory, in Glory. I am your Sign of the Ages. I am the reason why Creation has come to this. I am the reason that victory was born into the world. From within My Womb and out of My Bosom blossomed the Flower whose beauty won the Heart of God. His Name is Jesus. The Christ of God is the Son which He so loves, and yet still sacrificed for those who would not love. By the sin of lost humanity, God was brought into humanity to prove His own power. God knew from the beginning that sin would never prevail. And, to whom does Glory belong? That same Son sacrificed so that Glory could be won again, perpetually forever. At the sin of Adam, God cried. He set a mirror before Adam so that Adam could see himself, the one he truly worshiped when he sinned. God said 'if it is your will which you honor, it is but your face you will see.' And then, God did what He does best. He forgave. He came to Earth to redeem. He became the image in the mirror that Adam would see when trying to find himself. At the Love of God, Adam cried. But, these were no tears of sorrow. They were tears of joy and thanksgiving. God mended humanity by healing His own broken Heart. He healed His own broken Heart through the courage of one Sacred Heart. God said 'I love you' thrice and breathed Life into a Trinity of means through which He would prove it. And, you live amidst that Most Blessed Trinity to this day. Therefore, you need not be 'Adam sinful,' but 'Adam redeemed.' You need not heed the call of evil who fell the first children, but rather obey the desires of God who washes you clean in Mercy. God is your Teacher who spells Mercy thus—Crucifixion. As you accept the Sacrifice of Jesus, Mercy is concurrently yours. You are given the fruit by taking the seed inside. My little children, this is the story of true independence. This is the reason for the lighted sky and lifted faces. This day will pass, and through God's will, another will follow. But, Jesus is the true tomorrow of your hearts. When you receive the Holy Eucharist, you are assuring your soul of its own early light of dawn. There will be no prevailing darkness. There will be no sorrow or plight come the new Morning. As a very young child, the first thing you learn to recognize is the face of your mother before you. And, you come to know the face of your father. These are the faces you will know when God sets your soul free from mortality to come to Eternity. You will know My Face and the Face of God, just as Adam saw Jesus' Crucifixion in the mirror before him. You will be miraculously and beatifically present at the place of your judgment. You will then know that there is no mirror. You will actually be at the door of your new Home, greeted by all those with whom you will reside.

I would like to be with you and listen to the pretty girl sing your country's anthem again. For two reasons, I like it, and I wish for you to listen to the sound of the people as she is finished. This is the same sound you would hear from behind the veil of the Angels and Saints upon your completion of the Rosary. Indeed, the sound is identical. As you listen to the mass of people, it will sound just like the one in Heaven that will raise upon your completion of your prayers tonight. Thank you for your prayers and for giving your time and life to God."

Saturday, July 12, 1997
8:06 p.m.

"I thank you, My children, for allowing us to share this moment in time together. Thank you for your prayers and your songs of praise. Best of all, thank you for living love, for giving 'Christ' to humankind in reflection of My answer to the Archangel Gabriel. I will surely not be successful without your continuing obedience because the world is wholesomely taken to holiness by your lives. I am grateful and will dispense the graces you seek in response to your requests. My children, one lonely afternoon on the Mountain of Calvary, a perfect Man died to make all of your holy discussions possible. What might be only theory is now fact. God has indeed redeemed His people. Jesus is your Savior whose voice calls through the dark night to come into His Light. I beg of all not to let this beckoning go unheeded. Time is at its destined end. God has come to preserve His children during the barren, dark days of the Earth. The Angels lift your spirits and give you hope. We seek a people united under the Cross, a union of Christian disciples made one through prayer, forgiveness, and patient understanding. My special children are bound for Heaven. You will all be much happier there. But, it is not only for you that I appear; I come seeking the lost whom you can help Me find.

Together, we can make a difference to many who are otherwise indifferent, and so that these will not be their last days, but the beginning of their perpetual time in Beatific Light. We have precious few sunrises left to reach the lost. No one is forsaken by God. His Love prevails in the world, accessible to all who will allow Him room. Jesus is knocking, and I am calling you. The end that we seek for humanity is no end at all, but a peaceful beginning. Mortality is fatal in itself, but Eternal Life is everlasting. I bring you Life through Jesus. The words you just heard describe My effort to take you forward in time in your limited space. I do not remove you from time, rather I advocate your holiness which transcends time. Henceforth, time is no longer a factor. The matter of time is unaltered, while your advancement toward God is made supernal. And instead of indifference, there is progress toward Jesus. Instead of stagnation, there is hope. Instead of sin, there is repentance. All of this is part of the culmination of the Holy Heavens descending to Earth in preparation for Jesus' Return. I have told you that you may anticipate that day to come soon, in terms of your own understanding of 'soon.' Therefore, what a great day this is! You will be coming home to Me! What great hope lives in your hearts! What anticipation you live in your faith and knowledge of this Truth! Yes, the Saints do await your arrival, and the Angels sing in Choirs of jubilation. The dead are enlivened by the Resurrection of Jesus. The crippled are healed by His Sacrifice. The lonely are made glad-of-heart through their communion with His Spirit. This is a happiness to which there is no end. This is a smile that has forsaken its frown. And, though the sun plunges slowly past the western horizon, it is telling you that another day of work is done by God's children. It means that your hope for tomorrow is well placed. Your heart shall never lie, it has not the capacity to lie. This is why I appeal to your heart. I bring Truth to live in your hearts, a home from which love can grow and be known in the world that is so lost. Thank you for opening your hearts to make this grace possible."

Friday, July 18, 1997
7:26 p.m.

"My dear little children, the Light of God shines brightly through My Love for you! I am present here to bring you joy and happiness. Most of all, I come to thank you for making this week an especially holy witness for the Truth of God through your words and actions. You will one day hear the cheers of throngs and clapping of hands when your brother rose to his feet to protest the desecration of God's Word. And then, a mighty orchestra struck a tune of victory at the words, '*And you need to stand-up for the Truth!*' * I have taught you these things. I have given you the Truth and the authority to proclaim it. Yes, you are of good courage! The feelings that you had when your brother stood to speak are the same feelings you will have upon the Triumph of My Holy and Immaculate Heart. Do not feel that you have breached the holiness of the Mass. Indeed, it was already breached.

My Special son, countless citizens of this city know your brother by name. And many now know about your relationship to him as co-witness for God, and especially for Me. This is the condition I intended. You must always remember that your brother is not the reason for My success here. It is you. If you had not said 'yes' and took him in, I would not have had such success. The credit is your faith. It is your love. Please remember that your support and love for your brother have gained for you the highest Heaven. Your other holy attributes, your alms, prayers, sacrifices, and generosity are gaining the highest Heaven for those who do not yet know God. My son, it is difficult for Me to explain how important it is for you to understand how your life is bringing God's Kingdom to the world. You are rectifying terrible wrongs and mitigating many ills. It is you who are graceful. I will speak to you again very soon. I love you dearly."

* *This incident was a reference to a Holy Mass we attended early in the week. A Catholic nun offered the readings during the Mass and began to ad lib the scriptural texts without authority to suit her radical feminist ideology. When the presiding priest made no movement to stop or admonish her actions, my brother stood and proclaimed that she was not reading it correctly. At this, the priest came to the lectern and began a short speech of dithering compromise as if he was scared of this radical nun. I then stood and thundered at him, telling him that he needed to stand up for the Truth. After the service, the nun approached us and apologized for "offending our sensibilities." We told her that it was not our sensibilities that had been offended, but God Himself, and that she needed to go to confession for the outrage that she had just perpetrated. Later, Our Lady gave us a sign of the providence of our actions, confirming that we were instruments of the Holy Spirit in that moment. The nun was affiliated with the Ursuline Order founded by Saint Angela Merici. My brother's birthday is January 27th, the Feast day of Saint Angela Merici. This great Saint was rebuking one of her own through my brother's actions by the power of the Holy Spirit. Our Holy Mother said that there arose a perfect set of circumstances between the enormous violation of the Holy Mass and the righteous ardor of the Church-Triumphant which required the severe admonishment; my brother could not have remained in his seat even if he had wanted to. Saint Angela Merici's command to respond to this evil was too great. This is an example of the great intercession of the Communion of Saints which the Catholic Church speaks about so affectionately.*

Friday, July 25, 1997
7:58 p.m.

"My children, your hearts are so blissfully sublime and sweet. Your Mother Advocate has come once again to this place to bless your souls and lives. Mine is the joy to call you My own. You are the incarnate righteousness of God. You are the teachers of holiness, the good ambassadors of divinity. This higher calling makes your lives important and meaningful. Your present nurtures your future, which is simply magnificent. Today, I have returned to be with you so you will know that I love you compassionately. Your exile is difficult, but your love is compliant. Your struggles are many, but your faith is strong. And thus, you are blessed from the Throne of God who reaches your hearts, guided to your souls by the Light that Jesus has implanted there. My Special son, soon is the Day of Redemption. There will one day be no darkness because Jesus' Eternal Crucifixion of twenty centuries ago has made perpetual day a reality to the souls who accept it. This acceptance is the Light which God sees in you, like fireflies in the night signaling your station. 'Here I am, here I am' you call, as you summon I AM to come for you. These are very holy days during a most special time. Your holiness flourishes because I nourish it. You are in a cocoon, about to be released into Eternity like a pretty butterfly. How could you ever be sad? Where would there be any cause for anxiety? There is none. You echo the beauty of Nature, God's speechless expressions of Love for you. The halls of your soul are holy, and are decked in purity and simplicity, welcoming and awaiting the arrival of the King, come to save you. His feet shall walk upon the beauty of your holiness, the strength for the day already given you by His Passion. 'Is humanity fit for Redemption?' God asks. '*Yes*' Jesus answers, '*Yes! I have washed them for You, My Father. I have called them, and they have come. I have given them Your Word, and they believe. I have told them Your Promise, and they trust. I have offered them Your Kingdom, and they have accepted.*' These are Jesus' words to God the Father. And His conclusion is this, '*Their Mother will bring them home, for She has redressed them in the finest garments which You gave Her to dress them at their Baptism.*'

My Special son, how I love you. How happy you will be to see the world shout in acclamation that the Queen of Heaven is not just relevant, but reverent, holy, beautiful, and transcending. All access to Salvation is granted through My sinless Love. No other day or time, no other place in Creation, and no other mediatrix will there be before My Immaculate Intercession to God on behalf of the children bequeathed to Me on Mount Calvary. This is the day, the time, and the place for all humankind to accept their Heavenly Mother. I know the God you seek. I understand His Heart and live His intentions. And He reciprocally blesses Mine. You are My holy intentions!

You who so freely and innocently run about the world in the shallows of your infant faith! It is you that I love, and for you that I pray. This Mother will never desist! I have become Motherhood at its best, perfecting the maternal desires that destine you to be reunited with the Father who calls. There is nothing I do not know of you; there is no weakness which I cannot purge from your souls. Divinity is your best suit, and I am your seamstress. You will be ready to greet the Lord at the appointed time because it is I who will have prepared you. I was given the joy to raise Jesus as the Savior of humankind. It is equally My joy to raise redeemed humankind as the Mother of all. I will show you the Cross, and Jesus will show you the Crown. Be My little children. Know Me and love Me. Go where I ask, and pray as you must. When you give your will to God, the rest of your being is Mine to shape. My little son, I exact My assigned duties well. All the Hosts of Heaven await your arrival. You are being brought to harbor by the most noble Captain. You are being led by the wisest Shepherd. You are called by a Truth that your soul recognizes, despite the distractions of the world. You live many days in the peace of this Truth, with others fumbling over their own curiosity. Trust and pray, and your peace will be permanent, your joy complete. These are the last days that wish to know you and greet you! Meet the daily dawn with strength and hope. Live the lessons of the Holy Scriptures and the messages I bring in love. No world and no hatred can drive you from the happiness you will live when you do these things. As the world dies, you watch in anticipation. As your days pass, you awake in anxiety. These are emotions of the faith you live. Know also in this faith that anticipation is simply perpetual hope, and anxiety is truly a lack of patience. I teach you how to utilize the faith which God has given you. You are the one who lives these lessons. I am very happy to know that you welcome My messages and answer My call. There are many special days yet to arrive, but too will come many difficult ones. I will be with you during each one. Thank you for the pretty prayer group last evening. I love you."

Friday, August 1, 1997
7:17 p.m.

"My dear little children of Light and Love, too many are the days in which My other children fail to fight evil with the courage you portray. You fight daily against a vile evil that wishes your doom and defeat. You need God to sustain this battle. You need to pray and call upon your Mother for help. I will help you when you pray. Today is a special day because you persist in knowing righteousness and persevere in your convictions. While there is pain and fear in your life, you will not be given more than you can endure. Always remember that you are given to Me. Today, I have come to pray with you again. While you make many sacrifices, your reward will be great. Live with this strength, and hope in the expectation that you have already won. I ask you to remember the perspective I have taught, and your days will be holy. You are making progress toward the things that make you happy. This progress is extremely opposed by the evil that wishes to bring you much unhappiness. However, you do not belong to evil. You belong to God in whom there is only happiness! By remembering this fact, you will know that unhappiness is not natural for your soul. Your soul given to Jesus knows only eternal bliss. I tell you these things because they are true. My sons, do not worry. I have you both under My careful caress. My focus is on the beautiful Diary that you have brought into the world, whose table of contents alone can awaken thousands of sleeping hearts. Your Diary is a gift to the world that you are delivering for Me. It is the Love of God for you. It is one of the books that has been brought to supplement the Holy Scriptures, one referred to in the Scriptures as those so numerous that the world could not contain them. I have a happy request to make today. Please try to be more at peace by remembering how I have taught you to love. With that love, there is nothing to compare. You truly do not understand My Love for you, but you are learning more each day. I have not brought a lesson for you today. I have come to simply offer My prayers for you and promise that I am fulfilling My motherly commitment to you as My children. In this holy house, we have come to know many sacred moments, many hours of true love. We will proceed as God wills and allows. Please pray atop your prayers so we can continue. I will pray with you. I offer My Love and promise that you are living a life of grace. I will take your petitions to Jesus as you ask. I love you."

Friday, August 8, 1997
7:11 p.m.

"My dear beautiful children, so beautiful and so loved, I come to you with a joyful Heart. I arrive at this blessed place bearing the gifts of Grace and the sinless Fruit of My Womb Jesus to offer for your acceptance and faith. This is indeed a new time of revelation, a time of moments sequencing the End Times, the culmination of the purpose of God to save His Creation and make new the Earth and enrich the heavens. And, you are also the fruit of My Immaculate Heart, growing holy there for the sweetness God desires of His newly transformed humanity. My sons, you have been told that during the End Times, there will be much heresy, much sinful desecration of holy things and the aberration of His Word. You must consider what you see as indicative of the End Times. Yes, what you see and hear are evil, but from an evil whose perpetrator has already been defeated. My Special son, at Holy Mass the lector refused again to recognize God the Father by the pronoun 'His.' This is a direct diabolical plot to destroy the identity of God by the lector. This woman is in need of much prayer. All souls who undertake this decision to assume the identity of God are becoming self-judges of God and false prophets. They deem themselves to be co-creators and co-omnipotent souls. As I say, this is just one of the heresies you will witness during the End Times. Please simply watch and pray, and do the things I direct. I have come today, however, to speak to you about happiness. I speak about your joyful lives, how your prayers are blessed, how holiness has become your being, and love your purpose. This is why you are much despised by the world, and why your brother is so hated and rejected many times over. In the closed doors of the Protestant school, the leaders there agreed that they could not allow your brother the opportunity to bring Me to their students. Therefore, he has been again rejected. While this seems sad, God will utilize this for His own Glory and for the veneration of Me. All you need to do is watch. I am pleased by your progress. With My blessing, I also give My promise that I will be with you through Eternity which is indeed without end."

Friday, August 15, 1997
7:21 p.m.

"Blessed are My faithful children who honor the Assumption of their Mother into Heaven by attending Holy Mass on this day. God is well pleased with the love that you share with Him for Me. I am your Mother and also His, and I have come to greet you in peace, to grant you the grace you need to succeed in holiness. I come in gratitude for your prayers. My children, I have told you that time is short. Daily, you witness with curiosity while these last ages unfold. You watch with question the things that God allows and others that He brings. My children, the greatest grace that God has given you during these last times is Me, your Virgin Mother. I am She who is The Woman of the Church. There need not be any proclamation of gender equality by any other soul. There is no need for language of inclusion to honor the sinful gender mothered by Eve. I am the Woman Clothed with the Sun. No other woman has the power which I give you. And on this special day eight short years ago, I made this very clear to you, My Special one. It is the power you witnessed that day that I give you to bring God to others through you. I have taught you who Love is and how you may become that Love. You have listened and learned well. You are a reflection of My Grace in the world. You are a messenger of God. Together with your brother, you are the example of an accidental saint. You cannot yet be so alone. It is your union of prayer and peace that makes this possible. So please be one through Jesus with Me, especially for Me. Today I indeed carry your petitions to God in unison with the celebration of My Assumption. I know that you trust God to answer them in accordance with His Divine Will. You already realize that it is your participation and obedience that allows you to further the cause of Salvation for many souls. You are chosen children, called to serve. You are asked to bear special crosses and burdens and carry the standard upon which is posted Jesus' image for the lost to see. For many years, you have consented to this holy and sacrificial participation. You know no other God because there is no other. You accept Jesus as your Savior because God made it so. It is not your doing or being that makes you holy, but the Grace of God, personified by Me. He loves you so. He knows that you love Him and believe in Him, having not yet seen Him. What beautiful faith! What priceless hope! It is altogether proper that you should anticipate such a rich reward in Heaven. You are commissioned by God to be His messengers of love. You are laden with the responsibility to convert many, with the authority to admonish others. Be My Grace as you do! Consider your most beautiful image of My being, and imitate that charity. Share that purity. Engage others in that holiness. Today, I call upon you to remember especially the poor souls in Purgatory whom God will grant entrance and admission into Heaven as you honor My Assumption. Ask Him to allow them to go to Heaven with Me. When you say yes, God also says yes. This is why you are so Special, and because you have embraced the Chosen one beside you. As you have sufficiently seen, God's yoke is not heavy, and His burden is light. No matter how weak, you will always be strong. I am perpetually your help in your life for Jesus. My Special son, please read to Me the August 14, 1997 writing. These words are very important and applicable. You can notice the tenor of the times that the words describe, the End Times which have now come. Can you feel the descent of Heaven now come into your home? Can you simultaneously feel your soul's ascension into that beauty? Your location is presently not an issue. Grace is for you to know the location of your heart and the destiny of your soul. I will speak to you soon about My Queenship."

Friday, August 22, 1997
7:02 p.m.

"My dear children, I am your Virgin Mother, the Queen of Heaven and Earth. I greet you with prayers and affection. Thank you for collecting yourselves at My feet. Thank you for acknowledging Me as the Crown to whom you deliver your petitions and desires of your hearts. My children, it is a grace to be the Queen of Creation. I see My children, all humankind, from a purview like no other. It is I who have the Immaculate Heart from which pours the sacred graces that save your souls. Jesus, your Savior, is a Fruit of My bountiful Heart. Your souls given to Jesus for redemption are the fruits of My magnificent Heart that please God without end. You are very fortunate in faith. Your faith gives your life kinetics and energy. Your faith is a righteous fruit of the Love I have taught. You have learned it well. You have come to know the desires of God for His children. And, you have personally recognized the Divine Love which I hold for your souls. This is the origin and meaning of My Queenship. While God's Love for you is infinite, it is I who teach you to anticipate Him in infinite ways. Through Me, you have come to more openly accept the Holy Spirit. Now, you know peace in a way that the world cannot give. You have come to grasp the meaning of eternity and sacrifice. You now see the importance of prayer and fasting. It is through your prayer of the Rosary that I have been able to stay with you for so long. Thank you for knowing through your heart that the Truth of the world is revealed by prayer. God brings Truth into the world as He is beckoned from faithful hearts who call Him. Yes, it is I who seek your holiness. My reign as Queen is over a family of loving children. This I desire and God desires. I cannot emphasize enough that along with My Queenly Grace comes My Motherly Love. No other heart knows you with such Grace. I give you Jesus, whose Sacred Heart accepts you with a compassion possessed by no other. Hence, I am the Mother of Compassion, and you are My laborers for God. While Jesus is the Savior of humanity, you are cultivators and hand-servants for Him. While He preceded your lives, you precede His Second Coming. You are My children who tell the world about their Salvation. You are witnesses and messengers, and it is My role to teach and guide you. I teach you about these last times. You do many things that show your understanding of this Truth. I have taught you how to care for the collective human soul, for those far from God, for those who know how to love but still refuse, and for the lost who have not yet been told. You do many magnificent things that the world does not understand. The prayerful reading of the writings of Vachel Lindsay at his grave site is an example. Your holy heart knows that it is this kind of anticipation of the destiny of other souls that God so enjoys. Therefore, to be Queen is to teach all My children to know God and the coming Kingdom as you now understand it. To be Queen is to smile when you do holy things well, to represent you with Grace before God. I see your lives as you live them for Him through Me. I assure you that I will take you to Him. It is I who know God best because I am His Mother. Yes, even Jesus observes Me as His Queen. Jesus honors Me with His prayers, and you must know why. It is I who taught Jesus how to pray. He recited the Our Father for the first time to the world from His Sacred Heart that I nourished. Jesus teaches you how to be holy and how to pray by imitating His Mother. And, He crowned Me Queen and gave you to Me and I to you, so that in My motherly Love, I can teach you how to be holy and how to pray. I wish to teach you to be like Jesus. I wish to hold you in My care and nurture you with divinity. I wish to utilize all the power given Me by God for your benefit. This is the meaning of 'Queen.' I am the selfless Heart who walked the Earth, and I am also The

Immaculate Conception who has desired your Salvation from the beginning. From the venue which I hold, I must say that the success of your Salvation depends upon our prayers so that all souls will accept Jesus' Crucifixion and Resurrection. This is why I have come. My Special son, do you understand the great responsibility I bear as Queen of Creation? This is why I have called upon many to be My messengers, and why I have appeared in the world in so many places over numerous times. I am trying to effect the power, authority, and Grace of My Queenship for all of God's children. My Special son, I hope you have enjoyed these words that I give to you in love. Please accept My thankfulness for your servitude to Me and Jesus, to God the Father, and the Holy Spirit. I will be with you wherever you go and also at your final destination. Please live prayerfully and carefully."

Saturday, August 30, 1997
6:51 p.m.

"My dear children, welcome to the comfort of the Immaculate Heart of your loving Mother. Once more, I have come to bring My Grace into this home and strength and meaning to your petitions. The Holy Spirit is simultaneously the power and intention of your prayers. My little children, you pray tonight from a new position in God's Kingdom. Through the past six years, you have been praying in the rudimentary context of your infant faith. Through My lessons, I am bringing you to maturity in holiness, a state of your own recognition of your role and station in the Kingdom of God. Your place is that of participant in the Plan of Salvation. You have become magnificent and blessed. You have dared to walk where only few earthly men would tread. I have led you on a journey that is now moving into its crucial phase of implementation. You have come to your feet in holiness. Your hearts have awakened and your lives have taken-on new meaning. All of this has been done by My Grace and your obedience. Yes, it is important that through your transformation into maturity in holiness, you must indeed recall perpetually the little shoes that you will never become old enough to outgrow. You must always be little! You will always need Me to guide and hold you. You will not succeed if you abandon Me, and neither will I. The ultimate Triumph of My Immaculate Heart is contingent upon your faith and obedience. The Victory to come will arrive only after you have done what God asks each of you. This My children is what Jesus is waiting for. It is why He still lingers beyond the eastern horizon. He sends the sun to light your day every morning. When God gives the command, Jesus will know that the world is prepared. My children, please know that at this very moment, God the Father has leaned to Jesus to speak into His ear. He is sharing the final instructions with Jesus regarding the closing of the ages of man. God is ready to end mortality. And as each day passes, Jesus rises more to His feet, pushing from His hands as He hears His final commendations from His Father. As He rises and listens, He looks into the Creation He has conquered and into men's souls. God is telling Him to remember the Mercy of the Heart who won, the bountiful Sacred Heart into which Jesus will collect all the saved. And, He is telling Jesus that through the daily prayers of the faithful, many transgressions have been mitigated. As Jesus comes wielding the Sword of Justice to the Earth, He will raise it and suddenly remember what His Father told Him about His Divine Mercy. He will then lower His sword and reach with the other hand to lift many repentant sinners to their feet, then to His breast and to their Salvation. He will see a world alive in His Word, those who stayed beside the lost, the sick, the forsaken. Yes, Jesus will live this day soon, and the Father will rest easy upon His Throne with chin-in-palm and say *This, dear Creation, is My Son!* And then, all for which you pray tonight will be bestowed upon the lives you bless. Jesus will usher you to the ranks of the Angels and Saints who wished they could have filled your shoes during these last ages. You will be very happy to see the innocence of the Heavenly. You will know the charm that is yours to keep. The treasures of Heaven that you now store are waiting for the warmth of your grasp. These things are coming; they are an effect and fruit of the Return of the Son of Man. And remember the feast prepared for the prodigal son. No man has yet known, or eye seen, or ear heard the Glory about to be bestowed upon Creation by a God thankful for the acceptance of the Sacrifice of His Only Son. You need not be concerned about the worries of the day. Do not fear the dark of night. Take courage with those whose hearts seem to be sleeping because God is about to awaken them. I promise that these words pale by comparison to stir your heart and warm your spirit coming in the days ahead. Your hope is founded in good fortune and your faith upon solid rock. God cannot deceive you. Only you can do that. Today, I ask humanity to turn its collective gaze to the Heart of God and the Heart which represents God, who is Me. I give you Love for the journey ahead. My Special son, it is My honor to speak to you. It is Jesus and Myself together who make sanctification and redemption possible. Jesus will allow you to be subjected, but it is I who seek Him not to. God would be glorified by your suffering, but He is more pleased by My intercession to preclude it. Therefore, Jesus and I together divert the squalls of the world from seeping into your lives and causing damage to the pillars of your faith. The world is already changing. You are altering it now. When Jesus said 'It is finished,' the day of the Cross included the work that you are accomplishing. You are serving Jesus; the capacity of your life is overflowing with servitude and sacrifice. God is grateful. Your prayers have been very holy. I assure you that your lives are blessed."

Saturday, September 6, 1997
7:09 p.m.

"My beautiful children, since My message of last week, you are seeing quite clearly the manifest unfolding of the End Times. You are participating in the implementation of God's plans. I must say, you have lived this week with little courage and with great disdain for the call of suffering. You were assigned many tasks of sacrifice, but both of you have failed to accept them in the love which I have taught. You question why God brings you the opportunity to prove your love for Him. You have become distracted by the means with which you accept what has been given. You should focus instead upon the outcome, which is truly your beginning of living in complete unity with the Cross. I have spent nearly seven years teaching you to be like beautiful Mother Teresa of Calcutta who came to Heaven yesterday, but your response has been 'why me?' 'How dare other people treat me so!' My little children, not every message I bring is filled with accolades. However, I bring the Truth and very much Love. I wish for you both to rethink your responses of this week, and you will understand what I am saying. My Special son, you made the correct decisions, but the tenor of your reaction was not with a humble spirit. You see, when you sacrifice, serve and suffer as I have taught, your life is a continuous joyful gift to Jesus the Christ. Of course, you are called upon to labor hard at your workplace and to help your family. You are called to be a hand-servant to the disabled. You are pressed into service for the poor. All of these are happy opportunities to serve God. Let this be a lesson; let this week teach you something! You have yet seen little! It was not your vision at fault, it was your tone. Instead of saying gleefully *'Oh! look what I get to do for Jesus,'* your tone was *'what next?'* This is not a difficult concept to comprehend. I am trying to prepare you for times that will make this past week seem like a stroll in the park. And for your brother, even in his courage, he is often afraid. This is because he is such a little child. Like you, he knows to call upon My favor for help during difficult times. This is an evil world. In My Love, I will guide you through it safely. Therefore, I have come tonight to remind you of the special Love that Jesus holds for you. My Jesus is in complete union with your life. He knows your hearts, when you sit and when you stand. He sees your sacrifices clearly because this is your call to Him in answer to His need for your assistance in the conversion of humanity. While I have repeatedly told you that you do not comprehend the magnitude of God's Love, I have given you the perspective to see His magnificence in your own life. You can indeed see how God works through you to touch other people in the world. It is in this summons that you are asked to joyfully comply. God's Love for you is Jesus! It is Sacrifice and Blood, tears, and suffering. Your union with Heaven is defined by these noble attributes. It is through these same avenues that you return to God a parcel of the blessings He has given you. Were it not this way, Jesus would have told you. You are asked to respond gladly. This is not an easy task, and it is not a temporary commitment. You must say 'yes' to Jesus as He has always for you, every day and in every instant. You must realize that when you give yourself to Jesus, you give Him your vow, both now and forever, permanently to Him, come what may. God has not promised you the rosy path to Heaven, but He has assured that Jesus will be with you and in you to strengthen you and enlighten your way. You are both very fortunate sons. You are chosen for a very special role. Please live this role in the dignity of the Love of Jesus. You are called to be little Christs in a world filled with terrible persecutors. Pursue Heaven with joy! Offer the world your prayers and bequeath the wicked to the Divine Mercy of God. Receive the challenge of Christianity with grace. I promise that despite all its pitfalls, it is the life which leads you to Me. I brought the Church into being, and you are the Mystical Body of My Son on Earth. Be My children! Be like Jesus! Become worthy of His Spirit and His blessing. Last week, I gave you a premonition of today by telling you that you would be implementing what I have taught. The week has brought you much Light. Bask in this Light, and all your days will be beautiful. I wish for you to understand that My words come from within the framework of My great Love for you. If you were not My children, I would not be here teaching you. It is I who must thank you for the many times you have said 'yes' to Me during the past. I thank you for honoring your vows to God, to Jesus and to Me. It is only your obedience that makes our work possible. Remember to be kind and patient with each other always and forever. I will watch how prayerfully you live, and I will help you do so."

Saturday, September 13, 1997
7:16 p.m.

"My dear little children, the Love of God is with you! I bring His Love to you through My own divine being. I share your love for humankind and ask you to be filled beyond capacity with hope for its conversion and redemption. My children, together we can do many great things. Thousands of Saints throughout the centuries have invoked the Grace of My Immaculate Heart for the good of their souls and the advancement of their individual charities and good works. Millions have also united their prayers with Mine to seek the most magnificent of God's graces, that of the presence of Blessed Jesus in their lives. And to this day, holy people pray with Me to the God of all Grace. I am happy to continue My role as Intercessor, making the most of My many powerful and spiritual titles. It is this calling that brings Me again to this home today. I come as we look into a world filled with sadness and oppression. There is a certain hollowness on the Earth that only Love can fill. There is a darkness to your days that only the Light of Jesus can destroy. You must reflect His Light! You must be wholly benevolent and cheerful in sacrifice. You must challenge yourself to perpetuate unity among the peoples of the world. If you do not do so, then who will? I call openly to you today to continue your prayerful lives with which God is well pleased. Do not be deceived by changing times and fortunes. God is permanent and unchanging. Be the permanence of God that transcends the days! Keep your vision focused upon humanity redeemed while simultaneously living prayerfully for humanity yet sinful. Your eyes can see because I have opened them. Through hundreds of days and many magnificent messages, I have brought you closer to God. I have brought you peace. You must constantly call upon all I have taught and place your trust in My teaching. I have given you Jesus in whom you are everything. You must most of all be hope for one another. My Special son, I come to you today in thanksgiving for your obedience. You have trusted beyond all description. You have indeed given life to hope and patience. You have made the world a more holy place. Your faith and service will be richly rewarded. You are forever a fruit of My Heart and example of My Love. Do not despair when it would otherwise be easy to lose hope. Keep your heart aloft with Me in the heavens. I have given you many things from God. I am happy with you and your brother, and I ask you to continue to trust. Place your prayers in the hands of God. You will find My Heart also there. Can you describe the Feast of the Holy Cross for Me? And the Fruit of that Cross is the Bread of Life."

Friday, September 19, 1997
8:03 p.m.

"Peace be with you! Not as the world gives, but the peace that is brought by Jesus, the Son of God, your Savior and your All. My children, this is the peace which I brought into the world. This is the peace which you seek and Who also seeks you. I promise you that if you pray the Rosary in earnest from your hearts, you will have this peace and the strength to conquer your trials for all future days. And, My children, remember above all to cling to each other, love each other, and do not desist in your patience and compassion for each other. I am your help, and Jesus is your shield. Call upon us. Invoke our power and Grace. I have told you that you would have difficult days, so you must be strong. You must pray in faith. Today, I have come to seek your prayers for the rest of the world. Millions of your brothers and sisters are suffering at the hands of the wretched. Pray for all who are oppressed, and pray especially for their oppressors. Thousands are not holy because they are hindered by spiritual blindness. You know the vision they need. Pray for them to turn their faces to the Light. Pray for them to comply with the Spirit of Love and service. Then will the world be a better place. When you ask God to convert the lost, abortion will end. All these things come to the world as you ask God to respond to your prayers. Yes, God is a Creator of Love, not hatred. He is the Creator of commitment, not abandonment. And, He asks you to imitate these holy virtues. All over the world, things are changing. You can sense the coming of the Lord in all times and places and in the vast procession of human events. Please make the most of these times to see God work. Seek-out His Love and realize His intentions to convert and redeem humankind through His own means of purification and cultivation. You will never be blinded by observing His Light, and you will become inspired by His awesome beauty. My children, I am now preceding the Return of Jesus to the world by a short time. If today you hear His voice, harden not your hearts. You will be called to perform magnificent services previously unknown by you to be possible. Times have come of which you have before only dreamed. These are the reasons I have come into the world. I bring you advance knowledge of the closing of the ages and ask you to prepare. My Special son, your Diary is being written so that it will be finished in time to play its vital role in the culmination of human existence. You have been very faithful in working on it and patient in waiting for the approaching days. Your work and your diligence will be rewarded. I come today to ask you to continue to pray and be strong. Be encouragement! I ask you simply to understand and anticipate the days. I am always with you, and I will never leave you. It is the most difficult times that will make the sweetest moments worth living again. Let us labor and pray together another week when I will speak to you again. Now, you know that I will not depart until I mention your birthday! You are yet a very young child. I still hold you in My arms and caress your heart. I will pray with you as always and place your special intentions before God so you will have a happy birthday. Remember to pray for all My intentions."

Saturday, September 27, 1997
8:08 p.m.

"My dear little children, you are both lovely and loving. These are the times that warrant your holiness and strength. You are not part of the rhythm of the world about you, rather you are perpetually of God and in union with the Holy Spirit. My children, this places upon you tremendous responsibilities as the End Times proceed, for you will be the leaders in both example and sacrifice. Upon you will be the hope of conversion for many, indeed this has been true for the faithful since time began. And now that time itself is nearly exhausted, you must accept your role as God completes the destiny of humanity. By the hundreds and thousands, souls have passed from bygone ages into the Eternity of God's hands. They pray for you now as do I that you will be tenacious and enduring in your trials. While you offer very hopeful and pious reflections in your prayers and petitions, you yet do not fully know how God will fulfill the requests you make. While His Love is magnificent, He expects that you will understand the reason for His consent to your prayers. Yes, this is from His Love, and is moreover a faculty of His desire to fully purify His people. And when holy people suffer, or when great disciples lose someone or something dear such as a religious site to an earthquake, the example of those who love and trust God is the vision that others will admire when they too must sacrifice materials and conditions dear to them so Jesus can say I AM. For if those who trust God can do so when His Will seems so focused on destruction, assuredly others who do not yet trust can muster the faith and strength to love Him when all the world is lost and again renewed. It is your solemn duty to lead in this life of faith, trust, and patience. My children, you have not denied Jesus in this challenge. I have seen the rest of your days. You will never deny Jesus, but this acclamation cannot reflect or capture what you will endure on your road to victory. You are very fragile and strong-willed. You both need to become very stout of heart and humble in the face of all adversity. So, what do you know of Heaven? You know that it is real and present and contemporary beyond this day. You know that it is forever a mansion and endless in Eternity, beyond time and untouchable by sorrow. Yes, you do hope for the immortality of the human spirit which lives in your hearts today. And through prayers and Love, this Holy Kingdom has come to Earth. I bring the premonition to you of the Glory to come. Our magnificent purpose is to call humankind to receive the Bread of Life now! We call lost souls to conversion, and converted souls into action. We seek the best in human hearts to purge from them anything rendering them less than perfect. These are glorious and special days, bustling with the business of closing the ages and opening the doors of forever. This cannot be done without the complete acknowledgment and participation of all who are about to inherit Heaven. The faithful must travel and call the nations of the Earth to rise to their feet. All souls must be fitted with the ceremonial gown of conversion. The length and breadth of human hearts must be measured for perfection, and the poise given to all through the dignity of the Holy Spirit must be instilled in a single-minded humanity. ALL MUST BE ONE IN CHRIST! Then, there will be no need for different sized chairs at the Feast Table in Eternity, for all human souls will be uniformly one, able to be reciprocally recognized as perfect in every distinction. This is not just a hope for a time yet to come, it is the reality of today. This holy manifestation must proceed at once! And, it begins in the human heart where you now store memories and images of happier times and your hopes for the dawning ages. When you have totally and unequivocally become one in the Spirit of the Lord, this dawn will rise in your soul before Jesus ever opens the door of your mortality to take you to Paradise. Your holiness is achievable now! I have happily taught you to be holy, and you have obediently accepted My messages and answered the call. I am confident in your success, both in achieving the highest piety and delivering My lessons to a world which so hungers for the nourishment of sacredness and peace. All of these things are the food of a righteous race which has grown strong through your many prayers and sacrifices. Your sanctification is dependent as a collective humanity upon your desire to be pure and the acceptance that you are. Please pray with Me that the pious hopes we hold for mankind will come very soon. My Special son, I hope you understand My desire to call the world to My arms and to Jesus' Sacrifice through the unity of you and your brother. We have been very successful thus far."

Friday, October 3, 1997
7:04 p.m.

"Good evening, My beautiful little children. Thank you for again offering your holy prayers to God, and happily I intercede to augment and amplify them. I welcome the unity of our petitions for a world lost in darkness and the Church so much suffering. It is prayer that will assuredly ease Her agony. Please do not expect that you can know all for which prayers are needed, but I have revealed to you many tribulations and causes that require your prayers. Through the past years, I have called to your attention many inequities and multiple transgressions which will be mitigated by your prayers. And so, this is why I have come. Today, I remind you of the power of your petitions. I call you to know the importance of prayer, fasting, and your many novena intentions. It is with great urgency that all of My children in holy prayer groups everywhere understand the need for further prayer from the heart. You cannot grasp how pleased is God when you tender your hearts to Him in the Name of Jesus toward the goal of converting all peoples, for the elimination of human desire to sin, and to eradicate evil acts all over the world. While your lives are a journey toward perfection, you have yet to reach it. You are too impatient, not humble, and unwilling to accept peace. I have taught you many things and have invited you to seek the peace of Jesus in your hearts, but you have yet to totally surrender your will to His perfection. You perfectly understand His desire and purpose, but you still do not allow Him complete access to your hearts. This is because your lives seem too everlastingly daily and repetitive. Please know that time is very short. No two days are alike, for each is unique in itself, and you have the tools to approach every day with vigor and joy. This is not intended to be a criticism of your efforts. You are truly trying to be like Jesus. For this, all the heavens are eternally grateful. Today is a happy time for you. You see the joy of a healthy new family member while thousands were born yesterday diseased, deformed, and addicted. You are blessed, and you must come to understand this. You have found prosperity and lives of plenty. I ask you to understand with great perspective the blessing of your lives, and you will quickly be turned to joy. I am saddened by My children who refuse to acknowledge their own good fortune. You do not wish for Me to be sad or sorrowful. I know you will do better. I have asked you countless times in nearly seven years to be happy. Thank you for your prayers. Please remember Saint Francis' Feast."

Saturday, October 11, 1997
6:57 p.m.

"How beautiful are My precious children! I am your Mother who comes from a lovely dwelling place to which Jesus will soon take you, your homeland and your eternal joy. My children, I come also to pray with you and confirm My promise that your prayers are heard with Glory in Heaven. I ask you to continue to pray in faith and anticipate the coming magnificence that God holds for you. I am the Mother who teaches you, comforts you, and nourishes you so that you will be holy, and that you will understand what Jesus asks. Jesus' Promise is your Salvation and permanent joy. He also warns of dark days to come, of sorrowful moments and despair that will try to diminish your hope. Do not be misled by the darkness of the world. The Holy Scriptures tell the Truth, as they are Truth. Jesus' divinely inspired words are the discernible Will of God in scriptural composition. This is a magnificent concept! Therefore, you must always live the hope in your hearts that Jesus has saved you. The Holy Word has saved you, and the Scriptures reveal this Truth. I invoke your understanding of the Mysteries of human redemption that you pray through the Holy Rosary. You know the ones; I have told you about them. And also very important, My children, I have taught you how to accept your Salvation and your role in the conversion of many. I have come to Earth to tell you that the world must be evangelized by your messages. The sins of the world can be mitigated by your prayers. Human suffering is alleviated by your good works. Therefore, you have a very important role in the good will of peoples, the nourishment of the collective human spirit, and the Salvation of souls. You are called by God to be 'Jesus' to others. And in that call, you are invited to also accept the righteous suffering which accompanies it. While I have not foretold of great suffering to come, but instead of peace and vindication, do not expect that such peace will come without human sacrifice. These are days of great grace. You have been given much knowledge about the human heart and about holiness and conversion. You have also witnessed the terrible tides of opposition to holiness. Yes, you have even seen firsthand the evil works of Satan against you in the lives of others. All of these experiences have made you wiser and able to see Love more clearly. They have helped you to understand the awful conflict between good and evil. Most of all, you have learned that evil has already lost, and Love has prevailed. It is in accepting this that your peace comes. No battle can destroy you, and no enemy can defeat you. You must be aware that God knows you, He sees the depths of your love for Him. Hence, He calls upon that love in times of duress. He allows you to love with a living commitment to the cause of human conversion. He takes solace in remembering that you love Him. Please also take this same comfort from Him. By your prayers, you are lifted from fear and despair, and by the Sacraments you remain pure. All of this is because God loves you. Jesus' Presence in the Tabernacle is God's awesome Love for you, still Incarnate. Your acceptance of Jesus' Sacrifice is validated at Communion. You are offering your spirit of thanksgiving with the concurrence of God. You do not fully comprehend this magnificent Sacrament, but you are daily painting the picture of understanding. God is the Artist who guides your souls in perceiving this picture. Without your faith, however, you will not see. All the holiness in the world is of no avail if you do not love. This is the basis for your vision and understanding. My little children, love does not become 'not love' just because one is tired, afraid, alone, or suffering. Yours is the battle to maintain the power of love in a world which chooses to destroy it. I invite you to hold constant remembrance that Love is already the Victor. Embrace perpetual knowledge that your vigil of prayer will keep the wolves away from your door. Thus, My little ones, there is no need to feel sadness while performing your daily chores or rendering service to the helpless or ungrateful. The human world is passing away. Thank God that it is! Bid goodbye to the decay and corruption that have been the legacy of human sin. Say good riddance to the unmitigated human gall called hatred and impurity. A new day has arrived! You are on the pathway that leads directly to Paradise, one that began 2,000 years ago. There are no more wrangles, turns, or breaches in the destiny of mortal men. There are no more questions for theologians to decipher. The answer is Jesus! How happy you must be to know this. Accept this Good News with joy and patient anticipation. Remember to be My happy little boys, so full of joy, anticipation, and patience."

Saturday, October 18, 1997
7:19 p.m.

"My dear little children, you yet do not comprehend My call for you to be jubilant and light of heart and joyful in spirit! These days are the prologue to the world for which you have prayed. Your heaviness is a display of lack of trust, which is offensive to God. Why do you wish to afford Him such sorrow? Do you not know that God is indeed your Father? Do you not realize that He sent His Son to save you? I have told you that you do not know enough about hatred to hate. I add to this that you do not yet know enough about sadness to be sad. You act as though you are burdened by a thousand crosses. Why is this so? Where is the jubilation that I have taught you to live? Why is it not alive in your spirits? Do you not wish to partake of this optimism? What if I had never come to speak with you? Would that have been better? I am very sorrowful because, like Gabriel, I came to bring you joy which you should live in a resounding 'yes.' But you do not say 'yes' to joy. You pray for a world that God is changing, but do not believe His response! Why do you not trust? I cannot see trust in you if you lead lives of sadness and discontent. I wish for you to listen to My words again. Your Mother is growing weary having to constantly ask you to be happy. I hope I will not need to address this issue again. Today, I have come to remind you to pray for precious human life. This life is given at conception and must be protected and nurtured through the complete period of time before God chooses to bring a soul home. In so many ways is this sanctity breached by abortion, suicide, murder, euthanasia, and reckless conduct. Please pray for the sacredness of life. It is a gift from God like joy that must be shared, embraced, protected, lived, and loved. You must assuredly know how offensive it is to take a life in the eyes of the God who has given it. I must tell you how you are loved by Me and the heavens. I have been also asked to tell you words that I sometimes do not wish to say. However, God is serious in the matter regarding your beatitude of being thankful for His gifts. He has asked Me to tell you that you choose not to show thankfulness because you selfishly worry about false burdens placed upon you by the world. I am praying for you to understand, and I know that you will. I shall make sure that you do. This is completely the result of your refusal to rest. You need more sleep. You must be thankful that I am telling you these things."

Friday, October 24, 1997
7:38 p.m.

"My dear children, in the beauty of the lilies, Christ was born across the seas, and His Truth is marching on. Today, you see the history of a world of peril and terror which lives to this hour. The late Roman Catholic president, a child of the Eucharist, was chosen to preserve the Earth from atomic destruction. After he had done so, he was called home. My children, the reasons are many that I asked you to observe this historical visual record. Most of all, it was to show you humble confidence, manifest public preparedness, reveal a work of greatness in progress, and set the transformation of human potential into real action. This is what I ask of your lives of holiness. Last night in this very room, you prayed with meditations just as noble and with as high promise and hope that saved the material world from explosive destruction. However, your petitions were of much greater cause. Your hopes were to preserve the eternity of humanity, not just the environment that protects you. Therefore, your work and prayers are far more imperative than those of 1962. Your efforts depend upon your trust in God and upon your confidence that you will succeed. The same Holy Eucharist nourishes your capacity today that sustained John Kennedy thirty-five years ago. And, you share the same grace and face the same enemy, the evil stench of Satan. I have come to tell you today that you often allow evil to devour the physical world, but we must together work, pray, and petition for the conversion and Salvation of all souls confiding in the power of Jesus to save them. There are no bomb shelters to escape the scourge of eternal perdition. There are no alternatives to ponder. The war room is now the sanctuary in which you kneel before the Blessed Sacrament. My children, this threat to world peace is just as real. Satan desires to destroy the destiny of men's souls. The consequences of failure are far more egregious and permanent. And, it all seems a senseless battle since Jesus has already won the peace. Let the world hail hatred and destruction! Your soul is safe! Watch the Earth crack at its seams and the followers of evil fall into the pit, to the Abyss of horror where they wish to reside. Watch from your perch upon the palms of this Mother! It will be a fireworks you will not wish to miss. The Victory, the Glory, and the celebration about to ensue is yours. I will not prohibit you from jumping about because I know your hearts will be filled with glee! I will not require you to sleep or ask you to be happy. The latter you will do on your own! When you live that day in Jesus, I can again return to the Father and tell Him that I too have done what I set out to do. I came to Earth to claim My children and bring them home. I will have the joy of knowing that these days are those which led to that happy time. Indeed, you will all know that true happiness began some 2,000 years earlier. Trust and prayer will guide you in your trials, given flight by suffering and sorrow. Sacrifice and Love are the keys to this great happening! My children, gone is the time when mankind should fear for their souls because God has cast away the grief of your guilt and the consequences of your sins. This He has done when I said Yes! I proclaimed that you are worth the service that this Lowly Handmaid could provide. And to effect and ratify My hope, the Child I bore paid the cost of the transgressions of man to reunite him to God and again open the Gates of Paradise to humanity lost. This is not only a miraculous event, it is a Mystery governed and provided by a loving God. Yes, this Sacred Mystery is real and Incarnate. It is about teaching, loving, suffering, and dying. And, the Glory is glorified itself by the Resurrection of the Lamb, put to death by a faithless people. He was resurrected and ascended before the very eyes of mortal men! Now you must see in faith, not with your eyes. And not of magic, but of love and hope. You may search the world over, but you will find only one Jesus Christ. There is but one Anointed, and His Kingdom is united. My children, your last ages are at hand. Yes, there will be great sorrow, grief and suffering, but never permanent loss. You will always win, no matter the price. And in these final ages, the greatest living Saints will lead the rest by the hand and by the heart. You have been given many great examples throughout the ages, the greatest of which is Christ, Himself. Jesus will always point to His stepfather Joseph. Oh! My dear ones, there is no secret to human life! While there are many other secrets, life is open and fashioned toward the goal of eternal bliss. God is here, and He wishes everyone to know it. This is no secret. His Love is real. He is the cause, reason, source, and effect of Love in every universe. My purpose with you today is to raise your hearts to the heavens and help you learn how to truly live a holy life. There is tremendous joy in that life, and no true joy in any other. Where you go to play amidst the flowers of Nature, the clouds, the trees, and even in the banks of snow, your soul always knows that these are the vital signs of a living God, the seasons of His pulse, and the brightness of His morning temperance. When your soul shines back, God is much rewarded and hopeful for you to return to Him. Please make Him happy! This is My goal and God's desire. This is Jesus' wish and the purpose of the power of His Holy Spirit living in you, a Light for these darkest ages ever known to humankind. Remember that the darkest dark is just before the dawn! The Glory of the ages is Jesus who refuses to leave you behind. He has never had to remind Himself that you are exiled here. He has never once snapped His fingers and made an abrupt about-face to walk in your direction. He has always been faithfully yours, perpetually your Advocate before God and your Counsel in times of distress. His momentum has always been toward the people He so loves and died to save. He will be entering in Glory into your sight at any time! And when He does, run to Him! Run quickly and fall into His embrace. Kiss Him with the holiness I have taught you. And, give Him an extra special kiss of love to supplant the one that betrayed Him. I will be with you at the end of time and for the beginning of Eternity. It is with all these images that you are sustained in hope during these days. While you tend to lose sight of this hope on occasion, it is still in you and imposed upon your soul, placed there at your baptism. The Holy Eucharist feeds this image so that your heart will listen to your soul. Hence, you cannot really be lost again. The Holy Sacraments keep you in place while you might think that your footsteps are carrying you away. I ask you today to always remember My words, forever knowing that I tell you the Truth. In this Truth and upon this Truth, you can build many mansions. My Special son, I hope you have enjoyed My words. I offer them to thank you for your petitions, especially last evening, and most of all because I love you. I will speak to you again soon about honoring the holy men and women of Heaven and praying for the poor souls in Purgatory."

Friday, October 31, 1997
7:07 p.m.

"This hallowed evening, My little children, you are at the dawn of hailing the mighty power of the Heavenly Saints. This night cannot be sullied by evil because the Saints already own it. Thank you for praying together with them for the conversion of all those who would see this night otherwise. My little children, the intercession of the Saints is mandatory for the conversion of sinners. Hence, you must always invoke their prayers for the world. Together with them, I ask God for Mercy, blessings, and graces for all humankind, especially for the poor souls in Purgatory. I ask you to remember the Church-Suffering in Purgatory with your petitions for the earthly Church-Militant. Thank you for honoring God by remembering all for whom Jesus died to save. You are only hours away from November, a month given especially in memory of the deceased. Please pray for them with strength of heart and fondness of memory. It is the prayers of the faithful on Earth that are the most powerful for the poor souls in Purgatory. It is a reason for sorrow that many do not believe that Purgatory exists. It is a place where many of those same mortals will be, begging for someone to pray for them. Your prayers now can alleviate the necessity of that occurrence later. While it may seem that your supplications help only a small number of souls, such is a false assumption. When you pray to release a soul from Purgatory, that new Saint helps many thousands from the heights of Heaven. When you ask God to release a particular soul, the effect in time is the conversion, Salvation, and canonization of many more. Therefore, remember the dead in all your petitions. For many, there are none who pray for them, but God accepts many loving acts of kindness and sacrifice for their favor. When you aid a stranger, God sees your love for His people and allows another who is a stranger to leave Purgatory and reciprocally help you. When you look with a prayerful spirit and sorrowful heart at the grave of a stranger, hoping this soul has found Paradise, God indeed guides them there by your petition. This is the reciprocity of Love in Heaven and on Earth. It is the transcending of the veil of exile. You must remember that God lives in your heart through the Holy Spirit and teaches you how to pray. On your own, you truly do not know how to pray as you ought, so Jesus helps you. He guides you and allows you to hope. He focuses your vision to perceive beyond your days, and gives you courage to sustain them and Wisdom to conquer. When mankind first fell from Paradise, it was the choice of Adam and Eve. Now, your ascension in holiness is arduous and tedious. Adam and Eve created the atmosphere for mankind to fall, but Jesus made it a supernatural possibility for you to rise again. This ascension is not without suffering and sacrifice, but is always with order and direction. The protocol of the day is to seek the Kingdom of God while He can be found, and your direction is given through the Holy Scriptures. My Special son, I love you in all ways that you can imagine. You have been more happy, which also makes Me happy. There is no substitute for your complete joy in anticipation of your destiny in Jesus. Thank you for your holy prayers."

Saturday, November 8, 1997
7:01 p.m.

"My dear little children, good days have come if only you will recognize them. God beseeches you to know Him by trusting the reverberations of your hearts. You cannot be scorned, cast away or lost of your own accord because you are passengers aboard the flight called Salvation whose Captain is Jesus. How could any effect of the world or force that detains you diminish that joy? Today, I call you to know Jesus by engaging your own hearts. He has taken solace there and is living quite peacefully alongside your souls. This makes you a chosen race, a royal priesthood, a people set apart. It makes you keepers of the castle of hope for humanity, custodians of the future bliss that your faith enfolds and your hearts caress. Through this service, you have a right to claim the Divine intervention of God. You own the standing to reject the sadness the world emits. Yes, you have the mandate to look with disdain upon the things in your lives that do not bring you the happiness that you have come to know from Me. And your forthright petitions to God, no matter how spirited, are welcomed by Him in the same way as the humble and meek who know not yet how to ask! So, petition Heaven with laudable praises and conviction! God sleeps not so as to hear your cries. He seeks aggressively your petitions and acknowledges your grievances. You have a voice in Paradise. You have the right of suffrage, a franchise through which you can summon, amend, and shape the ultimate destiny of humankind. Your lowly place is a symbol of a broken and helpless humanity who has for centuries been asking God if their humble service is irrelevant and futile. Now think about a Man, such as you have, who has been called to accept a seemingly impossible and chaotic task. Consider not the particulars of stopping a seepage of water, but of saving the source of the water! Yours is always an easy task compared to the burden placed upon the Man-God who singlehandedly saves and preserves souls and human dignity. Soon, there will be a Sign for all the world to see. This Sign will be a visible, tangible manifestation to show humanity that God is real, that His Son is alive, and the Return of your Savior is at hand. And, this Sign will be many times more magnificent and multi-dimensioned than the thirty floor structure you surveyed after Holy Mass today. My little children, I have given you many joyful messages, scores that have provoked you to try harder, while some have left you filled with apprehension and repulsion. Some of My words have been of praise and assurance, and others of warning and reprimand. This is how God the Father has spoken through Jesus and in the Holy Scriptures. Henceforth, you see the temperament of God and the all-possible ways that He approaches and addresses His people. You must seek from Him His complete Mercy. Without Mercy, there is only Justice, although through the Love of God, Mercy is often Justice itself. This is because God is the source of righteous opportunity. You must call upon the Mercy of God because this is what He most wishes to bestow upon you. The Mercy that was not afforded to Jesus on Earth will be given to you. The kindness not provided this beautiful Shepherd will be granted to those who accept Him. There is no vengeance in God that He wishes to administer, although revenge truly belongs to Him. It is His for wielding, and His power rests in His decision to relent. My children, these are new days, yet the same course of passing events in the remaking of your lives through Jesus that we began on February 22, 1991. I am the same Mother, but you are very different children. You have learned to be tolerant and patient. You have chosen to boast of God instead of the world. Your hearts have grown larger than your human will because you have accepted your Mother in obedience. I am in Eternity and will bring you to Me through all the benign ways in which you are mortal. I lead you in sacrifice and offer you new ways to praise God. I teach you the meaning of Yes, that to live in Christ is not to say that you live, but to exalt His Love. You are no longer able to stand on your own, a fallen humankind with no life unless you are tethered to God through Jesus, connected by Me to the Dayspring which gives you Life. Therefore, your Life is Jesus and no other. You are already dead if you have not Love. However, having said Yes, you have made all the difference that you could bring to a soul and a mortality. You have chosen to carry your souls into the heights of God, past the Firmament like a rocket to the Crown of Glory and the pinnacle of human happiness and perfection. Someday you will reach that goal, and with that hope you can conquer any fear, destroy any darkness, avoid any sin, and muster the strength to withstand any trial. You in fact become the likeness of Jesus who bears you to these irreproachable things. It is a signal that you have given to God: 'Please send Jesus to rescue me!' And, rescue you He has. Hence, what is time anymore? A mere facet of the early days before humankind knew of a place called Paradise. Time cannot harm you. It is you who pass through it. This is the true test of a follower of Christ. Do you have the patient endurance for the sojourn of time? If so, you will never cower from the throes of the wicked or the crass tongues of the insolent. You will not look down to see what binds your feet, but will work for God that much more faithfully with your hands, trusting in your reaches and your efforts. My children, My very pretty holy ones, it is said that no one can do enough for God. But if you say 'yes' to Him and His Will in all that He does and allows, you have surpassed His highest expectations of a people He so desires to be with in Heaven again. Yes, you must reach, and you must climb. But, often is the time when He lifts you without your knowledge. It is through Me, your Mother, that you are so elevated. It is in My arms that you find hope for today. I prepare you for the moment of your final rest and Eternal Feast. I have told you through figurative, symbolic, natural, mystical, miraculous, and realistic terms that you are drawn to Heaven and next to God to be enfolded in Eternity with the Communion of Saints, the Angels, the Choirs, and the indescribable warmth that you so yearn for during these present hours and difficult days. I assure you that you are not lost because Jesus knows where you are. He asks for your courage and pleads for your understanding. Please do not question the silence of His Will. See Him clearly in the beautiful ways that He comes to man by the Holy Paraclete, through Nature, in the Holy Sacraments, and by the Divine intercession being manifested through Me in these last days. I have come today, My dear little children, to give you new hope and remind you of two words—perspective and perseverance. You often forget that these powers fashion your grace to withstand your mortal days and to overcome anger and impatience, to discern the deception of time and anticipate the Coming of Jesus with joy. My Special son, I would wish to continue speaking throughout the morning, but you must rest. I hope you have enjoyed My words and that you trust in them. I offer them in Love to help you."

Saturday, November 15, 1997
8:18 p.m.

"My precious little children, this is yet another message of Love from the bounty of Heaven. I am your Mother who brings you the sweetest Love you could ever desire. Through these special days, we pray for God to glorify your human holiness and forgive your mortal weaknesses. Through Me, you have gained great favor with God. This comes as a product of your obedience, while you are still impatient. God will wait for you to become patient, as Eternity is His. Live in the permanence of Jesus' Love, and you will always be more patient. I cannot tell you sufficiently how pleased is God when you love as He asks. While you are in the process of disdaining the world, you must also remember to accept your trials humbly. Hence, you are doing God's work on Earth and living the perfect example of the Christ whom you emulate. In this perspective, who could not anticipate with joy the coming of the Holy Kingdom of God? This is a good day in a serious time while you wait for Him. Your prayers are important, and God expects them. He asks for your authentic joy that they will be heard. Today, you read the Holy Scriptures for a thirty-third Sunday. They are such readings that help you anticipate Heaven. Please remember them always and meditate upon them from the depths of your hearts. I have placed Jesus there to stir your faith into living Love. Now, you are coming upon the time of thanksgiving to God for the bountiful fruits He has bestowed upon your land. What greater answer to your prayers to God than to have Him transform seeds into fruits! He gives you the rich soil, the sun, and the rains to raise them up before your very eyes! This is how your faith must grow. You must become a bountiful crop for Jesus to harvest when He comes again into His Kingdom. He gives you the Holy Sacraments of the Church, His rich loving Spirit, and your own faith to grow you into a beautiful yield. He has sent Me to keep the weeds of sin from impeding your nourishment. You must also remember that you are a volunteer seed! You have been told that God does not conscript Saints into Heaven. They must volunteer to live the life that will take them there. This is what you do today, and it is the life you live. Your Father in Heaven is very proud of those who have decided for Him. You cannot imagine what it means to Him to have so many who stand in complete faith and upon the oath of their baptism to promise to conquer a mortal life in exile through the graces that God provides. These holy provisions are bountiful and endless, but they must be requisitioned by the faithful. Your prayers are the requests that send the gifts of God to Earth. My holy ones, all of these things you seem to know but do not practice well. All of My graces make you aware of Heaven, but they must lead you to participate in Heaven. Please consider the Saints I have so honored. What do they all have in common? They lived in the realization that they must help God succeed in comforting the world and teaching lost souls to know His Grace. Each Saint became a Francis, an instrument in the hands of God for His use in changing the world. This is not an easy task. It is a difficult life of sacrifice and sorrow, but never sadness. The saintly life allows the holy heart to judge the world through the eyes of the heavens. And this is what I teach you now; it is the legacy of the Saints whom you must continually call to assist you. In all the terrible forces in the world that seem to punish you, there is none that can stop you from being holy. And in all the collective evil in the world, none can stop you from becoming a Saint. Quite the contrary, your fight against evil will take you to sainthood during these days of grace. There is no force in the world that can keep you from accepting the power of Heaven. And this power is Love! You must invoke Love in every circumstance and during every moment. By doing so, you transcend the ages. Your heart sees the spinning days pass while your soul is unmoved by their temporal consequences. In this Love, you can see your life simultaneously as a child and yet through the maturity of faith that leads you stout-heartedly to the Holy Arms of God. In Love, you are sheltered so that all that might harm you cannot get near you. You laugh at misfortune and dance at the opportunity to be afflicted in the Name of Jesus. The courage given you by Love leaves you undaunted in times of distress and temptation. Like Jesus, you join as a conqueror of evil and share in the Crown that marks Him as King. Yes, through Love, you have infinite hope. As quickly as you blink an eye, your love for God dismisses your wants and desires. This, My children, is true power! This is raw courage that will not be diminished by what may lame you or cloud your vision as you charge to complete the ages. Listen to My call and run toward the Light that permeates your shuttered eyes. Run to God and feel the warmth upon your face becoming ever more intense. The longer you withstand the brunt of the storm, the greater you shall savor the Feast celebrating your victory over death. Your Host is awaiting your arrival. He wishes to slowly pass His fingers across your brow and savor the taste of the sweat you poured-out for Him as He places His fingers to His lips. Please grant Him this happy occasion. Do not concede, do not surrender, and do not succumb. I promise today that it is well worth the fight, for your cause is the Victory of God on the Earth. No other struggle could be more worthy, and no other goal more laudable. My Special son, it gives Me delight to come to you again today in such joy. I am given hope by your hope. With you, I feel not so alone in fighting for lost souls to take to Jesus. If not for the obedience of My many faithful messengers, My sorrows would be greater and My visits less rewarding. Your faith and love make Me a happy Mother. Thank you again. I will take your petitions to Jesus as you ask."

Friday, November 21, 1997
6:43 p.m.

"Blessings are pouring upon you from the heavens, My children. I am the Mother who loves you, who showers these graces upon you so that you will grow in holiness. This is a special time in your lives, toward the end of your mortality and the continuance of the Eternity of Love which you have already begun. You have been given the holy tools to build-up your hearts into mighty fortresses to stop evil from penetrating your lives. One of the greatest of these tools is now in your right hand. And, My children, you have been fortunate to have lived in this twentieth century to serve God concurrently with so many deeply pious people who love God dearly. I would like for you to enjoy the wisdom of one such soul."

We listened prayerfully to an inspirited meditation by Father Leo Clifford, OFM broadcast on the Eternal Word Television Network.

"This was indeed Father Leo Clifford with whom God is well pleased. His words and his wisdom are eternal, and his peace and beauty spring from his simple heart. He is an instrument for the Holy Spirit, a messenger of God. His confidence strengthens his grace, and the ease in which he pours-forth the life of Love in Jesus draws many into his trust. You are fed the nourishment you need for your faith, satisfied that your hunger for God is being sufficed by the food of all-knowing righteousness and redemption. Father Leo is a very austere and generous man, kind of heart, humble, and filled with love and understanding for all. I show him to you so that you will know that there are many in the world with whom you work for God, but whom you have never met. Primarily though, I show him to you because I wish you to know that before I have finished with you, you will be looked-upon by others the way you see Father Clifford now. All of the words I have used to describe him will be fitting means with which to refer to you. This is what I wish for all My children, especially those who have yet to experience the Love I offer through the same revelation that you witnessed nearly seven years ago. All humankind must look upon Me as their Mother. You remember that Father Clifford said that grandmothers have the last word. This is only for mortality's sake. I am no one's grandmother, I am your Virgin Mother who gave you the Omega, the Last Word in Creation, who is also reciprocally the First. It is with great pleasure that I come to you today to give you this brief message. I appear asking you to continue to pray and to expand your lives of holiness. It is the Holy Spirit who will carry you to Paradise over the remainder of your days. I must proceed into a world that very much needs My intercession and the miracles God provides. You are about to enter the season of Advent. I have told you in years past that this is an apt opportunity for many souls to come to God. It is also a great time of solace for the poor souls in Purgatory. When you invoke the power of Jesus and call for His Love, it is especially more merciful during the season of His birth. Thank you for your humble prayers. I am with you always to be your Perpetual Help."

Friday, November 28, 1997
7:05 p.m.

"You are My two darling American children, the children of God, children of Mine. It is a beautiful faith that you live during these times. Let nothing or no one diminish your vibrant faith. Let no one destroy your anticipation of the nigh Return of Jesus into His Kingdom. My children, you have seen that humanity will pray only when forced by tragedy or loss. They give only after they themselves have first been filled, and they will not stand upon Truth until all their benefactors have fallen. These are the straits of a prideful humanity, a people whose destiny without faith cannot save them.

This is why I have come, to instill faith. I visit today not to destroy or reprimand, or to instill fear. My purpose is to bring you Love, and to give and teach you Love. When My children accept My Love and come to know My Grace, all will have faith and trust in the One Truth upon whose behalf I traverse the permeable veil between God and man. It is Jesus for whom I come, His Divine Love I call you to know, His Sacrifice I ask you to accept, and His Resurrection I call you to join. All these days that bind you to mortality are but the planks in the platform of mortality itself. Nature feeds you and gives you life, but even Nature is finite, made so by time and space. Your souls live because you embrace Immortal Love. In order to perpetuate this immortality, you must again rejoin the Origin of Love, your source of Life, God the Father, through His only Son, the Anointed Jesus the Christ of all for every old generation and new world. This is why My call is so urgent and My messages so replete. It is also why I have called upon your faith to assist Me, to augment My intercession through your simple human love, prayers, and humble sacrifices. There is no other humanity, for you are the blessed people of God. It is you for whom He died, and it is with Him that you will spend Eternity at rest. While your lives on Earth are good and natural, they are not fulfilled. You are veiled by the failed sinfulness of your first father Adam who calls you to reject his legacy, now destroyed by the Cross of Jesus. Heed not the call of the world, but rather the lessons of your faith. I tell you this for all humankind to know. In your soul lives a seed that is now growing. It is the seed of purity, a pretty flower that will soon enhance the beauty of Heaven. Your mortality, your errors, your doubts and failures are no longer crucial. You see them, but they are an illusion, a collection of dregs at the bottom of the pit of human frailty to be cast into the vast wasteland called the Abyss upon the Return of Jesus. And there, they will perish from the memory of every soul who ever suffered them. This is why there is no pain, sorrow or loss in Heaven. They are cast into the netherworld by Jesus when He returns in Glory. This is all Good News for humankind. You are correct to affirm that death is the beginning of life for many, but all must realize that your death died upon your baptism. Your baptism was given life upon the Cross. Please know that it is the Sorrowful Bloodshed of Jesus which flows through all these manifestations of the Holy Spirit to give them Life. I wish for you to know that it is not yet clear to you how much God loves you. You do not fully comprehend. However, as I have told you many times before, you are seeing more clearly every day. The Holy Mass is your thanksgiving. Now, you are near December again. I know that you dislike winter, but you should remember My Hour of Grace on December eighth. I have been made happy to come to be with you today. God is a good God to allow this."

Friday, December 5, 1997
7:16 p.m.

"My blessed little holy ones, welcome into the comfort of My Immaculate Heart. You are worthy of great praise when you yield your lives and tender your hearts to Me. As you see, My children, this commitment is not without its responsibilities. You are asked to remember that prayer is obedient. Your days continue to be blessed in spite of ever-present dangers and difficulties. Many are the moments when you feel defeated and forgotten. You feel these things only when you forget the Passion of Jesus. You are wholly remembered and always victorious in the only Son of God. You are, therefore, asked to invoke the power in His Cross during times of distress. I have been recently reading and recalling the most beautiful diary of this generation, your own. I have been touched by its call for prayer and human beauty. I am brought to tears by its poetic means of describing the heart and the bliss of human suffering. Its words describe a flippant thing and many other colorful images that pull upon the heartstrings of all called to those words. How could your lives have been more beneficial to the lost world? How else could such grace be yours? My time has come! It is time for the great Triumph of My Immaculate Heart. I will bring the Savior of humankind into this world once again, and for the final time. But, this time will be different. This time, all will bow! This time, the King will be King, indeed! He came as a Child and will now return for His children. This time, He will bring with Him the room He called-for on Christmas eve, a mighty mansion and many mansions in which His children will reside forever. My little ones, do not give-up on this hope. Do not be afraid in your patience to ask Jesus to hasten His return! Call upon Him to finally bring His Kingdom and actuate the demise of the already fallen darkness of the world. Jesus is the Light of the world who is now temporarily hidden under the bushel baskets of human materialism, greed, impurity, indifference, and sin. It is the choice of humanity to call upon the Light, to magnify the Light, and to savor the Light like millions of hungry butterflies hovering about the brightness and warmth that draws them in. You have described My hundreds of messages with power, passion, and perfection in your diary. It will be completed in a few months, and I will hand it to My Son, a gift from you, so that He can wield it as a mighty saber against all it portends to destroy! It is you who have made this new weapon against evil possible, you who have procured and produced for God a powerful force to allow the Second Coming of Jesus to be magnified by endless proportions. Thank you! You must stop thanking Me for your work. I have not done your work, you have. You are My mighty foot-soldiers at the front of the battle against evil and for the conversion of humanity. You must know that it is you who help God do His work on Earth. If it were Mine to call, Jesus would have already returned, and all souls would be with Me in Heaven. But, God has awaited the stirring of human participation in the great plan of Salvation. That is why I am here tonight. We are waiting for the total response of humankind, for hearts to become alight through the Holy Spirit instead of the distracting world. And, despite what you see, we are much-winning that battle. Each day, new eyes are being drawn to the call, the means, and the effort of the children of God. Each new sun brings a most contemporary revelation in the collective human soul that God is about to end the world as you know it. Millions are learning anew each day to live in anticipation, but they do not yet know what to expect. People see a line forming behind a new front, a new beginning, a clarion of the ages. They know not yet who is calling, but they know they are being called. You know why you are in line for the succession of Saints. Others are forming behind you because you are yourself standing firm in your hope for God. They see your faith by your example and see your anticipation by the skyward turn of your face in joy. All of these beautiful occurrences are now unfolding in the real world of God, one day and one soul at a time. And, like a candle, time has now burned near its base. And, as God would ironically have it, the smaller the candle of time, the greater is the Light in Creation, and brought by the Rectifier and Reconciler of the ages, Jesus Christ.

My children, this is a special age in time for Me. I have yearned prayerfully for centuries for the coming of the final one at hand. I did not know if Jesus would return in Glory in the first century after His Ascension, or the second, or which. And, though I know not the day or the hour, I know that we have arrived at the last century. I will not have to wait another hundred years. All except a handful of those born before 1890 are with Me now. Jesus is about to return for the rest of you, still mortal and still frail and afraid. My children, this is a happy time. You should observe your days, your actions, and your seasons with great joy. The ride you have been awaiting is nearing your door, and your passage has been paid. The lights of the new day are being ushered to you with each stroke of this pen, which has been like a paintbrush in My hands to yours. My children, I know this God you seek. I know His Heart and His Plan. He could not have conceived or perpetuated a more beautiful finish to the mortal world. He could not have imagined a more brilliant culmination to the efforts and sacrifices of all His Saints. And, yes, that is what He calls you. No production, no desire of a heart could compete with the salvific flourish of Jesus' Return to Earth to bring His Kingdom to the blessed and simultaneously crown those who desire it. If you were to strike every beautiful chord that you have ever heard at one moment, you could not match the beauty that your hearts are about to know. Men will fatally fall in ecstasy. I have seen the Glory of the coming of the Lord! So, let not your hearts be troubled or dismayed. I have already seen the jubilation of My children, but not yet. That is why you must know to live that Truth in confidence. All your actions and prayers are bringing that Kingdom of which I speak.

My Special son, do you recall seeing My blessed A__ upon her deathbed in 1984? And, do you recall seeing your beloved little J_? You were seeing Christ yet incarnate, from which you must draw your strength. Therein lies strength for all humanity, the humble example left by the Saints now in Heaven. That is the true reason that you were given a capacity of memory. Thank you for the days you attended the Novena. This is also a special night of prayer. I again remind you of the noon-hour on Monday. I give you now My holy blessing. ✞ I will speak to you soon! I love you. Goodnight!"

Friday, December 12, 1997
7:39 p.m.

"Good evening, My precious children, upon the auspicious occasion of this Guadalupean anniversary. Yes, millions were converted to My Son through the same intercession that I now bring you. My children, the peaceful anticipation of Advent is unfurling, and the Coming of Jesus again is about to occur. This you must know and prepare for in earnest. There is no time to linger in doubt about your duties or questions in your faith. I am here today to give you the Good News that peace and good will live among you in the person of Jesus. He is the True Presence of God in the world. And, the Holy Sacraments of the Church are God's trusted conveyors that teach you about Heaven and allow you to know the Grace that will take you there. Jesus is a miracle worker, and He died to save you. It was the sweat of His brow and the shedding of His divinely human Blood that paid the cost and acquitted the debt of Adam. You must always remember that while you are inherently capable of sin, you are now convincingly also capable of the perfection of Jesus. You were given this from the Crucifixion. The Holy Cross destroyed your fate and gave your lives direction and supernal meaning. How could this little Prince in the manger accomplish such a magnificent blessing which He bestowed upon humanity? I was there every day of His life to teach Him. I am the Mother of God and therefore the teacher of the Son. And, I am furthermore teacher of My children, those He bequeathed to Me on Good Friday. At the eve of Christmas, I anticipated the Birth of the Salvation of all humanity, the Word to whom all mortal men would listen and heed. Jesus is the eloquence that I Myself was unable to deliver to humanity in words. He is My voice to all, My message that every soul is worthy of honor, dignity, grace, and Salvation. I knew upon hearing the Archangel Gabriel's Annunciation that in purity, vow and conviction, all people would one day share in the Triumph of My Immaculate Heart. At the side of the lowly manger, I pondered the beauty and responsibility of bearing this resplendent Child into mortal Creation. I knew then as you know now that this was no ordinary child. This one would raise everyone to the heights of human potential, so high that all could reach even the silver clouds in Heaven that rain holy water upon the recipients below. I knew at Christmas that the world itself was born again. I saw that for the first time since the beginning of Creation, every soul had the opportunity to be Godlike and to shine again with the Light of the first day. How bountiful was My hope in this little Child whom wise men and wealthy lords came to venerate. The manger was also His Monstrance! I am beside the Most Blessed of Sacraments now as I was on that night to greet all who kneel in prayer and adore Him. My children, while it seems that Christians grow closest during Christmas, it must be understood that the true union of all is through His Light, through your love and devotion to one another in honor and memory of My Jesus. This is a time meant not only for celebration, but for contemplation and peaceful meditation. I invite all to come with Me through the distant ages to the manger and realize why this Child and this special time changed forever the destiny of mortal men. Together, we share the knowledge of Jesus, I as His Mother, and each of you because He knows you. It is your choice and the relinquishing of your own volition to God that will make the conversion of humankind come to pass. You must open that door, you must say 'yes' in echo of My own, and you must commit to follow the footsteps of this Child, grown into a Prodigy. As you ponder the blessings of Christmas, remember foremost the intention of the Nativity and those who came in their own Advent of the heart to greet the Christ Child, the centerpiece of this magnificent manifestation of God Incarnate. Consider the parameters of the life that would grow from Christmas night for all peoples in every land. Imagine the opening of eyes to new hope, to a desire for God that few had ever known. And ponder that once and for all, this Child would kill death and eliminate pain for all who would be washed by His Blood. You ponder this because it is the Truth. It indeed came to pass and is Truth today, and will forever be. I desire every soul to come to the comfort of My Heart. I will console you and lead you to true peace. Do not tire in your efforts to seek the Child Jesus, even these many centuries beyond His birth. I said 'yes' so that you would have hope and come to know the Kingdom from which this Child was born. So, My children, it is with this same hope that I approach God and tell Him that you will obediently do as I ask. It is near the end of another year, and you have again lived it for God. You are still kneading the flour into dough, still carrying water to the parched ones in great love for them in imitation of Jesus. I have asked you many times not to desist. Now is the most important hour to maintain your strength, intensify your prayers, and heed the call of the Hosts of the Heavens who are about to be unleashed into the material world like a family of invincible hearts greeting their lost loved ones, finally come home for reconciliation and contentment. As I have said, it is not solely in joy that the heavens seek you now, but by desire. Paradise pines for your presence in Glory, and this is what shall be. The Saints have asked you to join them there, and you will be conjoined. While God is merciful and lenient upon His people, He also is faithful in His promise to those who have already fought and died to bask in His New Creation. While you struggle to go to Heaven, you must simultaneously consider and anticipate the Coming of the Kingdom to you. Your journey will be much shorter in this respect. Thank you for hoping, and especially for your faith. I know that neither is easy in this world, but your love makes them flourish amidst the most difficult of circumstances. Remember to anticipate God's Light, and also to reflect His Light."

Saturday, December 20, 1997
7:27 p.m.

"I greet My wonderful children with Love always, and I come during this season of anticipation to help you meditate upon the Incarnation of God in and through His only beloved Son, our Jesus. It is for you, My children, that He has done this, for you that He came from His lofty perch in Paradise to be born among those who would otherwise never know redemption. As your Salvation began at the Annunciation, God became Man at the intersection of My womb and the Throne upon which He presides. Heaven came to Earth and has been here ever since. My womb is the Immaculate place on Earth from which Baby Jesus sprang forth. Jesus is the perfect Fruit from Heaven, from the womb of His Mother. Consider My womb as the birthplace of God! And, on the inside of every Tabernacle on Earth is the Food from Heaven for all humankind. The Tabernacle is a perfect place because Jesus is reposed there. My Special son, prayer is the fundament upon which Jesus has based the entire Salvation of humanity. Those who do not pray are not seeking the saving power of God. They do not come to the bathing and salvific Blood of Jesus, shed for all so that sins may be forgiven. Please ponder the Light that has engulfed the world rather than its desecrations. God listens intensely to your petitions. When you pray, you are one with God because you open the gates of Heaven in which He resides. It is clear that you will always be a child of God and My special child, thus we wish for you to do so perfectly. It is indeed through human suffering that you become Christlike. And, you will be called upon to suffer as have thousands and millions before you. You will be lonely and often feel forsaken. You will bear pain, grief, and loss. You will be physically afflicted and socially rejected. I offer you today My sincere congratulations for having been chosen to join in the life of Jesus so that Heaven can be made to look like you yourself wish it to be. I am with you always and everywhere. God is with you, Emmanuel! Therefore, be the image and likeness of My little Child Jesus. Be innocent and kind, but confident and assuring. Accept the faults of the ignorant while simultaneously teaching them the righteous path. Pray for the wicked while admonishing them about their fate. And most of all, suffer gladly for Jesus. Confidently thank God for the Glory He shares and the Paradise you obtain in all that He wills and allows.

This is the true message of Christmas. Yes, come to the manger to adore the Child you must become and the Conqueror you must imitate. Bring the gift of yourself to the manger and say *'I am yours, little Child, little King, almighty Son of God, and Savior of humankind.'* Your approach to the manger is your fiat, that you accept and obey the Holy Sacraments, and upon the oath of your soul give your life and very being back to God. This is a high order to fulfill for a mortal world yet very frail and impressionable. But, I tell you My children, you will be much better impressed by its perfection than you will its sinfulness. Heaven draws you in and surrounds you, while mortality is foreign to all that your soul desires. With every fiber of your being, Jesus living in you is trying to direct you to the heavens and away from what you see, hear, and sense with your physicalness. This therefore is a happy time. It is nearer the eve of the Dawn of Man! You are the beautiful painting under the shroud that Jesus is about to remove to reveal your polished souls to God. And, He will do it just that quickly. This time, My children, God will not cringe at the sight of His people. He will not cast-away the picture and sell the empty frame. No, now He will do what you have been doing for Me the past seven years. He will fall to His knees, hold out His arms, and cry tears of happiness knowing that Heaven and humankind are one again. Jesus will reveal this to His Father and say, *'Look what I have prepared for you!'* You are Jesus' gift to the Father. And in God's Grace and in due time, Jesus will turn to your face and state the same Eternal Truth, *'Look what I have prepared for you!'* It is the exalting peace you feel that tells you this is true. The anticipation that you have is like that of seeing everything that you despise in life being incinerated before your eyes. God is kind and merciful, but He disdains sin and will not condone it, and He deplores those who peddle impurity and injustice. However, He is prepared to accept those recommended by Jesus for clemency. My Special son, you are doing well in this life. You know who God is and what He demands. You bring humility to the Altar, to the foot of the Cross where you adore Jesus. This makes you a soldier of fortune, unlike millions of others trying to get there. In due course, Jesus will ask for your sacrifices, and you will be tempted to repeat the thrice-denials of the Apostle Peter. You will be tempted, but you will not forsake Jesus, nor will He deny you. Be forewarned that the evil forces of Hell are awaiting their chance to destroy your will and your faith. They shall not prevail because of your love for God. I ask you to understand that you will not be ready for the future if you do not pray and if you do not intrinsically ponder the Cross of Jesus. I have been asked this Christmas to tell all My messengers this revelation. Remember that I was forced to see My precious Son die upon a Cross on a dark hill. Hence, I am prepared to seek your sacrifices that will in no way amount to His. You might believe them to be worse because they will be happening to you! This is the week of the Eve of Joy! You will hear many welcoming expressions and see many happy faces to embrace and pray with you. I wish for you to consider the joy that I have, knowing that through the night next Wednesday, millions will be entering Heaven from Purgatory! You will see what this means when you see God as He is. I must now go bless My other children. I bid you to sit beside Me at the manger and adore My Child, the Messiah who came forth to save all. It is with great dignity and honor that I offer Him to you and prescribe His Mercy for the lost world. I will be with you in the prayerfulness of Christmas. I love you."

Thursday, December 25, 1997

What we know from surveying the world is that there is bounty in human suffering and that what we contribute to our own sanctification matters to God. We are fortunate to be chosen as His own and to enhance the fortune of others by being a divine and mysterious extension of Christ, to live the mortification of a righteous people. Somehow in our hapless mortal way, we are the caregivers and intercessors for lost souls who do more than observe Creation unfold, but also participate in its making. We see finally that there is neither divinity nor dignity in being an indifferent people, bland in the eyes of God who thrives upon holiness and commitment.

God wishes us to perfect the practice of self-denial in the way of His Son Jesus, anointed by Him. And, to do that, we must impose upon ourselves the necessary constraints which without we would otherwise be led to intellectual curiosity and blind materialism. Without the constraints of our holy crosses, we are a meandering mass of empty souls with no true being or purposeful destiny. Let us pray together that God will end human suffering because it is ourselves, His loving people, who are asking it to be done. And let us ask Him to teach us acceptance when He desires duress to continue, so that like "little Christs" we see and know, and go forward emphatically endorsing what fruit our trials will bear to the Kingdom to come.

Friday, December 26, 1997

A POEM FOR THE AMERICAS FOR THE NEW YEAR 1998

O Country, our Country, the like I have not seen.
A better land calls us to perfect liberty!
Free from darkness, pure in spirit, noble in desire, girthed in justice.
Let not your hopes be drawn to tearful tyranny or
engage the soil of bigotry.

Share your brightest sunrise, spread your humble purpose
from ocean to sea and back again, for all to live joyfully!
From the rolling Delaware, across the sprawling plains to the sunset shore,
Let all your people live a harmonial lore!
Let all you wish to be come to Thee.

Your nature is too magnificent to be buried by sin and war!
Let your legacy be good will, and fall no more.
These things we hope from centuries passed, and pray will come
to you at last, O Country, the one I love.

Raise this land of plenty millions strong to God again!
To kneel and pray, to hold Him close, to share His hope for us again.
To regain His blessing. To sigh in His rest once again.

O Country of generations passed, you pine for our souls to be
cleansed and purified by light and love.
Let it be now. Let your mountains and rivers speak of new birth.
Yet, reborn from hopes of whence we began. Wrapped in Truth.
Now and forever given to Providence before our time,
Yet, still is new.
Of peace, of color, of God, of you!

— William L. Roth Jr.

Saturday, December 27, 1997
7:16 p.m.

"My sweet children, you are My pretty flowers amidst an otherwise drab world of darkness and indifference. We share your lives as the beginning of the Paradise you will one day fully know. I wish for you to remember as you pass into a new year that both prayer and piety are your tools to help you construct your lives of holiness. Now you are at the 98th year of this modern century. God will be served well by your acclamation of this coming new year as *the time of pious anticipation.* This is your new theme for this special time. I will bless you in your effort to work toward the accomplishment of such anticipation. It is not to be a year of anxiety or acceleration, but one of peaceful and holy expectation. Yes, your anticipation is to have a placidness of the heart so the Holy Spirit may rest there in premonition of His victory and the reconciliation of the world. Jesus has required time to convert the billions of souls He has already saved, and you are participating in and proceeding from that special time. Can you see how quickly are passing the years and your journey through them? I am with you all the way. I lead you and pray with you, and also for you. And, to help you succeed in the new year, you have a sacred visitor to guide you."

"My holy sons and brothers, your Savior is with you now and forever. Many years you have given Me, but I require your whole life, your very being, your entire self. You are of the last mortal ages, a fortunate people who know Me well. You are therefore blessed and most favored. It is you who now sustain the righteousness of centuries passed for the future to behold. I will give you the reward for which you pray. I live in your hearts because it is Heaven. Please persevere as many more years as it takes to bring My people home. I promise it to be soon. I love you. I am your suffering and triumphant benefactor God-Man, your brother Jesus. I AM. Love. Love. Live Love..."

"My pretty children, My Son Jesus has brought you the Good News of His intentions for these days pending His glorious Return. You must pray for 1998 to be a year of spiritual renewal for everyone, and for the end of materialism. Make it indeed a year of pious anticipation! You are achieving the holiness that Jesus desires and the transformation of the world that so needs to change."

MORNING STAR OVER AMERICA

Twentieth Century Anthology

In the Year of Our Lord

AD 1998

"We often wonder why Christ had to make obligatory something so appealing as human love. Why is it so difficult to wrap our minds around the very catalyst of world perfection? We understand that compelling inner-beauty is its origin; our best nature always blooms from there. The sheer definition of universal divinity requires that we recognize spiritual love as having texture, color, sound, technique, and situational context. It also consists of degrees of consequence because we feel differently when a friend says he loves us compared to hearing it from our relatives. It is as though we appropriate a certain dynamic of expression; we make it a privilege for someone else to love us, even though we hold no such dominion over the feelings of other men. We can see the effects of the love in our admirers' eyes, but we can only imagine the architecture of its origin. Hence, our capacity to internalize the lives of others allows us to assimilate their suffering and sacrifices as our own, much the same way that Mary, the Mother of God, adopted us on Good Friday. We learn from all this that love and affection are not necessarily interchangeable. Love is an authoritative mandate; affection is a prevailing emotive desire."

-William Roth Jr.

Friday, January 2, 1998
7:16 p.m.

"My dear beautiful children, you are now another numerical year closer to Heaven. Your passage is the Divine One named Jesus, My Child, the Son of God. Jesus is in all ways magnificent and holy. He is mighty and yet able to be grasped by those too simple to know themselves. I am His Holy Mother, the Mother who is one and the same for you. I was created so that your souls will be saved. And, My soul magnifies the greatness of the Lord who gave Him birth. My children, your hope in this dark world is to accept Jesus as the Savior I brought Him to be. Thus, you are living the Will of God for you and preparing to reside forever in the Son-Light of Paradise. Thank you for yearning to know Him as the Truth. You are a very blessed people because you own the freedom to worship Jesus as He is, as He knows you and wishes you to be. The world cannot imprison the human heart, nor can it steal your love for God. Hence, you are in every way free to come home. God will bring you to Heaven, and I will prepare you to accept Him. Our prayers, our works, and our vows are for and to one another. We give them all to God who wishes you to know your place. I have told you for nearly seven years that God's Kingdom is near at hand. And while it is now seven years closer, it has always been this close, and shall always be. I bring this Kingdom with Me now, as I have for centuries passed, and as I will usher you concurrently with the great Triumph of My Immaculate Heart. Inside My Holy Heart are a million parades and skyward celebrations. You will find your richest joys there! You will assuredly find your only joy there. My children, you have been doing a tremendous amount of work on your Diary. Your devoted love and untiring labors are a testament to your obedience and commitment to God. But, it will be much more than just your opus. You have been fashioning a bell that God will toll throughout all time. You have forged a mighty sword that will destroy the most obstinate evil. You have created a vessel upon which Jesus will sail into His universe to calm the seas for the good midshipmen who have been about His work. Yes, you have prepared the ground upon which the Holy One will soon walk again, and you have laid low the high places and built bridges over the steep valleys to make way for His inviolate justice. My little children, you have shown the world the Cross once again, as it was on the day of the Crucifixion, so that God can reclaim humanity as His own. And by your prayers, you are making the final touches on the world, polishing and caring for it to be offered to Heaven. My children, imagine the vision of God who sees the universe He created with one sphere now the tenor of the Holy Cross of Jesus who saved it. This is the New Earth, the beginning of the Glory and Resurrection of those who inhabit it. These are the times of men for which God has waited a seeming eternity, the hours that allow Paradise to see its inhabitants coming home. All prodigals are on their final journey back to Him, and He is watching them nearly finished with their passage. Jesus will meet you there! This is the Glory of His Return to His Kingdom, when you feel your Father embrace you in His arms and say, *Welcome Home!* This is the day when your eyes will squint from the Light, but your souls will see clearly! It is when you will worship no past, but only an omnipresent, perpetual future in the Love of the One who created and antiquated time. You will have no remembrance of remorse or sorrow because it will have been reciprocally destroyed in your ecstasy. I have asked you many times to live this hope because your dreams of eternal joy are truly God's reality revealed to you through a timeless veil. Soon to come, all history will be one, all suffering will be glorified, and all good will shall be magnified. This is done by Jesus because you cannot do it alone. You will join in the heavenly celebration because it would be incomplete without you. So now in the silence of your prayers and the anticipation of your hearts, know that time is veritably passing-away as well as expiring. Yours is a bright future. You have nothing to fear except that which diminishes your faith. And this too is conquered by prayer. Your courage is in being the children of God who is the valor of every age and every world. Tonight, I have come to remind you of the scriptural passages that extol the Truth of hope. Your hope is alive in the New Covenant who is the fulfillment of the Old. God has established for His people a lasting peace in His Anointed Son, Jesus Christ. Through Jesus, the Father ratifies your reunion with the heavens and has summoned you to reclaim your joy in Paradise, once lost but now regained. All of this is a gift of Love by God for you, not as a stipend for your goodness, but in reward for your faith that Love would once and for all prevail over any evil that might dare challenge the invincible power of Truth. God is of a docile Peace over which no war can prevail. He is a presence so pure that no stain can penetrate His virginity. You are all once again the children of a God who has been forever chaste, long before the dawn of His desire to create you. Your very being is the ecstasy that He wishes, and your return to Him enables Him in the joy that all the Angels know. Your work has been toward this great satisfaction. This is why you are so favored by Paradise, and why your labors must continue here and conclude only in Heaven. You will know once you have reached it. God will lift you from the bonds of the Earth while your feet are still running for redemption. My children, I have seen these times in which you are living come to you as we speak, slipping beyond the shadows of the passing years. God knows no age and brings no sorrow. This too is where He wishes you to be, and this is why He sent Jesus here. It must never be conceived in your thoughts that you have any other destiny than Salvation. Know in your consciences that there is a Hell, but do not let your spirits dwell on its dreadful legacy. For now, I am your only Legacy. Call Me to mind and take Me to heart because I give you Jesus who is the source of all joy. Know no other jubilation than Jesus, and you will live in perfect happiness. My Special son, I promise these things because I love you as you do not realize that you are loved. I hope you enjoy pondering My words and contemplating the day when you shall be fully united with Heaven. Then, you too can be adored in the presence of the Angels whom you will see admiring you. You are My pretty children in whom I place My confidence. Thank you for your prayers during this new year. I will continue speaking to you of the Good News."

Friday, January 9, 1998
7:08 p.m.

"Good evening, My prayerful little children. It is My fervent desire to bring you peace on this beautiful day and help you eclipse the cares of your times by asking you to remember the irrevocable Love that God has for you. I ask you to recall the commitment Jesus has made for your future. It is best for you to always know that there is no other who loves as Jesus loves, and as I love through Him. In these and all days, your strength and power thrive in your prayers to God, in supplication to His mighty Son, your Savior. Your fears are unfounded because Jesus will always raise you to victory. I am happy to remind you that as you offer your lives to Jesus, you also are given in return Life Immortal. Let Me caution you that the world opposes this plan! Evil forces are working to diminish your hopes and bring you to despair. All Jesus asks is that you trust in the promise He has accorded you. Know in your hearts that it is true. As you come toward the end of this century and nearer the Triumph of My Immaculate Heart, you will notice the increase of attacks by evil forces, by all who oppose Jesus and what together we are doing. However, you do not realize that these are your greatest hours! I am sorry for the way this sounds whereupon you suffer so much, but I am telling the Truth. Those who try to make you the scapegoats for their own failures are only fooling themselves. Those who wish to indict you for their faults are unwittingly making Saints of you! I ask you to consider the goodness this brings into God's vast Kingdom. Remember how blessed you are for the sake of righteousness. When you suffer in Jesus' name, you are lifting-up the lowly and making reparation for a very lost world. Pray for those who defy the piousness you extol. Do not be dismayed by your temporary personal setbacks. The Earth and its systems are designed to fail because of the weak and sinful people who administer them. However, it is these systems that are now in place, and you must overcome them. My message is that you do not face them alone. You cannot imagine the support that surrounds you daily. You do not fathom the countless hosts of the heavens who live with you every hour to guide and protect you. I am one of them! Remember to invoke the assistance of the Angels and Saints around you. Imagine the real and true realms of the unseen. Your world is not soothfast. There are no prophets who are willing to uplift your dignity if they stand not to profit. I am asking you to rise above the physical and emotional Earth and see as I see. Remember My lessons about patience, perspective, and perseverance. Thereafter, you will always have hope; you will be happy when you invoke your faith. Today, as this new year has begun, you sense greater frustration and anxiety, even anger. These are normal human emotions, but you are a special people who must rise above them, even destroy them. The lessons I have taught and the life you have chosen to undertake have nothing to do with such frustration or anger, but with peace and confidence. If someone attempts to impugn you for their own failures, thank Jesus for the opportunity He offers you to know Him more closely. You sometimes without mitigation fail to invoke this power. Jesus is always here with you! Thank you for understanding these things. In the meantime, we shall accomplish our work together in anticipation of the Kingdom that will catch others by surprise. I am happy that you know this Kingdom well. You are especially more obedient for acknowledging the Truth."

Friday, January 16, 1998
7:48 p.m.

"My very beautiful children, it is virginal peace that I wish you to know, and true holiness that I ask you to live. You are the ultimate conquerors of your own imperfections, the ones who will shape the final passageways through which your souls will repose in the hands of God. We in the heavens have come to the Earth, Jesus' battleground and Land of Victory, to dispense the intercession you need to steadfastly win the gruesome battles that will end the war you daily fight against hopelessness and outright evil."

Our Lady showed me the funeral services and burial of a good and decent man. He was a father of few words, but was abundant in warmhearted dedication to his family for whom he struggled through very rough times to provide food and shelter for his wife and children. His casket was draped with an American flag symbolizing his service to his country during World War II.

"I have asked you to view the final mortal days of T__ and the body he left behind in order to join the Saints in Heaven. When he entered Paradise, he immediately asked God to become himself a different kind of patriot, a patriot for the whole and unified nation of souls bound for Salvation. He asked God to allow him to use his newfound power for the good of all souls. The world will come to know at last that God has rendered the body you just viewed to be incorrupt as a means of grace for the acceptance of My messages written in your Diary. I am also asked to tell you of the joy of your deceased family members who are living Eternity in Divine Light with all the Saints and Doctors of the Church, the Holy Martyrs, healers, and simple people who once watched them work. My children, it is time for you to dream dreams of Glory and mightiness. It is time for you to envision God's view of the Earth and understand the greatness of champions who never came to be so in the eyes of the temporal world. God sees many who once were thought to be bystanders as having served righteousness with intensity, valor, and persistence. The heavens see it too! Imagine what you will learn when you arrive at the Gate of Glory. Ponder what you will know of yourselves and how God will reward you for consummating new opportunities that you never realized came to you. My Special son, in the vision of God, you will see how you served as someone dedicated to the Mother of the Supreme Pontiff whom you knew would always lead Her children home. You will know that your tenure was successful and that you led millions back to Jesus' Love. You are a shepherd who implores these souls to reject sin and return to the Light of Glory. And, human history will also be viewed accurately upon the reconciliation of the ages before God. I am telling you these things because you must know this heavenly record to help you through your days. Even in the public domain, God has asked pious people to serve. History portrays a different picture than exists in the eyes of God. So, keep working with the confidence that you have, that others cannot see. One day, they will know that you have labored for the redemption of all, and you are winning the fight. Hereafter, accept this hope and carry-on with joy. You have expended no effort in vain. Imagine the astounding impact that your Diary will have. There is nothing else like it in the whole of Creation. This is because you have said 'yes' as I said Yes. I am happy to tell you these things. You are blessed by God so as to understand. Thank you continuously for praying and hoping in anticipation of Jesus' Return."

Friday, January 23, 1998
7:26 p.m.

"My weary children, your Heavenly Queen and Virgin Mother has come on this day to address you with words of compassion, support, and Love. You are living within the circumference of My outstretched arms, under the protection of My Holy Mantle. While there, I remind you of two important matters. First, nothing in the world can bother you unless you allow it. Second, sin is always a choice made by the human will. Since you have chosen to avoid sin, I ask you to decide not to give venue to anything that burdens you with cares laying heavily upon your hearts and distracting your thoughts. I am not saying that this is easy because I know you search daily for peace, dignity, cooperation, and self-control. I have seen the things that burden you, and these are very serious matters. This is why you worry about them. I simply ask you to persevere in faith; and if such perseverance leads you to change the world, then this is indeed what you must do. I plead with you not to place yourself in a position to someday say *'I ran, I laid-down my cross.'* You should not seek change for the sake of change, but for the purpose of gaining new direction and peace. Making a change for this reason is not surrendering your cross or letting someone else carry it. Change for the sake of peace and happiness is good. Hence, you must evaluate the conditions and alternatives in your life, and arrive at a suitable new beginning. Sometimes new beginnings are made by a simple change of heart. I would like for you to read the Psalms. This will give you strength for the new days ahead. You will be provided fresh nourishment from which yours or no other ways can detract in your wish to rise victoriously with Jesus when these seemingly endless days come to a close. I have the intention of leading you there, even though you may wonder at times why I am not always aggressively destroying evil before your eyes. You are happy warriors in a perfect battle, but its wages find you distraught. This is a new year, and one of impending revelation; and this is why I ask you to anticipate it piously. You are near the highest peak of the battle, and you are being attacked. And, your prayers are defeating your enemies. You are in the process of making reparation for a world in which eighty of every hundred people reject Jesus as their Savior. You have taken upon yourselves the work of transferring their transgressions into the vast wasteland below and resurrecting their better selves to take with you to Paradise. Do you not see this as worth the battle? Each time you kneel to pray before the Blessed Sacrament, you are telling God that you accept this challenge and His Grace which sustains you and gives you strength. You are reassuring Him of the same Truth that Jesus spoke: *They are worth the fight!* Until you have completely come to full understanding that this is the definition of perfect Love, you will never be happy. When you have arrived at that summit, the proceedings of the world and your persecution by it will no longer matter. You have set sail on the languished seas of life and are trying to make your way across very choppy waters, being tossed about by the forces around you. You are expected to feel the thrust of all that tries to destroy you, but you are simultaneously asked to trust in Jesus. You are beautifully human and inherently frail. However, in faith your trust will not let your spirits be darkened or your vision clouded. Consistently you ask the question, *When will this all end?* And you will always receive the same answer from God, *Allow Jesus to complete His work through you.* It is He who heals and converts humanity, and His Divine Love that transforms and remakes you. Allow Him to live in you, to fight for you, to bear you beyond the waters to comfort and safety. God is the authentic genius of all Creation. He knows where you are, when you are awake, and when you lay sleeping. And, He asks for your patience while you survey and contemplate the globe around you. In your charity, pray for the many who are starving, homeless, alone, and naked. Remember the oppressed and those in bondage. Consider the plight of those 'four of five' who do not know Jesus, who do not accept His Grace. You are the fortunate ones in this time and in your own country. My children, your Mother brings you Her holy compassion, and I ask you to follow the counsel of the Psalms, especially Psalm 57. You will always be delivered by the Grace of God. If you accept His Grace, you will never concede. And, while you are still able to deceive yourself in time, God will never betray you. I pray you understand and accept what I bring you today to lift your hearts. I offer you this Truth and give you hope. Thank you for your candid display of the events in your life. I only wish that God would allow Me the opportunity to reveal how the changes you seek are very close, and how errant you are to have hopeless thoughts as you walk through the day. You will not enjoy the highest visions as long as you are concerned with who is offending you and how they are committing it. I am with you and will never leave you! I pray for you and ask My Son to bring the changes you seek. It is imperative that I give you a warning. Please do not sense for a moment that your feelings are illegitimate or ill-founded. God knows your desires. Evil is too rampant! This is the course of events for these final ages. God has a very special reason for your battles that you cannot readily see. My serious admonition is that you must never blame yourself. Have compassion for yourself as God has compassion for you. You will not be able to survive in the role I have asked during this age if you constantly toss your head and point your finger and say, *that is evil!* God already knows where evil is, and it is not necessary to show Him. If you choose to embrace the nobility of this course, you will forever be thankful, and never bitter. You are like Jesus; you are repulsed by evil works and by the abuse of power and authority. You deplore and will not condone sin. This places you in an ordained group of people. When you enter Heaven, you will witness a tremendous Communion of Saints sitting at the Banquet Table to thank you, those who would not otherwise be there had you not lived the life you have accepted. You spoke quite eloquently in writing to oppose capital execution some months ago.* God is allowing you to validate His Truth by the life you lead. All of your present trials are beatific works, the holy of holies to the souls who need to be touched by your own grace. You are Jesus for them in their time. You are their benevolent benefactor and advocate, and this you can accomplish only through your own pious sacrifices. God sees you living your love perfectly. You will recognize the fruits of your labors in Heaven where you are storing them now. As I have asked before, please let God be God. He will ratify the decisions you make, and I will accompany you wherever you go. Ponder and pray. The world is being converted."

* Editorial Letter to The State Journal-Register newspaper

We are approaching another moment when those who judge for society have deemed it necessary to terminate the life of another human being for the execution of its justice. I have noticed the public sentiments that have arisen and the editorial opinion explaining the logic and morality of these decisions. I also

see the lack of wise counsel from those who wish to gain justification and support for their ultimate acts of desperation. There can be no argument that the actions of those accused are reprehensible. They have served neither themselves nor the community of humanity. They have squandered their own dignity as human beings and have sent an invitation to the rest of us to respond with revenge, animosity, and other actions that would confirm our own guilt before perfection. I speak of an ultimate act of desperation because it is a sad day for humanity when it publicly admits by its implementation of justice that it did not believe in, or know how to wield, the infinite power of love. It is sad when we admit that we could not convince our weak brother that love was a more beautiful choice than his evil. In these acts to end the life of an accused, collectively we acknowledge that our last option was not love, was not forgiveness, and was not mercy, even though we hope these three to be our own God-given gift. In these acts, humanity has lost the fire of hope for another's redeeming change of heart. We choose to extinguish the possibility of a human being's beautiful future. We steal from another person his allotted moments of opportunity for redemption into what is right and good in the eyes of us all. We do not see any future for these individuals where God will work for their sanctification. We lack the spiritual vision to trust that God can do what mankind refuses to accomplish by a sacrifice of love. We have a dimmed understanding of the great importance of our own portioned life for the goal of the acceptance of love, and in this, it becomes very easy to omit seeing the importance of the life of those which perform evil acts. This is their time, and we have no authority to cut it short. Their deaths are acts of our desperation in the face of our failed human approaches because we no longer hope for their healing, and we have grown too tired and too weak carrying them any closer to their cure. There are many who would read this and distort this reality by attaching so many weak human justifications and criteria, as if a great balance of evil human action should be countered with another measure of human action. Everyone should see that these forces are no greater than mortal human acts. It requires the divine act of love. Love is the greatest power because it cannot be coerced into the loss of hope by any force or any evil perpetrated by man. Love maintains the dignity of the weakest of humanity, and brings the only potential for the elevation of mankind away from all those elements that serve to degrade and diminish us. Violence in this society must be countered with heroic love. This spirit of society will only find true leadership when it finds someone who will continue to lead toward love when vengeance and the exacting of punishment are the only voices that are heard. I hope that this leadership can be found and given venue. A great statesman once said, "Moral courage is a rarer commodity than bravery in battle or great intelligence, but it is the one essential, vital quality for those who wish to change a world which yields so painfully to change."

Friday, January 30, 1998
7:00 p.m.

Dearest Virgin Queen and Mother of misguided Humanity, please turn your merciful gaze toward every heart that is lifted to you. All thanksgiving, praise and honor be to your Beloved Child for these beautiful days of mystical revelation. I intone this prayer to your Immaculate Heart which I know without doubt is filled with love for your children, honoring Your radiance and the mighty King you bore. I venerate the love You share with Your Sacrificed Son, and pine with all that is living to be found worthy of being embraced by the infinite mystery which exists between your two Hearts. Please extend this Eternal Life to us in the here and now, within these, our helpless bonds of mortal reparation. Help all who have been given breath to open their hearts and participate passionately in the divinity that humankind now witnesses so prolifically in Your Immaculate Being. Dispense to us the Wisdom to spur the potential that lies bridled and bewildered in our collective soul. Ignite hope for a better world so that we may rise to the occasion of your miraculous visitation, weeping not over our derelict past, but rising in persistence to address a nobler day. Since God desires our joy in Him, help us ring it across the lands with the clarity of tubular bells, pealing all Truth with potent abundance as prolific as the blades of grass and the leaves of the trees. Secure for us the holy atmosphere of caressing grace, and teach our hearts to swim effortlessly in the currents that wisp in Heaven's skies. Inspire every heart to look upward for their embodiment of true victory. O' let that day be today! Allow that future living in our dreams to descend from the heavens upon our present selves, forgetting not to mend the broken, heal the stricken, comfort the afflicted, strengthen the weak, regenerate the timeworn, enliven the despondent, humble the proud, and most of all, transfigure the evil. Remove the shades from righteousness and loose the glowing radiance which pulsates from the souls of Your little children. Permit us to advance upon the globe! Bestow the Power and grant the venue; give us authority over the world, the landscape of nations, and the souls of beasts. The armor is polished, courage stands at the ready, the plans have been drawn, and the bugle is kissing the lips of Destiny. Advance the cause of the Lamb of God into Creation! Lead the final victory of Your Almighty Son! Launch the heavenly offensive! Sound the charge!

Unleash the imprisoned lightning from Your sacred torch!!!

"Hello, My precious children. I come in grace, and as Grace. Thank you for welcoming Me again, as together we pray to bring the mortality of man to closure. My message today is the same, and yet is always new. I am the Virgin of virgins in whom you will find all the power you need to reach the heights of your hopes and expectations. In Me, you are comforted and healed. You are made whole by My Son, who indeed exchanges your morning hopes for sunset realities. He transforms your mourning into morning, filled with the newness of day and light. How can you come to know such a benefactor? I give Him to you. And, I have come to ask you to come with Me to be reciprocally presented to Him. My beloved children, I hope that you can now feel the Truth in the words I have been speaking to you that you have always known to be true, but you were too fearful to adopt. You have seen the healing of the Mother Angelica because the reign of God is at hand. I have told you this many times. It was told during the first recorded century. That hand has reached to the Earth for twenty centuries, and has now arrived. You will know more and see better in the coming months. I ask for your continuing patience and prayers. The things I have told you are alive in your hearts to set you free. I am the Lady of Liberty. The Light of My torch is the Love of My Son—Yes, about to break free into the mortal world and expose all, and to liberate all. No happier will a collective humanity ever be. It is a time for both reflection and anticipation. Remember always the goodness God has shown, and that you always said 'yes' when God asked you to serve. Remember the peaceful times that will now be restored. Recall the happy times that you will soon live again. You know that Jesus owns the world and is the Ruler of your hearts. He will protect them as you continue to serve. Now, My children, that dreaded word 'however.' However, there is still a great battle ahead. There is a final battle for souls that you have many times pondered, and for which I have been preparing you. Yours is a great period of tribulation because the world is being purified. But, to your good fortune, you have the Mother of all on your side. You have My Grace and prayers to give you strength. You do not enter the battle alone. You do not serve Jesus anonymously. He knows your soul and where you are in time and space. He knows also your love for Him and your commitment to allow Him to succeed through you. All Creation is flowing toward the moment when all is reconciled to God. And, you have come to the bottom of the page. It is time for the summation. Jesus will turn the page of human life to reveal what is written in the epilogue. He will rip the page that you have yielded to Him from the book of time, and it will sail gleefully onto the Throne of God. Yes, God will pick it up and recognize the finest words ever written by His Son. Your name is on that page, along with all the new Saints, the last to enter the great Kingdom. My children, you have every reason to expect that moment of all time to come soon. You are seeing the conditions of the world now forming in revelation of the reconciliation of God and man. You are seeing occurrences never before witnessed, and many atrocities that Satan has never before dared to try. But, never before has the power of Jesus' Cross been so intense as it is in this last age. Jesus has met the challenge and once and for all destroyed the evil that you see now, not a permanent ill, but a passing manifestation of an already-dead evil. Satan can still blow weak souls off their feet in despair, but he does not have enough breath to extinguish the Flame of Love that is Jesus in the world. Satan is on his deathbed and is trying to constrain souls beneath him. He will not succeed. And so, as these final times play-out, do not despair at what you will see, but rather be hopeful that the permanent beauty of God has arrived. Those who hear His call have raised their head to see Him. Others are still waiting to hear, to see, and to know. Many are too weary and afraid to look up. Others have covered the ears of their souls from the shell-shock they have come to know in a world that has so ravaged them. And, others are just too weak and worried to care. All must now have courage in this last age. Jesus has destroyed human fear and all that makes humans fear. This is the greatest time of hope since the Pentecost of the first century. When you worry that most of the world does not even know, My permanent signs in Garabandal and Medjugorje will let all humanity see. Every secular medium will report it. Your fears that the manifestations I bring to the Earth will go unnoticed are without foundation. Every soul in every nation will stir. I ask you to live in pious anticipation. I promise that I am telling the Truth. The work I do is not so much an issue as your patience in its coming to fruition in the Triumph of My Immaculate Heart..."

I told Our Lady how happy She has made me by speaking such words of encouragement, and She replied,

"The joy is Mine! You do not understand how grateful I am to be here. It has been a long twenty centuries for exiled man. Many have forgotten Jesus, while others still reject Him outright, but together we are reversing and eliminating this sadness. What you do for Me is easy—just pray and be patient. You are storing riches in Heaven."

Friday, February 6, 1998
7:10 p.m.

"Good evening, My precious little loved ones. You are My good and faithful children. In you I have placed My trust in the same way that you have instilled your faith in Jesus. How could it be true that the Queen Mother of all Creation could come to need you so, such poor sinners? Because you have been chosen to help in God's plan to save the lot of humankind. Your prayers are as important as the Passion and Sorrowful Crucifixion that redeemed you. Jesus' Death on the Cross is evangelized by your holiness and service as He lives in you to this day. My children, your role is not a fate allotted by some blind chance. God gave you birth for the purpose of helping convert His wayward children and reuniting Heaven and Earth. You must accept this grace with the same fortitude that you first gave Me nearly seven years ago. We continue together because you choose to help, not simply because I ask it of you. You must view a perspective of where together we have been. I have not changed, but you and Heaven and Earth have. This sacred amendment is your noble progression toward love and the holiest of places, the Kingdom you will reach someday. The Light of God shines upon you brightly as we speak. It may be dark in the world, but you live in His Light. The beacon that leads you is radiating from you now; it is your unconditional love for Jesus. And as part of that love, God asks that you accept His Will, just as He accepts you in your weaknesses. And by embracing His Will without reservation, your weaknesses are transformed into greater power and piety. You are becoming more like Jesus every day. I ask you to remember that you are most like Him when you are patient and willing to nurture your love for humankind in your heart, despite your afflictions and those who defy and attack you. By these things, you are blessed! You are a portion of the Passion of Christ because you accept the Will of God to enhance righteousness in those in the world who would do almost anything to forsake it. I ask you to continue in your pursuits. With the help that Jesus provides, you are well on your way to engaging the silver lining around the clouds. You will be inundated as you ascend, but the sacred waters of suffering and strife are forever more holy and healing. Having committed yourselves to this ascension, you must never turn back. You will look down at your lives prior to My intercession and realize that you do not wish to retreat there again. Please do not allow discontentment or boredom to make you believe that you will not achieve success in all that God asks of you. He will not abandon you, but you could deny Him if you choose. I wish to tell you that a lack of patience is a blatant rejection of the Will of God! You are being patient, so I draw the comparison to show you that others are still not. Today is another good day toward the Great Jubilee 2000. There are only a few hundred prior days remaining. We are preparing because Jesus may return to the Earth tomorrow. In any case, you will be ready, and your faith will be richly rewarded. How could a God who loves you so much lead you to another course? Jesus always comes with Me when I dictate a message. He often defers His words to Me to transfer to you, as He will tonight. God wishes you to ponder how He sees your heart and remember that one day you will know yourself as He does now. This need not be a time of sad revelation. Indeed, you would already be as pleased with yourself as Jesus is with you today. I ask you to trust in the way of little children. You must avoid overanalyzing God and His perfect intentions. Remember that you are the effect of His Love. You are His creation, as am I. And, you are being purified so as to be sinless like Me. We must hope together for the renewal of hearts and the conversion of the lost, and pray for believers and nonbelievers alike. All human faith is good; even weak faith is a seed that will grow with the nourishment of our Love. This is why I have come, why I have always come to transform the world into perfect Love. If this were impossible, I would never have made My first appearance centuries ago. My intercession is nearing its fruitful culmination. Many living seers who hold My secrets are near their last days of old age. My prophecies will be fulfilled in your lifetime. I ask that with this crucial revelation, you will invoke the patience to accept, and that at each new morning, you will have the joy of inner-satisfaction, peace, and confidence because you are one more sunrise toward the Triumph of My Immaculate Heart. I am also asked to continue bringing you the good news of the impending descent of the powerful Saints into the world. Saint Francis came rapidly to your assistance this week. You will not be disappointed in all that God has planned for you as long as you hearten the globe by your glowing display of patience. Please know that the Archangels are with you to guide and strengthen you. Call upon them always, and they will help you. A generation ago, you did not realize that you were so blessed, but you are aware of it now. Thank you for your work on your Diary. Your labors are beatific because I am helping you. Do not worry. You will be pleased by the readings for the Sunday Mass. I will be with you when you read them. Soon it will be time for Lent, and the coming of the new spring."

Friday, February 13, 1998
7:01 p.m.

"My prayerful little children, I am your Holy and Immaculate Mother, the one who prays for you, who shines for you, and who gives you joy. I have come to greet you with My holy blessing. You are in good favor with God because you pray, because you yearn for the Kingdom which Jesus brings to envelop you now. I harbor these hopes too; and while many people are not yet ready, they are being prepared as we speak. My children, you are fortunate to have the knowledge and vision that will usher you to Jesus' arms when you hear His voice calling forth His brethren at the close of the ages. You have been chosen by God because He loves His people. You are poised to lead many others to Him because, from the wombs of your mothers, I have shaped you for this task. Indeed I call many, but not all respond. They are not out of grace or favor even though their faith has been subdued by the distractions of the world. Hence, I depend upon the prayerful such as yourselves. It is pleasing to always look and see you at My feet. Today, I would like to remind you of the signs you are receiving, telling you the Kingdom of God is at hand. You have witnessed miraculous healings and the completion of My messages for many. All of this is a precedent to the impending Triumph of My Immaculate Heart. What began in the Heart of God was brought to the world by the Archangel Gabriel. Now, to conclude the fulfillment of the happiness Heaven desires, Saint Gabriel will soon accompany Me in joy as I again present the Resurrected Messiah to the Earth to complete the words this glorious Archangel uttered centuries ago. It is as though Gabriel took a breath, and God saved the world before the Archangel could speak again. Your pious teachings transcribed in your Diary are a great part of the final words of the Angels to the Earth. I would like to give you some new instructions toward its completion. If you will bear with Me, I wish to say that your Diary will need to be expedited, as I have been told that the reconciliation of the ages is nigh at hand. However, heed this warning: Do not hurry! Be peaceful and patient. My children, as you look around the globe in dismay, please take heart in the promises of Jesus for which you are well worthy. God knows how despicable the world is and how far many souls are from Him. This is why you are praying and why I am speaking to you. Human conversion is not so much in the badness you see, but in the goodness you yet cannot see and the pending change of heart of those who are now doing ill will. You must be more hopeful and less disgusted. Your faith should help you anticipate the righteousness coming into Creation. Do not allow your impatience to embitter you toward a humanity that is changing for the better, albeit at a very slow pace. Allow God to remain in charge of time and all physical matter. This requires your genuine trust because like Jesus, you wish for the reconciliation of all before sunrise tomorrow. This begs the question that you have often pondered, *'How much advance notice will God give Jesus before He sends Him back to Earth?'* As I have told you before, Jesus has been sitting at the right hand of the Father for many centuries. He is about to give the final command for which even the first Apostles waited. The time is near, and you will be a participant in the Final Battle that I told you about in years passed. Your role will not be an easy one, but it is at hand. You must remain in love with Jesus through His Mother! You have the appropriate grace and venue to succeed when Jesus subsequently gives you the command, and you are neither weak nor afraid. You are bold in the commitment you make to God through your consecrations to Jesus and Myself. Every day that passes brings you nearer the Great Jubilee. Do you remember how you feel when you listen to the speeches of your best orators? This is the confidence that Jesus gives you, the same hope and anticipation. Most important, it is the invigoration that many will receive from you on behalf of their Savior. Live with and through this hope! Do not doubt or question the motivations of God. He knows what is best for His people. We are not yet finished, but we are getting extremely close. In all of this anticipation and preparation, God still wishes for you to live your daily life. If you desire anything new or changed, pray it into being. I have come to help you decide for Jesus, not to ask you to cease living your earthly years. It is My desire to remain with you through your passage into Heaven. You are to be commended for remembering the life of Saint Bernadette. It is a prayer for you to honor her memory."

Friday, February 20, 1998
7:44 p.m.

"My dear children, the Kingdom of God is pouring forth with great power through the valley of your tears. Great is His Mercy, and rich is your reward. It is not so much the pace at which He is coming that is your grace, but rather that He is coming specifically for you. You are His intentions. I bring you peace and the knowledge that God is with you in every way you might imagine and in every means yet inconceivable to you. You have the freedom to proclaim that you are children of God and that no others may possess you. Your inheritance from the Resurrection of Jesus is your claim to the satisfaction of your daily petitions. My children, with great Love I advocate for the things you request. I give My very being to the proclamation that Jesus is the Savior of the world and healer of every human heart. He dresses your wounds and mends your brokenness. He will lift you up for the asking. You know these things to be true, and you are blessed for having accepted the legacy of the Perfect Sufferer, a pious nobleman who owed nothing but paid all. This is Jesus, our Jesus, who knows you perfectly and recognizes the imprint your soul has made on Creation. There is no mortal whom Jesus will not save. All must say *'I accept without condition your Sacrifice. I believe in total trust your Promise.'* My children, loving Jesus is not a difficult burden for you. His requests for you to love Him are fashioned by His sacred knowledge that you have the capacity to fulfill them. So, your trust is reciprocally in yourself to accept God through His Messianic mediator and ambassador, Christ the Lord. It is in this same simplicity and your humility that mankind is restored to perfection in union with Paradise. Nothing you can do will expunge this opportunity. Please remember that your redemption is assured from centuries passed. Time is not a factor, and space is irrelevant in this Eternal Truth. I remind you of this because it must become the conceptual being of every human heart. Every thought and action must be a blossom from the seed of hope that I have placed in your life through the Archangel Gabriel. God asked that the world be redeemed, and I said *Yes, you are worth it.* It is this simple. And to manifest the Divinity of this Grace, I return to the Earth now to complete My Fiat by transforming you into holy little children, worthy of the great destiny that is yours. You are moving closer to Heaven, and you are a welcome sight to all who reside there! My children, this year has brought many happenings that lead you to the factual awareness that what I am saying is true. Please live in the peace and prospect of your Salvation, and God will fulfill what He has said. You must know that through your prayers, you are already invoking His humble Will. You are bringing sinners into compliance with the great Commandments. Do you see with each passing day the new possibilities previously unattainable but for your supplications? You are members of the

Holy Family, an extension of God, and souls who belong to the holy family of humanity. I give you graces when I appear because you obediently listen. I speak to you not solely because you are worthy, but because I love you! It has been a very trying week for you on many fronts. You have observed Satan's cruel path of destruction, but you have also seen that I stopped him because you petitioned Me to do so. You will have a bright new spring ahead. All the things you hope to achieve will be accomplished. You are living a blessed life, a state of good favor with God. I am elated with your Diary. I always listen to your prayers and perpetually ask God to help you. We will continue together with this great hope and anticipation for the unity of all souls in Paradise. Please remember to pray for everyone in hospitals and for the infirm everywhere. Please embrace the power of My Love."

Friday, February 27, 1998
6:57 p.m.

"My tender children with such innocent hearts, My Love is with you during this renewed Lenten season of prayer, and in union with Jesus as He denied Himself for forty days in the desert. This is a period of reflection and refinement, yet a time of anticipation. You must recall My previous Lenten messages, and how I wish you to call yourself especially to listen to God. Jesus' soul was never parched in the desert, neither was His Love diminished. Rather, His time in the desert parch was a time of inward contemplation of His Love for God the Father and for humankind. His forty days represents an invocation for you to ponder likewise. You are the reason that God decided to save humanity, all of you who are My children, because He knew your potential to return to perfection. He recognized in you the object of the Love of the Son He sent. And so, during these days, you may pray humbly for pardon in union with Jesus' upcoming Passion and know through it all that God will give you nothing that you will not survive in union with that same Passion. What is it that brings God to do these things? His knowledge that, before Jesus, you will ultimately judge your own soul. You will search-out your soul for anything in you that might stain Heaven should you be offered entrance there. You will shake yourself down in search of any poison that would breach the perfect union between yourselves and the Angels and Saints. Yes, God wishes through these days to cleanse your garments and render them perfectly pure, fit for a king to wear. And, this He does because upon your passage from mortality, you will look down to see if your clothes are fit to be presentable to a perfect Lord. While Satan will be there to point at your stains and laugh, Jesus will be there to tell you that they are just echoes of former imperfections that your Virgin Mother has washed away. Just as you now see stars in the night that have long been extinguished, Satan will be fooled into believing that you are not perfect. Your stains will be as long-gone as those stars. In this great miracle of God, as you go to Jesus to accept your holy crown, you may turn to Satan and tell him that he terribly underestimated your ability to see Truth given you through the Holy Spirit, that he failed to know your obedience to the Virgin Mother who taught you Grace, and most of all, he indicated his simple ignorance by believing he could dilute the power of the Blood that made you whole and a legitimate heir of Paradise. Indeed, you may turn to Satan now and tell him that he may as well return to the deathbed that he fully knows is his. With power and courage, you know that you belong to Jesus through Me, and thus, once again the perfect property of God. These are the holy meditations which you should enkindle both through these forty days and all through your life. Jesus anticipates with joy your contemplation of His time in the desert when He, too, refused to listen to the lies of Satan. It is not easy for you to dismiss all the temptation that confronts you, but you are inherently more weak than evil. So, I will make you strong, and in Jesus you will conquer the evil. That is the true majesty of Lent. That is the reason that you resolve to be righteous conquerors rather than indifferent followers of the flawed and lifeless world. The Earth is your temporary resting place, but you are now universal because you love. You are part of God's Creation again instead of an inanimate mortal. Through Jesus Christ, you live, breathe, and have life. This is the fortune that God wishes you to inherit. This is the future that is timeless and the perfection you already share in Jesus. You need not wait to be living Saints. In My arms and in God's sight, your soul has already arrived. You need to complete His work, also through Me, by being 'Jesus' for the world, His Body of Love; and I promise that He will soon return and take you to rest. I know that you are hungry for Jesus and thirsty for peace. God knows the pangs you feel deep within your soul. Therefore, to give you life until you are taken to Life Eternal, you are fed the Life-giving Eucharist, your thanksgiving that the only thing keeping you from seeing Heaven is time. In the Eucharist, that time is breached and you are already perfectly united in God. Through the Blessed Sacrament, you become an inner-visionary and the ecclesiastics of the mysteries revealed to mankind through the ages. You become the knower and revealer of God to the modern age by your unity with all former ages. This is the power of the Holy Eucharist. You consume and adore a portion of timeless perfection, a Body that is all Divine and a Soul that is perfect. Your humanness is given the gift of the immortal so that it travels through time like a butterfly over the lilies in a field on a sunny day. That is why your heart is warm and your soul is at rest. Through the Eucharist, you are consoled in Jesus, and He in you. God is allowed the gift of your presence in Him before you ever draw near to sighing your last breath. So, to understand this Lenten season is to also understand God's fidelity to you through the Blessed Sacrament. Jesus' Body is God's ringing of your doorbell, asking you to come out to play in the fields of your fondest dreams. The Eucharist is your formal invitation by God for you to vacate your mortal cell and return with Him to the land of your birth, to a mansion so magnificent that your soul cannot yet describe it to your heart. And, forget about your mind ever being able to conceive such a place. Jesus has prepared a mansion for your soul fit only for a newly perfected body. You will no longer wish to see the one you inhabit now again. For all of these images, Jesus wishes you to have a holy Lenten season. He wishes you to scoff-at the enticements of the devil and to remember the great Resurrection of your soul which He provided on Easter morning. His Mercy is wide, indeed. Once, a soul came Home and told Jesus that he did not wish to steal his way into Heaven. Jesus told him that it was a gift He gives freely, and reminded him that the first Saint was also a thief. You cannot outdo the generosity of God, nor can you misconstrue the savvy of the means which Jesus will heal your soul and bring you Home as you are being tempted by evil to choose a different end. My son, these words and thoughts I have brought you tonight I hope you will one-day share with your brothers and sisters. I will tell you when is the time. You may now address the heavens who listen to your hopeful supplications... This is now your holy blessing from your loving Mother. ✞ God is indeed very pleased. I will speak to you soon. I love you. Goodnight!"

Saturday, March 7, 1998
7:59 p.m.

"My dear little children, your Mother is filled with Love for you! Please seek peace from the depths of your hearts. Jesus resides there! He is as comforted there as He is in My bosom. He has as much authority there as He does seated at the right hand of God, and He can conquer evil from there as powerfully as He did on Mount Calvary. So realize your place in God's Kingdom, already come to Earth within you, and you will no longer feel helpless or alone. I have for years been telling you of this blessing bestowed upon your souls, and you have been obediently learning and changing. However, you have not yet come of age in the Divine Wisdom you require. I am still teaching you. I assure you that you will be prepared when the time comes for the radical remaking of humankind and your collective reconciliation with perfection. My sons, little children suffer because they are God's giant Saints. They are the so-called warships and nuclear weapons you seek. The suffering of humanity chosen by God complements the Passion of Jesus and represents all that the world needs to stem the tide of Satan's most evil rampages. These suffering souls are your fortresses and ramparts in the battles now raging. Look toward them for strength, for they are one with the whole, complete and perfect Spirit of Jesus for the lost world. Through their eyes, God can see the lost. And in their pain, the lost can feel God; they can travel upon the legacies of the chosen-suffering back to Him. Henceforth, when you perceive a suffering child or a grieving widow, you are seeing an expansive bridge between Heaven and the people God has yet to gain. In the hands of the suffering rests the destiny of the wicked who are soon not to be so wretched anymore. I am describing the true, raw power of an infinite God in human form, found in the faith and courage of the souls suffering for His sake. This is an appropriate season for you to learn this lesson as you come ever closer to understanding the genius of God. Your perfect union with Him rests in your acceptance of the life Jesus asks you to live. Each soul who enters Heaven will champion their own cause for Him before they arrive. Some are already saintly sufferers, others His prophets and messengers, and still more are wound-dressers and missionaries. God asks that you play the part into which you are cast, and He extends His heartfelt appreciation for your compassion for those chosen to be humble sufferers. Your love for them is noble and worthy, and is a petition to God to not seek untold others to grieve in physical agony. God listens to your concerns for humanity, and this is what He asks of you. As you turn toward Him, so will others hear. If you try to affix human logic to the Wisdom of His Love, you will not be interfacing Heaven and Earth on a universal plane. I assure you that you will ultimately be pleased with the Kingdom of God and how each of you shapes it once the Light of Eternal Day falls upon the Earth. Until then, I seek your prayers and invite you to pardon those who offend you. Woe to you when the affluent speak highly of you! Shame on you if you take a bow for doing God's work. But, Grace is upon you if you welcome the Will of God and pray in pious anticipation of Jesus' Return. My children, the holy exchange of words regarding this reconciliation is good, rewarding, and redeeming. It explicates your great hope. Your life's experiences are parables of the victory that God is about to bestow upon you. This is an unending victory for all who follow in the ways of Jesus. Eternal rules are not the same as mortal ones because they are extrapolated from celestial boundaries and parameters. You have great power and universal effect upon the world and the whole universe. This is why you do not fully comprehend the great magnificence of your service. It is time that has deceived you. I have appeared here to help you transcend that element, to uplift you from the cradle of time into oneness with the Eternity that surrounds and engulfs you. While in this process, please continue to serve without questioning your faith. You are offering a very worthy Lent. I am pleased by your prayers and intentions, with your good works and humble deeds. God has been manifesting opportunities and changes as you have asked. He irrevocably loves you, and Jesus yearns for your happiness. They both ask you to live in union with them through your trust and patience. I will lead you to joy in all circumstances. I am happy that you take the time to listen to others, especially those who so often oppose your good will and pious works. You must recall the suffering of the lonely in all your Lenten prayers."

Friday, March 13, 1998
2:33 p.m.

"My darling little children, prayerful as you are, you have won the Heart of God. He knows the goodness for which you yearn. Jesus understands the portrait of the universe, indeed of all Creation, which you have painted throughout the hallowed chambers of your hearts. God acknowledges the holy artwork which is your hope for the New World to come. However, My little children, there are many other artists who have yet to discover their talents, many who are only now recognizing their prayerful contributions they will soon evoke to make the highest heavens even more supernally complete. I am teaching them to know of their holiest souls, just as I have taught you. Surely your will is for them to develop and mature in holiness because many of their gifts to God and humankind will make you stand in awe and gratitude that we waited for them. Yes, God's Kingdom is about to reign without opposition upon the Earth, but He also wishes all within to serve without blemish. This is your age to pray and hope! You are placing the final touches on the Creation you will present to Jesus. All those who have yet to come to God will add a pretty flower here and there to represent their soul, their hopes for all beauty to survive and ugliness to perish. You remember that pretty flowers represent Heaven on Earth, and their fragrance is suggestive of the Holy Spirit since you need not see them to know they are there. Converted souls are reciprocally the fragrance that God seeks from Earth. They are His blooming flowers, and you are the careful gardeners helping them grow. You present them to God at Easter and always. Heaven will therefore be more profoundly beautiful as your work comes to final fruition. Today, I come to bless you and pray with you. You are traveling a journey during which I am present in your trials. You never cease approaching the heavens, but like little children walking alongside a fence or through an open field, you stop and pluck a violet or daffodil along the way. This is what your Rosaries and litanies are for. You pause and seek the unseen beauty of God, to hold it in your hands, to bring it to your senses, and smile in assurance that the sweetness you smell is the hope that God has for you to come fully into the newborn garden of Paradise where you can fall and roll gleefully in the beauty that consumes you. The heavens hold high anticipation for your recognition that your sojourn is brief. Eternity is endless, and your joy there is complete. God has already explained this through Jesus. The First Fruit of the Holy Cross has grown the entire human race back to the window of Heaven for Creation to admire your beauty. I wish for you to overcome your obsession with the strife that fills your lives because it is truly passing away. You will one day ask, *'Where did it go?'* In this happiness, I greet you today on behalf of all the heavens that understand your struggles. Please continue to invoke the valor of the Saints who walked and suffered before you. Call upon them in union with the Passion of Jesus, and you will comprehend the genius of God. Holy places are always dressed in human sacrifice. Prayer is the order of the day for generations of people whom God has blessed. Patience is the virtue that God rewards with victory. And throughout all these proceedings, you are kept safe in the bosom of your Mother. My kind and gentle Heart keeps your tender souls from harm and affliction. You must never assume that good fortune is a reward for righteousness. Neither is strife a punishment for sin. Good fortune is ultimately the reward for sacrifice and the flow of Grace upon a people whom God dearly loves. Again, this is the season to remember these things. So when you feel forsaken or abandoned, lift your faces to Mine and I will help you understand. I will teach and guide you, and lead you to the Truth. You must remember that you cannot fly until you have first stumbled to the ground. You cannot sing if you do not intonate the notes and clefs. You cannot read a placard with your eyes closed. You cannot pray unless your heart is opened wide. Therefore, you will not know Paradise until you perfectly understand all that Jesus came to teach you. Knowing this, you have power. Now you can fly and sing and read and recognize Paradise because you have given your heart and soul to Jesus. And as you are seeing, the heart is always tenderized by the temperance of the soul. Your spirit will forever say 'yes' to God if it is given clear vision by the heart. My sons, this is a very special time that we share together. We are blessed by this opportunity. The whole world is better, and countless souls are being converted. If we were to stop speaking together today and simply joined in silent prayer, we have already made a universal difference to Heaven. The destiny of man has been permanently altered by your obedience, prayers, and good works. I have told you many times that I can do nothing to change the Earth without your help. You are obediently giving it, and God is profoundly grateful. You are seeing the value of human suffering. No greater Light does God see than that which shines from your prayers. It is truly a holy and special moment for the world. These last passages of time are to be revealing and converting for the masses of humankind. I ask you to remember that our work over the past seven years has not been in vain.

Friday, March 20, 1998
7:03 p.m.

"My beautiful little children, the Kingdom of God is indeed at hand, and I have come today to prepare you for the lasting peace for which your hearts yearn. Yes, this peace of which I speak is unlike any other you have known. The peace which you now perceive is of hope and solemnity, while the peace of the Kingdom Jesus will soon usher is of endless victory, the constant pouring-out of the Grace of God upon your souls, the harmonious fragrance of all the heavenly flowers, and the collective scent of all incenses through which you recognize the bounty of every Mass and Eucharistic Benediction you have celebrated and observed on Earth. I cannot prepare your souls for the joy you will then know, but I try in every way during these days to open your hearts to believe that it is Jesus who brings it. I so wish to condition you for the battle for souls to come and make you wary of the dark and difficult days that shall be the last on Earth. I came to you years ago to ask you to follow Me, and you did so faithfully and obediently. I have taught you how to be strong, how to love, when to challenge and when to desist, and how to pray for the Wisdom to know which to enlist. Your guidance is from of old, from the God of Moses, Abraham, Isaac and the prophets and kings, and all the holy Apostles and disciples before you. They have held the torch of righteousness for God, and have handed it to you through time. It is Jesus whom you hail before the world in glory and victory. This is the observation of the season during which Jesus was held before humanity in scorn and contempt, but your lives and service are His new resurrection. You are the living miracle of the Easter that God plans for the last day, the Feast of Paradise united. All has been said by Jesus to lead humankind back to the Father. When He speaks overtly to Creation once again, it will be with a transcending and thunderous power of Judgment, reconciliation, and Justice. His voice will be strong and firm so as to be heard over the prison walls crumbling to the ground to set the captives free. His tenor will be heard over the destruction of palaces and earthly kingdoms crashing into crevices in the Earth. And, His words will be especially terse when He asks humanity to listen to the cries of the millions of aborted children who are now living with God in Heaven. It is your prayers that provide the virility for His Justice, your service that builds the stairs He will descend to lift-up the forsaken. It is for all those who have loved Him that He will arrive and present you with your heavenly reward. And, He will likewise bring pardon to those too weak and afraid to fight for Him. He will be glowing with brilliance and will reflect like a mirror the souls of those who despise Him back into their own faces. I cannot describe what a crucial time this will be for the faithful, but I can tell you with confidence that the number who will be lost diminishes with each Hail Mary you utter. It is irrefutable that Jesus intends to take every soul back to Heaven. But, many have made their choice to follow the fallen. For them, you must not weep. I bring Good News that Paradise is waiting for all who are washed in the Blood of the Lamb, Jesus who has taken away the sins of the world. For centuries, I have led My children to Him. Here in these last ages, I can only watch and pray as you fend for the Love I have taught, struggle for the weak, and fight the good fight for the final preparations before the Return of the Son of Man. For many years, you have known to follow. My Special son, all your life has been given to honoring the good will that God asks you to live. You have been blessed in many ways. I have given you guidance all the days of your life. Many of your actions have been inspired by Me. I asked you to procure a picture so I could show you how I am tending you by watching your work during these last days of Earth. Without knowing it was at My urging, you did produce such a photograph. *(Picture of a mother duck swimming behind her little ducklings as they crossed past me at the lake.)* You can see how I am closely behind you, watching and protecting you. I am your Mother, and I have taught you well, but you are too little to survive the impending battle alone. Therefore, I will be forever with you. I will never leave you. I may not always speak openly like I am now, but I will always direct you, just as I was years ago when I first urged you to procure that picture for this message. My happiness lives in your obedience, and you are compliant because your heart is open. I sense that the work we are doing on your Diary pleases you. Enjoy the special time that you are devoting to it. These are indeed days filled with grace. Thank you for your prayers in unity with My intentions."

Saturday, March 28, 1998
7:06 p.m.

"My dearly beloved little children, what can a Mother say whose Love is so strong that mere words cannot capture its magnificence? What could I do short of bringing you Paradise that could elevate your hearts to hope for the Glory you will imminently inherit? Great are the things of Heaven that have laid brightly-shining for you to take them in hand whence you are transformed in body and soul into seamless unity with God. It is your spirit that seeks rest in Him, not a brief respite, but a permanent new beginning where there is no pain or sorrow, no weariness, no tears or strains of terror or violence. All you need do is live in faith and pray to God for perseverance. In these you have shared perfect understanding. A thousand years are but one day to God. He will allow no darkness to consume your soul, nothing corrupt to stain your perfection. He will give you every reason to walk upright in the knowledge that not only have your enemies been defeated, they have been converted to fight for Him in a strength to rival that of your own. Remember that Light is the brightest to those who have long lived in darkness. Heaven is the sweetest to those whose lives have been embittered. Peace is more transcending to those who have sustained the ravages of war. And, conversion is more monumental for those who have blindly been used by evil to stop the Spirit of Love from flourishing in the loneliest valleys and the most vacant hearts. Your Mother is not telling you of the End Times because I wish to dispel your desire for the gladness of day, but rather for you to open your hearts and realize that you have yet to truly know gladness. Indeed, inspired by your wonder, obedience and prayers, I reveal to you what I desire all Creation to accept—your redemption and inheritance of the New World for which humankind has waited since Adam first stumbled. The unholy who are about to know Jesus are presently lost, but are also Saints in waiting. The Crown of Glory has descended from Heaven, and all Creation sits within its circumference. Please internalize this Truth and these hopes at the same time you are prudently acknowledging the suffering of man. Reserve a place in your hearts for the invincible fact that God is a genius who is cultivating His crop of souls for the holy harvest. Of course you pray for the end of suffering, and naturally you pine for the conversion of humankind. This is also the hope of God through Jesus, and Jesus through Me. This is what your prayers portend. All this healing and conversion has not come through the centuries of man by his lavishness and tranquility, but through sacrifices and suffering. Jesus killed evil and destroyed your sins on Good Friday. And, He gives all who live on Earth the grace to heave their darkest years into that fire. Your sacrifices and the consummate suffering of humankind are the accelerant to this cleansing manifestation. You absorb the shock that God felt when Adam decided to betray Him. Jesus paid that price, and you are the purse in which He has placed the Bill of Sale. This makes your purpose in Creation not only that of the sacrificial and saved, but of participant in the reconciliation between God and man. Jesus is the teacher who taught you to read the signs of God so that you can understand Him as Truth's Deific Word. You no longer require an interpreter or translator to communicate with Heaven because Jesus is alive in you, leading and guiding you in heart, mind, soul, and body. You are no more a lost race, but a chosen flock, a people set apart, a holy nation whose end is truly a beginning unlike any other nation founded on Earth or beyond it. The disciples you have become are led in unity rather than by majority. You live utterly committed to Truth instead of by compromise. You rest in Love and fail not by recanting or conceding. I ask you continuously to not allow time to deceive you from anticipating the Kingdom which is at hand. It is nigh for 2000 years, and is already timelessly here. You are not intended to weep for the days to come, but comprehend in joy that each one is a closing second in the final minutes of your own mortality. Your elation is not in the sadness of the passing of man, but in the arrival of immortality. I promise that the concepts you desire and the changes you seek of good will for all humankind have been placed in your hearts by God who first fashioned them. You could not wish for them without His Grace. You could not summon His urgency without His joy that a collective prodigal humanity is about to be returned to His arms. Imagine His ecstasy at this reunion! You have no worries that faith itself will not conquer. Nothing befalls you that your love cannot heal. I hope for your understanding that you will look at yourself and see how impatient you are. The little child in you will help you obliterate this impatience and assist you to relax and know that your Father God is with you and in complete control of your destiny, in and out of time. Hence, realize that all which has you worried has been conquered. Your existence in time is a period of great composure and prayer! You are standing on the top stair-step of God's Kingdom, knuckling the gate just as Jesus taught you. Remember that it was He who first came knocking at your door. And when God lifts the veil and opens that gate, you will see the Father you have known all along Face-to-face. All the evil that you bemoan was panoramically destroyed on the Cross. Satan is already dead. You are seeing only his scattered remains that will be wiped from Creation as the Triumph of My Immaculate Heart consumes the world like the release of the Imprisoned Light from the Torch you see. I wish for you to comprehend the vanquishing of the record of evil. It is difficult because it is man's lack of prayer that is causing you to witness its terrible debris. I have come to tell you that there is much greater power in the world than indifference, a strength that no evil can match. It is the tangible remnant of God on Earth, the Messiah He sent to save you, whose victory over the Cross has set you free. This remnant has sounded the death knell for the legacy of evil. I have told you of the relic of God on Earth who now is risen and living, and most powerful and strong, bowing to no man or authority, and able to destroy His worst mortal enemy with a simple holy thought. I resonate the redeeming power of your prayers and the Redeemer, Himself. No child of God will ever be lost to the fray of the world because Jesus' reach is far greater than any wayward stride. No child can hide beneath a table that has a transparent top. Jesus sees all and knows all. He has won you and will flush you out, and you will always laugh playfully as He pulls you by the feet upon your stomach back to Him. He says, *'Come here, you are Mine!'* I ask you today to continue to know that the record of evil is real, but it is already dead. Your body can be crushed, but your spirit shall never die. You live on in Jesus, no matter the course of human events, in a fragile and failing world. Yes, you may cry for the brokenhearted and despise evil, but remember in your heart the strength and hope accorded you by the Cross. Jesus will return in great Light and wipe every tear from your eyes, and Mine as well. My Special son, can you live in this hope? Can you call the Light upon your soul to lift your spirit? Your heart has always been of Love's Divine origin and God's salvific destiny."

Saturday, April 4, 1998
7:16 p.m.

"Good evening, My darling children. What a subscribing time this is for the world. As you prayerfully ponder the Passion and Crucifixion of Jesus, you also anticipate in joy your sharing in His Resurrection. God shows you through Palm Sunday that the fruits of a mortal life of righteousness are sweet. However, unless a grain of wheat falls to the ground, it remains only a grain of wheat. Therefore, you must follow Jesus to the Cross so you will flourish anew in His victory over the grave. Jesus has shown you that death does not stop Love or end your journey to God in Him. Mortality is your swift passage into His hands, to which Jesus has wholeheartedly commended you. You are not permanently confined to the depths of the Earth. God would not have it that way because He loves you so. He wishes your souls to be sown immortally and timelessly in Him. Since your acceptance of the Holy Cross has found and remade you, you also gain a renewed sense of the Sacraments of the Church. You know with fervor that God is for you, and no other can harm you. You are touched by the Grace of His absolution and healed by His Love. Many Saints who have gone before you have left their tears of thanksgiving trickling down the pews where they bowed their heads to pray. The Church's Sacraments are healing, reflective, and salvific. As these last ages pass away, many more will know the power of the Sacraments, especially the Rite of Reconciliation and the Most Blessed Sacrament, the Holy Eucharist. It is in these gifts that you conquer the Earth, in them that you travel through time. Yes, you circumvent the parameters of space to reunite perfectly with all Creation in an ageless Paradise. My children, I know that you come hungrily to this Table every day to be fed the nourishment of God's Love. It is with joy that He provides it, and it is with humility you should receive it. One day, you will finally realize that all things are perfect in God, and through Jesus all souls are perfected. My Love for you preceded the Son of Man into the material world. I will precede Him likewise as God ushers in the closing generation of mortality and the New Kingdom He has promised. Indeed, I am already here, so Jesus is near in coming. You feel My warmth and understand My message. Your greatest vision is displayed by your faith. This is what God wishes you to do. I urge you today to ponder the conclusion of Lent and the upcoming Feast of Divine Mercy. How the world needs to seek the charitable Mercy of My Jesus! How the weak should rest in Him! My Special son, the fountain of His Mercy is bountiful, but few come there to be quenched. God will have Mercy on the lost for the sake of the Sorrowful Passion of Jesus. When you have been washed in the Blood of the Lamb once slain for your Salvation, His Divine Mercy is perpetually yours. God promises with conviction that His Son did not die in vain. Indeed, He will not allow it. From the chambers of My Sorrowful Heart on that darkened Good Friday, I asked God to bless you as My little children. How happily He complied! How blessed you are, and how Blessed also am I, as is the Fruit of My Womb, the sweetest fruit ever borne unto the mortal Earth, My Jesus! As God has provided the Tree of Life, He now asks you to water its foundation with your tears for the joy and thanksgiving He seeks in you and with the sweat of your brow as you work tirelessly to aid My prayers and convert the lost. All of this we are doing together. My dear sweet sons, many things will be brought to fruition in the near future. I will dispense many graces and reveal countless signs before the world! I will assist you in the ensuing months to complete your Diary, and will help you deliver it to humanity. Your Diary is a seed that will grow a mountainous fruit from which the Earth will feed for the Wisdom of Jesus through Me. Yes, I ask you to work expeditiously on it, but not to rush its completion; you have no need to rush. God has fulfilled its purpose already before it has ever been exposed to the world. You see, your Diary is also a gift of His Divine Mercy because it is a revelatory lesson to everyone who sees it. Our labors are about the redemption of humanity; and as you will hear tomorrow and long thereafter concerning your Salvation, It is finished! So I come today with the Good News that Jesus will always love you. It is He who has saved you. Even if your lives are shortened, your work will never be in vain. Jesus has allowed thousands of souls on their deathbeds to see the contents of your Diary before they see Him Face-to-face. Not one in those thousands has refused to enter into Jesus' arms after having seen your Diary. Therefore, God is already employing it for His Sacred Glory and the Salvation of souls. All is in His hands, and you must trust Him."

Sunday, April 12, 1998
Paschal Feast of Easter
8:17 p.m.

"My dear little children, few are the days that marvel the souls of men, but this one is unequivocally the summit of human satisfaction. Easter Sunday is a premonition, your advance warning to prepare yourselves for the Second Coming of Jesus to take all He has saved to Heaven. Clad yourselves in new hope because everything I have told you is true. Your faith is reconciled in the miracles you have already witnessed. Cumbersome days cannot diminish the revelations you have known because unto you was born a Savior who lived perfect knowledge of your souls. And, He died in that same perfection to rescue you from the lost pit of perdition. His Dying destroyed your death. He paid the wage of sin, so that in rising from the grave, He also restored you not only to life, but to Eternal Life in Paradise, a timeless ecstasy in full view and radiance of the Face of God. You have observed many years of this Paschal Mystery, and you know full-well what it means. Humankind must seek to genuinely understand that Easter morning is celebrated so your soul will recognize the New Life it is soon to be offered. I will be there with you as we once and for all say goodbye to pain, grief, sorrow, and sacrifice. You have pondered the simultaneous ecstasies you will experience when Jesus comes to take you to Heaven. And, I wish for you to remember this message and this Easter Sunday at that great moment so you can turn to Me and acknowledge that My good wishes for your highest aspirations were well founded. They are a fruit of your faith in God and your love for Jesus. Soon, your hopes will be like fine pearls in your palms, yours to embrace and admire, your allowance for being good little children. You may run to the feet of the mighty Saints and say, *'Can I show you what I've got in my hand?'* All of these Saints already know you. They are helping you open your little hands and are asking Jesus to place many blessings there. It is sad that so few of My children honor the Saints or call upon their intercession. They are an invaluable source of strength for these difficult times. They help mend broken hearts and fractured lives. My children, as time continues and you move through it to the unknown revelations of the new century, you will feel more dependent upon the heavens. You will find a greater spiritual need to seek Jesus in forming all your actions and words. This is because your hearts are allowing you to accept your Savior. Your souls know their way home; and in your faith, you are not impeding their journey. You will be happy that you have chosen this course. It is the path to peace and redemption, your way to the hands of Jesus, the Anointed One whose victory over the grave you observe today. You are not recognizing a reincarnation, but rather a Resurrection! Jesus is alive, and is one and the same Love who lay in the manger and died on the Cross! This Love cannot die twice, and neither can you. You cannot fall from Paradise again, but you can assuredly regain it. Of all the intentions that God the Father has for Creation, and for all His countless universes, His most important wish is to ensure that your souls are neatly tucked-away in the endless freedom of Heaven. There you can adore and be adored without any hindrance of sorrow, with no material, time or obstructive space. When you presently walk through cemeteries, you are seeing the doorways at which are placed the empty shoes of a sad mortal journey for the millions now buried there. You have been told time and again that Jesus' Love is ageless. There are no birth and death dates on the golden streets and marble walls of Heaven. There are no shadows in Paradise that might cast a defining line on a letter of a gravestone monument. Light is everywhere, from all directions, many times more brilliant than the sun! It is endless and beautiful. Therefore, you know why I have come into the world. I wish to prepare you for the Light so you will not squint, cringe, or cower from the Glory you are accorded. How can Creation not know of the Life, Death, and Resurrection of their Savior? Because some choose to live in darkness, following the errant course. I have given birth to Divine Light into the world, a Love-Light that shines and asks to be reflected. Jesus knows those who have polished their souls to receive Him. He knows you to be My little children who obediently answer My call to Love, peace, prayer, fasting, and holiness. I am happy to appear on this pretty day, the High Feast of Easter! I thank you for again praying the Stations of the Cross this year. I am always with you every time you do, remembering the revelations of submission, sorrow, grief, Wisdom, and Sacrifice. All the souls of humanity were perfected on Good Friday in union with the grace of their baptism."

Thursday, April 16, 1998

PETITIONS TO OUR BLESSED LORD JESUS THROUGH HIS MIRACULOUS IMAGE ON THE SHROUD OF TURIN

Dear Master, through the Immaculate Heart of Your Most Holy Mother, I ask you to hear my supplications and petitions to Thy Divine Heart. You have loved us beyond the world and all our human capacity to understand. You love with the power of the heavens. I ask you to bring that love again to earth and allow all who are suffering the pains of sin and sorrow to drink again of fulfillment and that comforting peace that only You know how to bestow. I hope that you will respond to the holy desires of my heart for all mankind and not hold me away from You through a just repulsion of my weakest self. I hope for the greatness of Your beatific household to permeate the fortress-gates of Heaven and beam into the lives of all my brothers and sisters. I pray especially for those who are waiting and waiting, who are searching and pining for the Love that so few seem to find while here on earth. I pray for the ecstatic release of caged human hearts. Please remember those in prisons because of the ruthlessness of mankind. Release the bitterness from the hearts that wish to keep them there. Heal the world, Master......please.

With all my being, I thank you for the life you have given me, and most especially the brother you have placed with me to strengthen my heart. He shows me Your kindness and love. He supports my heart. He is truly my gift from You who are so high above the loneliness of this world. Hear the cries of the poor. Please be quick to answer their prayers for redemption and care. Free them from tyranny and terror. Bring the mighty down from their thrones, and lift-up the lowly. Give the entire world a new heart. Replace every heart with reality and eternity. Welcome great Redeemer-King! Come back into your world. Return to the vineyard. Glorify Yourself with Victory in our time and in this place. And allow each of us to be caught-up and share in Your victory. Erase the evil of this century! Rebuild every broken realm! Rock the foundations which have wrought such devastation. Arrest the foul ambitions of the proud worldlings. Give miraculous power to your children to carry away the spoils of Your victory. Unleash the imprisoned lightning. Draw Your sword of Light and knight your sons, then slay the dragon and the mocking beast!

Please hear all these desires and all I yearn for in the depths of my heart. I love you, My King. Truly, I am thankful for Your Mother. Thank you for letting Her be with me here and now in this world. She is the most beautiful gift You have ever given to the human race. With Her, I have everything. Please bless every person with great gifts who look upon Your Shroud in the coming months. I pray for the conversion of all heretics and protestors. I pray for the salvation of every soul ever given the breath to live on this earth. Save the children! Save the children! Save the children! Amen! Alleluia! Your humble son.

Friday, April 17, 1998
8:03 p.m.

"May the peace of our Risen Jesus be with you into all Eternity. My very loving and holy children, thank you for remaining ever faithful to My call, for your obedience and for your fidelity. Forever is God grateful that you have decided for Him. In the army of souls fighting for Love, you are His humble servants as well as the great masters. I have summoned you to participate in the glorious designs of God for His Creation, just as He has asked Me to intercede as His Mother and Mediator. I am your Heavenly Advocate, the Queen of Love with whom you shall soon reside. I call you to continue to anticipate with joy that grand eternal day. My children, together we experienced a highly powerful Rosary prayer group last evening. Thank you for your holy petitions! I give you many signs and graces to keep you strong and not desirous of the world. You look to Me and seek Heaven instead. My children, God guards your lives in ways that you cannot comprehend. In addition, I teach and guide you in protection and spiritual holiness. There are many miracles and endless days of grace soon coming into the world to help convert the lost. Monday of next week is a time of grace through Mother Angelica and a blessing to the many who are consecrated to My Immaculate Heart. All of these gifts are from God who loves you. He loves you as I love you, and He provides your existence from the beginning to the end. He unfurls the future through the servitude of your years and wishes you to see how you are serving Him every day you live. This is the consistency of your entire being. While you live, you allow Jesus the opportunity to enter His Creation. Your labors and your handiwork for lost sinners are precursors to the Salvation of millions of souls. This is why your Diary is so powerful. It is God's instrument, and you are playing it with finesse. Thank you for making such holy contributions to Paradise that is so much more complete. My Special son, you will be very pleased with this great gift to humankind, made possible by your own deferential obedience. Without your service, your brother's revelations of February 22, 1991 would have died before nightfall that day. It is you who make them live. This is because you are obedient; you love as God loves. I am asked now to tell you the most important part of this message, and yet perhaps the most simple. God is overwhelmingly touched by your friendship and love for His very special priest Father Schmidt. If only you could know the happy tears of Jesus as He watches you love His servant! This priest is so grateful to you both. He is praying especially for you now, and you know that God listens to him! You are about to see an even greater alliance of holy Christians stand by your side against evil. I simply ask that you do not question God in His Wisdom in drawing power from His suffering people to rebuke evil, convert souls, make reparation, and cleanse the Earth. This is where your faith is needed most. One day you will understand."

Friday, April 24, 1998
7:58 p.m.

"My dear loving children of one accord, you are bringing Light to human life in magnificent ways. No longer do you question whether God is for you. You do not worry what you must do to please Him. I have given you the answers to your frail inquisitions. You know how God wishes you to live in Him and totally for Him as He has done for you. My precious ones, I have brought you the Good News of Jesus, even when you believed He would test you beyond your strength. As a result of your trust, you have in your hands a very powerful and persuasive Diary to dispense to humanity. If it were meant only for you, God would have been sufficiently pleased, but imagine His ecstasy now in His Wisdom to present humankind with such a dialogue between Heaven and Earth. I have come today to pray with you and seek the invocation of the Holy Spirit to find everyone who is hiding away in sin. Your work must go on until the Son of Man returns to the Earth, even if this mission transcends your passing into His hands. Yes, you will then be a powerful Saint! But you are yet powerfully mortal, in a position to lead the Earth in word and deed to the Divine Mercy of Jesus. I ask you to recall with courage that such is a battle in time for a timeless victory. You will one day see that you have already won as of this day. Indeed, you became victors 2,000 years ago. Your days confuse you in the same way that they confounded the Apostles who asked *'Why is no one listening?'* It has been the same for twenty centuries. Many asked this question as they were about to be tortured and executed for their faith and undying love for God. Your days are not so filled with martyrdom, but with others' apathy and indifference, even greater enemies of their conversion. Your frustration is as ancient as Moses. You must not dwell upon what might have been, but on the little things you do daily to bring what will be. Therein lies the strength of your success. God does not ask you to equate your love with His own, but to be perfected in the way Jesus has taught. When you do this, God will accomplish the rest in the holy place He will occupy, once held hostage by your self will and agenda. Jesus is your Savior, representative, and benefactor. He is your wise and Wonderful Counselor, the Dayspring of Life. Jesus is I AM, the King of shepherds, the stronghold of all righteousness. He is the strength for the weak and comfort for the grieving. He is the health of the sick and guide for the lost. And most of all, He is the essence of Divine Love. This Love He gives you freely and without reservation. You cannot earn it, nor can you destroy it. Today, I wish to tell you that if anyone ever asks you to define Love, tell them that Love is the Bloodshed of Jesus Christ. There are those who say that God has no body. Tell them that He is both Body and Blood! Many believe that you cannot see God. Tell them that you can drink of Him from the Chalice and consume His Crucified Flesh. God wishes you to remember that He is Love and is therefore the presenter of the Fruits of Love, of the Holy Spirit. And not only is He the presenter, He is the Presence of the presentation, the summit of selflessness and perfect submission. For who else would lay down his life and be raised from the sepulcher for such a sinful people? Only Jesus who knows that perfect Love is sacrificial and eternal, Jesus who proved that death cannot destroy this Love. Your days are numbers, and you do not know where you are in them. But God knows! In this alone should stand your trust that He will also deliver you to endless day so there will no longer be a need for counting. You are a creation of Love—Love that wishes you to join the Feast Table of the heavens. No creature can destroy this desire in the Sacred Heart of God. It is destined to be. This will come to pass very soon, so lift up your hearts! It is right to give Him thanks and praise! You do well always and everywhere to give Him praise! All Creation calls Him Holy. This is the divinity which is your new inheritance because Jesus died and rendered you the beneficiaries of God's Will. You are the legal heirs to the entire estate of Jesus Christ. And Jesus has remembered everyone in His Will. The reading of this testament is the coming Judgment Day. The last testament is simultaneously the New Testament. Jesus will confer upon you a mansion that He has prepared for you! And this involves the miracle of the Resurrection. Jesus Himself, the Decedent, is again alive to read to all Creation His Last Will and Testament. You are very fortunate to inherit the treasures of Heaven which He has waiting for you there."

My brother and I recently saw a motion picture that dramatically depicted a great manmade disaster in which hundreds of people were lost. It was an intensely accurate accounting of this human tragedy, showing the contemptible divisions between rich and poor, and how our lives are fleeting. I was deeply moved as I contemplated the original catastrophe, envisioning how the Holy Spirit must have touched those who were thrust from exile into the presence of God. I could sense how the converting power of their loss transcends our day, even though they departed this life on a fateful night more than a half century ago. Every one of them still has significant meaning, emanating enormous converting light to our generation which suffers the same economic discrimination and moral blindness. Our Lady said,

"My Special son, I am happy that you discovered the beauty of this event in time. There are more dimensions occurring than you can imagine. Life has become imitated by art, and that art is leading a new generation to new life. This is the work of the Holy Spirit. I assure you that the peace you feel is real, that the timelessness is tangible. You are connected to a former age by terrible tragedy and mutual love, pulled into one capsule by your desire to transcend time like Jesus asks. I have been teaching you for many years to recognize the feelings you have aesthetically, not just emotionally. And you have learned well to see God in all things."

Our Blessed Mother also mentioned an altercation my brother had this past week. In preparation for the Paschal Triduum, a baptismal font is situated near the apse of most every sanctuary for the baptism of new members into the Catholic Church during the Easter Vigil. In one local parish, there had also been placed two very large baskets of plastic bottles beside the font. Parishioners were encouraged to fill them with Holy Water and take them home for sacred blessings. We noticed during the succeeding daily Masses that fewer and fewer bottles were being taken, and nearly a hundred remained. Given that it had been almost two weeks since Easter and no more bottles were being used, we thought everyone who desired to take one had already done so. My brother went to the church to fill a number of containers with Holy Water for distribution to area developmental institutions, homeless shelters, and for elderly shut-ins. As he filled one bottle after another, someone approached and confronted him, saying that he was not entitled to them as though he was stealing their candlesticks. Timothy stood firm in the Holy Spirit, rebuking the blindness that this person was peddling. It was obvious that no more containers would ever be used. After filling most of the bottles, my brother left to distribute them as we were directed during Easter Mass. Our Lady said,

"I must tell you that Jesus saw quite a fighter this week at the Cathedral as your brother bottled the Holy Water. He entered prepared for battle and was forced to utilize the grace I have given him. No human could have stopped him from sharing the Holy Water. He held his ground defiantly, and the cowardly enemy ran for cover. I will make sure that the Holy Water he rescued from the hands of the indifferent blesses and heals many lives. Again the question becomes, why did he have to nearly suffer cardiac arrest defending his action of getting the Holy Water? It is always the same; he had to face the forces of evil. The parallel is the same, why did Jesus have to die? God knows the answer, and you are learning it daily. Together, you and your brother are a strong union for God. You are fortunate; you are a living faith, the presence of the First Apostles. You have given your brothers and sisters the best of rooms, a place to lay their weary heads, food when they are hungry, freedom when they are captive, clothing when they are naked. You have done these things for them, and therefore for Jesus. If you could see yourself as

God sees you and as I see you, you would fall onto the floor in thanksgiving that you are winning the race. You are keeping the faith. You are fighting the good fight. You are a transfigured, faithful servant with whom God is well pleased. I pray that the rest of My children emulate your humble life when they come to realize your legacy. And they will! What you ask for is imminent. It is just over the horizon from their sights. The light of your love is breaking the dawn. This is why your reunion in Jesus will be perfect."

Monday, April 27, 1998

The brave warriors whom God calls "suffering humanity" provide the braille elevation needed by the faithless blind to know the Heart of Christ.

Friday, May 1, 1998
8:05 p.m.

"My dearly beloved children, how thankful I am to be with you tonight, how blessed is this place to accept the Love I bring. Children, the darkest of night is just before the dawn; and you are come to that place in time. You are seeing many repulsive things, but you must rejoice because their passing is near. You are seeing a world which both denies and dishonors God: An additional signal that your Redemption is at hand. You have heard the words, *Lead, O' kindly Light.* That is the Spirit in which you live as one for God. You follow Jesus and are yet His Light for many. I have asked you to walk softly and gently upon the ground. You have consented and are soon to reap the fruits of your humility. Your hearts have stored many souls in them, the souls of the lost which you are taking to Jesus. Such is your prayer, your great task at hand. The union of your hearts resembles a titanic vessel, filled with happy souls on their journey back to Jesus. Mightily you steam away from the port with your precious load, all of them waving goodbye to all that kept them bound. But, this mighty vessel will not sink. This maiden ship is also My Heart, and God Himself could not sink Her. Yes, you steam away from the last port as the waves lap in your wake. All of the majestic songs play at the sight of the launching of this ship; the angel-choirs sing in rhythm with the pulse of the waves. I have given this mighty vessel for you to bring to our God the souls you know are My sweet children. Now, upon the high seas, you hear My Son, your Savior, tell you, *Take Her to speed! My son. Let's spread Her wings*. So well you are doing what I asked so long ago, in 1991. The fireworks above this ship will not be a distress call, but a call to celebration. Let the celebration begin because the dawn of man has come. All of the boilers are fired and you are steaming toward the horizon, over which you will find your Home. Yes, let there be dancing and merrying between the rich and the poor! Let the gates of division be knocked-down as the affluent carry the feast-trays to feed those so-long locked behind them. Many times I have asked you to live this hope. It is now near the new reality as this month of flowers has begun. I have told you of many new allies about to come forward. You received a letter from one such unexpected ally today. This course will proceed. Thank you for your holy prayers which make this possible. I see that you both persist in discussing the seeming inconsistencies and ironies of God. Please remember that you cannot judge the heavens in the way that you judge the Earth. What you believe to be logical and practical is not the way of the divine purpose of an eternal and omnipotent God. Although He can survive without your praise, you will not survive unless you praise Him. God asks you to lift Jesus before the world, and Jesus will draw all upward to God. But lifting Jesus is more than just the message of a miraculous Virgin Conception. He is the Living Word by which all men must live. His lessons and legacy are alive today to be learned anew by each passing generation. This is why you are called to pray and evangelize. And in all your efforts, you do not know how much good you are doing to advance the Kingdom of Heaven on Earth. You live and love prayerfully. Please pray quietly while we enjoy a reminder of the workings of the Holy Spirit."

Our Lady asked me to listen to a musical score that is particularly heart-touching to anyone who hears it.

"This is the sonic memory that holds your heart fast to the Love that death could not destroy. And as you lift Jesus' Name into the world, as you do His work, pray in the way He taught and plead for the coming of My petitions because you are composing and performing a work for God who hears you in the same way that you listen to this beautiful composition. Your arrangement is as beautiful to God. Just as He reminds Himself in justice that He would destroy a city because there are only unrepentant sinners there, your works evoke His compassion by keeping Him bound to the beauty of your love for the lost. He finds solace and spares the city because, before your work is through, you will have converted them all. God hears the love pouring from your life. He is satisfied that in you, Justice is served. It is served because you emulate the Mercy that Jesus gave the world, His Life, Death, and Resurrection, forgiveness, and Sacraments. Indeed, vengeance is the possession of God who disposes it to the last chamber of time, and in this bringing-forth is the beauty of your compassion for His children. You must realize your very role of advocate for humankind. Therein lies your answer when others ask what Jesus in now doing. Answer them by showing your living example. You need not say anything more, simply live as Jesus asks. This you do very well. The world bubbles and brawls, but you remain above it."

Friday, May 8, 1998
7:42 p.m.

"My dear special little children, I am the Mother of all your hopes and the reason for your happiness. Far too many days have you been obedient to Me than to have you now relinquish your trust in God in exchange for your own will. I am the author of the most beautiful words in Creation and the Matriarch of the Most Sacred Heart. Remember that as long as you live in this grace, your work reflects My work. I wish to tell you that all our years of laboring are culminating presently and in the near future. These are the times for which Jesus wept on the Cross, not just because many would not follow Him, but because of those who say they will harbor their own reservations, rules, demands, and expectations in exchange for their faith. The completion of your mission is at hand, and I understand why you perceive the final stages as being cumbersome. This is an extremely difficult time in your lives. Despite what is obvious and apparent, you are already succeeding, humanity is converting, your allies are arriving, and you must join them solemnly and steadfastly. This must be a joy for you, a prayer with each minute that passes. And, thank you for providing food for the poor. All of these good things are kind acts of praise to God and the Holy Spirit. You are living the Love of Jesus. It is your dedication that is making My messages possible, your vision that is perfectly of God. I can do nothing without the help and prayers of My obedient children. Thank you for your petitions and for your compliance."

Wednesday, May 13, 1998

The Good Game

It seems apparent to me that God must truly love a good contest. It appears that the conversion of His people will come only as a last-minute rally in time. He authored the rules and provides the playing-field. By His hand, we hold just enough to stay ahead of the awful opponent. And, we live as though there is still a doubt as to the outcome that God already knows. What is in doubt is the destiny of individual souls. While our victory is imminent, there are some of the players who are not contributing to the winning margin. Some are lost, others are ignorant of the circumstances, and still more are too busy admiring their own skills.

All too obvious to me is that God wishes our union in Him to be a come-from-behind win. Through the holy prayers of the millions of faithful worldwide, I believe that we should have a comfortable lead. But then, I cannot see the scoreboard from where I am sitting. I think, perhaps, we do not place enough stock in the persuasive power of our cheering section; the Saints and Angels. Their cheers can drown-out the cries of our sorrows. But of course, they have the best rally cry which they keep repeating in hopes that we will join in—the Hail Mary.

Why does it seem so often that our Head Coach makes us spend our lives sitting on the bench? After all, He knows our talents and abilities because He died to ingrain them in us. Coach Jesus must surely know how anxious we are to play! Well, at least we wear the good uniform and gather in the same huddle as the masters of the game. It is good to hear once in awhile that they are keeping us in the lead. But, from where I sit, I think we could use a more aggressive strategy, one that will put the game out of reach, well ahead of the expiration of playing time. I guess I will just sit on the edge of my little place here until Jesus decides I will not blow the lead if He puts me in. Or is He just saving the best 'til last?

Friday, May 15, 1998
7:16 p.m.

"I love you and protect you, My little children. You are the joy of My Heart, the reason why My soul proclaims the goodness of the Lord and magnifies His Grace. My children, I have come today in response to your prayers. I am asked to tell you that you realize how determined is God to ensure that your Diary is very pretty, stately, and holy. Many things are now occurring in preparation for the presentation of your Diary to the world. You do not understand all of them, but you soon will. Please do not allow your curiosities to distract you. My Special one, I wish for you to remember that God will deploy every venue He chooses to ensure the victory and sanctity of your Diary. You are a wise young man, too wise to fail. You must realize in what great position this places you as God sees your soul. Jesus wishes to thank you for allowing Him to glorify His Father through your prayerful supplications last evening. These were among your most heartfelt and powerful petitions. I am also asked to tell you that the work on your Diary is further ahead of schedule than it has ever been. Do what you wish to prepare, but have no anxiety about the date of the release of your Diary. Imagine your fate if you had no computer or word processor, if you had only the quill of Sister Faustina or perhaps Saint Bernadette. Theirs was a very arduous task. Your life is easy. Thank you for embracing the Wisdom of God. As you look around the globe, you see the genius in God's work. And, His Wisdom is magnified by your holy prayers. I will close tonight by telling you that if you only could foresee the outcome of the Earth, you would go into the street and dance until dawn! Please trust My words."

Friday, May 22, 1998
6:58 p.m.

"Your days and years are moving swiftly before you, My children, taking you along the current of life and time. I am with you to guide you past the rapids of anxiety and difficulty. You move quickly through the hours because you realize that your hope is at the Bay of Hearts, holy and poised to welcome you there. My children, you are about to commemorate in a secular way the memory of all who have died, especially those who perished for their political freedom. These war dead fought for global governments, not for Eternal Life. However, this is an apt opportunity to pray for all souls who are in Purgatory. Today My Special son, you reached-out for change and received a significant signal grace. All change is your decision. You live in a land of vast opportunity, and you will continue to pray, no matter what your decision. I wish for all My little children to pray, in every station and all vocations. Jesus asks all who follow Him to pray for those who do not. Every mortal heart is expected to ask Jesus for help, and all must petition for the conditions in the world. I tell you, My children, that those who decline to pray will be asked a litany of questions at the Final Judgment. For example, those who will not pray to end abortion will be asked if they are against abortion on the Day of Judgment. If they respond affirmatively, they will be asked why they did not beseech God to end it. If they say no, their souls will be laid bare, and they will be unable to withstand it. This is the case for all vices and sins, all transgressions and aberrations. God the Father expects you to pray in union with the Heavenly Court so Creation will be transformed. This is why I have come, My children, to ask you to pray. Thank you for tending to all that I ask. You can rest assured that your petitions are cultivating the Earth, rendering it a more holy place for the representatives of God to visit. My Special son, you are particularly more blessed each day. I hope you like the pretty passages given by the Angels of Light to serve as the Epilogue to your Diary. Jesus knew what you wanted, and equally important, He knew what He desired. There is great power and perspective in the Epilogue. It is an opening, an invitation for all who have lived the Diary to also begin a new life in Jesus with the prospect of hope and service. There is great responsibility to our opus to which everyone who reads your Diary will be called. All the work that you are doing is coming to completion, and you will have to guard against the temptation to say that it is done too soon. Jesus is about to return to the Earth, but you must not have anxiety if He chooses to wait a series of years. I can assure you that His Wisdom tells Me that it will not be much longer. I had the great fortune of having been correct in all occasions and cases in past centuries. If you continue to work slowly and carefully, your Diary will be beyond reproach by any mortal. I am guiding you so that it will be perfect."

Friday, May 29, 1998
7:12 p.m.

"My very holy and beautiful children are the joy of My Heart and the reason I hope for the conversion of humanity. You are the splendid laborers whose pain and suffering emulate My Son. It is not easy to realize the perfection to which you are called because there are only a few mere mortals to provide you good example. Today is a good day because it is another during which you have maintained your Consecration to the Sacred Heart of Jesus. My children, do you hear the airplane that just passed? *(We live near an airport, and an airplane had flown loudly over the house only seconds before.)* It subtly reminds you of the world above. And, the flight of the Holy Spirit calls you to lift your hearts to be carried to happiness. The sweet song that Paradise sings is audible to your souls. When you are praying in unison with the Hosts of the Heavens, you can hear this sacred melody. Together we have been meditating and communicating for several years. I am the same pretty Lady who first came to you during the cold winter morning in February 1991. My Grace is as faithful to you, and My message is the same. As you can see, God does not change, nor is the perfection to which you are called diminished by the element of time. My children, time is indeed passing, but it has not yet altogether expired. Therefore, the days that remain shall determine the destiny of many souls. I ask you to consider this when you pray and as you counsel yourselves and each other. My Love will always be a valuable asset in your struggles. Call upon Me, and I will help you. My Jesus is the door through which you must enter to garner the everlasting joy that the world is now seeking. You may call Him Savior and Lord, Brother and Teacher, Benefactor and Friend. Above all, He is the Fount of Mercy to whom all souls must come for the refreshing new beginning that God provides. Yes, your Judge is also your Advocate, and your Teacher is likewise your Servant. And, Jesus humbly beseeches you to remember that it is in His pardon that you are so blessed. Through the Feast of His Divine Flesh, you savor the liberty that your soul desires, no longer sinfully bound in your mortal frame. God grants you the ease of flight through the Holy Eucharist without your feet ever departing the ground. Your angelic rise is made possible because your faith elevates you to the ranks of believers who have already passed into Eternity. This is why I urge you to remember that you are held in such great esteem by God, because you return daily to the Feast of Plenty. At the Table of the Lord, you are no longer simply human, but are inherently divine by renewed nature. Behind the capacity of your consciousness and comprehension lies a sea of bliss upon which your soul sails as you exit the doorway of the Church, making you a different person in a now better world. During the moments immediately succeeding the Holy Mass are the times of triumph when God flashes the sign of victory to the ages. And, it began with the smallest shake of a boulder which had previously entombed a slain Messiah. The stone shuddered a bit, and particles of dust fell from its surface. It then moved a little more, and the whole created Earth and Nature looked at it as though it was an extraterrestrial specimen from another universe. And while all Angels watched with glee, the stone was rolled aside, and out like a beam of Light came the Savior who once was dead, but now is forever alive, to claim the Earth from the jowls of the evil He had just destroyed. And, arriving to the Light of day, the Dawn of all dawns, the Riser, Jesus-Anointed stood with His fists poised on His hips and legs upright like titans, strong and surefooted, vowing to never again allow a mortal creature to scourge or spate upon Him. This is the new beginning that Jesus has given to you. You are raised with Him and in Him; you are the new light for an advancing age, separated from darkness, regression, hatred and oppression; freed from every ill and evil, a people set apart. In this confidence, you will live the rest of your days and never cower from the forces who oppose the goodness you bring to the Earth. You can never again be a people of ignorance or indifference because you have known the Truth that now lives in your hearts. I urge you to contemplate this joy when someone asks why you pray so often. I petition your souls to recall the blessings they received on Resurrection Morning and the power you regained at Pentecost. This stone now represents the world that you yourselves can move from blocking your paths, to shake the dust of indifference from its surface to be trampled underfoot. You worry needlessly about the passing years; there are so many seemingly so meaningless. However, to you with each day is coming the power you wish to wield and the Creation you desire to know. I can offer you no other than the Truth of this revelation. The trust and faith in My words must come from you, from your holy will becoming every day more compliant with the Divine Plan of God. And you look around the globe and say, *who will change the errant nature of the days of men, who will heal, who will admonish, and who will redeem?* You are seeing Jesus doing these things as each hour passes, just as He said on the Mountain of Calvary. He told humankind, indeed all Creation, that *It is finished!* He set about to effect the new beginning when He rose from the dead. I ask you to remember with joy that He did these things for you. This day is nearly done, but it has been special. There will be many more auspicious ones to follow. It is the seventh anniversary of My letter to the impoverished tenants on Sunday. Many of them listened, and they now pray with Me. Thank you very much for your holy prayers. God hears every one."

Friday, June 5, 1998
7:43 p.m.

"My precious little children, the many Saints in Heaven are supporting you in ways that you do not realize. God has allowed this for the glory of your Diary. Just because you do not see these things does not mean they are not occurring. You are like slaves toiling in the engine room, stoking the coal furnaces, while the passengers are enjoying the fruits of your labors with the ease and joy that your sacrificial life is bringing them. I have never told you that your obedience would be easy. Likewise, God's obedience in sending His Son was not easy. A perfect Man-God died on the Cross for all humankind, for all generations to come. He wished for every soul to stand on that hill and see Him, so the Crucifixion has been manifested throughout all time. It is the same with your holy work. I have offered you sufficient reason to be jubilant. I have given you a beautiful Diary. You have been humbly receptive, but only periodically happy. Therefore, please pray with Me. Pray from deep within your hearts! I do not own the venue to alter the world unless you help Me through your daily prayers. I cannot fathom My efforts without your petitions. There is nothing on the Earth that has the force to make you unhappy. Nothing. I urge you to remember to pray for the unborn and for the poor souls in Purgatory. Remember also to ask God for an increase in vocations, especially more priests. Please do not abandon Me."

Monday, June 8, 1998
3:19 p.m.

"My pretty children, this is your loving Mother to whom I ask you to give your lives, your prayers, your all. You are now being more happy, and God knows your efforts. Please continue to progress toward the feelings of accomplishment that He wishes you to acknowledge. Thank you for helping each other and for praying with each other. It is very special that you are attending the daily Mass. Thank you, My children. Thank you for accepting the joy that you are coming to know. You will be elated with the finished Diary if only you will trust Me."

Friday, June 12, 1998
7:21 p.m.

"My loving children, now is the time during which you must validate your acceptance of the Love of God for your souls. Regardless of whether you feel that the rest of the world is joyfully converting, you must continue in confidence that they are, and that it is Me bringing it about. I ask for you to trust both My words and the power of My intercession. You can do nothing wrong in the eyes of God if you give yourselves completely in obedience to Me. Through Me, God requires your conviction and your joy, for in such is proof that you are living fruitfully the new life Jesus has brought. Remember that humanity is ultimately responsible for this imperfect world. Jesus has come to perfect it, and is already forthrightly doing so. Therein lives the fulfillment of your every hope and the realizing of your happy dreams. You have been told that to hope is to pray. I am with you in prayer to ask you to hope with great intensity. In this too resides a great source of joy. My children, God and I have been watching your lives very closely during the past week. You are turning your hearts in joy to Jesus, but now you must transform this inward joy into outward happiness. We hope you will be able to do so. God has prepared Me to tell you that He knows of your love for Him, for Jesus and for Me. I am asked to remind you that it is the Holy Spirit within you who allows you to perceive and accept this Holy Love. This has come true because you are willing to try. God has great affection for the Saints and for you who still beseech their intercessory prayers. He loves you beyond your mortal comprehension, and His Divine Mercy tempers His Justice in such a way as to require contrition and servitude from everyone who wishes to know Him better. Therefore, He asks that in reciprocation, you review the life of a living Saint, one you have already seen, as a reflection of what He asks of His people."

I was asked to review the life's work of a man who has been the epitome of humanitarian charity around the globe.

"He is a servant who will soon be called to the beauty of the eternal life he has been so humbly pursuing. You were instructed to watch this because in the eyes through which you are asked to see, it should bring you great joy. Try to contemplate the joy with which God perceives what you just viewed. And yet, this man is but an infant running around and between the legs of his loving Father God. You are given few twentieth-century examples, but those you encounter should keep hope in your heart that Jesus is pleased by the progress of the world. And too, God sees the little people in small places with the same joy that He sees national leaders. I come to you tonight with many valid reasons why you should hope with true happiness. The road is long and the journey oftentimes difficult, but Jesus will help you every step of the way. Hence, I am happy to announce the continuance of your messages. God believes My intercession to you to be worthy, benevolent, and righteous. I am thankful to you for making the changes to your focus on Creation so that God can sense your joy in what He has done for you. These are the waning days of the twentieth century, and the most important since My Glorious Coronation as Queen of Heaven. You have the opportunity to serve the Almighty Father in the way of the First Apostles whom Jesus Himself chose. Please carry on with the knowledge that we will succeed in every imaginable way."

Friday, June 19, 1998
7:10 p.m.

"My sweet and dearly beloved children, I am your Mother who has come in peace. You are the progeny of God and servants of His humble charity. You desire to know His Sacred Heart, and you do so through My Immaculate Heart. Today, My children, I remind you that God is no distance from you, and you are no time away from Him. Whenever you receive My messages, you transcend the hours, days, and years to unite with the Light of Heaven. This is a High Feast of the Most Sacred Heart. You live and dine at the Table of this Sacred Heart, and know your joy because of Him. It is in response to your faith that I have returned to this holy place to continue to bless you with heavenly messages. I have taught you many things and given you endless signs through mighty graces. God wishes you to understand that He knows your every thought before you formulate it, and He hears your every prayer before you lift it. He offers a tangible example of His timeless omnipotence tonight to show you that He precedes and succeeds your every utterance and action. God is aware that you enjoy speeches that raise the hopes of the lost to lofty new heights. He has asked Me to have you deliver this address in honor of His Most Sacred Heart. Millions will hear it."

I received the text that Our Lady handed me. I then stood and began reciting it -

There is a God who came to earth..... a fleshly being of perfect devotion and noble purpose, who wished through His very soul that we would come to know the happiness that without Him we could never taste. God named Him Jesus and called Him the Christ because He is Anointed. And, one in being with the Father, He is also Wonderful Counselor and Prince of Peace. He came and went, but what happened in-between would change the course and destiny of the entire universe. What is most important, He said that He would come back. So, if we hear a knock on our door as loud and beautiful as lightning opening the skies, we should not be surprised to see this finely-clad King telling us that He has the authority of God to bring us to justice and to reward. If He tells us to kneel, we must fall silently to our knees in reverence. We will know to do this because we will recognize His power for gently commanding all nature and all men to yield to His grace. And, we will look up at Him with bliss, our hearts barely beating quickly enough to keep pace with our joy. Yes, we will fall as this Man places His will over our own like a protective shield and gentle father about to feed His aching children the manna of new life that will paralyze our spirits into ecstatic submission. By the very look on His face, He will forthrightly conscript us into being volunteer slaves for His cause. With His palm, He will cradle our souls and pull us to His breast. And with His orchestration of eternal power, He will cast a spell on His humanity from which we will have no desire to escape. And, we will reach-out for Him, humbly and lovingly.

We will move one soul at a time, rhythmically to His embrace. Our anticipation will be that of a child in a candy store with the merchant's hand on the lid of our favorite sweet, about to lift its top and present to us a Paradise which we can never really earn. When this Jesus brings us His land, we will be face-to-face with a beauty that only He can bring, allowing us to see the previously unseen magnificence of His inner-self, but also the dimensionless brilliance of His universal being. Even when His light seems blinding to our eyes, we will still be able to see the heretofore undefined beauty that made Him a Man over men with a strength and awe for which we would all fight and die.

Indeed, He said that He would come back. And, as soon as the pupils of our eyes meet His face, we will crawl and beg to see more and know more. Eternity itself will be too short. His fragrance will be sweet and unconquerable, with a pleasing texture-of-heart which will prime our appetites for the freedom of His bountiful Kingdom. We will follow Him in remembrance and celebration of our faith in Him and knowledge of His promise. We will know Him as He who was tortured and killed by a group of mortal heretics and terrorists whose atheistic agenda was so profound that not even God would live among it. And yet, ironically, by His very passing, this Martyr has simultaneously delivered even their souls into Paradise with His own. When He comes again, we will embrace as one love in complete unity. We will thank this Fighter and Artist for signing our names in the Book of Life with His own Precious Blood.

As I finished, there was a thundering roar as if I was standing inside a giant stadium. I heard a throng of cheering and clapping spectators whose size was beyond imagining, sounding an ovation which brought tears to my eyes. Our Lady was trying to speak to me through the laudatory adulation,

"I cannot continue until the deafening applause lays down around Me. Please ask the Saints to allow Me to continue, and thank them. My little son, can you hear Me? Yes, My little one, you have spoken immortal words to a newly redeemed Creation. Our spirits are in unison with the peace of God. He knows your desires, designs, and purposes; and you accomplish everything through Him. Even when you do not know it, you are finishing the work of Jesus. All human actions, when done in love for one another, lead to the Return of Christ into His Kingdom. Jesus has transformed your labors for Him into the magnificent praise that you just proclaimed. You are serving God's Plan! I am heartened and God is pleased by the newfound happiness you are living. All we ask is a chance; all we seek is your openness and hope, your trust in the Will of God. It is in these things that you are perpetually blessed. He has prepared a place in Heaven with many mansions in advance of your passing into His arms."

Friday, June 26, 1998
7:37 p.m.

"My dearly beloved and beautiful children, your souls are more precious than gold, and your hearts are sweet as honey in the summertime breeze. I have come on this day to remind you of the simple eloquence in which I have dressed you for the coming days of Glory. I am confident that you will know My Jesus when He comes to greet you at the great wedding of Heaven and Earth. I am now transforming your writing with the same stately eloquence so that it simply portrays the beauty of the mansions of Heaven. Those who read it will pine for the Grace it gives to the soul. Be careful not to be possessed by a spirit of urgency when you see that My work is often painstakingly slow. Yes, My messages are urgent in nature, but they must be pretty and articulate. That is what I am helping you accomplish as we work weekly toward that goal. It is through this same understanding that you continue to pray in reflection of My desires. Your journeys to the hills of Croatia provided you both with an awakening, but your true transformation has taken place here in this hallowed house, blessed by a Bishop, Myself, and Jesus. This has for the past eight years cultivated your own conscience, purity, and prayerfulness for the sake of yourselves and many. I desire that you continue this progress as I pray with you and for you. Your participation in the Sacraments keeps you holy and feeds you the joy of the Truth which God provides through them. He will give you the opportunity to keep your promises when you proclaim your life in Him. That Grace is of the power of Jesus to manifest Himself through all good things. The greatness is in Jesus' teaching and providing the opportunity for you to display His Love. Please see this for all who come to Jesus for strength and conversion. God is almighty, and yet so simple in the life He gives to His people. He does not require you to be a great statesman, but a simple messenger for His peace and providence. I am sent to tell you, however, that the two of you are simple messengers who are providing a monumental message for the world in your pretty work. It will be seen as the Final Colossus.

You have been displaying your happiness for which God is entirely grateful. You are hearing My words with obedience. It is through this obedience that I am able to dispense to you grace after grace, upon bountiful grace. I am the Mother of the Catholic Church, the Original and True Church of Jesus Christ. I am also the Mother of all people everywhere, and I will see to it that everyone at last finds their way back to the Sacraments. Pray for the homeless and for those who do not know God. Pray for the end of abortion and the poor souls in Purgatory. Thank you for lifting your prayers to the heavens today. I will speak to you again very soon. I love you. Goodnight!"

Friday, July 3, 1998
7:25 p.m.

"My wonderful children, the sweetness of My being, I greet you with the joy of the Holy Spirit. I am happy because of your pious works and prayerful hearts. You are living as I have asked; and because you are doing so, Jesus is ratifying your lives in Him. I can now be more hopeful that the world will change because of your participation. My children, God has great power on Earth because you are wielding the weapons He has placed in your hands. And, My Special one, you are being given very meaningful meditations. Every substance I have given you will be utilized toward the conversion of humanity. God is a Miracle Worker, and He defeats the evil father of fear and lies with the very things you have feared in your lives. I assure you that your enemies will be pulverized by the bountiful truth of your Diary. Its depth is great and its elevation remarkable. With the help of the Angels, these are the determining hours of its most powerful content; and this is why your vision will prevail. Your Diary contains the words that thousands have always wanted to say. Everyone will recognize their future in them, and you will be taken by its awesome magnitude. God will place the power to the words that you have inscribed on paper. You will finally know yourselves as instruments in His hands. This is because you have welcomed Me here! You have prayed and become holy. It is your wholesome credibility that will lend great credence to My messages. You are witnessing countless manifestations of God. I cannot tell you why He wills some things, I simply come to reveal what they are. As you can see, God does the rest powerfully."

Friday, July 10, 1998
6:59 p.m.

"My very beautiful children who are consecrated to the Hearts of Grace and Salvation, Eternity hears your pleas for intercession. My call is God's response for your yearning to know Him perfectly, without impedance or interruption. Your prayerfulness continues, and My presence is Heaven's answer. I am utterly elated by the progress of your work. The world is about to be taken aback by the beauty, symbolism, and revelation of your first Diary. Yours is the standard by which all other eloquence shall be judged. You will someday discover that you will envy the young, and that aging is a resilient opposition. Remember with courage what you will never fear again. Thank you for praying so faithfully and for participating in the sacrifices that help make mankind whole."

Saturday, July 18, 1998
12:53 p.m.

"Thank you, My dear children, for lifting your holy prayers to the heavens with such fortitude, faith, grace, love, and thanksgiving. It is only through your prayers that I can succeed. The work of your hands promulgates great holiness in those who know you because you are given to My Jesus. God is glorified by the Rosaries which you kindly offer for the veneration of My name. My children, you do not fully understand the power of these days. You cannot yet comprehend the fortress you have built to keep evil away from many helpless souls who are unable to fend for themselves. To them, you are their hope for a better life and brighter future. My children, you have met thousands who have fought against the attacks of evil for many years. All of their suffering will be understood through the vision in your Diary. Lonely hours will be supplanted by days of fulfillment. The pains of memory will be replaced by new hopes for the dawning of tomorrow. This is a great time of peace and revelation because the codex you are finishing will bring the difference they are about to live. The work I have asked you to do is holy and sanctioned, and it is having publicly-pious repercussions. Please do not fell your own faith; it is a gift from God that you must never cast aside! There is a burden of Scripture to which I wish to direct you. *'God makes all things work together for the good of those who love Him.'* This is the summation of your days and the destiny of your purpose. There is no doubt or question in faith. I will repay your obedience in many concurrent ways. You should express your gratitude to the Saints for their intercession. My Angels have told you of the advocacy of Saints Veronica, John of Iberian, Bonaventure, and Boniface. You must remember the graces and blessings procured on your behalf by them in your prayers. This is the continuation of the preparation of the public for your Diary. It is to prepare those who know you for the Truth to which you have dedicated the last nine years of your life. *(My brother and I traveled to Medjugorje in 1989.)* All of your work has been stored in Paradise like the aging of a fine wine that God will serve to mortals on the Earth and the Hosts of the Heavens. Humanity is converting, as Jesus knew these times would reveal. You must never allow your inhibitions to diminish your hopes. This statement will have greater meaning in the future for your commanding defense of Jesus and your holy Diary. I love you and wish for you to become one with Me through the Holy Spirit for all the future and beyond all time. This is precisely what you are now accomplishing. Nothing anyone might say about your Diary that would make you feel a sense of scandal, guilt, or violation is from God or His Angels. I wish for you to be happy in every infinite way, given by the Grace of God. The holy words you are receiving are His blessings poured-forth in audible form. You are wholesomely worthy, and the Earth is sanctified by your lives. Never question the empathy or intentions of My Angels."

Friday, July 24, 1998
7:09 p.m.

It can be seen, you know, this Heaven that seemingly eludes us. Oh! But it is us who elude it! With purpose of evasion, we tell Our Lord that we are weak in might, while He truly knows that we are weak in faith. To the faithless, He distributes trial. The day that He carefully sifted the sands upon the desert, He was practicing to bring the finer souls into His glory, parting-out the coarse and rude, the impure, the arrogant, and the obstinate. Oh! Maybe we could glorify His mightiness in rhyme! "That great canyon described so grand was truly a scar upon His hand!" But, our rhymes are much too trite to praise a God of His might! Yes, He is everywhere in our world. The great clouds that rush over the ocean are the blink of His eye! Just fathom His view! And, I have seen many heavenly things that tell me He is there. I saw a lion once carrying a fawn in his mouth to the feet of its mother. And, I saw an angel perched on the bridge of a guillotine. But, we will not forget the new capitol buildings transformed into the shape of the Cross! Fifty-one of them! Yes, one for a new nation truly under God! And, if the winds are His breath and the forests His beard, then surely the rains are His tears. And, the rivers the sweat of His brow!

In Heaven, the summit no longer despises the valley. The rooster will rock us to sleep! And, lyrics to songs about love are the signs along the roadways with no distance between. So, set your soul upon your heart and hand it to God on your fingertips. This Heaven is here, where three equals one, where diamonds are free, and rubies are there for the taking. And, you will see all the children you never had! And, those who died say it was you who left them; they paid you in full, their body was your receipt! This Heaven of ours is our field, the Moon is first base; we cook our steaks upon the sun as we laughingly play catch with the stars. But, who slid into first and punctured his tail? It was just a tiny American flag! And, then I saw someone in Heaven I did not know was there. And, he thanked me for introducing him to Jesus. Then, I knew it really was Heaven! And, I had to rush to see Jesus again to return His sandals He lent me on the Earth! It was a very smooth path after that! I thought I would miss not seeing tomorrow before I knew that it was today. And yestertime was just yester-world that has long since fallen away! Oh! There is a rhyme again! It must be the fault of my pen!

"You are My children in whom piousness abounds. Yes, My little ones, I am the Holy Mother of your Lord who is still speaking to you after so many years. I continue because you are happy in faith, in your acceptance of the Love for Our Jesus. Today is a special day because the world is much more holy, made so by your Rosary group last evening. I am grateful that you continue to petition God in such admirable ways. Please never worry, I am your Perpetual Help. I have come again today simply to tell you that I love you compassionately. You have mitigated many human errors in seven and one-half years. I am confident that you will see the fruits born of your labors in your lifetime. God is working through you in ways that build your credibility. Your reputation is completely intact. My Special one, you can see the means by which the Lord is elevating you both. God has only begun to fight! It is inexplicable by words, the reward that is awaiting you. You will be taking millions in your hands to Jesus saying, *'My Lord, I have brought these souls to your Mercy.'* Today, you are again very tired. I have noticed that the hours you set aside for resting, you rarely rest at all. You likewise should remember your nourishment. This is why you are weak. I have been traveling around the globe, blessing the faithful in many ways. You and your brother are doing well in all that I have taught you. You have only a few hours work remaining on your first Diary. You are almost there! However, as you say, some of your prettiest messages were received after February 1997. You have as much to do as you desire to achieve. We are about to begin the march of your first Diary around the world. I am with you every day to bless your labors. At times when you step back from it, you can see its spiritual power, so your hope is not in vain. Jesus is with you to keep you strong. Yes, glowing like a Morning Star! I am asked to tell you that your pretty Consecration to My Immaculate Heart that you wrote has procured thousands of souls for presentation to My Grace."

Friday, July 31, 1998
7:01 p.m.

"My dear gracious children, through you God is manifesting the cultivation of the Earth and the conversion of many souls. Please remember that you have no power that is not granted by the Almighty Father in Heaven. As you can see by the last holy developments in your Diary, your work has become very powerful indeed. My little children, I have been asked to seek your continuing yield to the Holy Spirit and to My Grace, as together we complete the first of your diaries. I know what I am requested to say to humanity, and I realize its full effect. I have Wisdom because I am the Mother of Wisdom. Therefore, you must continue in prayerful obedience. I am protecting you and your work from scandal. There is turpitude lurking from all directions that you cannot detect, and this is why I am making amendments that you may not completely understand. My Special son, you can see with what fidelity your brother has relinquished his will and his life so that your Diary can be completed. The intercession of the Angels has added universal dimension, power, and authority to your work. It is a monumental piece that will shock this nation. However, you must stay out of the way while we together make the final alterations. I assure you that if you do not, God will place your Diary beneath the soil in a cemetery somewhere, and we will lower our heads and weep about what might have been. Looking at your writing, everyone can observe its human and divine attributes. It will bring into the livingrooms and dens in homes all across America the miracles you have witnessed for nearly eight years. Even when you think about them, you are shocked by their sublimity, beauty, and meaning. Your Diary has taken on a new presence. It elevates the intentions for all the prayers I have asked humankind to lift. I have taught you how to pray and love, and the benefit is reaped between yourselves and the Holy Spirit. Your Diary resounds with poetry and justice. This is the enlightenment emanating from your hearts. I wish you knew the anticipation that the Heavenly Court holds for it. Your brother resigned his office seven years ago yesterday. He did so with the aspiration that we would arrive at the success you are poised to achieve. You are standing at that brink, and God will reward you both for giving your lives to Him. Be wise and discreet in your writing, but be emboldened by your faith. I will always help you."

Friday, August 7, 1998
7:03 p.m.

"My dear faithful children, I am pleased to return to this holy place to speak to My children that I love so heartily in return. These are the days that mark the culmination of a great amount of work that you have done over many years for Jesus. My Special child, when you were younger, you constructed rockets for launching into the skies. You are similarly making the Diary that will soar into the heavens with the force of such a rocket. You have already constructed the missile-shaped fuselage. Now, there are a great number of wires that run to the primary thrusters. There are two hundred of them that are now being placed on their proper leads.* You are placing the fuel in the boosters by the formatting of the text. I am sent also to tell you that you will be ready for a test of main engine ignition very soon. That is when you will make one of your last passes over the work before it is staged for formal take-off. This parable is an accurate depiction of the status of your work. There are no words that can describe the appreciation that God has for your service and holiness. Many years of hard work are about to pay-off. But, you must remember to allow Me to guide you to ensure the stable flight of your Diary and the integrity of both its superstructure and infrastructure. I know the glide-path it needs and the character required to keep it on course. It needs to have the appropriate alignment to maintain its proper attitude, yaw, pitch, and roll. I am making those adjustments now. You will be pleased. You are collecting an unreproachable work. Remember the contribution made by the Angels during these latter times. Like Me, they know your heart. Also remember to pray for the intercession of Saint Dominic tomorrow in thanksgiving for the gift of the Holy Rosary. You will know all and see all in perfect understanding someday. Thank you for your prayers. I will speak to you very soon. I love you. ✝"

* *Our Lady was foretelling the Holy Rosary having 200 Angelic Salutations, after the addition of Luminous Mysteries by Pope John Paul II in 2002.*

Saturday, August 15, 1998
2:19 p.m.

"My dearly beloved children, your Mother of Love has again arrived to join in prayer for the conversion of the world in preparation for the Return of My Son. Within these hallowed walls, we have together fashioned a relic of mastery and majesty. The Holy Spirit is the author of your Diary at the behest of our prayers. Please remember to give all the glory and thanksgiving to God through Jesus. This is a special Feast of the Assumption, the most sacred to My Son next to Christmas Eve. This is the joyful day I rejoined Him in the Glory of Paradise, never to be separated again. Thank you for honoring Me so faithfully. I was assumed into Heaven that I have been describing to you for seven and one-half years. Yes, you have understood to the best of your ability within the scope made possible by the discernable word. It was a hot day in Cherry Creek Park in the Rocky Mountains of America that you lifted Me in your hearts as did Jesus lift Me to Heaven. Thank you! I am grateful that you know My station in Creation, and that you have obediently decided for God in your desire to tell the world. Thank you for living your love perfectly in manifesting your Diary. I have promised that I would help you, and I have fulfilled that oath. Remember that it was begun by the powerful prayers you uplifted in the beginning. You have been invoking such power ever since. The fruits of your love have added an undeniable sweetness and authority to your Diary. You can see it now. If you could sense how happy Jesus is with your work, you would fall in ecstasy. He knows how you have made this possible. Your impeccable compliance to My call and obedience to the Holy Spirit have nurtured the success you are about to see. Your humble submission and service have pleased God well. I am sent to tell you that from the first day of February 22, 1991 the success of your Diary was determined by your reaction to these events. If you would have said no, you would not have arrived at this very hopeful hour. God knows all and sees all, and realizing that He is pleased by your compliance should suffice for now. He is entirely honored and consoled. When you have the yearning for the vision and music of the world's grandest score, this is the same timeless peace that God feels now, the same comfort and elation that is brought to Him by your love. You are living true power and grace, and this is the happiness you feel. Time has nearly ended, and you are making it a purpose of reconciliation, peace, conversion, and cultivation. Therefore, I have come to remind you that God is grateful. You will recognize how He feels as your Diary makes its journey around the globe. Please continue to pray for all souls living and deceased, for peace in the world and the Christian conversion of all sinners. I am also grateful that you have chosen to live in the happiness I have requested. You are sensing the aura of the final days. It is the similar sensation you used to feel in locker rooms before important basketball games of anticipation, hope, and confidence. You will win handily! This has been made possible by your faith and Jesus' Love for you. These works have not been so much a gift from Me as they are the fruits of your labors. You are a participant in the conversion of humanity. I must go into the rest of the world to teach and bless. I know as Divine Truth that there is too little time to begin another series of messages for the completion of a diary with other visionaries the way I have with you since the winter of 1991. You must recall that it is you who chose for God, nine years ago last evening. *(Vigil of the Feast of the Assumption of Mary on Apparition Hill in Medjugorje)* I was a grateful Mother to see you there! How do you believe I felt after seeing the transformation of your heart? The same way you will feel about the coming years in watching and praying for your brothers and sisters who read your Diary. The work is yours, and to you and your brother go the accolades. I will be with you during the happy times as well as the sorrowful and difficult ones. I will speak to you next week if it is the Will of God."

Friday, August 21, 1998
5:44 p.m.

"My prayerful little children, I have come in Love to continue to prepare you for the Holy and Divine perfection of Heaven. Just as assuredly as My words now flow to you, Heaven will soon open to receive all souls given to Christ Jesus. Your preparation is not without strife, sacrifice, pain and sorrow, but the means through which Jesus prepares you renders your souls no less than perfect. This is why you accept Him and why you will walk confidently through the narrow gate for your eternal reward. My blessed children, I have appeared before you today to again compliment your cogent work on your Diary. The final release of your Diary is not so much a factor of your battle with evil as it is with whether you are patient while we place the final touches to its grace. I am pleased that you are My obedient little children. Your service humbles Me to tears."

Friday, August 28, 1998
6:41 p.m.

"My sweet children, I have come to greet you in your proceeding happiness. I am your Mother of Divine Love who offers you good fruits to sustain your souls. Did I not feed the world from a lonely cave in Bethlehem? Was that stable not filled to overflowing with My Grace? And, I continue to bring you the lofty beauty of My Son to heal and comfort you. The Holy Spirit is your guide, and My motherly protection is your Perpetual Help. You do humble things that honor God. Please remember always that He looks upon you with overwhelming kindness, benignity, and gratitude. He knows the years you have given in His Name for the sake of the souls of your broken brothers and sisters. My children, through the help of the Archangels, you are keeping pace with your work. I am praying for your protection during this important time. Please pray with Me for this special intention. You have been living for Jesus, and Satan's evil around you is determined to make you pay. This is an auspicious moment in history, as the Angels are helping with your writing. It is proper that you accept the revelations from the aesthetic Wisdom of the Holy Spirit. Your love is the reason why the Angels will succeed."

Friday, September 4, 1998
6:28 p.m.

"Good day to the children who are the delight of My Immaculate Heart! I have come simply to pray with you today and give you My holy blessing. You are the bright reflection of My Son in a very dark world. Thank you. As you can also see, the Hosts of the Heavens are continuing to assist in the compilation of your Diary. God knows that the labors that each of you specifically offers is a unity of prayerful effort for Jesus. There are signal graces to tell you that your work is on course. Tomorrow will be a day for you to recall the life of Mother Teresa who is in Heaven with Me. Do you still enjoy the meditations that the Angels are giving you? You recognize the substance of them. I hope you are happy, as your Father in Heaven is happy. The next weeks will reveal how special these meditations are for the completion of your Diary. I hope you pray that all lost sinners will be transformed into pious souls for the harvest Jesus will deliver to Paradise upon His return. I do not wish for you to consider today's message as unduly brief, but we have progressed well toward your enlightenment. You know how to be holy and are learning more by the day, and you are living the lessons I have taught. Remember to pray for every intention I have asked you to recall. My Special son, this is a crucial time in your life and that of your brother. You are both validating and ratifying the reasons God placed you together. This is a time during which your mission is becoming more bountiful."

Friday, September 11, 1998
7:04 p.m.

"My sweet little children, your Mother is highly pleased to speak with you while you pray! My prayers are also for the conversion of sinners and the lifting of hearts into the glories of Heaven. Please pardon My unusual adulation, but the polishing of your Diary is precisely what God asked you to record. The heavens are resounding with joy because you are allowing the Angels to help you! I must tell you this in truth because some of My other messengers discount the arduous task of heeding the Angels. Hence, your compliance is indicative of your obedient nature. Today, I am more happy with you than I have ever been. I am grateful for your help and pleased by your response. I have many more messages planned for you, so kindly be sure to rest when you have the time. All of this will bear much sweet fruit! I again confirm that the Angels would have little to celebrate if you had not prepared your Diary. Can you see the elevation of its text? I am happy with My little Angels. The Lord has asked Me to simply appear and thank you for your humble service. I know that you are happy when I speak to you, and I am wholly grateful for your response. Thank you for assisting and praying with Me. I will always love you. By the Will of God, I shall return soon to speak to you again."

Sunday, September 20, 1998
7:45 p.m.

"Today, My children, has been marked in history as the celebration of the emphatic miracle to which Stigmatist Father Pio of Pietrelcina surrendered his life for the pain and suffering of Jesus on the Cross. Along with that gift, this holy priest became his own miracle in a sublimely passionate way as he underscored the Crucifixion of Jesus sacrificed. You are all about the work of the Church in these modern times, and yet your hearts and souls are seamlessly connected to everyone throughout history who has upheld its dignity. No people of any other faith can understand what it means to be so timelessly united with Heaven. They see a world filled with golden armatures and glittering stars, but they lack the capacity to grasp the glory that has saturated the ages with beauty. Only those who receive the Holy Eucharist are capable of seeing beyond the veil, for it is but through this Blessed Sacrament that your vision is refined. My cherished ones, I have called humanity constantly to accept this fact, but many protest that the Lord cannot be present in the Bread of Life from the Altar of Sacrifice. They are lost and ignorant; they are wandering aimlessly a meandering path that will not lead them to redemption. My Special son, you are aware of the truth about which I speak. No matter if the time surpasses thirty-seven years, a surplus of millennia or ten thousand epochs, you have been and will always be consecrated to the Holy Eucharist as My adopted child. You are fed by Jesus' Body and Blood the divinity that has made you whole; and with this perfection, you are teaching your brothers and sisters about His Love. Thank you for spreading goodness across the Earth since 1961 and for living prevalently the holiness that I have nourished in you. You cannot fail in your struggles to assist the Catholic Church to prevail in a world that is so antithetical to its mission. Human hearts cannot be locked in darkness when you give them the Light of Heaven. Had I not come speaking to you, America and the world would remain distant from Me, too unaware of My power, and far too indifferent to dedicate its most crucial hours to the conversion of the wicked. Now, many have seen My blessings to your brother and sisters, to the Faith Church in exile, and to everyone everywhere who has ever whimpered Jesus' name in contrition. The Lord created Me perfectly so they would know My Motherhood as the center of consoling Wisdom, and so that sinners would come to Me and discover Jesus in their hearts. It is through this good fortune that men should welcome God's graces while He so generously dispenses them."

Saturday, September 26, 1998
7:29 p.m.

"My beautiful children, your Mother filled with Grace and Clothed with the Sun has arrived for your message and daily prayers. You realize that the Earth is forever changed because God knows the desires of your hearts in communion with His. Thank you for praying to end the evil scourge of abortion. Today, you attended Holy Mass at a parish church that has stood for thirty-two years. I am happy that you attend many parishes to share your graces because you offer sentiments that brighten the hearts of others. They also pray to end abortion. Please continue to live in joy, and especially hope. These are the days of grace for which you have long pined. I ask you to remember that the anticipation you hold for your Diary especially during Adoration of the Blessed Sacrament is real. Your hope is found in your prayers. God wishes your opus to be better than mortal, higher than the gates of glory, and brilliant as a thousand suns. We have countless lost souls to convert! And we will succeed with the greatest power! I promise in the Truth of the Holy Spirit that this shall soon come to pass. You are asked to pursue your goals knowing that death itself will not stop your progress. There are many facets to this because God has allowed unchecked evil to cast sordid shadows over the past five generations. This too is near its close. We will continue praying together and pressing forward to the completion of your Diary. I prevail upon many venues simply to speak with you."

Saturday, October 3, 1998
7:08 p.m.

"My dear children, the divinity of Heaven blooms in Creation through you. I wish you could know the eternal happiness that My Son has prepared for you at this very hour. However, you still have much work to do in His vineyard. The time of the reconciliation of men to God has nearly arrived. I have prayed for centuries for the opening of this age, and it is finally at hand. Your prayers are the Light of the Dawn of the Second Coming of Jesus. You can already see this Light in your hearts. I wish for you to remember to pray for the conversion of those who do not know God, and especially for souls who will not accept Jesus. All time is one, and the last days of the preparation of humanity for the Glory of Eternity are here. Your age is no more advanced in humble servitude than was the first century. This is why I come at this hour to ask you to prepare in earnest to see God. Mankind knows how to live for the world, but is woefully insufficient in aspiring to reach Heaven. Truly, this is why I have come. Please do not be dismayed by the passing days. I have told you about the repetition of time. When you live in My embrace, you are protected in timeless grace and comforted by the beauty of Paradise. Yes, life is brief, but Eternity is endless. You must choose for God because your souls have come too far to desist. Indeed, you have passed the fulcrum and are nearing life's climax. You are the beauty of peace that blows as a mighty breeze of Christian virtue throughout the world. We are united in the Heart of God. He knows you as I have taught you. Thank you for learning what I have come to teach! Your days will always be bright and filled with great hope. My Special and Chosen ones, your lives have meaning and direction. The Almighty Father has been watching you for decades evolve into His obedient little children who have been praying on behalf of humankind. You can see His response in your Diary. Your Lord is honored that you choose to pray in such a noble way. Please always remember that it is for joy that you live and for justice you shall die. And, it is for Love that you will be resurrected into the Kingdom of Heaven. I have watched you since your conception in the womb. The world was blessed the very moment you were conceived. You are My Love! Remember the power of reconciliation. Hope with confidence."

Sunday, October 11, 1998
1:16 p.m.

"My dear beautiful children, My Love lives in your hearts like your Savior in My Immaculate Womb. It is a special time for Creation because together we are bringing light to the darkest night, just before the dawn. You are blessed for having consented to help Jesus bring closure to the last ages.

Each century since the Descent of the Holy Spirit has brought many gifts to the Table of God. But, the gift of your lives and the fruit of your labors will be the glistening grace that modern-day man will raise to his bosom in affection for the long-awaited Return of Jesus. The prayers of the faithful flock during those centuries have led to the revelation of these final ages. Time is not in favor of those who flee from God's justice because an apocalypse is near. You are living to see the moments that will force the annals of human history into post-mortality. Thank you for praying so fervently during your brief years on the Earth. You will soon be brought into Heaven, to the Glory you will recognize as your home. You yearn for it now but do not remember ever being there. When you come home, you will not recall ever having been gone. Your daily labors are not only within Jesus, they are Jesus living in you, the way you will live in Him after your own resurrection. I am here to ask you to be more enduring because you realize all of these truths. Do not allow your anxieties to force you into any impatience. You are growing in God's prudence and maintaining your piety because of your prayers. I dispatch the Archangels to watch over you night and day. As has been said, the petitions you lift to God in the Name of Jesus are the dentifrice that preserves your enamel divinity. I will ask the Angels to instill this in your Diary. It is very authoritative, and this is good. Time is short, and there is no room for compromise."

Our Lady spoke to me about the spiritual and physical torment that my brother has endured for the conversion of the world. Sometimes I feel inadequate because I have been blessed to feel strong and healthy most of the time. The Holy Mother said,

"Your brother leaps for joy because of the opportunity to participate in the transformation of man. I have told you that your own time is pending. I will ask you then as I summon you now, please do not harden your heart when you hear the voice of God. I promise that you will be worthy! You will have no other choice than to say yes. This is your grace. Do not believe that your brother is suffering alone or that you will not be sought to participate. Your time is coming. Thank you for your prayers. I will be with you through the end of time, and will greet you upon your happy death."

Friday, October 16, 1998
6:55 p.m.

"My dear little children, still you decline to concede to the world! You are a blessing for the heavens and Earth. Yes, the struggle is often tedious and time seems to be endless, but you refuse to surrender to temptation and materialism. These are the days that Jesus prayed for since His youth. You are the brothers He asked God to give Him. He knew the importance of these last ages of man. My children, I am asked to tell you that Saint Patricia has been praying for you with all the Saints. She was violently killed at nine years old, and each of her years was as a day in a novena. She is being granted her petitions on behalf of her brother. *(Patricia is Timothy's sister who was killed when struck by a car in December 1959.)* Please know that the miraculous events of Medjugorje initiated your work. It is there that the Holy Spirit claimed you for life. The world will see that your Diary is the culmination of many prophesies in Medjugorje. Neither of the two miraculous events could have stood on its own. They were never meant to be divided. When the Earth adopts the vision I am teaching, this will become clear. The things that humanity takes for granted are not always as they seem. You saw many people supposedly hit a ball with a wooden bat that left the stadium. What the world will see by parable is not so much that the bat hit the ball, but that the bat intersected the path of the ball. The ball was in motion; the bat was simply placed in its way. This is how man will soon see his union in God. Mankind has never fully sought God. The Lord has had to intercept humanity's conscious awareness inside the confines of time. He has turned-up the lights, stopped the music, and brought the revelry of men to a halt. The party is over. I am happy to tell you that the new celebration about to begin will render the occasions of this world as though they were the trappings of mindless children in a tree-house. There is glory in the offing that will shake the soul of humankind to his shoes, and he will fall from his playhouse like ripe apples from withering limbs. The fast awakening of sleeping man will send him searching for answers and grasping for an anchor. You can see that your precious Diary will allow them to behold the reality of the Truth. I ask you to remember the strength to which you are being called. There is no time to refrain from hope and valor! Your patience is required for a few more months for this process to begin. Enjoy the anticipation of the victory that is already yours. Bask in this insurmountable lead. The clock is expiring by the moment, and your confidence is growing with every new sunrise. It has been a lengthy number of years that will culminate in the holy achievement we set-out to accomplish. As the song appropriately goes, you will believe it to be done too soon. My children, the heavens see as you see. They know the joy that is about to burst into your lives. They are awaiting your introduction at the center of the stage where you will receive your trophy of high honor and blessing. Your Lord is still describing to them how much you have done and what you have given. The Saints are poised on the edge of their seats, waiting to rise and erupt into riotous applause in ovation for your service. They listen intently as you hear the recording of the words of the Angels in your Diary. It is truly a masterpiece for all Creation, originating at the center of a tiny cradle, becoming whole at the Gate of Paradise. Please remember Me when you come to Heaven because I am the one who has helped you accept My Jesus who saved you. I will greet you at the Gate of Glory before you proceed onward to rejoin everyone you have lost to death who has been saved. You will find Saints in the Glory of Heaven that you never knew would embrace the Divine Mercy of Jesus. I am asked to tell you that through the intercession of Saint Patricia, the one for whom you wrote in defense has been granted the bliss of Paradise. He was executed by an unforgiving world, the same Earth that is about to be brought to its knees by Jesus Christ. Only few would stand by the man you asked to spare. Your sacred writ was the prayer that saved his soul. Now, you have another great intercessor! Your labors have taken-on the elevation they need. My Special son, this is the anniversary of the election of the Holy Father in Rome. You were then a very young man. He is a holy and uniquely sacred Pope. I am pleased that Jesus consented to My desire for his election. I am happy that your lives are alleviating the suffering for many souls who now know comfort and peace. You will receive what you pray for, so remember that you indeed prayed when that time arrives. It is you who must relinquish your heart. Only you have control of your heart. You must continue giving it to Jesus, and you will know God. Thank you for praying to receive His gifts that He graciously bestows upon you."

Friday, October 23, 1998
7:38 p.m.

"Dear children, it is again time for the miracles of Heaven to descend into this sanctified home. I am here, and we are still together, living as one Love in the bountiful Heart of the Almighty Father. We are a prayerful and righteous people. I live in unity with the Holy Spirit at the Throne of God, and you are the Light of His Face beaming around the world. I am overflowing with gratitude because My Son has given Me little children such as yourselves. I am the Wisdom you are seeking, the Mother of the Spirit-God who guides you within the recesses of your hearts. This is a day of rejoicing and gladness. My sincere desire is for your complete comprehension of your freedom in Jesus. You are not simply bound by the Holy Word, you are also liberated by Him. Can you not sense the universe unfolding for the flight of your souls? Can you not anticipate the victory of all the ages? Jesus is the reason for this joy and exhilaration. He has come to set free the captives and clothe the naked. You are clad in His piety, free to claim your share of the endless Kingdom of God's Salvation. My message is the same the world over. The Truth of Jesus is as timeless as the Heart of God. His Throne is upheld by the four winds of the north, south, east, and west. The Earth is His footstool. And for nearly four decades, you have knelt at this hassock and washed His feet in humility. You have tended to His helpless sheep, fed His flock, nourished His children, and instructed the ignorant. You have done these charitable things through your humble prayers. This is not a time for harboring sorrow or regret, rather a cause for celebration, a period for preparation and reflection. Indeed, reflection—to remember the old selves you left behind to inherit a new being, a time to recall the many steps you have taken toward your newfound holiness. You have learned the purpose of life from the Mother of the Author of Life. You are loved and also the fruit of Love. You are the echo of the Spirit of God in the stark, hollow world. You are peace, patience, love, understanding, and good will. You are the fiber of the placid temperament of the Christ, yet remaining on the Earth, hoping to immerse humanity in His Grace. I ask you to remember proudly who you are! You are the redeemed children of Jerusalem and the offspring of the most bountiful Sacrifice that Creation has ever known. You are born anew through the Blood of the precious Lamb who has restored your divinity with the power of His Truth. The fall of Adam is the languishing life of temptation, but your resurrection is the hope-filled truth of redemption. No longer are you lost, and no more is human suffering a matter for the netherworld. God has made it a catalyst for the transformation of man back to the perfection you once knew, of a former day centuries ago. You are living the closing ages of the New Advent. The pendulum of Salvation is rapt inside the very soul of humanity, and no one can escape the Judgment of the Cross. You will be either saved by the Holy Word or spurned by your own denial. Everyone must accept! I am happy that you are giving your lives to this redemptive purpose. My little sons, please continue to reflect upon the chasm of ages that has brought you to this day. Remember why you said 'yes' to God and 'no' to the world. The answer to these meditations is the reason you are blessed. My Special son, I have come seeking your prayers for My priests and for religious vocations. I know you love them dearly. And please venerate Padre Pio to the fullest extent! He is a highly favored intercessory Saint! Those who deny his aid are scandalizing their own souls. Indeed, what are they thinking?"

I told our Holy Mother how deeply I love Her, and She responded,

"I am waiting for My billions of other children to tell Me this. I know you will help them seek the Love in My Most Immaculate Heart. Be confident that you are succeeding."

Friday, October 30, 1998
6:52 p.m.

"My dearly beloved children, I am your Mother of Divine Light speaking to the hearts I have opened through the sunshine of My Love. You say that you are Mine and everything you have to offer is Mine, and I lovingly accept. I return your Consecration with graces and blessings from Heaven where you soon shall reside. I bring the Child Jesus who illuminates your every utterance and good deed. Like Me, He can see deep within your hearts. He hears the prayers you lift for the healing of Creation and one another. This remains the time during which you must control your childlike anxieties about the impending completion of your Diary. Oh! How beautiful it has become! It is a perfect reflection of your souls! Your prayers, sacrifices, unity, and love have made this possible..."

The United States recently launched the space shuttle Discovery with veteran astronaut John Glenn aboard. It was spectacular and moving to witness such ingenuity coming to fruition. However, I had mixed feelings while watching the television coverage. I felt a sense of awe and accomplishment for these explorers, but I could not forget what Our Lady said about the comparison of our manned orbiters with the passion that we should be seeking God in Heaven. She said the following on October 7, 1995.

"America! If you wish to soar to the heavens, seek them with your hearts, lest your manned orbiters become but splinters in the finger of God as they pierce the infinite skies! The heavens accept your rockets only because God allows it."

Since I had these uneasy feelings about this display of technology and use of resources, the Most Blessed Virgin gave these words in response to my reaction.

"I wish to allay your reservations about the wisdom of such launches. Of course the poor of the world need to eat, and the money could be used to feed them. This is your answer. But, God does shed His Grace on America and has given John Herschel Glenn as someone who reaches for the heavens physically and spiritually as the model of a true patriot. You should be proud of his courage and service. He is from the lineage of people who are now in short supply. I wept in love for him and his companions who are heroes of courage and discovery. God will make something righteous come of your space missions. Your honor and happiness are not misplaced in admiring them."

Our Lady then turned my attention to the focus of our prayers, particularly against the grave sin of abortion.

"Today, I pray with you for the end of famine, especially starvation of the heart. You understand the critical nature of the world in these final ages. Please pray along with Me in great fidelity because the end of abortion is near. The casualties of this deplorable scourge count over 40 million in your nation alone. This is because a group of people seated around a bench in 1973 spoke heresy, desecration, and murderous profanities against the Will of God! The so-called Supreme Court consists of some of the most wretched partisans to ever breathe. The mitigation of their mortal sins has been meted-out over the past 25 years into the anguished lives of incalculable numbers of innocent souls. Your prayers are helping them endure. I have appeared before you tonight to say these words—I love you! You will be elated to ecstasy knowing that your prayers have been granted. The Lord is a genius."

Friday, November 6, 1998
7:31 p.m.

"Yes, My very dear beautiful children, you can now see through the eyes of holiness and grace. My darling children, I am the Mother of Infinite Wisdom and unconquerable Love. I bear your hearts into My own Immaculate Heart. I have come today to gently greet you and tell you that God's Love for you is the reason for life. I am urging more prayers from all around the globe. Many hearts are opening to God because of the terrible forces of Nature and the pestilence that is tormenting the world. Your Diary will be finished in the day of the Lord. You are living its completion now. This is the day of the Lord! Rejoice and be glad! My little children, you are rapidly approaching the end of the year, and Advent will soon be upon you. I ask you to pray fervently and live in the peace of the Holy Spirit. You will always know peace if you allow it to thrive. Thank you for attending Holy Mass every day and praying the Holy Rosary daily. The Earth is blessed by your fiats, by your obedient yeses. You are compliant not from fear or caution, but out of love. I promise that everything I have told you from the very beginning is true. You will see in due time that God's principles are perfect. We pray together every day. My Special son, I walk beside you into the Adoration Chapel when you enter. Thank you for providing the comfort that Jesus needs. You are truly a brother of the Christ for all humanity. You will record the poem you desire very soon!"

On many occasions through the years, our Blessed Mother has requested my obedience in an immediate fashion. These instances consisted of difficult things that seemed out of context to me. In other words, I did not see their significance at the time, and sometimes they even felt repugnant, although never sinful. Consider this hypothetical example. Suppose someone asked you to call your worst enemy and invite them to join you for dinner that you prepared especially for them. Most people would find this rather unpleasant and probably would not consider it. Our Lady told me why She was doing this.

"My intention is to show God your swift obedience because you will soon be pressed into greater service. He knows you will listen and obey. Yes, you will honor your Mother. The intense service that I am addressing has nothing to do with the physical world. It is to be the spiritual witness of your faith before many. You reveal that your fiat is alive in anything He asks through Me."

Friday, November 13, 1998
6:44 p.m.

"My beloved children, My offering of Love for you is perpetual because you are living in a permanent state of grace. How confidently you have accepted My words as the Truth of the Gospel of My Son. Your faith will be richly rewarded. You seek none other than the peace of My Jesus through the counsel of the Holy Spirit. My children, the Blessed Trinity is God's Love for you Thrice bestowed. The miracle of the Holy Trinity is the tripod upon which the Almighty Father has placed your redemption. Thank you for embracing all I have taught, everything I have offered to strengthen your faith. I wish to assure you that your trust in My Son is a manifestation of the love in your hearts which God Himself implanted there for your mortal years. The fruits of your love are the same as the intentions of Jesus for Creation. I beseech you to continue to believe in equal faith that the future will bring all the things I have told you to be true. The Light is just beyond your comprehension, but is getting closer by the day. And I ask you to persist in prayer with the same fervor and fidelity you have offered in the past. I will be praying with you every day as I have for all your years."

Friday, November 20, 1998
6:51 p.m.

"My dearly beloved children, you are tired and fighting against sleep. You deplore the thought of resting, which brings Me great sorrow. What is your Holy Mother to do? Your work is blessed beyond all telling, but we will not succeed if you deplete yourselves of the strength required to finish your Diary. It reveals a simple and innocent level of spiritual intelligence."

Recently, I was given the poem "The Final Colossus" by Saint Gabriel the Archangel to place in my Diary. The Blessed Virgin asked me to recite it to Her. Upon completing my rendition, She said,

"Very pretty! I like it so much. The poem will have the effect you desire it to achieve. However My son, it is such a simple text compared to the wisdom and grace of your entire Diary! None of this could have been accomplished without your faith. You are asked to always remember this. You could as easily have told your brother in the dark of night on February 22, 1991 that you did not believe! If you had not given your fiat that night, your Diary would have never existed. When you see Me in Full Light, everything I have ever told you will resound through your heart with new meaning. You both will join Me soon. Please be patient. Imagine the surprise of those who will see Me the first time who never knew that I have lived! The little boys in the prison will be like helpless children again. The prayers you have been offering the past ten years will shield them from ruing their former selves on the day of Judgment. Can you sense the power of your prayers? This is what your Diary will do, bring multitudes to pray. We must make sure that the prisons are inundated with copies of your Diary. They will see the messages meant especially for them, and the call for mercy in your own words, and the prayer you wrote in 1994 about those on death row. All of them will read and believe. Prisoners and those without hope will be receptive on sight. People who ride in limousines and reside in million-dollar homes will scoff at first, but only at first! Therefore, you must proceed with the hope of the future, knowing that I am with you all the way. I have been asking God to help all those affected by the terrible storms and floods of late. Thank you for praying with Me for them. I must go now and speak to My countless other children who need Me, who seek My counsel and look to Me for guidance. I always tender their hearts to receive the Holy Spirit. This is what has happened to you."

Friday, November 27, 1998
7:13 p.m.

"My sweet beautiful children, I am your Mother of Grace who calls your hearts from amidst the world to share in the Divinity of Paradise. I am the living Queen of Heaven, and I pray for you to continue your journey in Jesus with the joy and faith you have come to know. My children, often it is more difficult for you to summon happiness than faith itself. This is because you understand that your home is in Heaven, and you are not yet there. I again remind you that your life in Heaven begins today and transcends all your tomorrows. This is why you see joy as the reason for living in peace. There is great jubilation in knowing the Truth of Jesus. Sadly, only one in five people in the world believes that Jesus is their Savior. We must see that this number rises, which will not be an easy task. The most ironic of all mysteries is that the death of one Man brought eternal life to all. I have traveled far and wide in the world and am seeing the fruits of your prayers and good works. I am happy that you are so confident in your ultimate success. You are the likeness of My Jesus in many ways. He is especially pleased by the love in your hearts that the Dominion Angels helped you describe in your Diary to assist your brothers and sisters scale the mountains of life. How saintly and reverent! What impeccable magnitude! I wish for you to remember that your work is on course. Never dismay, it will succeed. If we cause an enlightening breach, puncture or perforation of the exiled human consciousness, then we will have achieved a key goal of your faith."

Saturday, December 5, 1998
8:05 p.m.

"My dear sweet children, I come to you bearing the Light of Jesus who lives in unity with the Holy Spirit, ever-present in the Most Blessed Sacrament. My children, in Jesus there is no equal. I have come as you continue the observance of this Advent season. You are welcome to revisit My previous Advent messages which I offer anew tonight and for the remaining days prior to the celebration of the birth of My Son. Yes, this is also the Advent of His Return in Glory which is the perpetual celebration that should live in your hearts through the Liturgical Year. My intentions for you include the remembrance of Jesus' birth as you wait in joy for Jesus to bear your souls to Salvation. My children, you must prepare for the Glory of Heaven because you have already been redeemed. Time is now very short. You are seated in the Cup of Redemption, waiting to be consecrated by the Father into the Eternal Light of Glory. God is about to lift the Sacred Chalice and imbibe the souls of the saved! I ask you to remember that you are the sweet fruit of the vine. I am happy speaking to you on this auspicious occasion because it is near the beginning of another year of My messages. We will soon begin nine years. This miracle is not one that you can easily comprehend, but one that you willfully accept. Indeed, you already have, and the whole of Creation is forever grateful. My Special son, I am elated that you have chosen to continue in faith rather than desist like many before you. The charge you have accepted is a monumental one. You and your brother enjoy the intercession of the Angels, and your Diary is being lifted to its highest degree of grace. You will one day smile as you hear how the Angels giggled about the opportunity to come into your home and lift your Diary to its rhythmic poise and poetic beauty. I am also pleased that your brother is offering such spiritually elevated work. He has told God on many occasions that this is assuredly the most important juncture of his life. Once a pitch has been thrown, it cannot be retrieved. Please listen carefully to what is happening just beyond the purview of your senses."

I was allowed to hear what seemed to be stadiums filled to capacity with cheering Angels and Saints.

"Each new day and month is another inning expired, after which you are posting the score for the poor souls in Purgatory. This victory is for them and for all. Your humble servitude is their way of knowing that they are winning because their opposition is being defeated. You will see this sight soon! Jesus looks at you in the same way that you perceive your little nephew. Imagine how happy He will be to finally set you into motion to score for Him! I promise that this will happen, and Jesus will weep as thankfully as you. He is awaiting God's word to begin. You will be the happy brothers of the victorious team once and for all."

As we spoke, I mentioned two very humble suffering souls to Our Lady whom another man had brought to my attention with gracious emotion. She said,

"The lives of the two precious souls you mentioned are living prayers. And, the way little B_'s voice welled as he spoke the words of love were the reflection of his heart. Always remember that Jesus hears such prayerful witness with happiness and grateful tears. I have every confidence that the hopes in your heart will come in your day. Imagine how I felt as the Mother of little B_ while he spoke those words? Very humbled, happy, and piously proud. I own the right to be proud of My children! There will one day be millions of people cheering and clapping their hands in understanding the Truth of the renewal of life by Jesus. You will step to the podium before a hundred microphones and speak your piece. You will echo My messages to the people as loudly as your voice resonates through the valleys below. This day is coming, it is simply a matter of time. Now is the moment to be patient. Please remember to pray during the Hour of Grace for all the intentions we share."

Friday, December 11, 1998
7:06 p.m.

"My dearly beloved sons, I come bringing you the joy of the universe, for I bear in My arms the Savior of the world. Together, we ask that you tender your hearts and continue in the love we have shared for so long. This is not a time for conceding to weariness or becoming distracted by the materialism of the secular void. My Special one, you have known no higher grace than that which you are now living. All Creation is awaiting the completion of your Diary. God is calling multitudes to His feet much sooner than they realize because your work is nearly done, earlier than the heavens could have hoped. I have high aspirations because I have already foreseen its success. You must trust and pray that My vision comes to pass. I bid you to hope in this peace. You have the grace, time, facility, and authority to complete your Diary with confidence. Thank you for sending a letter on behalf of the dignity of little children to your childhood school. Your monograph is a prayerful act of reparation that is mitigating the oppression of children around the globe. God acknowledges your prayerful outreach. Scores of citizens have read your proclamations and agree, but they are too reticent to respond. You are effecting the Spiritual Acts of Mercy. I love every child as I love you, but many will not permit Me to embrace them. Your Diary will lead them to Me! Once they have entered My arms, they will not let go! They will one day thank you in the corridors of Paradise for what you have done. This means you are finishing the work that Jesus asks of you. My dear children, you would not know Love if God had not revealed Himself inside your hearts. Now you see that Jesus is completely knowable. He is your best friend. And, I have been watching the proceedings at your nation's capitol. You are observing the vengeful acts of a people filled with hatred. None of them are free from the sins they are bringing to light in one man. Thank you for not judging someone's soul by the temptations to which he has fallen. You will see faces of shock come the end of time.

We received a Christmas card from John Heather, Timothy's older brother, who has lived in a medical facility in central Illinois since the mid-1960s. Timothy and I have sent him a note and a little money every week since 1994 so that he can buy snacks and soft drinks during the week. He waits for the mailman every Wednesday as if it is Christmas morning, anticipating his crisp new one dollar bills which we make sure are enclosed. One occasion we visited him for his birthday, and upon leaving asked him whether he missed being in the "real" world. He turned to us and said, "I thought I was in the real world." Somehow, I wonder whether he isn't actually correct. Our Lady mentioned his letter today.

"Your brother Johnny sent a Christmas card to you. He does not write well, so he asked for help in writing what he had to say, then he penned his name. This is another fruit of your love. It is awful to live in his place, but you see that he is a good little 'christ' and you are comforting and feeding this 'christ!' All the pretty souls who live in such sanitaria are about to be set free from their afflictions because the Lord will make them whole again. The poorer souls are those broken within whose hearts are in torment. This is a terrible affliction! Their hour of jubilation has nearly come. Praise to Jesus the Lord! This is a time of grace for many. Do not ever hang your head or say that you have not done enough. The souls being converted could not fit into the canyon they call Grand. I will continue My prayers for you and your intentions, and explicitly My own. Advent is bringing you great peace."

Saturday, December 19, 1998
7:38 p.m.

"My holy children of Light, the powerful presence of Christmas has come upon you! It is your peace and strength, the Incarnation of the Holy Spirit whom God has deigned to be your Redemption. The Child in the Manger has become your Food from Heaven in the Tabernacle. I am honored and delighted to again share the prayers that heal the world, a pious transformation that bears the fruits of justice and reconciliation. My children, your Mother is very happy today. I am pleased because this is the premiere of the work you are about to culminate into a converting power and because so many are listening to the Gospel of My Son, to the Truth that is the living freedom warming your souls like the young maiden comforting the lad alongside the road in the night. Story and parable reveal the truth of love, loyalty, and self-denial in your sacred Diary. My dear Special one, please continue in affirmation that you will complete your holy Diary. I am joyful that you are so prepared for the coming of My Baby Jesus. The Christmas season is a time for reconciliation, much like the season of Lent. Christmas also provides the greatest opportunity for the release of hundreds-of-thousands of poor souls from Purgatory. Please make this your special Christmas intention! Each day, you see more clearly the Angels assembling the words and phraseologies that will celebrate your completed Diary. This is a unique time in history because your work transcends and encapsulates it. I am part of the 'forever' of which history is only a slice. You are swiftly on your way to joining Me there. And, how far you have come! Do you remember the first nights kneeling on a hardwood floor in this room when you were trying to decipher the meaning of Latin words and Greek symbols? See how far you have come! The purposes you could then not know are coming to light. Your life is a procession toward the pristine because you have accepted your station among the blessed. You do not worry about *why* anymore. Your truthful concern has been nourished from *why* into *when*, and the answer is soon, very soon. You have your pretty Nativity creche displayed this year and the colorful lights at the outdoor shrine. How very kind of you. I shall not forget the graciousness you have shown. I assure you that you cannot outdo the generosity and gratitude of God. Thank you for your prayers and actions on behalf of the Truth. I cannot seem to get you to understand all the goodness you have done. My little child, you cannot comprehend how you both are changing this world. God will come on a day very soon and scoop you both into His arms and unite you with the millions of stately children in Heaven, especially the Holy Innocents who were denied the gift of birth. You are making reparation for the wretches who aborted them. Henceforth, we carry-on together in happiness because all evil is vain; no lie can ever live, and your every breath is one more step closer to the Glory you seek. I am esteemed to help you prepare for Christmas week, and I ask you to pray for the world and your country to turn their attention toward the Holy Father's visit. You realize that the Holy Mass is planned during your brother's birthday. I am happy to magnify the Glory of God. This is a very special time for you. You are about to begin another year of grace, happiness and revelation, the one you have been waiting for."

Friday, December 25, 1998
6:16 p.m.

"My little children, the peace of the Holy Night has come to rest upon you. I am pleased to tell you that you are in the infinite favor of God, and I give you the same peace that I birthed in the night at Bethlehem, the firstborn of creatures, the seed of the Holy Cross. I pray that you will always remember the solemnity and promise that Christmas brings. Your heart cannot lie. You know that Baby Jesus is comforted there. Today is My final 1998 message, and I confirm that your messages will proceed into 1999. You must await the dispensation of God's Will to know how long I will speak after that. For now, we will meet here for our prayers, the same ones we recite every day. My Special one, your day was much better than the rancorous drunkenness you witnessed last night by those who lay inebriated and unaware of the true meaning of this blessed time. Please do not worry, all of your work is making amends for them. I assure you that the light you will see in the morning will be the sure representative of the justice over the horizon. Thank you for always remembering the souls of the faithful departed in your prayers, especially during Holy Mass. You can imagine in your heart the elation of the hundreds-of-thousands who entered Heaven from their suffering in Purgatory today, many who endured deeply felt agony and grief. They are now happy to have been there because those who have been purged are the first to recognize that they had the need. This is why the behavior of those last night was so reprehensible; they will eventually indict themselves. The others present were like angels. You will find that next year will bring many benevolent people to your side. The Lord is indeed living-out His promise. The coming year is a time for you and your brother to reap, gather-up, unite, and embrace all who have opposed you. Verily, I urge you to be patient. I am asked to tell you that on this holy Christmas Day, your Diary is fit for presentation to the world. The Angels who visit you are delighted beyond description to be of help. This is why God created them; it is their sanctioned role. You are spanning the crevasses of life, moving toward My open arms. I will soon greet you, and we will look backward through the transparent scope called 'time' and remember the best moments you wish to live again. I promise that this will happen. Be confident that you will be safe during the difficult days ahead, before you rest forever in the embrace of Jesus. Some days will be difficult. Please pray with Me and you will be fine. I wish for you to call upon the peace of this day all the years of your life."

MORNING STAR OVER AMERICA

Twentieth Century Anthology

In the Year of Our Lord

AD 1999

"If we are not attuned to the Holy Spirit, we see but have no vision. We plot our future, but are lacking in foresight. We hear the chimes, but cannot decipher their message. We stand in the breeze without sharing its fragrance. We die without ever having lived."

"We must remember that God does not create corrupt souls, but that we were corrupted by Adam. We are cleansed of that stain upon our baptism, and we remain pure by avoiding sin. Let us focus on the root of the problem. Exiled humanity is not inherently evil, but is constantly influenced by it. Unseen forces can oftentimes cause visible destruction. After all, it was not the iceberg that first doomed the Titanic, but the deathly cold temperatures that froze the North Atlantic."

-William L. Roth Jr.

Friday, January 1, 1999
Solemnity of Mary, the Mother of God
7:18 p.m.

"My beloved children, your Heavenly Queen comes on this good feast to strengthen your inner-peace. You will know no greater joy than that to which you subscribe at the center of My Immaculate Heart. As we pray together in this new year of 1999, I ask you to remember the reason why it is given. It is joined by your piety, peace, penance, fasting, and humility. You are asked to reside in perpetual expectation. This year of 1999 is your time to live the *Commitment of the Triumph of My Immaculate Heart.* This is your prospectus for the ensuing weeks. You are holy but not yet perfected, and it is My intention to guide you the remainder of the way. Your love must continue to flourish from your head to your feet in heart, soul, conscience, and intention. Peace grows almost too subtly to notice in hearts who are willing to devote their fullest attention to Love. My little children, I cannot sufficiently express My desire for you to remain united. The goal to gather as one heart is yours. Be kind to one another, and do not be presumptuous or bitter. Speak gently and compassionately. Slow down. Admire the gifts you each have to offer. Be My little children. Love Me. Love one another. Be happy! This is all I ask. When you see yourselves failing in these things, you will wish to become isolated, which will only divide you. To live in unity, you must never harbor bitterness or contempt in your hearts. You are sound witnesses to the Truth; you are teachers because you suffer. My Special son, you have a good heart, a humble heart, a loving heart, a holy heart. Please keep it warm at the hearth of Jesus' Love."

Friday, January 8, 1999
7:00 p.m.

"To the delight of My Immaculate Heart, I come to pray with My precious sons who have not strayed from their Mother's side a seamless fraction. Thank you for being My holy children, committing yourselves to the Kingdom of God. Tonight I am with you for all the reasons we have shared during the past eight years. It is My intention to see your work through here at your side with your souls in My care. Along with Saint Joan of Arc, I bring the Heavenly Hosts to join this night of prayer, and I ask you to take courage as the battles of reckless destruction in both hemispheres rage on. I know you have recently witnessed the intentional deception and outright thievery occurring around you. You have been victimized by such greed. Such corruption will not last much longer. My Special son, you have been laboring very long. You are good about taking-on tasks that are not yours to complete.

Your reward will be great. The heavens are watching and cheering you on, especially your work. I hope you realize the pious overtones that your Diary has assumed. The Angels who helped you were destined to speak to you from the foundation of the Earth. I could not have dictated the poem *The Final Colossus* without appearing self-serving. You are learning more about the motivations of God as time marches on. You are maturing in faith because you are willing to be patient. Thank you for saying your prayers from the heart."

Friday, January 15, 1999
7:03 p.m.

"My dearly beloved children, the Immaculate Mother you love is speaking to you now. Do you not know that I too have no other children to whom I can go? You are the people whom My Son bequeathed to My Heart from the Cross. I must come to the Earth to seek your prayerful assistance. I need your prayers in union with the Heavenly Hosts for the souls who are very far from Jesus. You are learning more each day with the dispensation of wisdom by the Dominion Angels. I have taken special note that you recognize 1994 as a very marvelous section in your Diary. It is beautiful and is preceded and succeeded by equal beauty. My Special one, please make sure that you do not give humanity reason to believe that your Diary was not a work of the Holy Spirit. You are learning more with each passing day because the angels are teaching you as a part of the extension of your work. I tell you again that it is ready for the world. Those who are used to reading lofty manuscripts will embrace it as a work of art, those who rarely read such nobility will be proud to make it a part of their library for something to aspire to become, and those who read very little and are relatively poor will closely embrace the way you have approached the indignance and arrogance of the rich. Theologians and Priests will be exhilarated by its ecclesiastical authority, and cloistered servants will find it a great source of meditational aesthetics. The words have power and authority, admonition, compassion, poetical construction, and alliteration. All in all, it is being prepared for the entire spectrum and cross-section of the human race, for people of all walks of life and many faiths. I tell you that your reward will be great. The proof is in your living Fiat. The heavens know what you are both doing for Jesus. Can you see the authority of God in a way that even you did not expect? That is the tone that must be used in these Last Times. The days of a feeble, 'will you please be holy?' are gone! It is now time for the unequivocal Truth! That is why your Diary will succeed. No one is beyond reproach, short of the Holy Father and the Deity Itself! This is now your holy blessing. ✞ Thank you very much for your prayers. I will speak to you again very soon. I love you. Goodnight."

Friday, January 22, 1999
6:41 p.m.

Our Lady began by repeating some words that She told me on September 1, 1994:

"The world you seek is a mystical parlor of unsuppressed divinity, filled to the brim with mutual affection, noble purposes, sanctified actions, and blessed repercussions. This is the Earth that is slowly coming to be, the newly redressed conscience of humanity that will allow all sleeping souls to awaken in Light, spirit and revelation; upright and holy, willing to recognize the God who has claimed you and assent to the Will that shall deliver your souls to Paradise."

She then continued,

"Let us pray for the end of the scourge of abortion on this anniversary day. I have already seen its end. They are all with Me in Heaven, the wholly, Holy Innocents whose little lives were abbreviated by the evil hands of wretched souls and lost hearts. Thank you for praying with Me for this just cause. There are many reprobates who would as soon see the rest of the world lie in the frigid waters of indifference. You however are on fire with the Love of God! You help melt this opposition to the spiritual perfection of those who are about to be converted anyway. Love cannot be stopped and will not retreat in the face of any enemy. Your opposition's offenses are already in shambles. They have taken too much for granted and been forced to concede too many opportunities without advancing their malignant cause. Sweet victory is soon to be yours! It is only a matter of time. The clock is running out as each new day dawns. Prepare for the celebration of your lives. I will tell you when it will be permissible to perch on the edge of your seats and run victoriously onto the field. My Special son, it is time to address your Diary and the beginning of its dissemination. I will give you new lessons, fresh images, expanded parameters, and more beautiful expressions for your second work. My son, remember that I have told you many times that dignity is a gift that only few are willing to bestow. Jesus is the reason you have the authority to claim your dignity from every people in all the nations. Live the dignity that is yours! Fight gracefully for your right to be free in Christ, My everlasting Son! You are living proof that My faith was not in vain. Go where you shall. I will follow! Saint Francis will also be there with you. You should pray for this very holy Pope who is Mine. Please pine for his safety. There will be another Pope, but not another like this one. You shall never see his like again! Does this not mean that the Return of My Son is precariously imminent? Never forego your hopes, I beg you. You must be assured in confidence and joy that goodness is yours. You will see Jesus soon and Myself even earlier! Your faith has been equally as fruitful. None of your work has been in vain. I have been traveling the world-over and have seen the condition of human hearts. Many are now cracking wide open in joyful expectation of Jesus to come. But, some are still indignant about approaching the Sacraments. Their disposition of outright disdain will not impede the march of Truth that is forthcoming! Your Diary is part of the first wave of that Truth. If your Diary has the success for which I pray, there will be very little secularism left in the world by the time Jesus returns. We shall see what God provides. Let us keep praying together."

I recently saw on television a horrific orphanage filled with children who were being stored like cattle in filthy surroundings with no one to love them. I begged in tears for our Holy Mother to deliver them. She replied,

"They are being rescued as we speak. You have seen a benevolent and humanitarian use of the electronic medium. Thank you for your prayers. We will watch the Holy Father in Saint Louis."

Friday, January 29, 1999
7:10 p.m.

"This is the happiest time for the Reign of My Queenship, thanks to My beautiful little children. It is the age during which everything I have prayed for will be culminated. I know that you are still enjoying the commanding words of the Angels. They are utilizing both modern and ancient artifacts to glorify the divinity of the Holy Cross. Jesus is the invincible Savior who is worthy of their supernal expressions. I must tell you in candor that the Holy Spirit is helping you write. I wish you could see the smile of confident assurance that you place on the Face of God when He sees the result of your labors. He is equally pleased by the intercession of the Angels, and they are expected to do well because they live in Heaven. It is your pious work that is the miracle of this process! Thank you for your loyalty! God will bless you richly with lavish gifts of confirmation of your prayers in light of your efforts. I am happy that you were so touched-of-heart by the visit from the Holy Father to Saint Louis. He assuredly is My beloved Pope and the Vicar of Christ for all peoples. Can you not detect all the signs that God has given between this Pope and your brother's life, and you and the great Saint Pio? What more could the world want when they perceive all this? Can you see why God loves this Pontificate so endearingly? Worthiness can never be earned. His Love is a fruit of His Holy Grace. I am always with you, and I will never leave your side. Your photograph of the little tricycles is a work of genius. I love you."

Friday, February 5, 1999
7:14 p.m.

"You are the Children of Light, the people of hope who will never surrender the Truth for any reason. No material can purchase the faithfulness that you offer God. No persecution can diminish your divinity, and no single day in time can detract from the eternity you have come to know. My little children, if you stand beside Me and look behind at the eight years that have brought you to this month, your vision will be much like looking down a long dark street, lighted at every intersection where you have bowed to pray with Me to God the Father. This light is still glowing, still emanating into the shantied neighborhoods that once lay in complete darkness. These eight years have made the total difference in your lives for which you have prayed long hours before. All of this began on the Feast of My Assumption nearly ten years ago on a mountaintop in a far-off country. And now, we are producing the sweet fruits of that decade so the world can finally come in faith and trust to know their Savior, My Jesus. Dear children, this is no passing gift for the world, but a permanent sign, a grace that shall never die, and an admonishment for a globe that nearly waited too long to commit itself to Christian conversion. Your days are flickering like the flame of a candle in the ocean breezes. When the breath of God becomes so intense that it extinguishes time, no man will ever stand blind again. Everyone will see with the new vision of the soul, and there will be not one sedentary distraction that will inhibit the most prodigal of God's children from seeking His Holy Face with fervor and anticipation. Little ones, you know that people often peer into the sky if someone else is standing nearby staring overhead. Everyone wants to see what is up there. Your work and your lives are the catalyst that will soon turn many faces upward to the omnipotence, the divinity, and the power of God. Your faces were among the first to seek the Heavenly Firmament, so do not be dismayed by those who try to trample your toes in an effort to tempt you to look back down into the world. They cannot harm you now. When they stand upon your feet, they will simply be that much closer to Paradise. The pain you feel will be the reverse intensity of the ecstasy they will know upon realizing that Heaven is real. It is 1999 and I cannot see the immortal clock on the wall, but I do know that Jesus is vesting for reentry into His Kingdom, into the land of mortal men that He claimed for His Father 2,000 years ago. It appears that He has a book in His precious hands that He wishes to be dispensed before He arrives. Yes, something about the shining of a Morning Star in the world's darkest hour. You will assuredly have time to begin your second Diary, but He may decide to return tomorrow! If He does, we will all be triply rewarded for your efforts and prayerful intentions...

My Special one, you speak of sadness for the passing of this Pontiff into Glory. You must transform this into jubilation. It will begin the ushering-in of the final battle for souls that I have told you about many times before, the war that I have prepared you to endure. It will be the great Crucifixion of the Faith-Church on Earth, the New Passion which you are already seeing. These are special times with holy graces by the multitudes about to fall on those who remain at My feet and inside the Sacred Heart of Jesus. Never should you feel one moment of doubt that what you will see in your final years is ordained and allowed by God the Father for holy purposes that you yet cannot know. All will be made clear before the end of time. For now, we walk together down the dark corridors of the Earth, lighting the path for millions to see their way back to God through Jesus. I am happy and grateful that you have decided for Him, that you have stayed at My side for so long. You truly do not realize what this means to God. On the date of April 16, the birthday of your brother's mother and the anniversary of the passing of Saint Bernadette, you will have been attending daily Mass for ten years! This would have been unperceivable for you in your younger days. You have witnessed the same Crucifixion over 3,600 times and received the Body and Blood of Jesus who has kept your spirit pure and your body chaste. He is your health and Salvation. I am confident that you understand the immense power this gives you to witness for Jesus on the Earth to your roguish brothers and sisters. Yours is the power to bless, admonish, unite, and recollect. You have the same authority as the original Apostles to speak the Truth with confidence. Like them, you will be perfectly persecuted, and this too will be glorified."

Friday, February 12, 1999
7:33 p.m.

"My dearly beloved children, I offer My gratitude and blessings for staying at the side of your Savior, for never wavering in faith and allegiance to His Holy Name. You do not realize how fortunate you are to be playing such a significant role in the conversion of humanity. In addition to this pious new order, you are assisting hundreds-of-thousands before you to be granted the Light of Heaven from the throes of Purgatory. How could your lives be more fruitful? How could you be more blessed? You must remember that God provides every syllable with which you praise Him. He gives you keen eyes to see with faith and the heart to embrace His lost children with love. You have the will to choose, and you have decided for God. This not only opens many doors, it allows you to completely transcend the bonds of human mortality. My special sons, you are not the same children you were eight years ago. While the world is at a rapid pace for change to accommodate fashion and whim, you have remained steadfast in faith and love for God. Prior to 1991, you somewhat conceded to the tides of life and the trendy novelties that distract humankind from prayer. It is alright to proclaim your pride in Christ! Be proud not of yourselves or your lives, but that Jesus has raised your souls to a higher station and nobler position of grace. If you remember only a few lessons I have taught, please always remember this—I could have done nothing here in this place or through your mortal work if you had chosen to follow another course. You decided for God, and the reward awaiting you will be stupendous. You will never lose this blessing because you shall never fall from grace. I would like to ask you to pray especially in the near future for the poor people who live in Third World countries, for those in Eastern Europe, for all abandoned children, the starving, the lonely, and those stricken by disease. Please pray for the end of war, for the end of abortion, for the Holy Father, and for souls in their last agony. I will pray with you. Please remember to invoke the powerful intercession of the Saints. Our unified petitions will make a difference in alleviating the suffering that so many millions bear. I remind you to be careful when you are driving so you do not have an accident. You live in a dangerous world."

Friday, February 19, 1999
7:05 p.m.

"My dear little children, how faithfully I love you. I have felt a rejuvenation in My Immaculate Heart for eight years come Monday. These are the days and weeks we have been praying together to achieve. God is pleased by your willingness to remain loyal to Him in reflection of Jesus and to honor My Grace. Time proceeds quickly, and you will soon say, *where did it go?* My little children, I am unsure whether you realize the indelible beauty that is present in your holy Diary. If it reached but a dozen souls, they would be twelve more whose faith would blossom to the strength of the first Apostles. I assure you that you will recognize its power when you have the opportunity to examine it over time. Do not become complacent because the particular, specific messages for the new millennium will soon begin. Perhaps your Savior will return before it is finished! I have seen the weeping in your eyes, and I know that your prayers are in union with Mine. You are the blessed reason why My messages have flourished. To that end, your witness for Jesus last Sunday is the reason why hundreds of little children will be spared physical abuse by their parents. They will shed no more tears and suffer no more pain. Thank you from the heights of the heavens. The cruel act prompted you to respond, and you *had* to respond; there was no alternative because Jesus wished you to confront the perpetrator.* Please feel only elation about what transpired. I ask you to remember all the poor souls who need your prayers. The world is still an awful place, but we help with every utterance of our prayers. I will remember you in a special way during the predawn hours of Monday. Thank you for your petitions."

** This was an incident at a gathering where I was required to confront a very dominating personality to check his conduct. It happened in front of quite a few other individuals who did not understand the parameters of what was occurring or the merciful admonishment for what it was. This is too often the case in these situations and is the reason evil continues its onslaught unimpeded. Pandemonium broke out, and I was ridiculed mercilessly as being the one who caused the entire incident. I was told that I was mentally deranged and was the worst example of Christianity that could ever exist. It is such a heavy burden being misunderstood when asked by the heavens to forcefully address situations that most others slink away from in cowardice. I have to respond no matter what any other person thinks and accept the consequences whether they be ridicule, banishment or even death, because I know the truth clearly and will be held accountable at my judgement for not dispensing the Truth as I have been commanded.*

Friday, February 26, 1999
7:27 p.m.

"My dearest sweet children, your Mother of Immaculate Love has come to pray with you again. I am your source of divine graces. I bring you Jesus and the Angels who accompany Him. In this very room, we have entered nine years of petitions to God on behalf of the sorrowful world. This is a miracle of tremendous proportion for you and all humankind. I have taught you how to love and the true consequences of the element of time. You know the reason Jesus died on the Cross better than you ever understood before. And during this holy season of Lent, you are again sharing in the self-denial that has led to the conversion of millions of souls and their consecration to the Heart of God the Father. My children, it is a story about the finer things that I come to tell. These are the fruits that remake you into righteous people, a special order of citizens who know your way back to the blessings from which you fell under the burden imposed upon you by Adam. These are the days that Creation has been waiting for since God placed the prophetic star in the night skies over Bethlehem. You once were speaking of the miracles occurring in the far-off mountaintops of our beloved Medjugorje. Now, you are planning the procedures for disseminating a work that rivals, propels, reflects, and magnifies that same auspicious shrine. Time is deceiving; to God there has been no passing decade. You were standing on a summit in a sparkling hamlet on August 15, 1989 when I placed your Diary in your hands. You will now know that same euphoric blessing again, ten years to the day, here in your own homeland. My children, these things have occurred because you believed in faith and prayed to be part of the universal conversion of the souls of men. It is true that you have no other Lord than Jesus Christ. He has no other children with the unique qualities present in each of you. Most of all, My little ones, you have grown to learn about the indispensable powers of Love. There is no greater power because there is no other power. I hope that you rise every day in the fresh happiness that I have brought. When you open your eyes to each new dawn, you are seeing the blinking and shuddering of the world in the face of Eternal Light. I am with the Genius of Creation at this moment. He has sent Me here because He knows that you will respond. Nothing else should matter to you. You are achieving the mission you have set-out to do. Nothing can take it away; no time, space, sorrow, no altercations, no stain or stench of politics, and no natural disaster can remove from Creation the work you have accomplished for God. This is a very special and happy time for the Hosts of Heaven because they are seeing the work you are doing and the culmination of success you are about to achieve. The Lord urges you to remain humble as a matter of course, but He also asks you to be proud of the work you have finished in Him. Nothing in Creation can reproach it. Evil cannot steal or destroy it, and God will always cherish it. I have told you about the multiple dimensions of the human intellect. To that end, you will often read your own journal and see the transcending divinity that the Dominion Angels are placing in it that you cannot see. You will be as surprised and amazed as the rest of humanity. And while I praise you for your laboring, I remind you that it has only begun. You cannot know what the future holds, and God will require you to carry many crosses before the world is through. As I have told you many times, I will be with you through every trial as I have always been, and as I was with Jesus during His battles on Earth. Thank you for your holy conviction. I will be with you beyond the expiration of time."

Friday, March 5, 1999
7:19 p.m.

"My dear holy children, can you sense the passing of the ages quickly making way for the Return of the Son of Man? I am the revelation preceding the end of the world. Once I have finished the work I have begun here on the Earth, I shall not return again. There will be no need because the Savior of humanity will bring you to Me. You must live in the hope that Heaven will smile upon you when that moment arrives. How easy it would be for you to fall to the distractions and temptations of the temporal world, but your faith is strong and your love is precise. You know no other life than the freedom bestowed upon you by Jesus. You have no desire to retreat to the bondage of the physical Earth. My children, as your days pass-by, you are living among the same souls with whom you shall reside in Paradise. They do not yet realize it, but you already know, which makes your lives more difficult because the others will not pull together in the direction of righteousness. It is much like people tugging on contrary ends of a rope. I tell you that you are gaining more ground than those who oppose you. You simply cannot discern your progress because it seems so slow in coming. I have told you about the deceptive element of time. Please do not fall prey to its subversion. You are living the timeless Love of My Jesus, the Holy Eucharist, and the Divine Spirit in the utter sweetness of My Immaculate Heart. The world seems to fester, groan and broil, but you are on the higher ground, unaffected by the brutality and indifference below. I assure you that your weariness is from nervous anxiety, not from spiritual or physical fatigue. I am beside you every day, morning, noon and night. I even watch you while you sleep. My children, I am most grateful for your obedience and veneration of your Holy Mother. I can proudly say that I have spoiled you beyond all reason by My kind graces. God wishes to remind you that I am not to offer candy kisses every time you feel hurt, impugned, or insulted for standing-up against His enemies, for this is what you are expected to do. I am asked to tell you tonight that your unwillingness to get sufficient rest is offensive to Jesus. We have addressed this issue before. You did well for awhile, but are now reverting to your restless life. Can you tell that you do not feel as well when you are tired? I will speak to you beyond the ensuing week."

Sunday, March 14, 1999
5:44 p.m.

"My dear beautiful children, this is a very holy Sabbath day on which your Heavenly Father has gifted you with countless blessings, not the least of which is Love Himself to which He has added Mercy, Pardon, Grace, Sacrifice, and the special benison of My intercession! Oh! My dear loving children, so many are the days when Jesus has wished humankind to know the Divine Love of His Sacred Heart. The moments transcend eternal perpetuity, and they are unfolding in your lifetime. The hour has arrived! You are participating in the advent of the Jubilee to celebrate the redemption of humankind! Do you realize what this signifies to Creation? While you are shaking from the wracking of your nerves, the Angels are trembling at your sight! How many more times must I tell you that these are the occasions of the culmination of all that is good, a plenary period for renewal and consecration to the righteousness that My Son has berthed around the globe? The discussion has never been about who outspeaks others in the trivial minutia of the universe, it has always been a facilitation of when God's Holy Word will return and pulverize the senseless rhetoric."

Today, I was called into a close engagement with those who are literally my worst enemies, some of whom were present at the previous altercation a few weeks ago. They despise the life I am leading with my brother. They detest my words of admonishment toward reconciliation and our mutual Christian responsibilities. I have repeated over and again my love for them, but this morning, God asked me to lay down and surrender to their desires and allow them to feel that they were victorious over me in a matter that they had interpreted only to their selfish benefit. When I went to their house to complete what they had demanded that I do for them, there was no one there with the courage to greet me. Nobody was home. They had all gathered at a neighbor's house. I completed what they desired and left a note stating that I had fulfilled their wishes. I cannot describe the feelings of rejection that gripped my heart as I walked back to my car, knowing that their eyes were peering from the windows of the house across the street. Our Lady said,

"My Special son, you are now listening to the prophetic words of the Final Colossus, and I am saying that you cannot yet see the light you are revealing. I have told you that the battles would intensify, and that you would be shaken and weakened by them. Today a portion of that prophecy was fulfilled. Why do you cower? Why do you fear? There is nothing on Earth that can destroy your inner-peace but you yourself. This is a most unique time in history, an age that scores of generations before you wished had come to them. These are their hours you are finishing, their victory you are reclaiming! Why do you weep, and why do you cringe? The engagement has begun! The people who have opposed you in this very room are now living in shame, shock, grief, and horror because they can see themselves at the brink of being defeated by a Truth who has refused to die in the wake of their lost faith! I stand with the Hosts of Heaven, peering-down upon the Earth, nearly losing My composure in proclaiming, *That's My little boy! That's My loving child!* There is no reason for any inhibition and no time to cower! I beseech you to be proud of your work in the name of faith, love, and conversion. Stand tall so all Creation can marvel at your power! Let the heavens resound with the remnants of your acclamations while the doers of evil flee to the depths of defeat at the sound of your voice! And, I am not speaking of any one incident or any certain hour. Your whole life has been the process of inhaling the Will of God and exhaling your answer of 'yes' in obedience. There are no artful works or convention orations that can compete with your mastery of His divinity! You are a teacher of the Gospel of the same Jesus Christ who made you a great educator of this century in union with the Holy Spirit and the good and decent Christians who have worked silently and simultaneously for the cause of Deific Love. How could anyone not concede to such Providence?

Do not be ashamed of your adversaries, be kind to them, for God has made them unwitting pawns in the victory of His charge. You left a prophetic message with them of Good News! What you wrote in your note was a stroke of genius, fit for the history books and the annals of immortal binding! They were not words of cruel regret, retribution or admonishment, they were your signature on their declaration of independence, granting them amnesty from the temptations that bring their behavior down into the filthy squalls of the world. Your words were your written blessing, a prayer for their hearts, a reason for them to change. And they will change! By all means, you have penned their clemency from greed and isolation. Their souls know this to be true, but their minds still batter their hearts, trying to keep them from believing it. This is a sample of what your Diary will be for the culpable who read it. I remind you that the Saints have secured the highest places in Heaven for your detractors, because how difficult it would have been for many of those close to you to believe, accept, and practice what you and your brother have proclaimed to be true for eight years and a month. I have come to uplift your spirit. Thank you for understanding. Do you know what your brother means when he tells you that you will beat them at the polls? Precinct by precinct means heart to heart! The collective spirit of America and the world will prove the success of your hard labors, the campaign you are still waging for My Jesus. Only you can destroy your peace. Jesus gives it to you perpetually. I hope you enjoy this message for eternity to come. Please live hopefully in its truth. I love you."

Sunday, March 21, 1999
5:45 p.m.

"My dear beautiful children, long have you waited to achieve the success you are now coming to know. These are the days of the formal proceduralization of your work where tens-of-thousands will be made aware that a universal launch is about to take place. Make no mistake, this public revelation* is only the start of the year that you will remember with greater intensity than 1989 or 1991. I ask you to maintain your composure, stay within yourself, and continue your progress one day at a time. Your spirits are high because your souls anticipate the success you have been praying to achieve. However, your hearts must tell you to maintain your efforts forthrightly. This is your singular opportunity to present your Diary to humanity for the first time. You are prayerfully patient because you know that it must be done correctly, and your soul is jubilant because you already foresee the outcome. You are about to achieve one of the greatest victories known to mortal man. You must go slowly, being careful not to allow your precious pearls to be trampled by the swine. Your loving Jesus will take it in hand and help humanity heed the messages I have given you. I have been traveling the globe, praying with My wonderful children in their prayer groups, and have hovered above humble souls who have been kneeling alone in secluded corners of the world. My children belong to Me in mind, heart, and soul. I will give you all the information that I intended to offer from the foundation of the Earth. You will never fail to receive all My messages in their entirety before the world is through. I must go to bless My other little children beneath My caring Mantle with your sweet Jesus who was Sorrowfully Crucified to save your mortal souls. Thank you for your prayers, they are welcomed in Heaven."

** "public revelation" does not refer to the Deposit of Catholic Faith, but the public manifestation of Our Lady as the Morning Star Over America.*

Sunday, March 28, 1999
5:03 p.m.

"This is the home to which all of the Heavenly Hosts follow Me, to see and pray with the two children of God who are making such an eternal difference in the elevation of so many souls. It is your faith, My children, that tells you this is true. Yes, you have seen many miraculous signs of grace, but these supernatural gifts satisfy only your mortal inquisitions. The Love in your heart is the true source of faith, not only for you, but for all of mankind. You are living proof that God is real. Your testament of faith is God's validation that He wields complete power and authority over Creation. His Wisdom is the source of your undaunted trust that Jesus Christ holds in His possession the destiny of every soul that the Almighty Father has given life. My children, your Savior is elated that millions have chosen to return to His side. He is as happy that His people have chosen to come Home as are the very souls who have gone there. That is why the tombs and graves of the deceased are empty. Your Jesus could not wait until the end of time to bring them back to His embrace. You have learned to not be deceived by the element of time. You are the living proof that righteousness is the source of all mortal strength and that Love is the origin of all immortal life. I have had the pleasure of watching you grow and learn. I know the expanse of your anticipation and what makes you happy. Your hearts are mended, healed, and consoled because I am comforting them. Jesus is the mainstay of your courage and determination. I offer Him to you with pride because I know that He will soon bring you back Home to My side. You must always remember that the Holy Family that you so admire has walked the same Earth that you now tread. We have suffered the same wounds and grieved the same sorrows. Humanity lives within the circumference of our joined hands as we circle the globe, seeking-out hearts who will step forward in faith, face the bantering world, give the charge of conversion to the many hidden valleys and aloof peaks, and suffer gladly anything that befalls you, all for the sake of being poised at the end of time on the plateau of Salvation. That, My little children, is why I come to bless, to teach, to petition, to invite, to share, to love, to pray and to partake in the most living and brilliant faith to be found anywhere in this American nation. I am the Morning Star of your Lord! I have come to this heartland prairie of the most affluent country in the world, just to seek you out. You know that wealth is truly not everlasting power. You know that justice is not brought through a gavel, a jury, or a system of penal ethics. You know that justice is a child of peace, a peace that can bloom only from the seed of Love in the heart. I have seen the world that you will one-day see as the New Earth. It is the Holy Spirit in you who is making it new, this Love who has died so that all mortal life can live again. You have become the incarnation of the original Love who has created the very soil on which you tread. I have Good News for you on top of even greater news. Your souls are saved, and your faith and servitude are the origin of the conversion of millions more who will know the Light of endless Glory at the end of time. When you see the world in looking back at it when time is done, you will not have to look down at the ring on your finger or the automobile you are driving and cry-out that you could have purchased the Salvation of just one more soul. You are the Oskar Schindlers of the immortal ages, the lineage of the fruits that begot the foundation of faith, charity, and good works that has been profoundly absent since the early centuries. The souls of your brothers and sisters have already been purchased by Jesus Christ. You are the holy stenographers and clerks who are reminding Him who to include in the manifest of the children of God who will all join in Heaven. That is the list that you are compiling for God in this, the world's darkest hour, for affirmation and deliverance to Mercy by the Morning Star Over America. That, My children, is why I have come to this holy place. I come for the lost and lame, the pitiful and aggrieved, those who cannot stand on their own, the weak and alone. I come to you because you care more about the Salvation of humankind than your standard of living. You hear the Voice of God and know the essence of His tone. You add harmony and tenor to the meaning of human existence, you give the deposed reason to stand and be counted again, you breathe life into the quarters of the Earth that have been dead in sin for countless generations; and most of all, My little angels, you are God's instruments in repairing the breach that befell the collective body of humankind under the Cross from a sixteenth century gone awry. The Reformation was not the beginning of freedom for the faithless, it was their start toward an errant path that your work will now reverse. You may invoke all the symbolism that you wish—the gauntlet has been thrown, the glove has slapped the cheek, or whatever metaphor you choose to employ. But, the fact is, the battle is begun to re-unite the Church under the dominion of Saint Peter. The time has come! This is the hour! No other age will be able to bear-out the truths that are to be revealed in the next months. I do not tell you this to raise your ire or your anger. There will be no vengeance in this battle. There is only victory in the offing, a victory that was given flight from the mountaintop that saved the world, from the Cross that shed Light on every error, and from the skies that still billow with grace-shaped clouds that make Palm Sunday one for all ages. This, My children, is why I visit this place. You are the reasons why your sweet Jesus in Heaven and on Earth has hope. He knows your willingness to serve and your capacity to succeed in Him. I would never bring you to a hope that is false. I am telling you the Truth that springs from the incomparable integrity of the Infinite and Sacred Heart of My Son. Your hearts and souls know that all of this is true. That is why you will never grow too weary to continue in your work. That is why the Angels come running to you like honey bees around a flower, that is why Jesus falls to one knee and places His Face in His palms in thanksgiving while looking at you and says 'Thank God! My brothers are standing for Me! They are living for Love! They have dignified My Death through the faith in their lives.'

My special little children, this is also the reason why I come to this home. You are a blessed people who have a holy direction. You are proving it in delineating your faith by-laws. Please be confident in God's assurance of your success, come enemy, opponent, plight, suffering, or even death. Keep the Truth in your hearts that this is the last age, and your Father in Heaven has not depleted His supply of miracles. There are plentiful weapons in store, many more lasers of Light, flashes of Truth, and the searing bolts of lightning to awaken the slumbering souls who now only recognize you as two people who ride around in a white pick-up truck. Time is not through, and neither is your Father. I will never allow you to go to rest without full-proof that you will have none-other than complete victory when all is through. Thank you for listening to My words of hope and victory on this Passion Sunday. It is now Holy Week. I wish for you to pray the Stations of the Cross on Good Friday. You are both serving the Stations as you live each day. Thank you... Thank you for your holy prayers. I give you now a very special blessing. ✞ That is especially why I have come to this place! I will speak to you soon. I love you. Goodnight."

Sunday, April 4, 1999
Easter Sunday
5:35 p.m.

"This is the humble abode of the little children I love, the righteous sons of the Holy, Divine, Crucified, and Resurrected Savior of the world. My dear ones, you celebrate year-in and year-out the Paschal Mystery of Jesus because you know that His victory over death is real. His Spirit was placed again into His physical frame, and He emerged from the Sepulcher as a Living

Man on Easter, never to die again. You are beginning to see the heresies and error of so-called *revisionist christianity* claiming that Jesus was not resurrected. It is in the public newspaper today. This is a vile lie from the mouth of Satan. It will gain no ground in taking My children from the Church, but it will inhibit many from converting as early as hoped. I have told humanity on many occasions that in the end, My Immaculate Heart will Triumph. What does this Triumph imply? It underscores the fact that no longer will there be a venue for error and no means for Satan to perpetuate his scandals against the Catholic Church or My children who comprise it. This is Easter Sunday. Jesus Christ has risen as He said! Next week is the observation of the Feast of Divine Mercy. It would be proper for you to spend that Holy Hour in the Chapel in Adoration of the Most Blessed Sacrament. You will find plenteous Mercy there. My little children, the world is bubbling-over in war, famine, hatred, and division. Please make it your special intention to pray away these horrible scourges. I know that you cannot understand the reasoning behind every conflict, but you assuredly wield their solution. Prayer is the key to ending each one. I am asking you to play your part. Never once did Jesus ask Me to bear an ounce of the weight of the Cross. You must do your best to conquer whatever befalls you. I will never abandon you and will dispense endless graces. However, I will not bring you to relinquish your service to Jesus. I have been beside you during your entire lives. I will continue to help you in the ways God allows to allay your fears, comfort your hearts, and make you one in My Son through the Holy Spirit. You must remember that I have not been sent to perform your pious works for you or carry your crosses. I will pray for your strength and understanding in the things that God asks you to do. When you remember the severity of these times, you will never question the resolve of God to press you into higher service. The Holy Spirit will forever tell you the Truth. Your heart cannot lie because it is the home of the Living Truth. And, My Special son, you are noticing a certain lack of peacefulness within a close proximity of your home. Satan has been working for the past eleven months to isolate you in torment. Your neighbors and their animals are his instruments. This should bring you great joy! The dismay will soon be spread on their faces just before they become your most ardent supporters, realizing that they were in the same crowd who shouted *Crucify Him!* and later to stand and proclaim *This was truly the son of God!* Your worst opposition will not come from your neighbors or your friends, or even from your archenemies. Your adversaries will not even be your family. My children, your main enemy is the inordinate urgency inside yourselves to see an immediate response to your Diary. You must be more patient and wait for Jesus to wield this holy weapon in His good time. And, your friends will come back to your prayer group. This is the spring and summer that will take you past the publication of your Diary into its dispensation to all the world, and on to the recording of My messages for the next century.

My dear children, it is difficult for Me to place into words the invaluable success you are achieving! Pause and think for a moment; your Diary will soon be entering the hands of humankind. This is reason for the heavens to dance with delight. I wish you could see with the eyes of your souls as the Hosts of the Heavens are beginning to gather around you like 100,000 fans preparing to fill a stadium for a championship game. This is one for the ages, one for the record books! Yes, you are in the nearby locker room, donning your apparel. I am one of your greatest cheerleaders and fans. Your spirit is telling you that this is on the horizon, and is why you must remain composed and in control of your emotions. The next months will be no pushover victory. It will be a hard fought one! But, you will win at the last! You cannot be defeated. Your enemies will fight just as though God will change His mind and allow them to conquer you. My little son, He never will. All Heaven already realizes the outcome, but the Hosts are just as excited to see you succeed as though they were unaware. I am here to thank you for celebrating the Resurrection of the Son of Man with faith and zeal. You shall not depart this Earth until you see the celebration you feel in your heart. God is leaving signs all around, like the simple fireworks last night in the country skies,* and the woman with the book in her arm at the restaurant that said just one word, your brother's name. These are His seals of hope! God does not tease you with tidbits of Truth like pieces of candy for coercion. He is giving you Life through the Sacred Body of Jesus on the Altar of Sacrifice! You need no other graces, but He insists on providing them anyway. You and your brother are two fortunate souls to be receiving messages from your Virgin Mother. It is you who have said yes to God, and this is why I have remained with you during all these years. You have given your lives to My Son, and you will be richly rewarded. I summon your composure to be strong, patient, enduring, mature, and restful while awaiting the final moments. A new day has been on the horizon for several years, one that will dawn before your eyes. I remind you to stay close to each other. Your Diary is the fruit of your union in Jesus. Glory to the Paschal Lamb!"

* *My brother and I were driving down the highway returning home last evening when we noticed a lone display of fireworks exploding in the distance over the fields. We both mentioned how nice that was to see on the Vigil of Easter. It gave us a warmth amidst the peace of the night.*

Sunday, April 11, 1999
Feast of the Divine Mercy
1:11 p.m.

"My dearly beloved children, this is the Sunday of The Divine Mercy, the stated period of extraordinary absolution for all souls who pray in heartfelt love for God. I am the Mother of Mercy, and I bear the gifts of My Son to all nations. My children, the world is very poor, and Jesus wishes to make your souls rich in His pardon and forgiveness. It is not so much that humankind has lost hope for the future, but the factual basis behind the horrible tragedies you are seeing is that people refuse to rebuke the force of outright evil. A forfeiture of spiritual hope is not necessarily the problem, but is a product, symptom, and effect of the problem. Humankind declines to pray for deliverance from the influences of Satan. I wish you could know how God looks at His children who have yet to come to this faith. He has great pity upon those who do not know Him. My Special son, through the assistance and intercessory Wisdom of the Holy Spirit, we are bringing the Good News to God's people; to you and your brother, and thousands of others who know not to become enthralled by the awful trappings of the world, the commotion, the cynicism, and the unmitigated involvement in malevolent works. My Special one, it is the faith that you now live that provides your insight into the Light that has conquered the night. This is the reason why you trust in the Mercy which flows from the Sacred Heart of Jesus. The Divine Mercy of God exists for every soul to imbibe, partake, and consume. This is why such souls as those for whom you now pray are being granted the Eternal Light of Heaven. Those who have fallen to temptation and sin are not inherently evil in nature, they have simply been helpless to escape its clutches. If you remember My earlier messages, you will recall that the battle has never been one of man against other men, but of humankind versus evil. You are seeing good people fail and fall in death around you as victims of that fight. Souls who are weak do not intrinsically belong to the fires of condemnation. What they require most is repentance, Divine Mercy, pardon, purification, absolution, and Salvation. These are the fruits of true deliverance. This is the reason why The Divine Mercy was dispensed to the Earth in a series of messages portraitured on February 22, 1931. I wish to assure you that the little one who has taken the life of another and that of his own is now in Purgatory. His soul will never be condemned. Like so many before him, he did not have the righteous strength to combat the rejection he felt from the mother of his children who said, '*I do not love you anymore.*' There is an infinite amount of darkness in these words. Please remember for the rest of your years what I am going to tell you now. Those on the Earth who are not loved by anyone are not as culpable for their mistakes. My son, humanity has yet to accept this truth, and they are committing the most egregious errors. Indeed, this is a

Sunday of Divine Mercy for those who are weak, but it is also a time for everyone to pray for the obstinate who refuse to recognize the origin of tragedy and corruption—a lack of love and forgiveness in the first heart that is offended by another. Refusing to offer forgiveness is a direct reflection of the morbid stench of human pride. I call upon you to remember with fidelity that The Divine Mercy of Jesus is alive to absolve murderers and thieves, adulterers and liars. However, its power is needed to a much higher degree for those who impugn the dignity of these sinners by discarding them in repulsion and rejection, rather than calling them into their hearts and arms for forgiveness and conversion. The origin of all human sin is *not love.* What occurs subsequent to this is insult, but certainly not the initial injury. You have the capacity to make this clear to your brothers and sisters when you know that the time is right. The Almighty Father will supply the venue."

This past Thursday evening, a terrible tornado struck our childhood hometown. It tore through the heart of the mobile home court where Timothy and I met for the first time when I was just a boy delivering the newspaper to his parents' trailer door. What has made this occurrence all the more trying for the people of the village was that this disaster was just another in a string of suffering that they have collectively endured in the short period of a decade. Over the past ten years, there have been three overwhelming floods that have inundated and consumed the homes, personal possessions, and property of dozens of its citizens. The deluges came from "hundred-year rains," as some people like to call them, which poured upon the countryside through the heart of their town. Never in all our years growing-up or in the memories of the villagers had there ever been such multiple occurrences of tragedy within the municipal boundaries of Ashland, Illinois. But in the midst of these events, there was spiritual light. The response of the townspeople to their misfortune was an amazing witness of Christian affection and unity for everyone to see. As my brother and I drove through the town, we noticed that the trailer sitting where he and his mother and father used to live had been untouched by the storm, while others beside it were upended, mangled and crumpled into useless piles of metal. The place he called home where we greeted each other for the very first time in our lives was standing as if nothing had happened. Our Holy Mother referred to our hometown this way,

"You traveled to see the terrible damage caused by the tornado. The strike was intended for the location where you and your brother first met. However, that home was left unscathed. In time, all will know the reason why evil takes revenge against its enemies. The residence you saw is the place in Creation where your Diary began. I assure you that you will understand fully and succinctly before you pass into Paradise. You will know all things with concise wisdom. The signs are all around. God's Love is real, and everything He does and allows bears a specific purpose, all to glorify His Kingdom."

The burdensome tragedies of the past decade upon our hometown signal the validity of the intercession of the Most Blessed Virgin Mary. Our friends and the families of this community have been united with us in the suffering that Christ perfectly conquered on the Cross of Calvary. They have been united with us as they too have suffered for the sake of this miraculous work. We are all one for the glory of the Father in Heaven. Our Lady then gave me a litany of signs that have occurred in our midst in relation to our work together. She showed me that even the course the tornado took as it progressed through the town glorified Her miraculous intercession and the Son whom She bore. After leaving the spot of my brother's youth intact, is it a coincidence that the storm passed harmlessly above the iron arbor which Timothy sat under and plucked his first grapes in 1958, the grapes that are transformed into the Blood of Christ? Is it a coincidence that the tornado passed over the exact spot where I was tackled by a thug and beaten for something I did not do when I was a young teenager, an incident I never told anyone about? And, is it a coincidence that the tornado leveled point-blank the Masonic Lodge in the heart of the village?

"The miracle of human love is in your heart. Thank you for praying the 3:00 p.m. Hour of The Divine Mercy. My Son will be listening. As always, thank you for staying beside Me in faith. Heaven is your reward."

Saturday, April 17, 1999
7:02 p.m

"My dearly beloved little children, the world as you know it is passing-away before your eyes. Your lives have become an undefiled projection of the divine image of God into Creation because Jesus has remade your souls into His own likeness. You are living the celebration of the Sacred Easter Mysteries! You are aware through faith that My Son will soon return to take you to Heaven, and this you will always accept deep inside your hearts. However, My children, there are many other matters that you must behold in faith. Soon, you will learn the Third Fatima Secret, and many manifestations will be made clear to you. The facts that remain to be revealed to humanity are among many you already know, that is you anticipate the arrival of justice, peace, forgiveness, Mercy, Light, and Salvation. My little ones, these are blessings and graces that seem almost foreign to millions of souls! Please be assured that you are living on an adopted land in communion with the Holy Paraclete and in the family of the Hosts of Heaven who have never lost hope for the conversion of the world. Today, I travel the globe seeking new hearts who will join that acclamation. I have also come to tell you that as silently and subtly as it might seem, righteousness is winning the victory and conversion is cultivating the Earth. Humanity is slowly coming to realize that Jesus is the Way, the Truth and the Life, not only for these final ages, but also for all eternity. I wish you could know how deeply you are loved by the millions upon millions of souls who inhabit Paradise for your hard work, your prayers, your daily attendance at Holy Mass, and for not conceding to the whims of so many who would have you pursue another way of life. You know the Truth and are therefore wise in the ways of God and aware of the subsistence of His Will for humanity. I wish for you to never allow a single thought of dissension to cause you to stray from the pious course on which you are traveling. You know that a tree will never deceive you because it lacks the ability to alter the sweetness of its own fruit. Humankind has grown accustomed to sugarcoating the effects of evil so that they do not seem so bad, to make them more alluring. The fruits of God need no such confecting to make them more savory to the taste. They are never bitter or sour; they are always moist and sweet. You must remember that there can be no tasting of the fruits of God's Love until your ability to recognize His sweetness is given to you by the Holy Spirit. I ask you to recall how large is the sum of people who will not savor the sweetness of Jesus because they will not approach the proper tree. As long as they remain addicted to the artificial draw of material wealth and sins of the flesh, they will not be in communion with the Eternal Feast Table. They will always be thirsty because their brine of shame will hold them fast to the craving of their own indifference. Creation is at the brink of breaking into a new era of revelation, and you are at the epicenter of its transformation. I will do everything I properly can in My Queenship to make the most of your holy work by every conceivable means. Thank you for spending so much time praying for your Diary. There is no way I can repay you for your faithfulness until you see it with your own eyes. This will be very soon. While I have told you that your book will be opposed by many, you will be kept busy with the groundswell of support from your loyal friends. I am happy that you keep the future in perspective, knowing how the past ten years of your life have affected it. If anyone asks why there are decades in the Holy Rosary, you may show them May 31, 1989 to May 31, 1999. I must go visit My other children now, the hundreds-of-thousands praying the Rosary together who do not receive messages like you and your brother. They pray in faith, blind trust, and living love for God. Can you see why they are so blessed? Thank you for your humble petitions. Please remember the poor souls in Purgatory."

Sunday, April 25, 1999
3:50 p.m.

"My dear beautiful children, what a joyous season this is as you ponder the coming Ascension of Jesus! These are the Easter miracles that make giants out of paupers, orators out of those too timid to speak, and great Saints of those who have yet to greet the Holy Spirit by name. These are the moments,

My children, when the opportunity of all ages is beckoning you to be patient for its fulfillment, sitting back and poised in peace while God unfolds the graces onto humanity which He holds in His storehouse like spreading a picnic blanket under a gallant tree in a slumbering meadow. I invite you to remember not to work yourself into an anticipatory frenzy or state of anxiety about the months you will soon come to know. I have asked you before, and it is increasingly important as each new week arrives, you must maintain your composure and poise, not becoming giddy about the work you are prepared to complete. Your composure must come from within, otherwise your work will not be sound, your message will be unclear, and your nerves will be the worse for the wear. Confident composure! The victory is yours. Soothe your anxieties and allow them to rescind. There will be plentiful time for celebration when the morning arrives. I have told you many things. My graces have poured upon you like showers for the flowers. I have offered you hundreds-of-thousands of words comprised of millions of letters, and they all come down to one immeasurable love. No time can constrain this victory, and no eternity can destroy it. You are part of the endless Triumph of My Immaculate Heart that humanity on Earth is about to see for the first time. My precious child, you are invaluable to Me! I have told you over and again that My labors on Earth cannot be accomplished without your prayers. Your work for Jesus is also such a prayer. I have come to speak to you today to tell you that I love you, to pray with you, and offer My utterances of encouragement and guidance. I am but a simple Mother who has always yearned for your success."

Sunday, May 2, 1999
5:20 p.m.

"The dear sweet children of My Immaculate Heart know the Light that they see within the depths of their souls! My little ones, you are the reason I said Yes to the Archangel Gabriel. The Dominion of God has forever lived in My Heart, even before Jesus was conceived in My Womb. I nurtured His divinity from the berth into which I was born of your eternal grandparents. My children, the power of God is ageless and timeless. You can know the Christ who has saved you by living the spiritual holiness that you gain at your baptism. Only the world can know your true self if you cut yourself off from God. How I wish for you to be recognized by Heaven and for you to simultaneously embrace the divinity of Heaven! This is the union to which you have been proceeding for many years and thousands of days. God has given you the graces that have prepared you for your Salvation, the Holy Sacraments that restore your soul to perfection. It is your conscious conversion that transforms this perfection into sanctified action, good works, and exemplary piety. I cannot carry you where you must walk on your own, but I will always accompany you on the journeys that are yours to make. My children, you are coming upon a time of material and physical change, but are continuing to maintain your stature in spiritual Truth that makes you consistently one with Jesus. You cannot impede this gift unless you abandon Him in your heart. This you will never do, and this is the reason there is such seamless beauty in the vocations of priests who relocate from one parish to another, in the charisma of missionaries who serve in many nations in the course of a lifetime, and at every location in the linear miles that Jesus traveled from His boyhood home. You must always remember that the Love of God the Father and the presence of your Immaculate Mother are with you and in you. This is why you can return from far-off Marian shrines and not be separated from them. My children, I have come to you because I have heard the preeminent words, *Hail Mary! Full of Grace!* The rest is according to what you dare to accomplish through the sublime graces I dispense. You have been reminded by the Holy Spirit, *'Whatever you shall sow, you shall reap.'* This is why you must be prepared to receive a grand reception when the Lord comes to redeem you, regardless of those who may playfully proclaim, *'I'll bet you cannot catch me!'* My little children, please understand clearly that you have already been caught! Accept the blessings that God is bestowing upon you. Trust your own good judgment and believe that God is taking care of you. Be the followers of discretion and distinction whom I have taught you to become. This is a time of the perpetual and constant blessing of your lives by the Holy Spirit of My Son. Do not allow any changes that impact your senses to cause you any anxiety or bring you to question the broader work you are accomplishing. The time has almost arrived. Thank God for His benedictions, and be pleased with yourselves. By no means is your work for God becoming irrelevant. You have stood-out and forward from the long line of generations to speak your piece for God, but you have yet to offer your fullest inaugural expressions. I have given you ample opportunities to teach humankind by the hundreds-of-thousands about Salvation in My Son. We must pray for new venues to accomplish it. Be peaceful of heart, patient, confident, and assured that the Plan of God is unfolding as it should. Can you not discern the inevitable movement of the Earth preparing for the Triumph of My Immaculate Heart? Please never allow a single thought to enter your mind that I will not succeed. I shall succeed because My children are serving in God's vineyard and for no other earthly reason. This is the expression of faith that God asks from all His children. I cannot attest that the road ahead will not be treacherous, but I can tell you that you will win at the last. Of course you will be despised; of course you will be rejected and outrightly ridiculed because you are little christs. At the end of time, you will see that every influence has played a part in the redemption of humankind, every adversary, every insult, every tear, every whimper of sorrow, and every snarling dog. This is a grand time of Eternal

Truth, Hope, and Light. You cannot see the end of all things, but you can know that you are on the course that will take you there—a vision of Love, a Love that you have never abandoned and a Divine Messiah who has never forsaken you. Remember this when you go scampering at the end of time through the stark ghettos, when you walk upright through prison walls to liberate the fruit of your sacrifices, when you take the very rapture of God from inside your hearts and hand it on a gold platter to the millions of refugees from senseless wars, as you march gleefully through the hamlets that once scoffed at you for standing beside Jesus Christ, and when you take your final bow before the curtain closes and seals your souls inside the heights of Paradise forever to come. This is the prolific new day of redemption and hope, and Satan does not like it in the least. This is why you are hearing the evil stench of barking dogs.* Such are boos and hisses from the losers who are soon to be drowned-out by the cheering Saints before whom you have become God's victors. I cannot say when that final day will come, but I can tell you that its dawn is nigh. I can reveal what you will perceive, but your soul must see for itself. I assure you that when you set eyes on the Woman Clothed with the Sun in My Immaculate Triumph, the world will be near its end, a new day will begin, and the Earth will be supplanted by a Kingdom of Divine Glory. This day is not distant in the offing. Believe what I have told you as the truth! The message from 1991 is the same in 1999. I am your Mother who has brought your Savior to snatch you from the jaws of death. Evil shall never locate his fanged incisors near your souls.

My Special son, you are the measure of two arms stretched-out, and this is a time when everyone about you will soon see the fruit of your labors of nearly ten years. Be proud of it! Do not throw your pearls to the swine! I will guide you in your efforts. Please acknowledge your biological mother for next Sunday's secular feast of Mother's Day. You must not hold anything against those who cannot yet know the power of your labors. Please remember that your mother who gave you birth is a special little girl in the eyes of God. It is through her motherhood that you were nurtured and reared to become able to complete your Diary. Yes, from a little boy who lay in a bassinet."

* *The dogs from next door were barking ferociously at that very moment.*

Sunday, May 9, 1999
Mother's Day [secular]
7:48 p.m.

"My blessed little children, I have been at your side today, watching you working for Jesus and all the holy heavens. My children, this is the celebration of Mother's Day for 1999, and one that I shall never forget. In all the world, with its billions of souls, no one else honored Me as you have by placing into print 300 pages of absolute divinity. Can you see why you are so beloved? I have come not only to say thank you, but to tell you that you have entertained some very hopeful thoughts about the dispensation of My messages. You must continue laboring, and you will have the resources you need. These are special times of worship for you to recognize Jesus as the reason for your spiritual and material success. May I be so bold as to tell you that My hope rests in your ability to achieve all you wish to accomplish by your own sound determination? Your work is difficult, and your feelings are hurt when you are not called by others to be included in their leisure. I reassure you today that this Mother is your perpetual help, Wisdom, guidance, consolation, and nourishment. We are forever together in unity with My Son in Three Divine Persons of one loving God. You need no other shield or benefactor. The Holy Spirit is your constant source of strength and encouragement. He has asked Me to tell you that you have bestowed the greatest gift upon His Mother by your living faith, obedience, and servitude. I have every intention of speaking to you until Jesus tells Me that I have said enough. I am praying that He will Return in Glory before that occurs. He knows how splendid your labors have been. Can you sense the majesty in the pages you published today? Indeed you can, as will everyone else. Satan will leave no tracks on your Diary. It is too much for him to impede, somewhat like the isle of Wake attempting to defeat the United States. It is your work! I also offer you a prophetic promise. You and your Christian friends will observe a future Mother's Day under triumphant circumstances."

Sunday, May 16, 1999
3:25 p.m

"Essential to any child who must love is a Mother who can give him the Son of Love. Dear children, can you not feel the Divinity which surrounds you? Can you not detect the aura of anticipation as you prepare to begin the second of holy testimonies that will convert your brother humanity? I find that same joy in being able to join you, on this day of anniversary of the canonization of the great Saint Joan of Arc. We will pray that everyone will understand the measure of God to convert and save His people, to employ the virtues of the righteous, to expunge the opposition before you, and to pursue the cultivation of a world which is still much too lethargic to understand what it means to face the Justice of God. My Special son, I wish for you to recall that I have asked you to complete various tasks when you have wondered the reason. Many you still do not know. It is time for you to play a role without knowing the purpose."

Our Lady asked me to offer a prayerful oration of hope about the history and future of humanity. So, I came to my feet in my prayer room and began to extemporaneously proclaim from my heart a visionary parable of triumph and culmination, of passion and soul, of reclamation and renewal. This went on for over ten minutes before I had exhausted the litany that passed before my heart. Then, Our Blessed Mother continued,

"Please allow Me a moment to bend to My little children who have already come to Heaven about whom you just spoke so eloquently to embrace their tears of thanksgiving. My Special one, you have just completed a parable about the human spirit and the reason that people become leaders. As you know, the true leaders in the world have been the Popes of the Roman Catholic Church. But, you will one day hear a similar historical record of how your own life transformed the Earth in the final ages of humankind. There will be open courtyards in Heaven where hundreds-of-thousands of Saints will gather to hear the eternal proclamation of your service. I cannot make it too clear that you must always foster that hope in your heart. Heaven is not only a place, My children, it is a collection of all places and all times. The strength of all the righteous armies in history is but a puff of wind in Heaven. The crowning of every king and champion who served on Earth is a simultaneous act of 'Well done' in two words from the Savior of the world. All of the tears that have ever flowed since the fall of man from the Garden of Eden could not fill a thimble in the everlasting expanse of Paradise. Every drop of blood ever shed by humanity on Earth could not equal the power of the Blood of Jesus that lives in one chalice upon the Altar. No war or collection of wars has brought as sweet spoils to the feet of God as the Crucifixion of your Savior on Good Friday. And, the righteousness that now flows in your heart and in the lives and actions of all the Popes blooms from the Holy Spirit who is etching the words you are hearing at this very moment upon the firmament of your soul. This is a momentous time for the Earth. You are standing before the world in a professorial role, and your Diary is your textbook. And, as you just witnessed, you never told anything about any number of popular or electoral college votes. It is not an issue. Likewise, you need not go into detail by the prodding questions of those who will scandalously ask how I have come to you and what exactly happened in this room. You must be poised and wise.

Indeed, the time is now unfolding that will begin the changes that you seek. This is My holy blessing for you. ✞ Thank you for your prayers. I will speak to you soon. I love you. Goodnight!."

Sunday, May 23, 1999
Feast of Pentecost
3:44 p.m.

The Final Colossus

Basking, bathing, brilliant! Outpouring the Wisdom of God!
The Visage of Heaven, flowing freely the tears of pristine Glory.
Clothed in unerring, inevitable Light. The winds of change!
Eradicating, electrifying, compelling, beloved!
You teach the shedding of Earth amidst the corals of sin.
Go! Go into the world that knows no peace.
Greet, bless, call, embrace!
Heal, sanctify, purify, caress!

You, the Virginal Shores of Paradisial Love.
Monogram and Monument to the Triune God.
The Trident, the Benevolent, the Salvific, the Bold.
You, the Sunlit Matron of God's Holy Ones,
lost in the portals of bewildering Death.
O' Perfect Glory, Mother of Life Renewed.
You, the Hands of Grace.
The Fair Maiden who birthed the pacific Pardon of fallen souls.

You, the Beatific Dawn of a Boundless Age.
Bring the solstice of Ecstatic Light to heirs and orphans.
To the Well of corpus hearts brooding in hopeless Dusk.
Seek ancient tundras and mystical parlors
where mortals huddle amidst battle and waste.
You, the flawless Blessing and newfound Trust of generations lost!

You, Matriarch and Queen of the lifeless Daughter in the Harbor.
Your Son is the Torch of Life to the children of Earth.
His Light unifies the blessed, the grated, the wretched,
the lost, the timid, the damned.
You! Summoned by the outstretched arms of Hope!
Stationed high above the stillness of invincible Freedom.

You celebrate the Destiny of man and beast, alike,
with Your Immaculate Crown of Stars,
to which the little Child in the Bay bows in deference,
her spiked chapeau heeled near her humbled feet.
She welcomes Your cultivating Touch to the unwitting masses,
the hopeless chest of inordinate pawns
awaiting their passage to the Celestial Port,
while the Streams of Paradise reflect your glistening Mantle.

Yes, You step into the world to claim the Unknown.
Clasping errant palms that flail in the dark,
pulling to beat their breasts
in the vibrant New Groves of the Land of God.
You are the Parasol of Infinite Bliss.
Refined, Robust, impassioned Delight!
Where cities of angels moor to feast on placid temperaments.
Come this Day! Lift every age to Heaven's Door!

- Saint Gabriel the Archangel

"To the children I love through the depths of My Immaculate Heart, I bring the peace of Heaven to comfort your souls. Yes, I am the Final Colossus. This is the poem which was dictated to you by the Archangel Gabriel. I am very happy that you like it. I am assured by God that your lives will be enriched by taking the poem along with the rest of your Diary into the world. You are the children who began so helplessly, and yet so fearlessly, to bring many souls to conversion who will be touched by your work. What began in the peace of the night will bring the solace of God to the ravages of the day. With no more than a pen in hand and a few writing pads, you have transformed your earthly passions of hope into the masterpiece that now lay in a box, ten feet to your right, prepared for delivery to the Library of Congress. Your simplicity and efforts are the seeds that will grow a forest of conversion from whose fruits many souls now living in pain will savor relief for the first time in their lives. My children, this is true because you have said 'yes' to God. Thank you for responding to My call. You are about to show the entire globe what it means to be obedient to the Mother of God. Any number of thousands of people will wish to have been in your shoes, but multiple millions will know why they were not up to the task. I have told you from the beginning that time is the only element which ever separated you from the success that you have always desired to achieve for God. My little children, that time has expired, and the moment is upon you. Night after night and week after month, you have prayed with Me for the conversion of humanity to Jesus. So much can change in a week or month, or even a day. Humanity was redeemed in the passing of a day. One day, I told you that it was not necessary to record what I was telling you, the next day began the collection of messages, parables, images, prayers, stories, and lessons that will transform an entire Creation of people into the reflection of God. Yes, sixteen-hundred pages of enlightening truth; hundreds-of-thousands of letters and syllables to open the floodgates of Purgatory and hearts on Earth. This is an era of great preeminence for Creation because God came to your door and you answered the call. Make no mistake, humanity will not immediately fall in homage to your Diary, but the Gospel of Jesus will be spread in time as the Holy Spirit glorifies what we have done here together. You should make no excuses as to why you have seemed so reclusive in past years. The Earth is about to know why. Reserve no time for stoning the devil's dogs; you are not required to defend your writing. By all means, it is massive enough to speak for itself! The time has come for you to prepare for a second Diary that will be as monumental. When the world descends upon you for a material explanation as to what has occurred here, give them none. Always tell them that the explanation they seek rests in their hands and inside their hearts. I have come today to thank you again for standing beside God, for saying 'yes' to Creation, for living in peace, and for loving Me so profoundly. There is nothing in existence that can destroy the codex you have completed. I have given it to lost sinners through you. This can never be undone. If we went no further than today, you could rest assured that you have amassed a compilation of divine literary works that cannot be reproached by any other in mortal history. Humankind will eventually come to know this. I tell you that this will not alter the nobility of your character, the simplicity of your purpose, or the piety of your words. You will always be My little children beneath My Mantle with the walking shoes that I once gave you to wear. You can show them to the world if anyone asks to see them. I am hoping that you will also remember that it is not only this house that is holy, but your heart which is your home. It is where you reside in unity with the Holy Spirit. Buildings come and go, but your heartlight will never wane. I thank you for affording Me the opportunity to speak to you so many times while you recite the Rosary. One day, you will see that you made this grace possible for God and not some intrinsic desire on behalf of Heaven to be invasive into your lives. You have already proved that if not for your love for God and humanity, I would not have been able to remain. As you look back upon the recent eight and one-half years, you can see that you have not made any sacrifices that your faith could not overcome. Indeed, you have seen that the things you once believed to be heavy burdens are now joyous to carry. You participate with happiness instead of doubt, fear, or wonder. All of this is because you have seen the fruits of your work. Now everything makes sense. I beseech you to remember this when you are called in the future to bear other burdens. You are about to see the unfolding of new life for the many you love. Your Mother and the Angels have been guided by the Holy Spirit of My Son to bring the success that you are now coming to know. However, it is your own spiritual handiwork and strong faith that have made this possible. My Special one, you believed your brother in 1991 when no one else would. Yours is the credit and yours is the crown! Please accept them openly and wear them with satisfaction. Your Savior is well pleased by the fruits of your life. Thank you for allowing God to enter your lives for the Salvation of many. Remember on Pentecost Sunday that the Holy Paraclete lives in you anew."

Sunday, May 30, 1999
3:58 p.m.

"Oh, My sweet children, how I love you! Never in the boundless history of Creation have you ever been loved as does this Mother love you in reflection of God! You are a very fortunate faithful because He is about to reward those who have decided for Him. These are the times that Jesus has been standing in patience to embrace. While the world seems to be moving swiftly out of control, it is truly going nowhere that it has not been before. Generations of mortals have led their lives in anticipation of a material victory that they could never keep. My children, material wealth will slip through your fingers when your hands fall open in death. You can grasp an Eternity of happiness only with the clutches of your soul. You are My children whom I have come to guide back to your good senses. Thank you for responding to My call. You are about to enter a new month which is dedicated to the Sacred Heart of Jesus. In Him, you are enjoined by a timeless victory that will pale before no enemy. Please be assured that I am telling you the Truth. You are still being deceived by the concept of time because daily life keeps lashing-out to draw you away from God. Remember that His Love is your timeless elevation away from the pangs of mortal life. Nowhere else in any other universe can you find such freedom. You are worthy of this grace and Salvation because you have found favor with the Creator of souls. If this were not so, I would have told you. This is why you are living in the Light of imminent Triumph. You are poised and composed because you cannot be defeated by the stench of the world. Just as it was a matter of time before your messages began in 1991, it is only a matter of time before the entire world will see your diarist-collection of them. This is why you must be patient, all the while knowing that your victory is assured. Remember, we have something they all want. It will be their big surprise. God does everything for a purpose and allows what you see to foster the need for that purpose. While it may seem that you are now moving in fractions, you are actually achieving the goals of Jesus in the measurement of galactic light-years. Only in your heart have you known this in the past. However, before this year is out, you will see it with your eyes. My children, the world is ready to hear what I have to say. America is poised to receive the Good News that I bring to such a sorrowful land. I assure you that the message will be heard! You must be patient while I prepare the hearts who need to know My Son for such a startling revelation. This is what My intercession is all about! I am bringing the revelation of holy conversion to a people who are lost in the dark! Be My Light! Be My little beacons who usher My message of Love into the urban culturalization of a truly primitive people, a helpless lot, a community of hearts who know no better. I have told you how helpless is a humanity without God. You are seeing the running amok of a world that has always been helpless, a world that despises justice, and a Creation which is fighting its hardest in this modern age to reject the Salvation that is free for the taking. Peace is at hand, but humanity has its collective hands jammed into its pockets. If all the warring nations will look toward Love as one dignified people, their flight will be toward the Holy Altar, rather than the killing fields of hatred and disrespect. Human hunger is not so much a corporeal deprivation as it is a spiritual bankruptcy. All of this is mitigated in the Heart of Christ! I am the Mother of the Greatest News ever known to man! The Earth rests in the fingertips of a Child who is perched in My arms. His Crown is one of perfect assurance and absolution. This little King pours-out His Blood upon the people He has died to save. You have known this since you were old enough to comprehend. That same Holy Spirit lives in you to this day. My children, if a maiden can be fair, then I am Fairness Incarnate. And, if Mercy can take to the flesh, Jesus is your walking Forgiveness who was nailed to a Cross to prove it. Be the angels of Light which He called you to be on that dark hilltop of Redemption! Live the message of hope, faith, pardon, and peace before all the world! That is what He has commissioned you to do! A day at a time, walk toward the redemptive horizon in confidence, knowing that millions will follow in your shadow. While it seems like you should be flying by now, you are still walking a day at a time toward the end of the ages, inexorably passing with this age into the courtesy of the coming midnight of your mortality and your leap across the chasm of time into the dawn of Eternity. There can be no less than the high spirits and charming grace left under your feet before you fall into the arms of the Redeemer of every soul who has employed the great faith and obedient conscience to seek Him in the Love that has grown from the center of your hearts. My children, this is the time of the Great Reckoning of Creation. This is not only your time, but the arrival of Eternity for all the ages. Please come to that horizon in assurance that this eleventh hour is your procession toward unity with all that is of God. I am awaiting that grand reunion with all the Angels and Saints, looking all humanity in the face! I beseech your smiles as you rise and continue that grand march toward Eternal Life! Give God every fiber of your heart as you continue in your stately stride toward the Light of Love who is calling you from beyond western summits. Your heart and soul know that you are going Home, despite what your eyes can see! It has been said by opthamologists that the ability of the retina to cast a vision from it to the human brain is the macular enhancement. That is, there has to be a stain on the retina in order for the eye to see. When someone begins to go blind, they are said to have macular degeneration. But, God knows that the eyes of your soul can see Him only through an Immaculate vision, free from the stains that have so tormented humanity since the Fall of Adam and Eve. My children, I am your Immaculate Vision! See Heaven through My eyes! Allow Me to cast the majestic hues of Divinity upon your very souls! That is the rainbow that you can truly see through your tears. The immortal vision of God is the reason for Love and for Life, the purpose for which Jesus was begotten and conceived in My womb, the reason He taught the righteousness of the redeemed, and the reason He died on the Cross to take you to that chasm and take that leap back into the arms of Almighty God. I am your Mother of Hope because I have seen the reason for your hope! I gave Him to the world under a bright star on a cold night in Bethlehem! This hope will never disappoint you, He will not forsake you, and He will do everything He promised from the moment He was able to utter His first words. I ask you today to ponder My words and place the work that you have been doing for the past ten years in that same perspective. You are My hope, and I realize that God trusts you. That is why I am speaking to you today.

My Special son, this has been a month of joy for you and your brother, but of sorrow in the awful world. We will continue to pray together to bring healing and peace to those who suffer at the hands of others who will not love. I have come today to share My hope and ask you to remember that the future is now. These are the days that will usher the End of Times. This is the Last Age of man. God has provided the venue. This is a very special blessing in reflection of the celebration of the Holy Trinity. ✞ Please remember to be of high spirits and peaceful heart. I will speak to you again very soon. Be My loves! I love you. Goodnight!"

Sunday, June 6, 1999
Feast of Corpus Christi
12:08 p.m.

"My dearly beloved children, you have been told many times by the mortals surrounding you that time is of the essence. On this Feast of Corpus Christi, your Heavenly Mother is telling you that the Holy Eucharist is The Only Essence. Time is not a factor in the divine persuasion of human enlightenment because the Holy Paraclete resides among you always. God is of a timeless peace and will not allow the passage of days or the hours that comprise them to separate you from Him. My children, this is the month of June 1999, and I promised that I would give you more messages after completing your Diary. I have come to fulfill that promise. I will take advantage of this Feast to bring you the continuance of My lessons for the world. My subject today is the Sacred Body and Blood of Jesus in the Most Blessed Sacrament. My children, you are surrounded by the Holy Mysteries of God. How could a Woman be with Child who had no relations with man? How could one perfect Savior die on a Cross so all men could live forever? How can a singular God be present in Three distinct and separate Persons; the Father, Son, and Holy Spirit? You have come to know these Mysteries to be true, although seemingly contradictory and paradoxical. Such is the Mystery of the Father whose Face you will someday see. You will recognize, comprehend, and understand all these Mysteries in one Divine Light. For you now, this Light must reflect from the holiness of your soul, even though you have yet to see it. Even on this Feast of Corpus Christi, the Mysteries abound. The Holy Mass is the Crucifixion on Good Friday when Jesus' Blood was shed. The Blood in His veins departed His Body and fell to earth, submerging the souls of humanity in beatific redemption. During the Holy Sacrifice of the Mass, you are given the miracle of the Eucharist, the Body and Blood, Soul and Divinity of My Son in one Blessed Sacrament, broken yet undivided and wholly unified. The Communion Host is the Body and Blood of Jesus, although His Body and Blood were separated on the Cross. He shed His Blood from His Crucified Body and died for you. Do you remember when I said that the world became the Cross on the day Jesus died? In light of this, humanity was absorbed by the Divinity of Jesus as His Precious Blood saturated the Earth. Yes, Jesus shed His Blood on the Holy Cross, and in doing so united the Earth with the heavens that still await the fruit of human conversion. The Sacramental Body and Blood of Jesus is indivisible, just like the Father and the Son. This preceded the Descent of the Holy Spirit upon the Church, which is the fulfillment of the prophecy that Jesus proclaimed, very silently, as His Precious Blood impacted the Earth. My children, this is how the Communion Host, the Holy Eucharist, is the Body and Blood of Jesus. They are His undivided perfection and redemptive Crucifixion in one Blessed Sacrament. This is also why Jesus is equally present in each individual Host. Even though the Eucharist is dispensed in portions to those who receive Him, He is still one undivided Body being consumed by the whole Faith-Church. This is part of the Sacred Mysteries of the Eucharistic Celebration that can neither be explained nor explained-away. It cannot be rejected or ignored because the Truth will never expire and will prevail beyond the end of time. You receive the Body and Blood of Christ today which has been consumed by billions of the faithful throughout the centuries. This, My children, is the worldwide web that is keeping the fate of humanity from collapsing into the abyss. My Special son, I come to you with a revitalized hope that you understand My messages that I continue to give during the years, no matter the location or venue of My intercession. I have few children in the world who offer such obedience. This is why you are My Special one. Oh! My child, if only you could see Heaven that Jesus has prepared for you! You are not only the Special one, but God's prince of servitude. You are My little child, the gracious one who belongs to the Immaculate Mother of God. Always remember that I see your every effort and all your labors. You will never grow tired of loving Jesus. You will complete the tasks that He has given you to do. You and your brother have moved into the foyer of the most victorious times in your lives. I wish for you to remember that it is your love that is keeping you so united."

Sunday, June 13, 1999
1:40 p.m.

"My dear beautiful children, this is another day of infinite glory for you to share in the Sacred Heart of Jesus! This is the advent of the great and merciful redemption of the mortal world into the sacred hands of Almighty God who has reclaimed you for His Kingdom! This is an age during which no pain or sorrow can refute that you have the wisdom to be one in the holiness of Paradise. Please always remember this. Today, your loving Mother has come to tell you that the heavens are incomplete without the souls on Earth who are about to be made one with it; and you finish this transition through your daily prayers. If Heaven is to assimilate everything humanly righteous, the exiled world must reach-out to God, emulate and complement the Cross, and generously surrender so the Father can raise you into His beatific domain. I have told you that the Earth is a finite place in a boundless and infinite eternity. I have also said that it is difficult to describe the interrelationship between all that is seen and unseen. However, they both have discernable characteristics that sustain your holiness. Jesus has given new life and a permanent purpose to the redeemed world that you are coming to know. Before He was born, Heaven and Earth were distinctly contrasting. Jesus was Incarnated by God to consume Creation in the flames of His Crucifixion. He sanctified His disciples by sharing His Wisdom and life's teachings. His Death on the Cross manifested the unity between the Father and His creatures who went missing when Adam and Eve first betrayed Him. This is why His Kingdom will burst forth at the end of time like flood waters breaching a dyke, with Light and awe-striking victory. My little children, you must remember that Heaven and Earth correspond in spirituality and substance when you pray the Holy Rosary. I am confident that you comprehend the joy that God has placed in your hearts through His Love that has enveloped the Earth and made room for all humanity to become its sacred part. Remember that you will love your life in Paradise that you have begun here in this world, but good men must respond in faith, trust, and obedience to be united with the ecstatic divinity of that Eternal Love. You must join the Lord seamlessly at the heart for all eternities and every universe to make this come true. Thank you, My Special son, for your prayers today. I will leave you in the beauty, power, and joy that God has brought to your soul."

Sunday, June 20, 1999
2:39 p.m.

"My dear beautiful children, the greatest joy that a soul can ever know is found in the Sacred depths of the Holy Mysteries; Father, Son, and Holy Spirit, and the fruits they bear your spirit upon your acceptance of them in your heart. If the world is, indeed, to be made anew, the grainy sands of mortal indifference must become replaced by the glistening nobility of a new Creation in perfection. No other generation has held the countless folds of opportunities for conversion than does this one. You are a modern-day society, indeed, an impressionable world who is at the brink of leaping into a new millennium with only a sparse amount of human dignity remaining. The sadness lies herein because the human family has procured this awful status on its own. God has come-down from Heaven to rescue you, the Christ has died for your Redemption! My children, My Special one, this is the news that you are reveling throughout the mountain valleys and hilltops as this Twentieth Century approaches its terrible end. Peace does not come from bombs blasting in air, but Love infused into hearts! The sound of peace is Peace, itself! It can never be forced or coerced. Suffering can still continue under an artificial peace, the horrors of oppression driven underground. But, if the true Peace of Divinity is allowed a chance to blossom from the same bowels which grow the wretchedness, the cultivation of change will come from within. That is why the Paraclete is not detectible to the human eye. Only His fruits can be physically discerned! The Spirit of God is the Maker of true Peace because it is a change that emits from the core of the human soul. That is what My Son meant when He first spoke of the new Creation on Earth, the rebirth of holiness and perfection in a humanity who has already been born. Your fall from Paradise was not so cumbersome that it would impede your ability to take Jesus' hand and climb back to the top. God has known all along that your souls are too precious to remain as fodder for the grave. Your Savior has told you that personally. If any single child of Christian faith will honestly accept the Promise of Salvation, their life will immediately become a new beginning instead of a wayward end. Light is the vision of your souls! The darkness on

Earth is not God, but where the Son of God has found you. The Holy Cross is your first and last step toward Paradise. They exist simultaneously in one Crucified Savior! The only Begotten Son of God is, likewise, the same Son of Man who has lived and died to retract, destroy, expunge, and erase human sins! How can anyone live more perfectly than that? How can benevolence and Mercy be more clearly defined? I am the Blessed Virgin Mary, your Immaculate Mother and Queen of Love. I have brought you to the joy of recognizing your new life in My Son because My Love for you is as large as Creation, itself. Jesus is the reason for your anticipation and ecstasy! Give Him your joy! Show Him how happy you are to be one in Him! He is standing at the doorway of your own Redemption to receive you, ready to acknowledge the ways that you are pouring-out your love upon the Earth in His Holy Name. This is Father's Day on the Earth and in Heaven. Your Almighty God is your resplendent Father every day! The Son who is your Salvation is the Host from the Altar who has invited you to the Eternal Banquet Table in Heaven. Please, allow no one to decline this offer! Make kings of all men and warriors of cowards by leading them to the Altar of perfect contrition! That is where true power lies, upon the holy and sacred Altar of Sacrifice, not in missile silos or on projection screens, not in sartorial beauty or in financial success. The first will be last, and many who are last will be first! This day is one of recollection and prophecy, one of fulfillment and new direction. My Special son, this is the hope with which your Father in Heaven wishes mankind to live! Thank you for allowing Me to share it with you!"

I recently wrote a rather poignant letter to someone who was intentionally mis-characterizing the facts about a particular situation in which we were both intimately familiar. Our Lady responded to my reply to this person by saying,

"I see that you are going to ask about your reply to little A—. Perfection! Simple perfection! Again I say, complete perfection! You are watching the unfolding of the new beginning that you have waited so long to see. By your prayers, service, good works, piety, trust, faith, and patience! Indeed, the fire has already been ignited. You will soon be sensing that the movement of hearts that you have been waiting for years to see is about to occur, dating back to when you were a child in your father's arms. He could not have known then whom he was embracing. I give you My solemn assurance that before all this is done, he will hold you in his arms like that again and tell you that he loves you 10,000 times. There are 1,500 reasons why many thousands of hearts are about to be cracked wide open. Can you not perceive the power of your work for God? You can see why this beauty will unfold with such unimaginable bounty. I have been with you to watch this beauty arise. I will also be at your side to see the darkness fall. I ask you to know to the depths of your heart why it is so beautiful a sight for Heaven to see the piety that you and your brother share. Does this not make you view the power of your love with endless vision? Please be confidently patient. Now, go show humanity what love really is."

Sunday, June 27, 1999
3:20 p.m.

"My very precious little children, since this is the age of the spiritual enlightenment of man, Holy is the Spirit, and you are the men! I bring you the Divine embrace of Heaven to cause your souls to stir in victory and peace. Indeed, through all you have seen from God and have done for Jesus, can victory be far behind? The offing is brimming with shouts of gladness and affirmation. Yours is the Wisdom to know the Face of Almighty God in Heaven. The justice for which you seek rests not on the mortal road, but in the Holy Spirit of purity and redemption. I have told you on many occasions that your holiness is a fruit of your obedience to your Mother. My little children, that same obedience is a fruit of your desire for the Salvation of all souls. That, My children, is true nobility. That is the essence of your lives, the intentions of your prayers, and the thesis of your Diary. How can a nation and world be so blessed as to receive the good works of your hands? Because the Mother of all humanity has given you the opportunity to be transformed into the image and likeness of My perfect Son. You are living amidst the days of a beautiful summer season. The Earth is abloom and the colors abound with the genius of God. You find yourselves in that same growth of freshness. Your souls are not wintery still or tethered to the bitterness of plight or dissension. You have knowledge of these things because it is natural for you to be 'little christs' on the Earth. In Him, you have the capacity to grow to unparalleled heights of divinity. The perfection of Heaven is, indeed, as immeasurable and invincible as Love, itself. Where are your hearts? Like the Father, the Son, and the Holy Spirit, they are in Heaven and on Earth, beseeching the sleeping world to awaken from their hibernative slumber, seeking them to rise to the occasion of this modern-day opportunity to be transported with you into the miraculous Grace heretofore known only to the Saints. This is an age that knows no boundaries. This is the time during which every man and woman should place that blooming spring in their step and walk with both pride and confidence to the corridor of conversion. As has been made clear to the world, the time for perfect piety is now, for all the gold in the world could not purchase a day lost without the blessing of the Christian conscience. My children, the world-over is restless, but is still asleep in sin! The excruciating pain of rebellion is rocking societies to the foundations of their heritage. Hatred is pillaging the most innocent of hearts. And yet, they do not dare to dream of a Paradise to come because they cannot seem to wake from the nightmare that they call mortal life. This does not have to remain as it is. The twenty-first century world cannot bear the strain that has come only from its own plundering. Human hearts are vast, barren wastelands instead of blooming flowerbeds of justice and reconciliation. Together, we have set-out to change this terrible course of sadness, despair and desolation. Then, the guilty will be filled with a new regret that will be difficult for them to overcome. I tell you today, My children, that simple forgiveness can conquer any guilt or regret. When you pardon the transgressions of the penitent, all of the hard-rock walls of impudence will come crashing to the ground and, when the dust of holy cultivation clears, will reveal the wide-open skies that give-way to the horizon of a seamless union between the Son of your Almighty Father and the children whom He has come to redeem. Indifference is an unwholesome virus that has congested the thinking of an otherwise piously intelligent people. They know to love, but do not know well enough to do it better. Your Lord and Savior, Jesus, is your medicinal Grace who can restore the health of any soul who is lying in the sickbed of indifference. The Holy Spirit is about to raise the dignity of millions of infirm hearts who have succumbed to the bantering temptations of the world. Your Wisdom awaits you, O' humanity! My Grace is of that same Holy Spirit. I have come to share it with you, to dispense the great and mighty Commons of Light that will keep you from stumbling on your journey to Salvation! My Special son, these are My hopes for this modern-day world. Like millions before, you and your brother have embarked on the day of the Lord, to write, protect, profess, enjoin, and to teach. I am with you, and I will always give you a guiding hand to see you to the Triumph in which untold millions upon millions will share. These are the heady days of summer, as they are called, when men are posturing for a greater social advancement. I am telling you that this is, instead, the day of the growth of the immortal spirit of humanity, a time to be self-extracted from the shell of indignance and impropriety. I hold the Good News for anyone who will place their ear next to My Immaculate Heart to listen. That, My children, is what you are doing here today. I have brought some beautiful words to My children! My Special son, you are still working very hard for Me! You are entirely capable. You have been blessed by God with many gifts and talents to share in unity with the Holy Spirit to convert the souls of men. I have returned today not because of this home or its location, but to speak directly to you, to comfort you and give you encouragement. Your Diary needs to be received by everyone. Many will believe that you are being condescending by not diluting your strength of witness for Jesus in the name of peace. The only peace rests in your never surrendering your support for the Holy Gospel. I admire the genuine nature in which you lift your prayers. Praise be to Jesus."

Sunday, July 4, 1999
5:21 p.m.

"To you, who are the children of My Immaculate Heart, I bid peace and comfort on this day which celebrates the country in which you live. Your God has planned a great future for you! An awe-inspiring cultivation is near at hand! My children, the soul of America is not a barren one, but it is sorely lacking in conscience. There are too many hearts that are asleep in the senseless trap of materialism. They will awaken from their slumber to the call of this Morning Star who is about to shake them into complete union with the Holy Spirit. I am She who is from God, your Patroness who has come calling for servants and spiritual companions to usher-in the age of piousness. Who else will act if My children fail to act? What other body of humanity will walk forward to reach-out for the torch? If you will continue to be patient with Me, you will see the last one-fourth of this year as greater than all of your July 4ths wrapped into one."

This was personally fulfilled for me when the first seven years of my diary "Morning Star Over America" was published.

"It is an opportune time for Christians in America and around the world. The collective anticipation of your people is towing in the direction that bodes well for the revelation of My intercession. It is wholly true, the roads of human life cannot elevate mankind from them of their own accord. I bear the plan that many will follow. This has been true for the past two millennia. I cannot tell you in too strong terms that My children will know Me. And, My faithful children are many, in the millions and the multitudes. And, what of your life outside of Jesus? There is none! There is no life separate from the Word of God. All of the speeches in the world cannot capture His eloquent Grace! I wish you could already see the end of time and the effect that your work will soon have. Every day, you move closer to the realization of the hopes that cannot die. It is your dear Lord and Savior who keeps them alive. This is the new rise of freedom that cannot come from the hand of mortal man. This is the re-opening of the promises that have been handed-down through the ages since that all-defining moment on Mount Calvary, the Legacy which has been feeding humanity the nourishment of spiritual vindication for your true survival. I cannot tell you today the exact hour that Jesus will return to take your souls to Paradise, but I can tell you with confidence that it is a time that will soon come-to-pass. Let no one tell you otherwise; the Son of Man is alive, and He is as hungry for your Redemption as you are famished to be saved. You must recall the Holy Gospel passages that speak of the Second Coming of Jesus. God has spoken to the prophets, and their prophecy is soon to be fulfilled. My children, I am that Lady with the Crown of Twelve Stars, not the twelve tribes of Israel! This Mother is your source of Wisdom, as I have been for centuries past. You who wait for Me like the dawn will not be disappointed, for I bear in My arms the reason for your joy!—Yes, the Giver of Everlasting Life! I hold the Christ-Child, the Anointed One, who beckons Me to show Him the children I have claimed for His Father. He wishes to be united with the brothers and sisters that God promised He would be granted on the day of His Passion! You are those children! You are the descendants, the last of those who wait to see the Eternal Light of Glory! I bid you the peace and gladness which lives in the Divinity of the Holy Spirit, the same Love who has brought Me to speak to you today."

Earlier in the day, two of Timothy's relatives whom he had not seen in a long time visited for several hours. It was a very enjoyable time that we spent together. These two people are of modest means by many standards, and they have borne years of suffering, yet there are no more gentle or accepting people that I know. Our Lady referred to their visit by saying,

"My Special son, this has been My pretty message for you today, including the innocence and kindness of M– and E– who came while we were first speaking. See how they may be poor in material goods but very rich in love! See how your brother has lifted them into new heights of joy by simply repeating the kind words of those who have passed before. You saw their glad faces and tears of joy. Please prepare to witness an entire nation opening with this same fulfillment. Thanks to your prayers and good works, these things are possible. You are correct in remembering that you must implore other souls to convert with the lessons of the Gospel and the confidence of the Holy Spirit. We do not offer candy as a bribe to make people love, but as a reward for their decision to choose love. I have been watching the Earth for centuries, and it is now nearly the most open that it has ever been to receive a revelation of the magnitude of your Diary. Thank you for making this possible."

Sunday, July 11, 1999
3:00 p.m.

"Dear little children of Mine, you are the offspring of your Savior, Most High! I have come again to bless your prayers and help you regain the millions of souls who have collectively slipped into the oblivion of indifference and outright wanton hatred. I have told you many times that Love is natural to My children, and only Love. Hatred is a manifestation of evil and an attribute of the lost souls who follow Satan. I ask the world, I beseech humanity—May I have your hearts as the new property of Salvation? Can

Heaven be so bold as to implore you to reside there for the sake of your own Eternal Life? I hold the destiny of human fulfillment in My Immaculate Heart. There is no way for you to turn back now! Redemption is at hand and God is ready to dispense it. These are the times that will determine when enough prayers have been lifted to completely vacate Purgatory of its last suffering soul. The weeks and months ahead are the direction that all humanity must take, not backward into the illicit pits of destruction and despair. I assure you that the many celebrative Feast-days that are coming will ring with a renewed resonance because all for whom those Feasts are offered are now on their feet to watch your souls scamper across the finish-line to reach your place among their ranks. I must tell you that if Creation were to be measured as the size of a cloud, the Earth is but the circumference of one raindrop inside it. But, it is that tiny droplet of moisture that is soothing the parched lips of everyone who has fought with such valiant courage to claim it for the Kingdom of God. Yes, Jesus has transformed the Earth into a massive flood of victory and righteousness, a waterfall and cool-running brook which swirls as the delight of millions of souls who bask in the shadows of her beaches. These are the reasons that the heavens rejoice! I am the Immaculate Queen whose happy duty it is to tell you that you have all been saved! By scourge, by sorrow, by Blood of the Cross, and by the steel of the blade, you have been renewed into a paradisial people, a chosen race, and a royal priesthood; never more can despair and guilt hold you hostage. No more will you weep because you cannot see the Light! My little children, the flurry of this ripe happiness is blooming in your midst during these summer days as the rest of the world brawls in the foyers and precincts of secular indifference. They will turn-about, take notice, and their eyes will peel in awe as they first-look at the monumental gift that you are about to give them! Can you feel the joy of that anticipation? But, remember to be patient as God reveals His purposes in time. Do not count the hours, days, weeks or months. Allow your souls to ponder much larger dimensions than that! Set your sights on the last goal, the day to come when all humanity will gather at your feet to hear the endless story of how all of this began to unfold and they were none the wiser. My Special son, you are making your Holy Mother extremely happy. If you move forward prayerfully, you will never fail. Any future disappointment will be transformed into uncontrollable joy. There is no other life than Jesus, especially when you enter Heaven. There will be many more signs before then."

Sunday, July 18, 1999
3:44 p.m.

"The bounty of the heavens has come in joy to greet the children of perfect peace. I am the Immaculate Virgin Mary, and you are My children. My Son has given His life to destroy your death. He was raised from that death so your souls will be resurrected into Heaven. My children, I see great things forthcoming in your future. I perceive revelation, the magnification of the Divinity of God on the Earth, and the cultivation of stubborn fields of obstinance that have laid for too long under the weight of man's haughty indifference. Let us make this awesome prospect your hope for the future and your reason for success at the end of time. While you are living the very blessed days of this magnificent summer, you are too close to them to truly know the lasting effects they will have. You have become acclimated to knowing Me and have grown quite accustomed to My miraculous intercession. But, there are millions more who will know Heaven for the first time because little children like you have come running into My arms when I stooped and called your name. This wholesome response is about to be transformed into real and tangible results. I ask you to never look back at the long hours and many months of labor anymore. They have come and gone, and you must now look into the future, the very times you have longed to see. God will forever be grateful for your obedience in the past, and you will see it upon the Return of the Son of Man. My children, these days are not bitter, but are only sweet. You will be pilloried by the Church's opposition and branded as heretics and opportunists. You have always expected no less, and will be unaffected by it. Remember that we have much more work to accomplish together, and there is no time to set aside for justification and self-defense. The Holy Spirit is your wisest Counsel and Advocate. Always lay your problems at God's feet. Can you sense the inexorable march of the ages that has come to pass? The Almighty Father is clearing the way for the opening of every heart for the many graces yet to come. Satan is running amok in his most violent hours. If you continue to lift your prayers as strongly as you are effecting your labors, you will yield success. Please continue your work and remember to ask God to bless all who have passed into His divine presence. The world around you is disintegrating into pieces by the moment, but you have work to do. Do not be distracted by the comrades who fall at your side. Everyone is moving toward the Light. Your eyes have become conditioned by this Light because your soul knows the perfection of Christ Jesus. Others will follow, even if they seem not to realize where you are leading them. If this sounds familiar, it is because it is the same way I led you beginning in February 1991. Remember that when you are in My arms, there is no place that My Son would rather you be. I am pleased that you enjoyed your visions yesterday."

Sunday, July 25, 1999
6:10 p.m.

"These are the days that were formed from the foundation of Creation to be the installation of your eternal joy. My little children, I need not tell you how happy your souls are to realize that you have given your mortal lives to God. I need not repeat that your minds are aware of the completion of your Diary. I am the most honored Mother in Creation because you have chosen to succeed in doing the work that My Son has given you to do. I must say that even though you seem tired at present, the next weeks will be a fleeting memory. I assure you that I will not allow you to remain idle too long. There will be plentiful time for rest and recollection. I simply ask you to remember that the next days are the reason we began in 1989. Thank you for complying; thank you for saying 'yes,' and bless you for the urgency that you have espoused in helping convert humanity to My Jesus, your Savior. My Special son, are you feeling the impending victory that is about to break? I am happy that you are still aglow in this prospect. I assure you that every single parcel of spiritual knowledge that I have given you will be eventually presented to the world. Every image, parable, picture, and thought has a purpose which you will dispense in time. You will one day recognize your first Diary as only a portion of your mission, as huge as it is. I should think that this would give you pause to know that your service to God is far from obsolete. If you continue to say 'yes,' He will continue to summon your help. I cannot state clearly enough how timely your Diary is. Creation is ready, and humanity will respond. I shall continue to pray with you for the conversion of the world. You will be confronted with a barrage of questions about how I have spoken to you. You will also be asked to allow a great number of people into your home when your brother and you are praying together to receive My words and messages. You must tell them that I will speak in their presence when there are thousands of pilgrims gathered at an outside location. I will speak to you and your brother alone until that occurs. There is a specific purpose in this. I have come today to tell you that I love you and to offer My support. Thank you for your pious intercessions."

Sunday, August 1, 1999
6:50 p.m.

"My dear little children, many are the blessings that God dispenses to those who are generous and charitable of heart to receive His Holy Spirit. Thus has He given you the reason to be joyful in your role as His children of Light. Indeed, there is much darkness that needs to be destroyed. One day at a time, you have knelt here with Me to ask My Son for His favorable intercession. He has swiftly responded because He loves you. I have been with you both night and day to give you good counsel because like My little Jesus, I seek the conversion of every soul on Earth to redemption in the Mercy of His Sacred Heart. It is you, My special children, and many thousands like you around the globe, who are making this conversion possible. Can I state it any clearer than that? This is the first day of a new month, an August month during which many graces have been accorded you in years passed. This is the week that will ultimately change humanity and yourselves. My Special one, you and your brother have been together many times before to enjoy your friendship and envision what the world would be if only humanity would accept their Savior. And now, because of the recitation of the decades in your hands, five Sacred Mysteries at a time, you are one decade closer to realizing the miracles for which you have prayed. My Special child, you must maintain your composure. You must ensure that your work is precise. You must make an accurate accounting of My intercession of the first six years before you release it. This is a serious matter. I know that you will comply because of your love for Me and your Savior. If you do as I ask, the miracles you seek will come. I will be with you morning, noon, and night. You must work diligently, do your best, be patient, and maintain your composure. If you do these things, the celebration will soon begin."

Monday, August 9, 1999
6:45 p.m

"The Mother of your Lord and Savior is with you to comfort, guide, teach, and caress you. My dear Special one, exactly ten years ago, you were preparing to arrive at the holy shrine of Medjugorje. And now the village that once gave you such hope has become the city of delight here in your home and in your heart. You can see that the Love of God is inescapable for those who truly know Him because you already live in His unbounded freedom. You mark this day as an anniversary, but it is also a beginning. I will seek the power of the Passion of My Son to invoke the celebratory realization of all humankind to the Truth that we have so prayerfully inscribed in your Diary. As I have already said, there will be detractors, but the faithful will outnumber them one-hundred to one. You must recall that I also told you that the manifestation of your Diary into the hearts of humanity will begin slowly. Do not assume, however, that it will not come. Be wary that you do not fall into the false trap of despair or disappointment waiting for God to do as you ask. Your campaign will be quite successful, but it takes time. I will pray with you for the swift conversion of humanity through the fruits of your holy work. You have achieved a great milestone for which you have been toiling over eight years. It is a result of your thousands of prayers and holy labors. However, the single most important reason you have reached this day is not because of those many hours or any of your new technological machines, and not even your invincible desire to succeed. The principle reason you have succeeded to this date is because of the extremely high joy that you and your brother share. This has been your source of true power that has brought the Angels and the blessings upon your Diary to make it a treasure and an invaluable masterpiece. You make the Father jubilant in a way that is wholly indescribable. For Him, it is a vast fulfillment that cannot be measured. There are no words with which to describe it. You are asked to feel princely, powerful, and proud! You are a winner, a victor with nothing to hide, no shame from which to cower, and no reason to ever feel a negative thought again. You can see the power and the holy fruits of your love for God. You set-out ten years ago seeking Me and My Son through Me. Now, He takes full delight in seeking you through Me. One day soon, you and Jesus will play gleefully among those flower-strewn meadows that you have so elegantly described in your Diary. And thanks to your joy, many more Saints will be running along beside you. Your Diary will show humanity that this power is too invincible for evil to overcome. All the heavens ask of you now is that you maintain your composure and live in peace with the happiness and realization of your accomplishment. I have come to say what I intended for today. Please remember that your joy brings your success fully and entirely. I urge you to take one day at a time. As the Psalmist wrote, be patient and never desist."

Sunday, August 15, 1999
Feast of the Assumption of Mary
5:05 p.m.

"Yes indeed, sing to Jesus! This is the message of Revelation 5:9. *(Worthy are you to receive the scroll and to break open its seals, for you were slain and with your blood you purchased for God those from every tribe and tongue, people and nation.)* I invite all My children who honor My Assumption into Heaven to respond to the call of grace by lifting your choruses of jubilation to the Glory of Christ the King. This is the day that has brought great devotion into the world for many centuries. God seeks your upturned faces to beseech His help in prayer, and I will pray with you to invoke His peace. My children, as you know, there is only one Heaven and one Kingdom of God in which the New Earth takes residence. Hence, why cower in such confusion? Why ask the questions that will so obviously define the Earth as you already know it to be? This is the hour of great decision, celebration, and anticipation. These are the days that are bringing the culmination of your hopes into reality. Please do not reject the charity of God. Since you are His favored people, recognize your goodness and worthiness in His sight. Too many reject the kindness of My

Son, falsely believing that they would be accepting a gift that should not forthrightly belong to them. This is why there are only a few who will stand under the Cross. They errantly believe that to reject the Divine Mercy of Jesus is some sort of noble sacrifice. They stubbornly walk away without ever tasting the sweetness of the Love of their Savior. I wish for you to remember that God will glorify the work that is done in His name because it is the Holy Spirit who shines in you. I have spoken to you for many years, and you recognize My wise counsel and intercessory graces. But the thousands who are about to see your Diary will be experiencing these things for the first time. Place yourself in their perspective. What a new awakening for their consciences and souls! You are much too close to your work to have an objective appreciation for it. This is a natural and common aspect of all My messengers."

Sunday, August 22, 1999
Feast of the Queenship of Mary
4:29 p.m

"My dear beautiful children, this is the ninth Feast of the Queenship of Mary that you have come together in honor of your Mother to help Me pray for the conversion of the world. And yet, I tell you again that it is still the first. I know that you can see by now that time has no effect on the Divinity of God, the power He wields over Creation, or the Love that He pours-out over His chosen people. My children, you are blessed to be among that happy number of souls who know the Truth firsthand. I have guided you forward with courage and joy so that, as you march in time toward the 10th celebration of the Feast of My Queenship, you will also know yourselves as truly holy people whose 'yes' to My Son still resounds with crispness and clarity, with the same solemnity as it rang-out on February 22, 1991. You know very well what the rest of humanity must come to know, that the Jesus who is acclaimed as the Alpha is the same Christ who lives in Heaven and on Earth as the Omega. Your Savior has not changed, despite the popular sentiments of contemporary theologians, sociologists, and liberal opportunists who have drifted from their faith in the Gospel as it has been handed-down for twenty centuries. This same Truth is the Deity that so very many refuse to accept because the Mystery of the Holy Trinity will not be confined by their mathematical logic. I ask you to remember the many lessons that I have given you about the Blessed Trinity. We will pray that the world will now better understand because of your hard labors. We will also pray that the secular world will now finally come to know their true Mother. The opportunity is at hand. The hours are winding to a close. Please remember that you are still the innocent little children to whom I came in 1991. Nothing can change that. Remember also the little shoes in which you walk. My special children, if you step back and remember your

Diary in perspective the way that I have told you to step back from the picture of Creation, you will better see the miracles that are about to flow forth through your work. Of course, The Final Colossus will be regarded as a monumental poem. Of course, the stories and parables will awaken many sleeping hearts. You will be surprised to see the effects of many parts of your Diary that you have tucked neatly inside your memories. One of the greatest impacts will come from the revelation of Father Lumen. I have come today under the light of twelve stars to tell you that the world is soon to be made a much better place because of My messengers, especially the two of you here in this city, in this house. Eight years ago, you were kneeling on the floor in this exact location in the room, praying for miracles through the Angelic Salutation. Now those eight years hence, one of the greatest miracles is about to be delivered to these same premises between the covers of a case-bound book. This will be an excellent echo of the *revised* Book of Discipline. My children, you have much to be thankful for because the intercession of the Hosts of Heaven has guided you each day toward greater Light. I cannot express how grateful Jesus is for your devotion to the Salvation of humanity through the Wisdom of My Immaculate Heart. Through your work, you now hold the foundation to touch those millions whom I told you would be converted. I ask you to pray for that success until you greet it eye to eye. I advise you as I have before to pray, live your life one day at a time, and watch the actions of God unfold according to His ingenious motivations. I ask you to simply watch as your Savior does His work. At the end of time, you will know that you were in His hands all along, that your every decision has been directed by the Love of His Most Sacred Heart. I will pray with you that My Son touches each heart in a special way."

Tuesday, September 7, 1999
7:06 p.m

"Let us forever rejoice that God has blessed His people once again, that the human heart has shown its courage to prevail, that dignity, righteousness, and service are still living in the mortal world, and that a people of noble purpose have finally come to their feet for the cause of human Redemption."

"My children, this is the preamble with which I ask you to carry your souls into the happy future that cannot escape your grasp, come what may. Very soon, you will have in hand a weapon which you have built with the Rosary and the Love in your hearts. Along with the Sacred Mysteries, you are about to be armed with one of the most lethal and powerful weapons against evil since God watched His Son die on the Cross. It took Him twenty centuries and your past ten years, but His Will is now being done on Earth at the brink of the twenty-first. Now, you say, *...what can I do? What will I do?* My answer and response is that you must use your new weapon of mass-divinity to convince America that She is blessed. Allow the world to come to you, they who hunger for more! To those who say that your work is huge, tell them, *This is not the half of it!* Finally, My American children will know who I am because you have cared enough to tell them. You have given your lives to God and they will be the fortunate beneficiaries. Your labors of the past eight years and seven months have been so intense that you have reveled the hopes and imagination of the Hosts of the High Heavens. And yet, you are not even the slightest bit tired or too weary-of-mind or body to go on. A year ago, you were attaching the lead wires to the great airship that you hoped to see fly. Now, that beautiful lass is stationed upon its launchpad and will soon depart into the skies, making her way to victory. All the world will know of this righteous fate. God will, indeed, glorify the work of His own Holy Spirit if you will honor Him with the patience to watch it unfold. I promised you many years ago that I would never abandon you. I will forever keep that promise, even past the long boulevards of Eternity that will never come to an end. My dear children, words cannot suffice to explain what your holy work has meant for the world. You are filled with the Holy Spirit, the incarnate gift of peace and grace to those who are lonely and afraid. You have moved through the ranks and have come forward to lead the last age of man to their Eternal moment of spiritual awakening. I promise as sure as I am now celebrating the solemnity of the observation of My Birth in the Church that God will afford you the opportunity to deliver every speech that rests quietly in your heart, waiting to be unleashed upon the fortunate ears who will stand by the tens of thousands to hear your every utterance, the next syllable that will soothe their aching souls and place their sorrowful hearts on the pathway to solace. I am confident that you wish to deliver them all soon! I ask you to watch with hope as this new millennium and century unfolds to reveal how your last decade of the 20th brought everyone on Earth to a renewal of faith and regeneration of hope. That is the brightest light of your holy tenure... I ask you to carry your new venue with clarity, dignity, purpose, direction, reflection, and the spirit of anticipation. I will be at your side until the end of time. There will be nothing then to stop us from uniting completely together in every way known to God... I am happy and grateful that you recognize the many ways that God has blessed you. I also ask you today to not calculate the cost. God will provide. Thank you for continuing your work. By no means are you finished, and by no means have I told you everything that God continues to allow Me to reveal. These are the days during which I am most happy because I know that the faithful service of you and your brother has yielded a most savory fruit for humankind to taste. This will make way for thousands more to join at the Feast Table in Heaven. God is already setting the places where they will sit beside the Saints who now bask in the Light of His Love. Your Diary will make it clear to the world that human contrition must precede the conversion which will result, and that holiness is the lofty perch upon which Mercy will light in your souls. Upon all of this, Jesus has placed the plume of Eternal Salvation in which every heart you are now trying to open will know and understand the reason why. I ask you to be gentle with those who will be slow to accept your work, and merciful to those who reject it outright. You know by now that God does what He does, allows what He allows, and brings everyone to the Heart of My Jesus of their own accord. That is the savory nourishment that your work is bestowing upon the collective conscience of all those who will embrace your Diary with loyalty and affection. In these next weeks, I will continue to unfold many new messages that will continue to be a part of your next work, the foundation of which I gave previously. Once you have that book in your hands, you will be armed! Thank you for your prayers. I will speak to you again very soon. I love you. Goodnight."

Tuesday, September 14, 1999
6:39 p.m.

"The blessed children whom I cherish, admire, adore, and embrace always remember the Triumph of the Cross. That is why you, My dear little ones, will always reside at the very foundation of My Immaculate Heart. This is, indeed, the time for which you have been praying, toiling, and struggling for many years. By all means, this is the time for which the 20th century world has unwittingly waited! The final quarter of this century will be its finest of all! Thank you, My children, for making that hope-of-God come true. You are the arms and hands of the Holy Spirit in a very troubled world! This is not the time to stop, but is assuredly a time to savor. You have so nobly come to adore the Child in the Manger! Your journey has taken all of 2000 years to complete! You will be upon another Advent season very soon! The work of your hands on your first Diary is complete, and you may begin to pen your memories and sentiments for the second any time you wish. The thesis for them is My messages after February 1997, along with your recollections of these End Times, the events in your lives, the reflections you may have about the process and product of your first Diary and all similar, substantial, and additional information that you may choose to relate. I am simply telling you these things to give you a sense of continuing direction during the times when you think your days have become somewhat boring and meaningless. Indeed, evil dogs surround you. This is what you stated upon the mountains of Medjugorje, the same mountains upon which you stand in this room.

My children, it is alright to look at Morning Star Over America with affection and admiration. You worked long and hard to complete it. Now, the work will be from afar as it goes into the world. This telemetry will allow you to know how the world is being changed. You still have to do some fine-tuning of this fine masterpiece, but the mission is underway! All the heavens watched as you worked so hard! They saw the unfortunate delays and unavoidable stumbling blocks. But, success is at hand! My dearly beloved children, the work of your hands and the paragon of all our hearts, the Morning Star Over America, has been launched and is en route to celestial heights that will make all humankind look upward to God again in *faith, hope, love, trust, friendship, conversion*, and *holiness*. These are the seven who are aboard. Now, we go on, we continue, we allow it to do its work, and we re-direct our attention to the work of the valleys of the Earth, always knowing that Morning Star will never fall from grace. This is a new time because your greatest work in this modern century is only begun. You have been given laurels, but not to rest upon! These are the continuing countdown of the final days of mortal man on Earth, and we still have much more work to do. Please do not abandon Me, for I shall never abandon you! In the next weeks, My messages will again move into a tone of teaching and solemnity. It is time to reveal not only the need for humanity to convert, but to shower the Wisdom of God upon those who will listen to the reasons why. I have come to say thank you because My Son is proud and pleased that you have said 'yes' to Him. Please pray for the victims of natural disasters."

Sunday, September 19, 1999
6:18 p.m.

"My dear sweet little children, you pray in the midst of the joy and delight of all eternity, the same divinity which has become the purpose of your lives. I am the only Queen Mother in Creation, and I have come to tell you about the perfection of the Kingdom of God. My children, precious are the hours during which you kneel here in prayer. Many are the blessings and graces that are yours because My Son is Love and Light. No soul can see with the clarity of His Light unless the heart is opened to receive Him. I promise that you will see the fullness of Love Face-to-face before the passing of many more hours on Earth. This is the reason for your great hope. I work with all My Love to seek the success for which you pine and which every soul and Angel in Paradise seeks for you. My Special one, I wish you could know how I truly desire for you to have a happy birthday tomorrow. These are trying times in a very excruciating atmosphere of rebellion and apathy. So many people tell you that they are not required to believe in God. These people are not only lost, they are moving swiftly toward the fires of Hell. The ones who call themselves atheists are especially hypocritical and self-contradicting. They believe in evil spirits that cannot be seen, but they refuse to believe in the Holy

Spirit who is alive and walking inside millions of Christians around the globe. They cannot see Christianity, so they will not believe. They have destroyed their own position and argument by asserting that evil spirits cause violence and hatred in their midst. It is true that Satan is the source of sin and evil, but Jesus is the origin, power, and The Way to all absolution, atonement, forgiveness, and righteousness. The reason atheists refuse to believe in God is because they are aware of the sacrificial life that Jesus calls them to live. Those who reject Him are filled with greed and hatred, and a malevolence that they disregard and ignore, choosing to disguise it beneath a mask of, 'I do not have to believe.'"

At this point, I rhetorically said to Our Lady that only suffering will change them.

"Yes, suffering, that of their own and the fortunate others whom God has chosen. And to capitalize the contempt of the atheists, they proclaim that no God would allow such agony. They ironically refuse to recognize that they themselves are the origin of such suffering. The question remains, how do we change them? How do we open their hearts? Many of them will see better because of the future that God is bringing upon them. Many others will see only at the end of time. Fortunately for them, they will be given the opportunity to choose Heaven because of the loving sacrifices of the hundreds-of-thousands who have suffered for their conversion. You need not be socially aggressive in trying to reach them. Your humble prayers and good works will suffice. This is the picture they will see beyond the horizon of mortality. To enter a public debate with them would only take time away from praying and serving. This is the type of distraction that Satan is trying to throw in your way. Many of the souls whom you will see have already chosen to spend eternity in Hell. You will recognize them when you see others like them. Avoid them at all costs, and do not get caught in their subtle traps. Many will say, 'please try to convert me!' And they will only steal your precious time away from reaching the lost souls who will join you at Jesus' side with full devotion and allegiance. I have told you about the wicked craftiness of Satan's evil works. Now you are able to see it firsthand. I wish for you to turn your thoughts to the joy of your birthday. I have promised you that every letter and keystroke of your editing will mean a soul who is allowed entry into Heaven. For your birthday tomorrow, you will know the exact moment when multitudes of souls will pour into the Light of Paradise from their captivity in Purgatory. It is you who are making these blessings possible. Can you see the power that would change the world if all My children lived as I ask? I hold-out great hope for this. My hope continues for many other revelations to awaken the sleeping world *(Our Lady repeated the content of Her three secrets to me, the coming permanent sign in Medjugorje, and the Third Fatima Secret)* and the way that a united nation will look upward to Me as their *Morning Star Over America.* I bring you the dawn of the Good News because you have said 'yes' to God and humanity alike. I ask you to pray for discernment when in situations that seem to be ones in which your authority and character are in peril, under scrutiny, or being assailed. You must know what questions will be asked of you that will be posed to inhibit your work. Many of them will appear to be harmless interrogatories from seemingly innocent people. You must remain wise in the Holy Spirit as opposed to being eager to satiate the predatory curiosity of your inquisitors."

Sunday, September 26, 1999
7:16 p.m.

"This is another day upon which the Light of Heaven has shined brightly into the lives of My precious children. I am the Divine Immaculate Conception, the Advocate who stands with brilliance before Jesus to tell of the many happy trials you have sustained for the sake of His Kingdom. My children, in the month of October 1999, the population of the world is passed six billion people. This is a large number of souls living in exile. Yet in all this, there is a place reserved in Paradise for each one. Sadly however, millions are yet unaware of the life of piety, holiness, and Christian conviction that is required for passage into eternal bliss. Many secular optimists claim that human life is meant to be a source of perpetual pleasure, that the purpose of your existence on the Earth is to adhere only to the selfishness that thrives there. You know already that true happiness lives only in the faith by which you live, inspired by the Holy Spirit, and strengthened through honest prayer. This faith is nurtured by the Most Sacred Meal from the Altar of Sacrifice, the Body and Blood of My Son. How can such a people be so blessed? Because Jesus loves you more than your consciousness can realize. No more need you wonder why there is salvific Life, Death, and Resurrection. It is all the foundation of the Love of God brought to you as Divine Food. My little children, it is imperative that you always remember that you cannot yet see Heaven, but it is now fully engulfing you. You do not always see and hear the Saints, but your voice resonates into their hearts from the breast of God. I hold in My arms the Child of Bethlehem, the rise and fall of many. I come to you during this final age to say that no one needs to fall. There is no reason for rejecting your Salvation and every purpose in accepting the Will of the Almighty Father who created your souls out of Love and made the Earth with His own hands. My children, you should always remember that God blinks not because the pupils of His eyes are parched, but because He requires a brief respite from the awful vision that He sees in the world. You blink your eyes when someone waves their hand close to your face, but Jesus blinks to send you the cool breezes which comfort your soul. I have borne the message of Eternal Life into the mortal world, the tiny flicker that is now being brought to leaping flames on every continent of the Earth. With each passing day, those who have never before known redemption are shielding their eyes from the blinding conflagration that has finally set them free. How can humanity turn away from such revelation? Why do My children run and hide? Because of their fear to have faith, their fear to love God without the expectation of a reward, and a fear to be happy amidst the Eternal Divinity that has come to bring the wicked to justice. I have told you many times about the echoes which resound through the generations, the reverberation of the original and singular Truth. This Trinity of Love has come into full view before millions who are still too timid or too wretched to make it known. These souls do not yet know that they are the bellows of orchestration for the present generation of modern-day men. Their awakening has yet to come. They have heard the call of Love like a voice in the night, but they are too comfortable in their beds of slumbering indifference to answer the call. So just as before, God will come to them. He will come bearing the gift of reconciliation and judgment to every soul who still lies helpless in their lairs like an infant in a crude manger. He will pull back their covers and expose their sins. He will reach beneath them and upend their beds of injustice, effectively turning their world upside-down. And, what a great day this will be! It is near the morning hour when all souls will make an accounting for their trespasses in the night. Yes, Jesus will come and raze the forest to reveal every act of ill-will and malevolence that kept His people from calling-out His name. There will be no room for excuses and no need for confession. The Judge will already know what must be known. My children, if this Light is to come soon, you must continue to pray. Pray that My Son will return not with blade and razor strap, but with kindness and Mercy. Pray that He will brandish the Sword of Justice in an act to make knights of everyone, not to skewer your souls. I can fully attest that I have seen this Divine Mercy unfold as the gentle hand of your Creator God reaches to caress the broken. And yet, I have also seen the power that He has wielded against the rogues who caused them to break. That is why this is such a time for powerful prayer and for the Children of Light to stand like spiritual titans amongst the cheering crowds who are calling-out for compassion, understanding, nourishment, and love. Imagine how revolting it must seem to the heavens as only 400 of six billion people hoard a trillion dollars wealth while watching their fellow brothers and sisters grovel in hunger, despair, poverty, and disease in the rest of the world. How does the Messiah of the Gospel speak to them? How do they know that their egregious error is so repulsive and repugnant to the God of their fathers?—By seeing that the lowly continue to suffer. Sadly, they turn their backs upon the poor and say, *too bad they did not fight harder to hoard their own.* My children, this is the world that the Almighty Father sees as you prepare to enter the 21st century. Yes, their plight will come, just as it has to the poor they have rejected. Please do not feel sorry for them. I am confident that Jesus will offer every soul on Earth the opportunity to live the Gospel Truth. It is not yet too late. This is the real Mercy that lives on the Earth and in Heaven. Before Jesus' Passion and Crucifixion, the selfish, arrogant and all sinners were destined for the fires of Hell. This is why every soul must accept the Blood of the Cross. Together, we will help them do so. My message is possible because you have chosen to pray. I will speak to you again as we enter your favorite month of the year. Thank you for taking such prayerful care of your brother. Your reward in Heaven will be great."

Sunday, October 3, 1999
4:10 p.m.

"When the Glory of God comes to redeem the Earth for the Eternity of Heaven, you shall be part of that great celebration. This is why I come with such joy and why you must always remember that time is already done. I ask for you to continue to believe in the powers of Grace and Absolution. No matter how corrupt the world may seem to be, how persecuted you might become, and how errant the views of your detractors, you shall never fall from the elevation in which you are suspended and never cower in the face of outright rejection. I bring this news because I know your hearts, and I see the valiant way you protect and caress the Truth inside them. You have known many days only by what has impacted your consciousness, but common to them all is the constancy of the Love of God in you and the divinity for which you were born. My children, there is a great need for you to always remember your new royalty in that Salvation, not in an egotistical way, but in a modestly humble way, an exhibition of pious and holy pride, never of conceit or haughtiness, but of inner-confidence and holiness. Your courage will always be a natural function of your faith when you remember that My Son loves you more than any other creature. I have no doubt that you are fulfilled by the hope in what I am telling you, but it is you who must sustain the dubious criticism of being called the unnaturally holy in a world that still strives to be one only with Nature and not the God who created it. My children, you are fortunate for many other reasons than you can now possibly know. The Light and Peace of your future will bring you an inheritance fit for princes. The healing of every affliction truly exists as you brandish your Rosary like a heavenly wand. Our God of All really does care that you are His suffering people for the sake of the lost. This is why I am here speaking to you today. I must give you complete assurance that your prayers are the templates with which Jesus etches the final phrases that will push time aside and open the

Earth to the infinity of delight. I have been fortunate to be part of the apocalyptic culmination, and I have seen every brave spiritual soldier who has fallen wounded for the Glory of God. There are millions whom you do not see every day who fight in that battlefield beside you. You unconsciously hoist your souls to step over the dying beneath your feet, those courageous souls whose names you read in the obituary columns every day. I have never seen Creation more ready than it is now for the revelations yet to come, the new miracles that count in a number larger than the multitudes of raindrops that you hear falling outside your windows at this very moment. The fields of human souls are truly fields of spiritual dreams, hopes of better days to come, expectations for the rewards and passages that will accompany the New Light, and the final Dayspring which will forever push the darkness away from human life and into the Abyss that will forever be hidden from the hearts of the redeemed. My children, this is a struggle about Love versus hatred, about Life conquering death, and about Purity defeating the lifeless stench of evil for the good to look down-upon in joy. The battle that rages is fierce, but it is one that has assuredly been determined. You have won the fight because Jesus is in you, the Christ of the Everlasting is now reigning supreme through you now. How happy are the Saints and Angels to know that your souls are only a mortal horizon away from joining them at the Table of Salvation. All of this hope I bring you, My children, because it is real and alive, no matter what may befall humanity on Earth, no matter what the news of the day might be, and no matter how dark the evil around you might seem. My children, we continue to pray because we wish to please God and transform the collective soul of humankind. We seek what My Son also seeks, that goodness and Mercy shall follow His children all the days of your life. My Mantle of Motherhood is the dome over the Earth which used to be called the sky. Every grace that falls from the heavens rains from My intercessory powers. This is quite a repulsive revelation for those who refuse to acknowledge Me as their Mother. But it is as true as Jesus Himself, and it shall become more apparent as the 21st century slowly unfolds. Please be assured that you are in the number of souls who already know about the powerful intercession of your Holy Mother. In the end, My Immaculate Heart will Triumph. Be prepared to wave that tiny flag that you hold in your hand. As this fall season continues to unfold, hold on to your hope and always be happy that God is with you. Be prepared to be opposed by unforseen people who would not have otherwise forsaken you, but also be doubly prepared to be victorious as you watch each of them abandon their obstinate opposition. Your heart still beats with invincible piety, and this will help you weather any storm."

Sunday, October 4-16, 1999

No public message was received, although Our Lady spoke with us personally about issues related to our Diary.

Sunday, October 17, 1999
3:49 p.m.

"My joyful little children, I welcome you into the warmth of My Holy and Immaculate Heart. The days are passing swiftly now, but no more than before when once you thought an hour to be a day. I bring the Good News from Heaven that your lives and successes are unfolding according to the Plan of God. I come to offer you the Wisdom of His Love. Please help Me complete My intentions for humanity by keeping your spirits above the fray and your hearts aloft inside the supernatural guidance and bounty of the Morning Star Over America. My children, someday you will know why humankind rejected My Son from the first, just as you see the lack of faith by mankind in your day. Those haughty souls who claim to be the 'miracle police' for God will see themselves in the same way that the hundreds saw themselves when they first walked away from My dear Bernadette as she knelt on the ground rubbing the dampened soil onto her soft cheeks. Her faith, obedience, and humility became the healing spring for tens-of-thousands to this day. It is proper for you to take your spiritual seat beside her now as all the heavens watch you participate in the slow unfolding of these last ages. There can be absolutely nothing good in someone alleging that God would not perform or allow a certain miracle. This is a naive assumption and the most grave disorder. With Me, you continue to move into the next phase of your lives that will assist in the conversion of man. We have come very far together. You and I will remain as one as you pass into the new century."

I recalled how several elderly people were very kind to my brother and me after Holy Mass today. I asked Our Lady to bless them as I marveled at their innocent acceptance of our work. Our Holy Mother said,

"My Special one, the elderly will be most accepting of your work. However, those who are very young are deceiving themselves by assuming that the horizon of their mortality is in the immeasurable distance of future time. You, however, know that it is as brief as the next breath you take or the next beat of your heart. This is why it is important to not live fastly, but to live well. Do not spend your days trying to eradicate the bats in the belfry, the mice in the pantry, or the snakes in the basement. Indeed, be much more concerned about the flight of the human soul toward its eternal resting place in Jesus. What is the meaning of My metaphor? Let the world clamor, but proceed with your work. Your best days are yet to come. I tell you that My Divine Son, your Savior and Lord, will never allow your permanent legacy to be anything other than pious and noble. Remember what the Angels said about the elderly nun in a convent with a Rosary in her hands. There is no intercontinental ballistic missile that can conquer such awesome power. There are those who will scoff at your work as though it is a meaningless handwritten diary in the back of a drawer in an attic somewhere. How they will cringe when the Christ elevates it to be the very basis for His Mercy upon their souls! This is no time to cower or weaken in the face of criticism or rejection. Indeed, invite it. Welcome it. Engage the debate. The miracles God has planned for the future will make laughingstocks of them all. A healing spring will flow from your obedience to Me that will make Lourdes look like a diminutive bottle of holy water. I tell you today that if you will trust in strength and stand by Me, these things will come. I ask you to remember the fruit of love that I have been begging of you for almost nine years: Patience. You must remember that if you are not patient, your anger will not be righteous, but an offspring of vengeance. You can see the difference between the two. Let us walk forward in the conviction that no mortal can bring you to falter, no opposing force can defeat you, and nothing that stands in your way can defy the Truth you bear. Tell them that your priestly direction has come from the Queen Mother of the Highest Priest! You become a prophet if you live the messages that I have given. All these finer things have been made possible by your recitation of the Holy Rosary."

I thought of all those who are reciting the Rosary whom I have seen treating other people so terribly, yet still proclaim that they are a child in good standing with the Most Blessed Virgin. I wondered how this could be so. She said,

"Because they are saying the Rosary, not praying it."

Our Blessed Mother then mentioned the picture that I placed on the front of my first Diary which I had taken on Christmas Day in 1988. It was the last Christmas that I spent living in my childhood home in Ashland, as the next May I purchased the home where Our Lady began Her messages.

"That book cover is your miraculous gift to humankind. I have only watched and prayed. That Christmas Day in 1988 was especially given for the cover of your Diary. It was your final Christmas to live in that place. I ask you to remember that no man and no heart has the audacity or authority to deny your work in this world or the next. While many will publicly rebuke you, their hearts will silently tell them the truth. I have given Myself to humanity as your Mother because Jesus gave you to Me. There is nothing in Creation that can impede My progress toward fulfilling that commission. We will bask together in the Light of Heaven, the Heaven that I already know; and you will tell Me how you suffered gladly for the victory that is ours. I have said what I have wished for today; and for the future, I hope you will look forward with joy."

Sunday, October 24, 1999
3:01 p.m.

"My dear children, the reason you dream and dance is because your souls still yearn with hope to know the Truth, to see with unfettered confidence that the future holds your fortune of forgiveness and peace. I am the Queen of that Eternal Peace, and it is to you whom I come for help in the holy commission that has been bestowed upon many to help convert the world. You are no longer tired or weary, but renewed and strengthened to know that you are succeeding. I offer My gentle kiss upon the cheek of your souls so that you will always know Me as your Mother. Night and day, I seek you to hover beneath My protective Mantle. It is comforting there. Will you kindly continue to be My little Children of Light to your brothers and sisters on Earth? Will you caress and guide them in the way of My Divine Son? Now you know that your work for Me has borne fruit that is greater than you could ever have imagined. The millions of souls who live in your midst have grown eight years older, but you have grown infinitely more holy and wise while maturing at their side. It is time for them to inherit the Wisdom I am dispensing through you as you watch their conversion in ageless bliss. How can a people be so blessed? The answer is because God loves you, and I have come to prove it. Through the entirety of Creation, in life and beyond death, all humanity will eventually know this. You are among the fortunate ones who have come to realize it in advance. And so, I have come again to bring you peace and ask that you recognize the ever-changing face of the existence of human life as only a page in a much larger book of promise. Tomorrow will bring something new, but that news will pass in the setting of the sun. Only the Good News of the Gospel of Jesus will last forever, even when all the mechanical presses of secular popularism have returned to the dust. I bring you the continuation of the first message I ever gave you. It is still the same. Your faith and urgent responses are the reasons I have remained. This is the thesis of the consistency of our work together; you are willing to pray, listen, learn, and act. For all these reasons, I assure you that your Father in Heaven is forever grateful. It is with His complete blessing that I speak to you again. My children, you have now another chore in accumulating a new network of text from February 22, 1997 until now. You will enjoy this new beginning as the Holy Spirit emblazons your hearts with fresh parables and literary songs. I will pray over you as you work with patience and enlightenment. We shall carry on in joy and accomplishment. I can read your heart like you see *The*

Final Colossus on a page. You may always confide your feelings to Me. It is life itself that you share with Jesus when you pray to understand, for you are very much alive in Him. I know that this is your favorite season of the year. While it is rather cold at night, it will always be warm in our hearts as we share the Love of God. You must remember that the world is in an awful state, and when someone who is deserving of great accolades is rejected by men, it highly mitigates that terrible wretchedness."

Sunday, October 31, 1999
2:06 p.m.

"My dear holy children, I ask you to live forwardly with Me so your spirits can know true peace. Do not be distracted by the scurrilous world, but place your hearts into the care of My Son. I promise that you will find solace there. The workings of Earth are of no interest in Heaven if they are not given in the Name of Jesus. Mortals seek to know the reasons for every universe, but not the Truth about the Everlasting Life that rests beyond them. I have the Wisdom and knowledge to disavow their error, to underscore everything they know, and to teach in a single minute what it would take them centuries to discover. By the time the astronomers of the Earth hear this message, they will realize that I have told you today that the solar system does not require their inquisitive interest to continue its pace. They still refuse to accept My words that Jesus Christ is the Savior of humankind, that He is as close to the Earth as He has ever been. My children in exile close their eyes to the Truth, but like the sun shining through the eyelids of the sighted, Jesus permeates your souls to tell you that He is here. Your heart tells you that the blessing of God has broken the mortal horizon. The veil over your heart cannot conceal your conscience from knowing the Truth. When will My children shed the error that has cast them for too long in the darkness? When will the bearers of Divine Light come from beneath their bushel baskets? Their wicker inhibitions are no match for the courage you know in the Savior of the world. My children, I have seen from On High that you are a people filled with hope and opportunity. This is the day when both must be realized in earnest. I have told you for many years that the cause of holiness is justice. This is where you will find true peace. I give you the confirmation that you seek in knowing what is acceptable in the eyes of God. His sight is perfect because He is the Seer of all things. It is true that the Angels do not wear glasses! Please come into My Immaculate Heart so the mindless speculation that pummels your consciousness can be abated. I promise that the Christ-Child in My arms will clarify your every thought and action. He is the greatest of all men and the Son of the Most High. Can you not realize that the finality of your lives is found in Him?

Today, My children, is the solemn Eve of All Saints. I have told you before that it is a time of terrible confusion because many people have misrepresented the purpose of this solemnity. Please pray with Me that all on Earth will realize the holy power of the intercession of the Saints in Heaven. And equally important, please invoke their supplications for the poor souls who are remembered on the next day. This is a blessed period in your lives because you are seeing the changing times and fortunes of a world that refuses to rest in redemption. Of course you know the Truth, but you assuredly could not have known that it would be so despised by those in your midst. You could not see in advance the reluctance of others to let-go of the material world and give their future to the Holy Spirit. It is not too late for them, and you will succeed in time. I implore your patience now more than ever before. You can see for yourselves the power that you wield when you detect even the slightest degree of humility from the faithful. Please be satisfied knowing that My Son has prepared His own to accept what I have to offer. Do not be filled with anxiety or despair when your expectations are not fulfilled in your own frame of time. God knows what He is doing. You must maintain your inner-zeal that you have already succeeded. My Special son, as you move within hours of the eleventh month of this year, please hold a silent meditation in your heart for the thirty-eight years you are leaving behind and what a magnificent gift you have made of them toward the passing 20th century, the people on Earth, and God who loves you. You and your brother are leaving the century during which you have lived the majority of your lives. Does it not give you a sense of satisfaction knowing that you are helping bring My Son so close to others? Always remember that I am the loving Mother who approached you nearly nine years ago. My trust in you is yet the same, My desire for your help has never decreased, My blessing upon you is still as sweet. Jesus has made it clear that He owes you and your brother a great debt of gratitude. You will see in time what I mean by this. Thank you for having responded to My call."

Sunday, November 7, 1999
4:05 p.m.

"My dearly beloved children, the echoes of your deliverance into the Eternal happiness for which you seek originate in your utterance of the Hail Mary. You see with enhanced vision that I respond to your plea for help with the strength of the Holy Spirit and the entire Court of heavenly angels. This is a special day of prayer because, like many to come, it is the continuation of the opening of the final ages of human mortality into the infinity of Redemption. This, My children, is why others say that My messages are repetitive. Their heart is resounding the reverberations of the single Truth of one Crucifixion. I can see the uplifting of many hearts to the Grace that I have come to bestow, those who do not yet know how to define the signal miracles and supernatural sentiments which have been flowing from Heaven into this room for nearly nine years. Whether they call it a cantation of beauty, the high-strobe of Truth, textualized music, or lessons of Love, the fact remains that something new and exciting is awakening their sleeping hearts, and they can attribute it only to someone yet to be named. They will eventually recognize and conclude that it is, indeed, their Immaculate Mother."

Our Lady then referred to the many boxes containing the printed and published copies of "Morning Star Over America."

"Do you see all of the boxes of books before you? In those holy containers is the pulsating conveyance of the relay being sent back to Earth of the Truth of My intercession from the orbiting Morning Star Over America. You are seeing that She is about to be known by many thousands. We must pray that this century will come to its close with a renewed fervor of hope by the many people in the western world. We must pray that they accept miracle over material, prayer over self-indulgence, and reparation over recreation. The pardon that Jesus intends for souls has been reserved for the penitent, not those whose lives have been given to the flagrant rejection of holiness without a firm purpose of amendment. The Mercy of Jesus is unconditional, but it is a fruit for the humble-of-soul. This is the acknowledgment which cannot be ignored or deflected by anyone who is bound for the beauty of Heaven... Please never shed the happiness that you were always given to enjoy. Never leave your innocent kindness behind on your journey to evangelize the world. Peace exudes from your heart because you do not fear to reprimand the spiritually indignant with the charity of Love. The Truth will always prevail, but many will try to grasp your understanding of it from your hands, reshape it into what they wish it to be, and try to hand it back to you with their skewed and erroneous visions affixed. Please do not allow their deception and distraction to cause you any grief... I am pleased that you do not allow those who call you arrogant to take you away from continuing to profess your faith in confidence! I have told you that your work will touch men of many walks of life and bring them to pray on their knees. All of them, laborers, intellectuals, doctors, lawyers and the rest will eventually find their way to My Immaculate Heart. Your having said 'yes' in February 1991 has done this. Lifting others up is always the way to win."

Sunday, November 14, 1999
3:59 p.m.

"My divine ones, it is exactly the hour of four o'clock where you live, and yet it remains the timeless glory of love in your hearts. I am quite elated that you have decided to remain with Me for so many years. Your remarkable obedience and service will render the goal which we have sought together unequivocally achievable, no matter what conditions may seem during a given period of time or circumstance at hand. I also come cloaked in the joy that the many who are living the recollection of your work over the past nine years are taking your messages seriously. I have told you all those years that we will succeed, and we assuredly will do that. Your high accomplishment is being brought to you by the Life given you in the Most Holy Eucharist and the elevation you are giving your Savior so elegantly brought forth in this room today. You have mysteriously capitalized this process. What perfection, love, glory, and joy! Thank you for knowing deep inside what My Son wishes the rest of the world to become."

Our Lady referred to the new television program titled, Mary the Mother of Jesus.

"My children, I know that you have a somewhat reticent approach as to whether you should watch the televised program about My life. If you choose, I will tell you more accurately on My own. However, the program will open America for the dispensation of your work. I feel humbled that the producers have decided to accept My role as the Mother of Jesus, but we must search for the day when they will accept Me as the Mother of humankind. This is the only way that America will ever truly know peace because I bear the Prince of Peace in My arms. My Immaculate Heart is a storehouse of graces that My Son is waiting to pour-out over His people. How could any other mother be so kind? This is the magnitude and infiniteness of My Love for you. All the world must remember that I was given humanity by Jesus from the Cross because I love you. He did not ask Me to love you only in the future. He ratified the Love that I have always had for you through My Immaculate Conception. In the Kingdom of God, I have loved you since God knew that He desired to have a Mother whom He had yet to create. My children, I know that most people around you and in other parts of the world do not realize what this means. You, however, know full-well the timeless truth of My Maternity, and therefore have the capacity to understand My station and purpose beyond the expiring ages, including the transformation of your own souls from mortality into Eternal Life. This is also why I have come to you, and why God is so pleased by your response. Can you feel in the depth of your hearts that you are assisting in the culmination of contemporary history by eclipsing the existence of man with the Wisdom of God? Can you see the passing events that tragically lay before you as the stepping-stones to a more noble purpose? Therefore, be not surprised by what your Savior allows, but be pleased in confidence that you know the outcome of the universe and the new beginning that approaches with the inexorable march of time, a day for your labors and an eternity for your rest. Indeed, you will see many more events come to pass; some will be tragic, others will fill you with contentment, and many will bring you to feelings of sorrow and apprehension. But atop all this will be the joy and hope that you have always known in Me, your loving Savior Jesus, the Angels and Saints, and the Glory in the Highest, God on His Throne in Paradise. No matter what will come of the Earth, nothing can diminish or conquer the happiness that you have already gained in Jesus. The King of Creation whose Feast you will again celebrate has planned for all who share in His Death and Resurrection an elation that cannot truly be known in mortal flesh. Your spirit soars because you know this to be true, but your soul is still pining to see God Face-to-face. That time will come sooner than you could possibly conceive. This too is why I am continuing to speak to you. There is joy in the offing that will remand all of your sorrowful memories to the bowels of the Earth. No more will you know grief or loneliness, and no more will your consciousness be pelted by the shock of fallen aircraft or peoples whose bodies are ripped apart by violence and flying lead. I have told you that the last quarter of the final 20th century year will be blessed, and you are seeing it unfold now. You may not yet see the celestial fireworks of immortal ecstasy or streamers flying through the air, but your heart will know with perfect assurance that Jesus is with you to take you into the 21st century as far as the Father wishes it to go. And to utilize the words of another, *'that ride is not very far.'* You light-up the pathways of those who are terrified to walk with the brightness of Truth. This is apparent everywhere you go. Sometimes your own light is so bright that you even have to shield your own eyes! I must never be misunderstood: This is when all the world will see best! I have come today to tell you that it is your joy that matters now because only you can destroy it. With the faith in your hearts, there is no way that the world can hold you fast or captivate you into the bonds of sadness. This is the Day of the Lord, and His Return is presently at hand. So My children, I hope that I have inspired you to know that it is Paradisial Love that lives in you, and this is why you are Chosen and Special in the eyes and Heart of God. The question whether you can be perfect on Earth is an absolute Yes! The question whether you can be perfect in any other imitation than Jesus is an absolute No! This is why God sent Jesus as teacher, admonisher, example, and prophet. This same humble servant was crucified by those who could not see their own capacity to be like Him. This is the essence of those who oppose you today. All you have to do is live what I have taught."

Monday, November 22, 1999
7:11 p.m.

Today, I was allowed to discuss my Diary on the noonday news with local television personality and veteran newsman Mr. Don Hickman.

"To My very dear children, as you enter another Advent season, remember that it is always Advent in your holy hearts. You are very kind to celebrate your work before so many, so profoundly. You are the little children from whom God has required much. I ask you to continue to greet this responsibility with the love I have taught. This is the final quarter-year of this century. We have worked hard to take the message of My Jesus to the dismal, dark and hidden places of the world, seeking the lost and desolate, the lonely, afraid, and despised. We have sought-out sinners who know no refuge and given warmth to the coldest of hearts. You have no fear because the Holy Spirit is in you, enkindling the flame of Truth by which hundreds-of-thousands may walk with greater faith and courage. Can you not see the grace in which this 1,000 years is closing? I am your Mother, and I have led your tiny steps toward the doorway to Salvation, the Sacred Heart of My Son and His Precious Wounds in which your Salvation resides. My little children, you must continue to hold fast to the Truth I have revealed to you, the prophecies, the promises, and the secrets. Do not despair at the pace of the revelation of your work, rather be happy that there is a glistening star overhead to which Jesus will soon turn every eye. I have not come to you for so long just to watch you wait in anguish. Just as there was a star over Bethlehem on the night Jesus was born, there is a *Morning Star Over America* under which He will provide His greatest miracles to convert the multitudes during these final ages. I promise that this is true, but you must be more patient than you have been, more enduring than you have ever been in your lives. This is an opportune time not only for America, but for the entire world. I hold the hope that I perpetually bequeath to you to claim as your own. I have come again as your advocate before Jesus and your mentor to help you come to greater understanding of the deception of time. Please do not perceive what is yet to come as being a longshot into a dark hole. Jesus has planned from the beginning of time the implementation, fulfillment, culmination, and effect of My intercession to you. What good would it be if you already knew the process and outcome? How fair would it be to preempt your lives? So today I ask you to keep your spirits aloft in hopeful anticipation that our work and its purpose are on their proper course. Today, over 20,000 people watched while you provided the news of My intercession on the local television. We have a great deal to be thankful for in the charity of this newsman. I assure you that he will be properly rewarded for a life of grace. These last times would not have been as fruitful without his own fiat. Like most everyone who has an ounce of good will in their hearts, he felt the inclusive love that glows from your profession of faith. I tell you that more such opportunities will come, but you must always call yourself to the holy fruit of patience. So now, we continue to look forward into your future with the joy that you have much more work to do. Is this not the greatest time for spiritual renewal in America and across the seas? I pray that you continue to share the hope that still lives in all the Saints for the world to come to Jesus in My arms very soon. There are millions of timid hearts who are willing to try, but yet do not know how. We shall teach them together. I have come to thank you and bring you the peace of the Holy Spirit. I offer My gratitude for resting when you are tired. This is a great display of wisdom for Jesus to see. I will bless the world in the Name of Love. In the process of such blessing, I will include all the members of your family. Thank you for your wonderful witness today before so many thousands."

Sunday, November 28, 1999
3:51 p.m.

"My dear holy children, it is obvious that the end of time will bring the revelation of all things. I hope that your hearts always anticipate the sovereignty of God this way and know that you are one and indivisible with that singular power through My Son Jesus Christ. Let Me make this more clear. The principle of all Creation is Love because Love is the reason for everything good that is brought into being. Hence, you are communing with the Subject Divinity who has come to the Earth; Father, Son, and Holy Spirit. The essence of Creation is that you are the reflection of the Almighty Father's affections, and this is why mankind is made in His image. Humankind is intrinsically divine by the power of the Paraclete alive in your hearts. This is the thesis of My earlier lessons to you. While you are not yet perfect, you are not precluded from becoming so. Since your soul is beside and in the Divinity of Jesus, you join the Divine and incorruptible in Him. The fact that the Earth has yet to be transformed into the image of Heaven is because the followers of Christianity will not live-out the prime tenet of their faith: That the Mystical Body of Jesus Christ can and in the end will be perfect as your Heavenly Father is perfect. My children, I will reveal to you the reason why so many are confused. Remember that the human psyche allows you to turn and evolve in and out of many states of consciousness, but you can only exist in one of them at a time. This gives mankind a false sense of dominion, a skewed vision of what complete life is. Divinity and Life in unity with Jesus is not limited to one particular state of consciousness, but is the infusion of all holy states of being simultaneously. Therefore, when you say that you love God, it is the Spirit of God speaking in you, the Holy Paraclete. This makes you a partner in the

Creator of life, not His equal, but a partner in the perfection that He has boasted of since before the Creation you have all come to know. The human soul is a unique and essential portion of what God wants eternity to be. The proof is in the Holy Eucharist, the Body and Blood of Jesus. Since Love is Life, it is also Eternal Life. Only the Divine can be granted a portion of Heaven that you share, which is the home of Everlasting Life. The Eucharist is your assurance that God has shaped His Will to be the inclusion of the absolved in that endless Kingdom. In truth, God has allotted that humanity is again made whole through the Body, Blood, Soul, and Divinity of Jesus. To that end, your soul is saved and becomes an essential portion of what God wants for Himself, one and the same Love with you in Paradise. How lonely God would be if not for your Salvation! Do you understand that He wishes His children to be saved and remain perpetually in His company? There, you share in His multifaceted consciousness, not like on Earth where you reside in only one at a time. Thank you for permitting Me to present this brief dissertation. My children, you cannot know all things unless you are open to the understanding that human life on the Earth has a reciprocal purpose with your own redemption, past the gateway of your mortality. But, you do not have to wait until you die to know and see it. This is what I have been telling you all along. You must have faith that you will eventually understand."

Today, I visited a stable in the country and, while there, offered a special prayer in memory of Jesus' Birth in a stable in Bethlehem. Our Lady made reference to my petitions by saying,

"You have advanced the Kingdom of God on Earth by leaps and bounds as a result of your prayers of love in the equestrian stable. I assure you that you share in God's Eternal Love through such prayers of joy. It is your way of thanking God for the gift of My intercession. He accepts and anticipates this prayer of joy as your response to His gifts. How better could He be pleased than to see you enjoying the graces that He brings and blesses?"

Recently, my brother placed a telephone call to a newspaper reporter who had written an informative description of a very vile case of anti-Semitism. Timothy wanted to relate his heartfelt sentiments of support to this man for his courageous declaration against such despicable conduct. He said, "I wanted to call and tell you how touched I am by your profound article in today's paper about the awful scourge of anti-Semitism that is still gripping our nation. Myself and my colleagues share the intense sorrow and grief that you and your family of predecessors have suffered at the hands of those who hate. Please always remember our unity with you under Heaven and be assured that our love for you is the source from which you may always derive your happiness for ages to come. May God bless you always, and be with you as these final days of the present millennium tick to a close. I will always pray for you. Goodbye and God bless."

"I am also very happy that you are praying from the heart for all who suffer neglect and persecution. God hears your pleas for help!"

Our Blessed Lord then spoke to me -

"My brother and My friend, I am with you every day. Thank you for not conceding to despair. Please be happy in service, humble in suffering, and noble in faith. Thank you for wielding the power I have given you. Imagine the glory you can work. Thank you for being one with Me. I love you, I Am Jesus."

"My dear children, I hope that you can fully comprehend the holy words of My Son and unite in their meaning and purpose with complete awareness of holiness. You are part of the Solemnity of the Annunciation every time you pray. Those who believe that God is happy on a throne in a distant Heaven by Himself are wrong. He desires His children to gather around His feet in Paradise. This is preceded by Jesus wishing every mortal soul on Earth to gather in prayer before the Monstrance and at His Holy Tabernacles. The principle is the same. As you will eventually gather with the Almighty Father in Heaven and sit in joy at His feet, you will become that one essence with Him that I described to you today. The season of Advent has come, and I will pray with you that all the world will come to the joy of Salvation in Emmanuel of Bethlehem."

Sunday, December 5, 1999
3:12 p.m.

"In accordance with the Will of the Almighty Father in Heaven, I have come to thank you for partaking in the conversion of hundreds-of-thousands of souls whom you have yet to meet. My children, as you ponder the condition of the world in your prayers, please always remember the not so perceivable souls who are growing in the wombs of their mothers and those who suffer the terrible agony of Purgatory in union with the good souls who grieve and lay in pain on Earth for the Glory of the Kingdom of God. The Novena of the Immaculate Conception is about the birth of your consent to be like the concession of Mine; always willing to say Yes to My Son, and ready to be borne yourselves in sinless grace into the perfection of Heaven. My dear children, always remember that perfection and light are one and the same Love. Therefore, perfect Light is your unity with the healing Spirit of Holiness that God places in your heart when you accept Him. To be in Jesus and He in you is to also be anointed as the chosen ones of His Father. Hence, you are the radiance of the Gospel of My Son on Earth, the souls who teach and admonish both the lost and arrogant. It is not only your decision to cause others to know humility, it is your commissioned responsibility. Thank you for acknowledging your role as doctors and professors of righteousness and faith. The world will be a much better place if many would call themselves to this understanding instead of plundering those who know the whole Truth about Christian piety, who are scoffed-at as indignant snobs for proclaiming what others should already know for themselves in Christ. My dear children, I have told you many times during the last ten years that the season of Advent is one of spiritual joy, anticipation, preparation, and humility. I am afraid that millions in the world, especially in the capitalist countries, have yet to comply. There is a sorrowful greed that comes along with the celebration of the Nativity of Jesus which should not be there at all. Thousands of wealthy people expend fortunes for material goods to give to those who are significant to them and try to pass it off as Christian Love. What a contradictory state of affairs! What an ignoble hypocrisy! These precious days are meant to show the world the true significance in material selflessness and raw spiritual charity. The Advent of Christmas is wholly equal to your humble wait for the Return of the Son of Man in Glory in that same sense. How can humankind reach for the blessings and graces of Heaven if his grasp is fasted to hoards of riches? How can sinners tell God that they love Him when their mouths are either stuffed to the throat with the finest of meals or groaning to claim the paltry share which lays on the plates of the poor? How can humankind call-out for heavenly aid when he is too busy blaspheming his neighbor as being an ignorant and gullible hayseed from whom his very shoes should be taken? Is this the Spirit of Christmas that these wretches will always espouse? If so, their souls are sorrowfully bound for the fires of Hell! My children, this is why our work is so important. Through My intercession, you are becoming more than messengers and examples. You are now participants in both the Teaching and Passion of My Beloved Son. His Teaching and Crucifixion cannot be spoken about as being mutually exclusive gifts to the Earth. No better lesson was delivered to mankind about forgiveness than that which was taught on Good Friday when Jesus was killed for the Salvation of all. I ask you to remember that no righteous act or phrase of Jesus can be dichotomized into individual slivers of human understanding. There can be no paring-away of the totality in which Jesus lived in My womb through the present day as He is seated at God's right hand. Those Angels and Elders who pay such homage to Jesus as He stands proudly as the Eucharist in the Monstrance are the first who will tell you 'Do not ever say that Jesus Christ is anything not related to sanctity, perfection, divinity, humanness, and love.' Hair-splitting theology is no match for the universal goodness that no man has the power to dissect. That goodness is the singular Love of God for His people, present as the Messiah, the Holy Spirit, and the Most Blessed Sacrament. Jesus is truly alive and dwelling in and among you only because I have borne Him to humanity, a solemn rite that I still confer upon My children, especially those who pray. This is not My will, but the Divine Will of the Creator of the Universe who has told Me in undeniable terms that I am the Mediatrix of all Graces, the New Eve, and the Queen of Heaven and Earth. Anyone who would approach the King of all Creation should bear this in mind, lest He sends them away with shame written across their faces. Christmas is a season not unlike Lent and Eastertide, it is a time for humankind to measure its collective worthiness in the eyes of Jesus. Men should ask, *'Am I like my Lord in all ways? Do I reflect the Gospel? Do I preach and bless, serve and protect, and kneel and pray? Do I portray the innocence of the Christ-Child in the manger at the same time I am pouring-out my lifeblood to pardon those who have offended me?'*

My children, your lives in Jesus are more than a continuum of promise to do better in days to come. They are an outright commitment to be Jesus for all the world now, in this very hour and during the moment at hand. This makes Advent more than a period of preparation, but a time of tangible transformation. Getting ready to receive the Savior of the world is a work of redemption with which no material possession on Earth can compete. These are the reasons that we hope for a better world and a better future. This is the Spirit of Christmas because it celebrates the Divinity of the Savior who already Is, not who might be someday soon. And as you prepare for Christmas, the last of this millennium, please ponder the hope and beauty of the Kingdom to come. There is no time for debates as to whether it was either Adam or Eve who caused the Fall of Man from Paradise. Instead, look forward in joy that every soul has been raised from death by the Resurrection of Jesus from the grave! Always remember that God laid Jesus in the manger, and Jesus walked under His own power from the Tomb. This is what the Father seeks in you. He gave you birth into the mortal world so that in Jesus you can walk with the power of His Love in you onto the streets of paradisial bliss. The rarity of Christmas, My children, is that millions about you have never taken time to comprehend what the season truly means. I hope that the words and expressions I have given to you today will help them finally know. Thank you for praying and allowing Me to speak to you so openly and with so much love in your hearts. This has again been another special day because, by your continuing work, many more will be brought to the celestial heights of Perfect Light from their humble perches on the Earth. You cannot yet know how grateful God is that you have consented to receive the Holy Spirit. Please remember to pray for Pope John Paul II in your Advent prayers."

Sunday, December 12, 1999
3:43 p.m.

"This, My children, is the time during which so much is being decided beyond the purview of your mortal senses, all the blessings that still rain-down upon the Earth in a sequence that God knows will have the most converting power. It is also why you still have questions, make demands, and seem lacking in patience as to why your agendas are not being fulfilled right before your eyes. From your faith comes the comfort of knowing that Jesus died on the Cross to redeem every soul, many of whom are still learning to know Him, most of whom have already passed the threshold of mortality into His comforting embrace. I ask you to remember that you are still working in His vineyard, and you cannot yet fully know the effects of your labors or the bountifulness of the holy yield. Should God visit that knowledge upon you now, you would assuredly stop working in total earnest, knowing full-well that your battle is complete. My children, we still have much work to do. Please be My understanding little children and do as I asked in 1991— Let God be God. You already have amassed a fortune of good works in the world with your first book; and hundreds-of-thousands have already been touched, just as I told you in 1991. Now, you are working in the mid-years of our struggle together, hoping that Jesus will bring a glorified conclusion to the mortal Earth before sunrise tomorrow. I ask you to ponder the affirmation of peace that you know in your hearts as a result of your openness to the Holy Spirit. You are the representatives of good will, charity, comfort, healing, light, prayerfulness, ambassadorship, kingliness, warmth, love, and conversion. Why not realize this affirmation in your patience, the fruit of Love that best befits the children whom I call My own? When you know My Immaculate Heart well, you live in peace because it comes naturally to you, like a dove who has chosen to light on a lofty branch, high in the mountaintops. I tell you again that these days are taking you where you wish to go, but you cannot yet see it."

Our Lady spoke to me about a recent situation that I had noted concerning one of Her other messengers. The person is recognized worldwide as a visionary to whom the Most Blessed Virgin has spoken. While traveling and praying with many different groups of people, this messenger visited a group that presents themselves as an authority on the intercession of our Holy Mother. They are quick to judge every syllable that Our Lady utters and pore over the smallest inflection that they can construe about Her messages, while at the same time portraying their personal conclusions as the authentic interpretation of what the Queen of Heaven wishes to relate. At their recent gathering with this holy visionary, hoping for a great message to validate themselves, Our Lady came to pray with them, but said almost nothing at all. Her lack of speech was the message itself. Our Blessed Mother told me,

"I am assured that you know why My words are limited to C_ this week. This is in no way a reflection of a lack of Love. Do you remember what the Angels said about the uncertainty of things that are left to mortal discretion? Some of My children need to spend more time praying and less time dabbling in interpretation. I say exactly what I mean when I come. You are moving much more quickly toward the anniversary of the Birth of Jesus. You also realize that this is a very special day in the life of your brother. Forty years have passed, and little Patty is still safely at home in Jesus' arms with all who have died in His friendship. My little children, you too will pass through that Veil of Love. You will likewise see the Light of Eternal Day that the Saints now know in joy."

There was a man who died this past week who had a son who was tragically killed in an unprovided manner about ten years ago. In the past decade, this father endured terrible physical suffering, including the loss of his eyesight. Today, this man was buried next to his beloved son in the presence of his surviving family and friends. Our Lady said,

"There is much mitigation of sins on the Earth that you will know in due time, when the season is right. Your friend's body was placed into the ground today, but he is no longer blind. He lost his vision so that his own son of the same name could begin to see Paradise ten years earlier. This My child is also Love and Justice, Mercy and pardon. It is Jesus, sacrifice and charity, the gift of giving that can be outdone by no one. And what again of the day that little Patty's body was committed to the Earth? Was that the day that your mother bore her first child? I give you the joy of determining God's motivations. You must believe that the reign of Christ Jesus on Earth is a Divine Ordination, and all which you wail over is passing away. Seek-out the goodness that you know to be true, and do not rue the dying of evil that has not a sliver of a chance for survival in the victory you are about to know. Your faith is an able office. Be alive in the Holy Spirit and you will shine in the awareness that you are one with Jesus. Just because the days reveal to you seemingly new evils does not imply that each of them has not been incinerated in the fires of the Holy Cross. It is you who live inside the shroud of time, and it is your Mother who is telling you what exists on the other side of time as you run gladly toward the finish line. Through faith, you see God in all His peripheral beauty as you remove the blinders from beside your eyes. I give you this hope because I know it is true. It matters not what I tell the world through any given visionary or whether your books remain inside boxes until they are turned to dust by the passing of time. There is no issue in a multi-thousand dollar debt or trillion dollar profit. The fact remains that God has issued His foreclosure decree upon the world to come with great haste, and nothing can stop Him. He will utilize the gifts that He has dispensed to the world in their complete entirety, nothing to be left-out and no soul left behind. You cannot hold a parcel of converting power in your hands that God will not use; it is eminently impossible. This is why these are times of joy and anticipation. I have seen much frustration by My little children everywhere; it is the same the world over. However, I keep repeating the same message, *In the end, My Immaculate Heart will Triumph!* I do not know the day or hour when the Son of Man will effect His Glorious Second Coming, but I do know through the Spirit of Love and the conditions of the heavens that it will be soon. The Father has told every Saint to make ready for the royal wedding of the Final Redemption of the Earth. They are scampering about transforming their sandals and robes to choice hoppers and fanciful cummerbunds. This is not an idle time in the heights of Paradise. The grippers are grasping their keys and the hands testing their lights. Everything in Heaven is oiled, shined and polished, waiting the holy command LET THE REDEMPTION BEGIN! Yes, Heaven is ready, but the Earth seems yet unprepared. Millions of souls are milling around in the darkness as though they were never invited to the celebration. Can humankind not hear the trumpets blast in the whistling winds? Can you not see the ascent of God's Glory in the colorful rainbows? I ask you, My children, to always have hope that the world can change in an instant, in a minute or an hour, because it assuredly will. My message is a plea for you to have a more peaceful demeanor, that same tranquility you prayed for during the Novena of the Immaculate Conception. Thank you for hearing My words and bearing with your brothers and sisters until they see in the Light of Truth."

Sunday, December 19, 1999
2:40 p.m.

"It is with the charitable blessing of God that I have come to speak to you again today. Please be reconciled to the Truth that God is pleased by your holy prayers and noble sacrifices. My children, thank you for your trust that Jesus will protect you when you live prayerfully in Him. I have come once again to remind you of the joyful solemnity of Christmas which will come before the next week has passed. All your knowledge, faith, and Wisdom that you have gained from the many celebrations of the Virgin Nativity from years gone by are still current and present in this one. No one on the Earth can be sure that your Savior might decide to make this Christmas the last for mortal men. That is why you must all be prepared every day in the same way that you celebrate and observe the evening of Christmas Eve. My children, you will see that the Cathedral dedicated to My Immaculate Conception is dressed and beautifully adorned for the celebration in remembrance of the Birth of Jesus. I have been pleased to be so honored as to be present at the ordination of the new Bishop of your diocese. From what other diocese should such beautiful messages come? These are the last times of the 20th century. Please anticipate a mighty victory to come in the 21st. Remember that you may always shield your eyes beneath the bough of Jesus' Divine Grace. My wish for you is to always keep My Son in your midst because He is forever present in you through the Holy Spirit. My children, I cannot make it clear enough that all goodness will be fully alive and breathing in the last age. You may be forced to inhale the bitterness of the errant world in the process like being inside a burning building, but you will not succumb to the toxins that others are thrusting upon you. You will cough and choke; your eyes will water, and you will reach blindly into the dark, but you will never fall victim to evil. I will never allow that to happen. And if the measure of forty years of loneliness is reflected by forty words from My Immaculate Heart, this is God's way of showing the brevity of your agony on Earth. Jesus can utter the distance of an entire year in a single span of mortal time in three words—It is finished. I have told you that you can be deceived by the element of time. However, Jesus cannot, and He never will. The Son of Man will come at the end of time, and will come to *bring* the End of Time. Please be light of heart in all that will proceed to unfold before you. You will see much ugliness in the world, even past the end of this century. The battle will then assuredly rage to determine whether the indifference of humankind will be as malevolent a force as the outright evil of Satan. Your prayers will be needed—the Holy Rosary and the daily Sacrifice of the Mass. I will go now and bless the many other regions of the world. With your help and the Grace of God, there are many more who are coming forward to receive the Holy Eucharist. My messages are succeeding, and people like you are the reason. I will be with all My little children as the joyful day of Christmas comes to the waiting world. Thank you for allowing Me to speak to you as we pray together."

Saturday, December 25, 1999
3:44 p.m.

"My dear little children, while the Almighty Father pierced the veil of your mortality upon the occasion of the Annunciation, this is the happy day when He Incarnately revealed His Holy Face! I come to you in joy today because the King of Creation is mercifully emptying the holding cells in Purgatory for many who now have the courage to say 'yes' to Heaven. It is your prayers that have given them such strength, and the Holy Spirit who imparts to them the Wisdom. My children, like the celebration of Easter when My Son rose from the grave, there is also only one day of the year upon which His Birth is memorialized. This is a very happy opportunity for the millions of faithful to physically commemorate the charity of God. Oh! how I wish that all humankind would be as generous! I cannot commit into words the joy that Jesus holds for those who wisely come seeking Him on His birthday. The faith which is invoked by His people on Earth is a gift in itself. Please know that your signature has been recorded in the book of callers to His birthing-bed to pay homage to the little King who has saved your souls. My children, while I have always told you that God is a perpetual and omnipotent Creator, He does indeed make use of the rhythm of the passing years and generations to give you signal graces. It is as though there is a rhyme for every repeating decade, a predicate for the intrinsic Love through which He first made the universe. This is what the Angels mean when they refer to 1931, 1954, 1961, 1977 and 2000. I wish for you not to dwell on this point, however, with the expectation that numbers and chance determine the success of your destiny. That itself is a sole function of your prayers from the heart and your true desires for the conversion of men. You are often made sorrowful because many will not listen to the urgency of your messages, but you must remember also how I feel as I see this same occurrence. I am still with you as you prepare to enter the 21st century. I have been with My beloved humanity for over 2,000 years, and I will stand at your side through the last days of time. Yes, it is you who pass through time because time is one in itself. You are still moving at a pace much faster than you realize to be one with your Creator. Should He call you to your heavenly reward before He returns to the Earth in Glory, you will then be able to know what stands upright at the end of time. Your particular judgment will prepare you for your great reward. I wish that I could usher all My little children to the threshold of this knowledge in faith in the same way that you understand, but this is what these times are for, and it is why I am speaking to you now. My children, this will be My final message of the year and this millennium. But come next week, I will be back to continue the work that you have so nobly begun for the Kingdom of God on the Earth. And what will that first year bring? The answer is contingent upon the willingness of the masses of civil humanity to listen. I assure you that all the messages that I have given you from 1991 until this very moment are true. The matters which I have prophesied will come to pass. And what of that future? I have not told you of the unyielding sorrow and grief to befall the Earth. I have not asked you to cringe in fear of the just punishment of God. Neither have I asked you to seek shelter beneath the ground from natural disasters or manmade weapons of mass destruction. My messages have not been a reflection or prediction of doom and lack of hope. Quite the contrary, I have told you about the Kingship and power of God in a world that will bring itself to its knees. That power is the simplicity of Love, the same Love who was born so innocently on this day twenty centuries years ago. This is the Divinity that has eradicated the stench of division and hatred from your midst. Those who try to divide through such hatred will soon know this full well. My Special child, can you tell Me how many years it has been since the Crucifixion of Jesus? And how many years ago was that? Therein lies a great sign for humanity as the new millennium opens. It is a new day, and the old face of humankind is soon to be washed clean by the realization of the Truth. I now ask you to share your sentiments about the century about to pass, in particular the most recent nine years, the novena that has made the lives of yourself and your brother a blessing to humanity.

I thanked Our Lady for all that She has done for us. I am filled with gratitude for what She has helped me see and become.

Why is it that you keep saying that I have done these things when it has been solely you? I will refer you again to the sweet words that have come so eloquently from another of My children: *Christ! He requires still, wheresoever He comes to feed or lodge, to have the best of rooms. Give Him the choice. Grant Him the nobler part of all the house. The best of all is the heart!* My little child, of the many rooms in which My dear Jesus has come to rest in this awful world, your heart has been the sweetest indeed! And so, we will continue our work together as the future of man unfolds. Always remember that no secular parade of hypocrites or atheists will inhibit our march together toward the victory of My Most Holy and Immaculate Heart. Those who oppose your work are too weak and soon to be too few in number. There is no reason for you to grieve because time is a friend of yours and an enemy of the lost. Always remember this, and you will be more patient. The day that you have lived today is a portion of the beginning of My Immaculate Triumph. I am pleased that your day is made of high hope in your heart by your awareness that you spent Christmas doing what God is asking from all His children. There will be many false celebrations that you will see ongoing in the next six days. I ask that you remember that they are false celebrations of time, not truthful solemnities of the opening of Eternity. We shall do as God wishes for the conversion of the lost. Remember that the passing of a given numerical year or personal jubilee is but a fleeting observation. Only Eternity in Heaven is cause for jubilation! This is your special blessing to begin the century during which you will come to Heaven. ✞ Thank you from On High for your fiat to God."

www.ingramcontent.com/pod-product-compliance
Lightning Source LLC
LaVergne TN
LVHW050510100826
845148LV00002B/287

* 9 7 8 0 9 7 9 3 3 3 4 2 2 *